"John Hannah's brilliance infused with ı
make his book exceedingly important in
Christian doctrine. This powerful, practical book will be an excellent
addition to your library and mine."
—NEY BAILEY, AUTHOR AND SPEAKER, CAMPUS CRUSADE FOR CHRIST

"In our day, when we are trying to change the world through every
method except through the knowledge of God, Dr. Hannah's book
on knowing God through understanding Christian doctrine is sorely
needed. I recommend it highly for those who want to help change our
world for the glory of God."
—ROSEMARY JENSEN, GENERAL DIRECTOR, RAFIKI FOUNDATION

"We can thank Dr. Hannah for helping us understand our spiritual
roots! This readable book will remind us that Christ's church is greater
than any denomination. We have a great need for the perspective this
book gives us."
DR. ERWIN W. LUTZER, SENIOR PASTOR,
THE MOODY CHURCH

"This overview of seven key theological themes is both wise and even-
handed. The author deals with conflicts in church history with an
irenic spirit that will make the book particularly useful for thoughtful
evangelicals. Pastors and other church leaders finally have a readable,
learned, and clear volume on the history of Christian theology which
is fully aware of both the modern condition and the importance of sub-
stantive historical debates. Highly recommended!"
DR. JOHN H. ARMSTRONG, PRESIDENT,
REFORMATION & REVIVAL MINISTRIES, AUTHOR OF True Revival
and Reforming Pastoral Ministry

Our Legacy provides an easy-to-read road map through two thousands
years of Christian theology. By organizing his material doctrine-by-
doctrine, rather than chronologically, Dr Hannah puts centuries of
thought at the readers' fingertips. This book clarifies the flow of ideas
of both the heroes and heretics of our history in a way that engages the
reader in their struggle. We need this engagement as the struggle for
truth continues to rage as fiercely today as at any time in history!
JIM PETERSEN, MISSIONARY AND WRITER.
AUTHOR OF Living Proof and Church Without Walls

OUR LEGACY

THE HISTORY OF CHRISTIAN DOCTRINE

J O H N   H A N N A H

A NavPress resource published in alliance
with Tyndale House Publishers, Inc.

NavPress is the publishing ministry of The Navigators, an international Christian organization and leader in personal spiritual development. NavPress is committed to helping people grow spiritually and enjoy lives of meaning and hope through personal and group resources that are biblically rooted, culturally relevant, and highly practical.

For more information, visit www.NavPress.com.

A NavPress resource published in alliance with Tyndale House Publishers, Inc.

NAVPRESS and the NAVPRESS logo are registered trademarks of NavPress, The Navigators. Absence of ® in connection with marks of NavPress or other parties does not indicate an absence of registration of those marks.

TYNDALE is a registered trademark of Tyndale House Publishers, Inc.

ISBN 978-1-57683-264-6

Cover design: Ray Moore
Cover illustration: William Morris
Creative team: Steve Webb, Eric Stanford, Darla Hightower, Glynese Northam

Library of Congress Cataloging-in-Publication Data

Hannah, John D.
    Our legacy : history of Christian doctrine / by John D. Hannah.
          p. cm.
    Includes bibliographical references and index.
    ISBN 1-57683-264-3
        1. Theology, Doctrinal—History. I. Title.
BT21.3 .H36 2001
230'.09—dc21   00-068973

Printed in the United States of America

19 18 17 16 15 14
11 10 9   8   7   6

Dedication

This volume is dedicated to my companion in life for over thirty years, Carolyn Ruth Hannah. She has made a house into a home for me, filling it with joy and peace. It is not easy to be attached to an obsessive-compulsive man, nor to raise his children and explain to them why Daddy was not always there, and yet she did so with such devotion and understanding that it inspired them to love their father and to share the same passion as he for the ministry of the gospel. Now Carolyn and I walk hand in hand in our empty-nester years, as much in love as at the beginning, though with much more wisdom about living life. To her, my best friend, this book is a small token of my thankfulness.

Contents

Preface

In opening a book on any topic, a reader may legitimately pose a pragmatic question: *Why should I read this book when there are several others on the same subject in print already?* And in the case of a book on theology, a second question may come to mind: *Why should I read any book about theology?* In our day, theology seems to be an irrelevant topic, one that may even be destructive to the health of the church. Parishioners appear more attuned to quick and easy solutions to their felt needs than they are to the reflection and mental exertion required in the study of doctrine. Meanwhile, pastors seem to view theology as a subject to be broached with extreme caution, even embarrassment, preferring instead to wax eloquent on topics that are hardly the central focus of God's revelation to us. Contemporary sermons deal far more frequently with self-help and psychological issues than they focus on behavior as a fruit of the knowledge of God's character. What, then, is the value of this volume among the many that have been composed on a theme that appears marginal even within the Christian community?

Let me offer seven reasons for you to read this book.

First, *while most other books on the history of doctrine have been written for the scholarly community, the intended audience of this book is not scholars but pastors, Christian workers, and an informed laity.* This volume seeks to avoid the perils of lofty but irrelevant intellectualism on the one hand and the superficiality of populist literature on the other. It arises from the beliefs that the quest for the knowledge of God is not an idle pastime, that spiritual vitality in any era is found in people who know their God, and that the greatest danger for the church is ignorance of God. Fears and adversaries come and go on the pages of history, but only those who know God can change the course of human events, bring permanence from impermanence, and speak a word of peace in a world that knows only the struggle for self-advancement and self-fulfillment. In a word, this volume is a call to the church to return to God as the center of our priorities and life.

Second, *this book is an attempt to assert the value of both history and theology in the life of the church today.* Having struggled for several centuries to deflect the attacks mounted by Enlightenment Rationalism, which denigrated the biblical notions of God, sin, and grace, the church shows signs of imbibing its cardinal characteristics of micromanagement (that is, the penchant for "steps" and "rules" for everything from church growth to personal happiness), pluralism, tolerance, gentility (theology—once the "queen" of all the sciences—is rapidly becoming considered "an embarrassing encumbrance"[1]), and privatization (the belief that truth is personal and private, not public or universal). Thomas C. Oden suggests that the current state of the church is that of "an ecclesiastical swamp" produced by three sources: the emergence of "an intellectual immune deficiency syndrome, a marked decline of Christian content with a corresponding emphasis on the emotions; an acceptance of many of the premises of modernity; and an ignorance of the roots of the church in classic orthodoxy."[2] It may be argued that turn-of-the-twenty-first-century evangelicalism stands under the same judgment as turn-of-the-twentieth-century liberalism, which also berated doctrine while stressing morals and culture. This book is conceived from the conviction that the church must be aroused to reinvest heart and mind in historic Christian orthodoxy. A Christianity separated from historical credibility is not a biblical faith; a Christianity without theology is mere morality and not the faith "once for all handed down to the saints" (Jude 3).

Third, *this book is rooted in the belief that theology has an important role to play in the life of the church.* While theology is not to be confused with the Bible, there is an inseparable linkage between the two.

As the Spirit of God and the Word of God are never severed (that is, God most assuredly speaks through His Word to our conscience), so the Word and theology are inseparable. Theology is the fruit of the study of the Word. The task of the theologian is to gather together the knowledge of God available to us with a view to the church's worship and service. Older theologians, particularly of the English Puritan tradition, did not define theology in cognitive terms (that is, as the science of the knowledge of God), though their endeavor to understand the Scriptures was remarkable as a scientific endeavor. Instead, they often referred to theology as "the art of living unto God" or "the art of living blessedly forever." For them, theology was neither a mere intellectual discipline nor the attainment of a body of knowledge; it was a means to an end—a godly life. Theology, then, may be defined as the distilled knowledge of God that is the foundation of a walk with God. No one can walk with a person he or she does not know; neither can we say we walk with God if we do not have an accurate knowledge of Him. Theology is not about an admiration of a series of gathered insights, however wonderful these insights may be; it is about responding appropriately and regularly to God.

Fourth, *this book springs from the belief that the function of theology—and here I have in mind historical theology—is to preserve the church from fads and novelty.* A knowledge of the past keeps the church from confusing the merely contemporary with the enduringly relevant; it distinguishes the transient from the permanent. In so doing, it spares the church from diversions that, while appearing promising at the moment, are in fact harmful. A knowledge of the past bequeaths a stability and confidence in a world where flamboyant voices lend credibility to spurious ideas promising success. In essence, it brings to the church a valuable accumulation of enduring insights (often acquired at an enormous price) as well as relevant lessons and warnings. It abounds in examples, both positive and negative, for the contemporary church. It thus helps increase the church's understanding of its own teaching.

Fifth, *a knowledge of theology in its historical context and development will preserve the church from error; it provides both apologetic and polemic weapons against deception.* The accumulated wisdom of the church can provide an arsenal of arguments as we struggle to preserve the church today from its opponents both within and without. For example, the church has at times swung between an arid faith full of knowledge but with little vitality and an experience-centered faith with little intellectual content. An overemphasis in either direction has proven destructive to Christian experience. Though this is a contemporary issue of importance, it is not the first time the church has been forced to articulate the relationship between "the faith as known" and "the faith as experienced." The collective insights of the past are instructive in gaining a perspective on life. Another question that has arisen in the church more than once is this: Is morality in some sense the cause of salvation, or is it the proper effect of salvation? This cause-and-effect relationship has been confused in the church before and continues to be. The struggles of the church in the past with such issues provide a lens of helpful insights as we attempt to handle the same controversies in a contemporary setting.

Sixth, *a knowledge of the history of doctrine will provide a bulwark against pride and arrogance borne of the thought that any one church or ecclesiastical tradition stands in the exclusive heritage of first-century orthodoxy.* While all expressions of the church today mirror some continuity with the apostolic church, they all evidence significant discontinuities as well. For example, in the area of church structure, various ecclesiastical traditions, whether they be episcopalian, presbyterian, or congregational, claim biblical warrant for their structures, yet each has evolved forms (some more elaborately than others) that do not possess clear biblical justification. Often a particular ecclesiology has emerged out of a particular historic setting and meets the needs of the time. While it may be argued that one form or another more faithfully reflects the Bible, each evidences modification and change from the embryonic structure portrayed in the New Testament. A knowledge of continuity in the midst of discontinuity should have multiple functions: First, it should cause us to be careful in claiming strict biblical precedent for all that any particular church does. Second, it should cause us to make continuity with the New Testament the ground of true fellowship. And third, it should cause us to focus on those areas of truth that are truly timeless and enduring, recognizing at the same time that we all cling to certain things that are more a part of our tradition and our own accustomed way of doing things than they are strictly biblical.

12

Last, *a knowledge of the history of doctrine supports the Bible's witness to the triumph of the church.* Through times of duress and trial, the people of God have been preserved and have steadfastly proclaimed the gospel of our Lord Jesus Christ. The devil has employed every strategy to destroy the church; armies have marched against it; unbelieving scholarship has relentlessly assaulted it; internal bickering has rent it; and martyrdom has depleted its ranks from time to time. Yet the church marches forward in triumphal anticipation of the great consummation when the kingdoms of this world will be put under Christ's feet and when the bride, without spot or blemish, will be given to the Bridegroom. History witnesses to the truth of the Scriptures that the world will not end with some false messiah making good on the ultimate threat to destroy the globe through a nuclear holocaust, but rather it will be consummated in the glorious reign of the King of kings. How would we know this without Scripture and without the doctrines of the end times developed from Scripture by theologians throughout the centuries?

If you agree with me that these seven reasons are important, then I invite you to begin your study of the riches of the past in *Our Legacy: The History of Christian Doctrine.*

Acknowledgments

Life is not lived alone; it is orchestrated in a community. The same is true of the writing of a book. Many have made a significant contribution to this volume. To the institution I have been a part of for more than twenty-five years, Dallas Theological Seminary, I owe a debt of gratitude for allowing me to study, write, and teach. It was in preparation for the classroom that this book emerged. To the students who endured the expression of my studies, who often listened critically and shaped my thoughts about the material more than they shall ever know, I express my thanks. To the wonderful staff of Turpin Library of Dallas Theological Seminary, and to Mr. Jeff Webster in particular, I am grateful for their personal kindness and professional expertise. Two students helped me with particular parts of the book: Graham Hunt painstakingly edited the endnotes of the volume, and Mark Harris provided the technical knowledge that allowed pictures to be added to it. Many read sections of the book as it was being written; particular recognition for their help goes to my friend and colleague Dr. Jeffrey Bingham, to my wife for her careful editing, and to my dear friend Mrs. Neatice Warner. Not the least of my expressions of gratitude belongs to my secretary, Mrs. Beth Motley. Every teacher, like every businessperson, knows only a little of the debt we owe to those who schedule our appointments, answer our phone, and edit our papers. A final word of thanks goes to the editorial staff of NavPress, most particularly I am indebted to Mr. Eric Stanford, the finest colleague I have ever had on a project like this. Errors of any kind belong to the ignorance and myopia of the author.

ACKNOWLEDGMENTS

1

Introduction: Historical Christian Doctrine in the New Century

"*It was the best of times, it was* the worst of times, it was the age of wisdom, it was the age of darkness, it was the epoch of belief, it was the epoch of incredulity, it was the season of Light, it was the season of Darkness, it was the spring of hope, it was the winter of despair." These famous opening lines of Charles Dickens' *A Tale of Two Cities*, a novel describing revolutionary times in France and England, seem an appropriate starting point for a description of our times. Today many in the social sciences alert us to the fact that we are living through a sort of revolution of our own, a time of transition from one system of values and assumptions (modernism) to another (postmodernism). Some suggest that the unease many people are currently feeling about the transition will subside as we make our peace with the changes; others argue that we are entering a dark, glacial age and approaching the destruction of civilization. I say that the church will live and flourish in the new era, as it has in every other, because its origins and power are not of this world but from heaven. The naturalistic optimists will be proved wrong because human engineering and political agendas, ennobled by access to vast amounts of new information, can never overcome the destructive potential of human greed and insensitivity. But the doomsayers will be proved wrong, too, because what we are so prone to forget, in the flurry of our religious activities, is that behind the scenes of history is the Lord of history, who "causes all things to work together for good to those who love God" (Romans 8:28). It is into this world, with a firm resolve to trust in the God of the heavens, that we step to face

17

with joy and delight, though also with seriousness and pain, the challenges of the new century.

THE PLACE OF THEOLOGY IN A POSTMODERN WORLD

We exist within a set of cultural values that has repudiated many of the assumptions of modernity, such as the importance of the rational, the propriety of the orderly, and the possibility of objective truth. We live in a world where personality has more street value than character, where psychological wholeness is more valued than spiritual authenticity. We find ourselves in a world where pleasures are embraced without moral norms or a sense of social responsibility. Christian truth is attacked not so much for its particular assertions as for its fundamental claim that there is such a thing as binding, objective truth. The quest for truth has been replaced by the preoccupation with pleasure and entertainment. Thus, we live in a world of the therapeutic and the psychological, where people are engaged in an endless pursuit of self-fulfillment and entitlement. Sin has become little more than the infringement of personal rights and privileges; there is little thought of defining it by the standard of the holiness of God. It is in this kind of world that we must ask ourselves about the place of theology. With so much interest in the management of life, what is the benefit of studying such a seemingly esoteric thing as timeless, transcendent, historical truth?

The question is complicated by the fact that modern evangelicalism is in a state of crisis. The very community that historically has been deeply interested in transcendent, timeless truth seems intent upon focusing on the merely private, personal, and temporal. If I may be so blunt, the church has lost its soul. The quest for contemporary relevance has led it down the path of increasing irrelevancy and marginalization. The evangelical church is on the brink of becoming another of the many social, do-good agencies whose purpose has to do with helping people to more fully enjoy this life while neglecting the implications of eternity. While our culture has shown a marked inclination to secularism, the church seems to have followed suit. One of our

Christian social critics has summarized the problem like this: "The stream of historic orthodoxy that once watered the evangelical soul is now damned by a worldliness that many fail to recognize as worldliness because of the cultural innocence with which it presents itself."[1] There is also an appalling ignorance, among the churches, of their rich Christian heritage. Church historian Mark Noll speaks of "the scandal of the evangelical mind," the denigration of the intellectual content of the faith, and the elevation of the subjective and personal.[2] Christian pollster George Barna complains that the average Christian is uninterested in life-changing religious convictions, having little more than the most superficial awareness of sin, grace, and redemption.[3]

This moral and intellectual crisis comes to the evangelical church when Christianity is without a serious secular opponent. There are no potent rivals in our culture making claims to having objective, final truth. Such truth claims have been abandoned in the postmodern experience. David Wells has found a general parallel to the situation in the church today in the era just prior to the Reformation in the sixteenth century. First, he suggests that the two churches are similar in that they each manifest a lack of confidence in the Word of God. In the fourteenth and fifteenth centuries the denigration of the Scriptures was manifested in the church's reversion to papal pronouncements; today the same denigration is manifest in business know-how and psychological counseling. Second, both churches reflect a flawed understanding of the seriousness of sin. One of our philosophers, having reflected on the decline of the discussion of sin within his own religious heritage, has stated: "The new language of Zion fudges: 'Let us confess our problem with human relational adjustment dynamics, and especially our feebleness in networking.' . . . 'Peanut Butter Binge' and 'Chocolate Decadence' are sinful; lying is not. The measure of sin is caloric."[4] Third, in both instances the church, having lost its grasp on sin, has minimized the glory and efficacy of the death of Christ.[5]

These very circumstances—the moralizing of virtue and the trivializing of sin, the psychologizing of the Scriptures to make the message user-friendly and inoffensive, and the marginalizing of the cross of Christ—are the reason for this book. It is a call for the church, including its pastors, teachers, and laity, to reverse the recent trends that pose a threat to the gospel of Christ by humanizing sin and speaking lightly of the work of the Savior. It is time for us to listen to the Scriptures for our message, not to the beckoning cry of a pleasure-inebriated culture. The need of the hour is not for revival; it is for something even more fundamental. It is time for a reformation in the church. Revival has to do with the extension of the gospel; the greatest need in the contemporary church is to rediscover the gospel, its glory, and its power. It is time to return to the fundamentals of the faith and be refreshed in its truths, to gain anew a love and respect for the Holy Scriptures. Revival without reformation is religious fervor at best; revival out of reformation is the only hope of the church. It is with this passion in mind that this book is written.

SOME BASIC TERMS

This book will represent seven key theological themes for the new century: (1) authority, (2) God, (3) the person of Christ, (4) the work of Christ, (5) salvation, (6) the church, and (7) the end times. But before we get to these topics in the following chapters, let me cover some preliminaries. First, I must define three basic terms to be used in this book: *theology, doctrine,* and *dogma.*

Theology literally means "discourse about God." The word was used prior to the first century by Greeks to describe their pagan gods. In the Christian era, the term was neither readily used nor precisely defined until Anselm of Canterbury in the eleventh century provided what has been recognized as a classic definition. While not suggesting the exclusion of reason, the scholastic defined theology as "faith seeking understanding." Theology, in the deepest sense, therefore, begins in the conversion experience and is the task of every Christian. It is the quest of the saint to know who God is and what He requires of the Christian as an expression of his or her grace-caused regeneration. And yet, on a more practical level, a theologian is normally defined as one who is professionally trained in the skills and methods of doing theology, or at least makes the claim of being able to do so. It is his or her duty to explain the knowledge we have of God and His ways to the people of God at the highest possible level of expertise.

20

The terms *doctrine* and *dogma* have come to possess meanings that distinguish them from the broader term *theology*. While *theology* may refer to the notions of any individual thinker on the nature of God, *doctrine* and *dogma* have a corporate or community aspect. The terms *doctrine* and *dogma* are, however, distinguishable from one another.

Doctrine, for example, may be defined as the response of the church to questions that have been posed either by heretics from outside the church (threats) or by the faithful within it (questions). The term is almost universally translated "teaching" in the New Testament (for example, 1 Timothy 4:16). It is that which is taught, put forth as true, and embraced by a school or group. In the New Testament, it refers to the teachings of Scripture relative to any theme.

Dogma is a term that, unfortunately, has come to be perceived as a negative word—a word that speaks of imposed authority and oppression. In the Greek Old Testament translation, the Septuagint, it is used of a decree or formal, public declaration (Esther 3:9; Daniel 2:13; 6:8). In the New Testament it is used somewhat similarly (Luke 2:1; Acts 16:4); that is, it is used of a particular decision of a community. *Dogma,* then, implies those doctrines that have been defined by a particular group or community as essential by its universal consent to them and articulation of them in creedal form.

The study of dogma embraces the confessional statements of a particular ecclesiastical tradition. For example, the study of Orthodox dogmatics includes the great ecumenical councils from the First Council of Nicaea (325) to the Second Council of Nicaea in 787. Roman Catholic dogmatics embraces the initial five ecumenical councils as well as the findings of the Council of Trent (1545–1563), Vatican I (1869), and Vatican II (1962–1965). Lutheran dogmatics embraces the historic ecumenical creeds as well as the Augsburg Confession (1530) and several other Lutheran symbols, such as the Formula of Concord (1560). The sphere of Reformed dogmatics is enormous, embracing the ecumenical creeds and numerous other creeds (for example, the Helvetic Confessions, the Belgic Confession, the findings of the Synod of Dordt, the Westminster Confession, and the Savoy Confession) and catechisms such as the Heidelberg Catechism. The Free Church traditions (such as the Baptists) prefer not to speak of dogma, though they have developed doctrinal statements that are binding to various degrees within their varied groupings.

This book is a study of theology through all three of these lenses. It is an analysis of individual theologians, such as Anselm or Wesley; it is the study of the teachings of particular groups (that is, doctrine); and it is the study of the authorized, creedal statements of various traditions in the Christian community (dogma). It is impossible to separate these terms in any survey of what the church has taught.

SOME BASIC ASSUMPTIONS

Having defined three basic terms, let's now turn to four of the basic assumptions that undergird this book.

The most fundamental assumption of this study is that *there is truth available to us;* it is found both in the Bible and in the church's study of the Bible. We are not left awash in a sea of relative truths, as many believe today. God has revealed absolute, universal truth to us. The Bible is the Word of God written; Christ is the Word of God revealed in it; and the Spirit is the voice of God in it revealing Christ. With childlike embrace, the church throughout the ages has clung to the Bible, searching its pages for direction in life and work. We can and should do the same today.

A second assumption of the study is that *the Bible has been accurately understood by the church.* The Spirit promised through the apostle John that He would lead us into all truth (1 John 2:27). While this particular concept has been the subject of considerable discussion, it cannot possibly mean that all the details of orthodoxy are universally known in the church. There is simply too much division of opinion in the churches to assume that is true. "All truth" seems to be a reference not to all truth without distinction but to all truth without exception; it embraces what Christians essentially believe and have commonly accepted across all traditions and denominations. It is a reference to Christ, His person and His work, which the Spirit reveals universally to all believers. While Christians have not been able to agree on a wide range of topics (for example, the sacraments, spiritual gifts, church government, and eschatology), there is common consent within the redeemed community about the Lord Jesus Christ.

A third assumption is more difficult to explain. It is the idea that *our understanding of what the Bible teaches has evolved both negatively and positively.* History tells us that theology often has deviated from the path of biblical permissibility while simultaneously maintaining a remarkable similarity with many aspects of biblical teaching. It is one of the duties of the historical theologian to demonstrate how the church has stood in continuity and discontinuity with the apostolic age. Theologians have generally found the path of orthodoxy difficult to traverse in recent times, having embraced the Enlightenment notion of the improbability of supernatural revelation. Consequently, the church has been victimized by the difficult, if not impossible, task of seeking a revelation of God from parts of the Bible rather than from the Bible as a whole.

While the evangelical Christian church has correctly understood the essentials of the gospel, this does not suggest that in every partic-ular the various evangelical churches are in continuity with the apos-tles' teachings. In fact, that is a logical impossibility. Since they differ from one another, either one particular community is in conformity with the first-century revelation of God or else none of them are in conformity with it in every detail. It is this author's understanding that no single assembly of saints or denomination, however orthodox, evangelical, or primitive, strictly follows the Bible. It seems that the church has always sought to be faithful, but the meaning of texts is often subject to more than one interpretation. Theology is often the art of establishing central, classic texts, and every system of doctrine is subject to attack due to a failure to give proper regard to certain other proof texts. There is also the factor of contextual circumstances, which can serve as occasions of profound insight into the meaning of texts (though those circumstances may also obscure permanent truths). No single individual, church, or denomination has escaped human frailty, though there is continuity and uniformity in the essen-tials of Christ, His person and His work.

A fourth assumption is that *theology has been forged within church history.* The content of our faith was given by the apostles and under-stood clearly through the centuries in the believing church. However, the *meaning* of the revelation of God, though not the *fact* of it, has emerged in history. It is in the context of the attacks of the enemies of the church, and also of the serious inquiries of those inside the church, that theology has developed. The Bible neither came to us at one time completely intact as today nor did it come to us with a topical index. The Bible came to us a volume at a time; it was the written expression of the oral message of the church. For example, some claim that the deity of Christ is not a first-century truth but was invented in the fourth century by the bishops of the church at the first ecumenical council, Nicaea (325). Our reply is that Christians have always believed in the deity of Christ, but it took serious reflection upon the Scriptures, as well as other circumstances, to explain (not invent) that doctrine. Theology is made in history; it is the result of study of the revelation of God. It is a human endeavor by fallible people who engage all their intellectual strength and Spirit-inspired ability to understand an infallible book with the sure promise that the Spirit will lead us into "all truth."

THE DEVELOPMENT OF DOCTRINE

Historians in the church have generally recognized the development of doctrine.[6] They have grappled with the fact that some of the teachings of the church have evolved over the centuries in both negative and positive senses. Recognizing that truth is derived fundamentally from the Scriptures and that explanation is interpretation and embellishment, they have faced the need to explain the "expansion" of church teachings over the centuries; they have recognized discontinuity and have sought to defend it in light of a static continuity. The motive is to portray the expansion of the church's teachings as biblically justifiable and as having taken place without altering the teachings of the Bible in the process. Some have struggled to defend the expansion by laying down tests for its judgment. It may prove helpful at this preliminary stage in our study to briefly look at several attempts to understand the development of doctrine.

John Henry Newman was a remarkable churchman in nineteenth-century England. Though he made a confession of evangelical faith in

1816, he died in 1890 a cardinal in the Roman Catholic Church. Enveloped in the issues of ecclesiastical authority in the nineteenth century and a student of the history of the early centuries of the church, he felt compelled to change church affiliations, though he was thereby forced to consider a rather profound question. How can one justify the discontinuity between fourth-century Christianity (as reflected in Athanasius, bishop of Alexandria) and the Roman Church of the nineteenth century? He postulated an answer to authority within the perception of discontinuity in an 1845 work, *Essay on the Development of Christian Doctrine.* Believing that the Athanasian church was, indeed, apostolic and that the Bible was the one and only revelation of God, he explained the discrepancy through a seminalist, organic, evolutionary theory of truth. For Newman, development was not a flaw but a sign of the life of the church. However, if development was to be warranted, it had to conform to criteria that did not deface the one true revelation of God, the Bible. Newman recognized the fact of an expansion of the church's teachings and developed tests to determine if a change was valid. Though one may dispute the validity of his criteria, one must admit that his attempt was erudite and scholarly. Among Newman's tests were the following: the preservation of core essentials, the power to assimilate new ideas without internal reconstitution, the early anticipation of later developments, the expansion of ideas through logical consequences, the making of additions that preserve and augment earlier teachings, and the long continuance of a development in the church. With this organic view, he was able to justify the discontinuity between the written revelation of God and later developments. Protestants, however, called Newman's developments evidence of decay and corruption—discontinuity from the core, not simply expansion of it.

Protestant historians countered Newman's organic theory with the construction of theories of their own. The Anglican scholar Robert Mozley (1813–1878), in *The Theory of Development* (1878), conceded to a law of organic development but argued that there was also a law of corruption. He suggested that there were actually three models of doctrinal development: healthy development, corrupt development, and exaggerated development. What Newman saw as healthy development, Mozley saw as encompassing the latter two models! Newman understood Nicene orthodoxy as an *expansion* of the Bible; Mozley understood it as an *explanation* of the Bible. The difference between the two theories rests on the issue of expansion versus explanation, that is, on the nature, not the fact, of development. For Newman, the Bible is the beginning point; for Mozley, it was also the ending point.

William Cunningham (1805–1861), a Scottish scholar, countered Newman's attempt at apologetics by arguing that his organic view was novel. The criteria of orthodoxy, he suggested, was in its conformity to the apostles' teachings, not in an organic development. He argued that there is development of doctrine within the canon of Scripture, but only corruption or explanation through expansion outside of it. Cunningham saw explanation in the fourth- and fifth-century controversies over the Trinity and Christology, saw corruption prevailing in the late medieval period, and saw restoration in the Reformation.

Robert Rainy (1826–1906), another Scottish scholar, explained his concept of development in a considerable treatise in 1874, *Delivery Development of Christian Doctrine*. He countered with an explanatory model of his own that in structure somewhat anticipated teachings of James Orr and B. B. Warfield. Rational reflection on the static revelation of God, the apostles' teaching, within the circumstance of cultural and theological threats accounts for the development of doctrine.

Later explanations of the concept of development in doctrine came in response to Adolf von Harnack (1851–1930), the famed German liberal, as well as Newman. Harnack followed Albrecht Ritschl (1822–1889) in seeking to discern a revelation of God within the canon of Scripture, a distillation of the pure substance of the Bible from its manifold corruptions. For him, the essence of the Bible's "true" message had to do with moral or kingdom righteousness rather than the righteousness of a wrathful God imputed to undeserving and hateful sinners. His model was one of pathological and sociological development from primitive naiveté and simplicity to nineteenth-century adulthood and complexity. Theology is not developed in any real sense; it is transmuted into ethics.

The responses to Harnack were several. James Orr (1844–1913), a Scottish divine, in *The Progress of Dogma* (1901), recognized the difference between the static revelation of God (the apostles' teaching) and what the church has taught that the Bible teaches. He understood that real progress in theology had taken place over the centuries through the manifestation and outworking of an inherent principle or force within history (a theory that was theistic, evolutionary, and adoptionistic) to explain the expansion of knowledge as consistent with the apostles' teachings, not away from it. Princeton scholar B. B. Warfield (1851–1921), in *Studies in Theology* (1932), seems to have argued Orr's point of progress or expansion without addition by delving into the Scottish Common Sense tradition and Baconianism.[7] He argued that progress is accounted for by centuries of the inductive gathering of facts.

Roman Catholic scholars have continued to argue for expansive development in doctrine. A seminal difference between that tradition and conservative Protestant scholarship is that the latter has consistently argued that development is explanatory in nature, not merely expansive. To Protestants, the apostles' teaching provides a static, non-expandable foundation from which the validity of development can be determined; experience is valid only as it reflects the apostles' teachings. Karl Rahner (1904–1984), a Roman Catholic theologian, anticipated the shifts in the nature of authority that were later enunciated at Vatican II by arguing that experience can expand the meaning of dogma. In other words, doctrinal development is the experience of dogma in a changing continuum. Edward Schillebeeckx (b. 1914), a Dutch scholar, has suggested that the conscious experience of dogma in the church expressed universally by it—that is, through councils—is authoritative.

With this brief excursus on theories of the development of doctrine, it seems appropriate to identify the theory that undergirds the chapters to follow. First, it is apparent that progress or doctrinal development has taken place over the centuries and will continue to do so. Second, the nature of this progress is explanatory, not expansive. There is a core of truth, which is the Bible or the apostles' teachings, and there can be no deviation from it. Development of doctrine takes place as succeeding generations of Bible scholars discover the truth of the Bible within their contexts and elucidate the wealth of the apostles' teaching, not going beyond it or contradicting it. Third, the catalysts of development in the sense enumerated are cultural and theological factors, the rise of a historic threat to the church. Fourth, tests

27

can determine when a supposed explanation is actually an expansion. Among these is the test of coherency. Is the new teaching organically related to, not simply consistent with, what is already believed at other points? Consistency may imply an addition, a parallelism, a separateness; coherency implies an internal oneness with it. A second criteria may be called the noncontradiction test. If a teaching is at variance with the apostles' teaching, it must be ruled out. A third standard is the universality principle. A new development must be embraced broadly in the church, not merely be the private judgment of a small group. A fourth test might be termed the doxological criteria. Does a development promote the worship and adoration of God, or does it promote speculations, rationalization, and division?

THE HISTORICAL AND SYSTEMATIC-HISTORICAL APPROACHES

Writers in the field of the history of doctrine have approached their task in one of two ways. Some have looked at the subject through the lens of the history of the church. That is, they have followed the general divisions of church history through the centuries as a framework or outline, making those the several chapters or sections in the volume. Others have focused not on the outline of church history but on the several branches of systematic theology. That is, they have traced separately the doctrine of authority, the doctrine of God, the doctrine of the person of Christ, and so on. Each approach has advantages and disadvantages.

For those following the historical approach, an example of their text division might be as follows:

The Ancient Period (100–600)[8]
The Medieval Period (600–1500)
The Modern Period (1500–1900)
    The Early Modern Period (1500–1750)[9]
    The Late Modern Period (1750–1900)
The Postmodern Period (1900–present)[10]

28

Within this framework, theologians would unfold the history of the development of doctrine from period to period, emphasizing and explaining the particular ideas that received intense clarification in each, then passing from one period to another, perhaps without returning to a particular doctrine in the study. In this approach the history of doctrine is subservient to the study of church history.

The disadvantages of this approach are several. First, as noted above, it is difficult to maintain the distinctive nature of the study when stressing the flow of history. History is the external shell; ideas occurring within it have a history of their own. Second, the emphasis is not so much on the development or progress of an idea as it is on the emergence of it; the life history of an idea is not the focus of the study. Third, in highlighting the particular instance of its greatest examination in the history of the church, there is the danger of failing to see later developments, whether positive or negative. The retrogression of an idea is as potentially important to understand as its greatest period of clarification. Fourth, it is an approach that fosters the continuity of history but the discontinuity of doctrinal development.

The second general approach takes a specific doctrine and then traces it through each period of church history, noting positive and negative development through the centuries. An example of this approach of using church history as the outline of the study is the following:

The Doctrine of the Scriptures, or Authority (150–400)
The Doctrine of God, or the Trinity (200–381)
The Doctrine of the Person of Christ (300–451)
The Doctrine of Salvation, or Sin and Grace (400–529)
Renewal of the Doctrine of Salvation (1500–1650)
The Doctrine of the Spiritual Life (1650–present)
The Doctrine of Last Things, or Eschatology (1650–present)

The disadvantage of this systematic-historical approach is that it may tend to ignore the context of an idea; theology can devour history. The advantages, however, outweigh the risk of denigrating context. This approach allows an idea to be examined in the course of its development through the centuries, not simply the point of its most profound consideration. It permits a concentration that can be lost in the myriad of details when other doctrines are simultaneously discussed.

Though there are disadvantages to this particular approach, it is the one that has been adopted for this volume. Various doctrines will be considered in succession, beginning with the doctrine of authority, and traced through the centuries. It is hoped that the historical repetition will serve as a pedagogical device for those whose memory of the history of the church suggests the need for review.

THE STRUCTURE OF HISTORY

Because the focus of this study will be upon the development of doctrine throughout the history of the church, and though the development of theology will be given greater emphasis than church history, some comments upon the structure of history are germane. While scholars throughout the disciplines of historical studies follow the same basic method of research (generally the rudiments set forth by Francis Bacon years ago), there are significant differences in the philosophical assumptions in approaching the task. The overarching assumption for the Christian historian is a belief in the sovereignty of God in all human affairs and the decreed outworking of His purposes. His or her work is a blend of the data derived from the Bible, including history and prophecy as well as the study of the events and various circumstances outside the Bible. A rather insightful attempt at writing a history of humanity employing this method was devised by the American Puritan Jonathan Edwards in his *A History of Redemption* (1739), to which I am indebted for many of my own views in the matter. In this book Edwards suggests that the divine purpose in creating and sustaining humankind through the centuries is that God is gathering a bride for His Son, the Lord Jesus.

The Bible describes human history from beginning to end, but it is selective of material and there are enormous gaps in the story. The Bible, beginning with a description of an unspoiled garden, concludes in the same fashion—one garden existing in time and the other in

30

eternity. The function of the book is also twofold; it is a revelation of comfort and condescension. It is about the comfort of God for His people through His condescension to them through prophets, judges, and kings, then most perfectly and completely in the Lord Jesus Christ; it is about His triumph in and through history. History is really a redemptive drama. If the subject of the Bible is Christ, the central event in the revelation of God is the cross.

The Bible is composed of two testaments or covenants, an old one and a new one. The Old Testament is a book of shadows. The ceremonies and symbols of the ancient people of God anticipated the coming of a promised deliverer. Beginning with the promise to Adam after the Eden catastrophe (Genesis 3:15), God progressively revealed the one who would crush evil. Gradually the person of Christ is unveiled as details about him are progressively disclosed (for example, he is to be a male; a Semite; a son of Abraham, Isaac, and Jacob; a son of Judah; a son of David). His work is gradually unveiled through ceremonies such as those for the Passover and the Day of Atonement. The epitome of the shadowed unveiling in this regard is the revelation of Isaiah the prophet (see Isaiah 53). In essence, the Old Testament era is one of anticipation of the coming of the vaguely explained deliverer, shadows that gradually take on substance.

No longer revealed in shadow as in the Old Testament (Hebrews 1:1), Christ stands in His wonderful beauty in the New Testament revelation. In clear relief, the person and work of the promised deliverer are unmistakably unveiled. The central foci of the Bible are the events of Calvary, where God's promised deliverer became humanity's redeemer, where He rendered a sacrifice—a payment in His own lifeblood—to divine justice in behalf of sinners, where atonement was made for sin, whereupon God could justly and freely forgive sin without a violation of His holiness. The first of two monumental events in all the Bible, one of two central foci of the book, is the cross of Christ. The long-anticipated Christ became our Sin-Bearer, enduring the wrath of God due the sinner (2 Corinthians 5:21). There the debt of sin was paid so that God could remain just and yet could justify sinners.

In the New Testament God revealed something of the early history of the church, though there is a huge gap of time in the story until

31

through prophecy we are told about His second coming, not as a Savior so much as the Lord and King of history. The second grand focus of the Bible is His return as King to rule over His redeemed in a renovated garden. If the great period before the advent of Christ can be called one of anticipation, the period between His comings may be called one of both anticipation and reflection. Christians the world over have a double view as they gather for worship week after week; we express expectancy of the Lord's return and we reflect in the study of the Scriptures on His first coming, either from shadowed, Old Testament texts or from the clearer New Testament revelation. At the end of time, when Christ comes to reign as King over the earth, the third era will commence—the era of fulfillment. All the promises of God, those of both testaments, will come to fruition just as the Bible indicates; righteousness, not chaos, will prevail.

The Religious Historiography of John D. Hannah

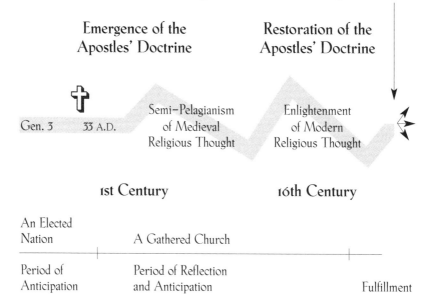

Theme: The Growth of the Kingdom of God in the Kingdom of Man

Emergence of the Apostles' Doctrine

Restoration of the Apostles' Doctrine

Gen. 3   33 A.D.

Semi–Pelagianism of Medieval Religious Thought

Enlightenment of Modern Religious Thought

1st Century

16th Century

An Elected Nation

A Gathered Church

Period of Anticipation

Period of Reflection and Anticipation

Fulfillment

The era between the two advents of the Savior comprises the period of the history of the church, the era of the development of the apostles' doctrine. Thus far, this period of nearly two thousand years has been divided into five segments. These time frames are not to be conceived of as rigid or exact; they are approximations having no consensus among scholars. It is important to grasp these basic divisions because the development of each doctrine will be traced through each era in this book.

The ancient period, beginning with the birth of the church through the desolation of the Roman Empire at about the time of Gregory I (c.540–604), has been subsequently divided into four eras. The first is the age of the apostles, which is the period from the birth of the church to the end of the first century. Second comes the age of the subapostolic Fathers, from the late first century to the middle of the second century, when the literature of the period was characterized by a pastoral, moral, nonpolemical tone. Next is the age of the apologists, or the middle second century to the end of persecution in the early fourth century—a time when the literature was characterized by its defensive posture. Fourth and last is the age of the theologians, a period of the triumph of the church in the empire and the early ecumenical councils.

The medieval period, a time incorrectly designated as the Dark Ages, is generally dated from the sixth or seventh century to the rise of Scholasticism and later the Renaissance in the fourteenth and fifteenth centuries. Often the era is subdivided into early, middle, and late periods.

The modern period is normally dated from the sixteenth century through the nineteenth century. It is divided subsequently into two periods, early modern and late modern. The subject matter of the early period is largely a consideration of the Reformation, which was deeply rooted in the multifaceted Renaissance. The later period, also rooted in the Renaissance, flowered not in a flurry of biblical studies and Christian renewal but in the Enlightenment, which resulted in a considerable attack upon the Christian faith (1750–1900).

The postmodern period (1900–present), which is our own, has been characterized by secularization and the desolation of Christianity as a shaper of cultural values.

The shape of the era between the two advents of Christ has thus far been characterized by two great events and the hope of a third.

33

First, through the mercy of Christ and the power of the Holy Spirit, the apostles' doctrine emerged in the initial several centuries of the church, displacing the pagan religions of the Roman Empire and triumphing from the fourth century through the nineteenth. Second, in light of the decline of clarity regarding the apostles' teachings on grace, sin, and redemption through Christ alone in the late medieval era, the Lord granted a marvelous divine mercy to His church in a restoration or recovery to prominence of the apostles' teaching in the era called the Reformation. However, the gospel endured erosion with the rise of the Enlightenment, which bequeathed to history the modern era and witnessed the end of the triumphal reign of Christianity as the predominant source of cultural values. The demise of Christianity as a cultural force in public life caused the apostles' teachings to become increasingly privatized and internalized; today new forms of old paganism predominate in the general culture. Thus, for the glory of God and the good of people in general (the salvation of souls in particular), we pray, hope, and labor for a restoration once again of the apostles' teachings that will grip and transform our current postmodern culture of despair and disintegration. In this book the history of the development of doctrine will be traced through these several eras with the hope that the gospel, the glorious message of Christ's transforming grace, will once more inform cultural values. The place to begin, it seems, is to retell the story of the orthodox faith once for all delivered to the saints.

2

Authority: Where to Go for Truth

When a young woman named Jennifer moved into the townhouse next door, Mary offered to help in any way she could. The two women hit it off, though more than thirty years separated their ages. Jennifer seemed to appreciate Mary's help in choosing curtains and planting flowers, and they fell into the habit of taking walks together in the evening. On one of these walks Mary found it natural to mention how her study in 1 Corinthians 15 had been comforting to her in accepting the death of her husband, who had died the previous year.

"I think that's totally great for you," said Jennifer. "I can see how believing in resurrection could make you feel better."

"Do you believe in life after death?" asked Mary.

"Sure. I mean, I'm mostly into reincarnation myself. But resurrection, that's cool too."

Mary was puzzled, not sure what Jennifer really believed. "The Bible teaches resurrection. Don't you agree?"

"Oh, yeah. That's what they said back when I went to Sunday school. And the Bible's what you believe in, evidently, so that's why I think this resurrection thing is so great for you."

Mary had to ponder this on the way home. She had been a Christian since childhood and had mostly associated with Christians. Frankly, it shocked her to realize that Jennifer apparently believed the Bible was true *for her* but not necessarily true for everybody. And if Jennifer didn't accept the Bible, where did she get her ideas, such as that half-baked belief in reincarnation? Mary decided she would have to get to know Jennifer better.

As Mary learned to her surprise, the issue of where one can go to find truth has perhaps never been more prominent than today amid the shifting sands of postmodern relativism. And yet, in one form or another, the issue of authority has been of concern throughout the church era. Historical Christian doctrine, in the orthodox tradition, gives us an answer as to where we can go for truth. It thus provides us with a solid foundation on which to build our lives.

The fact of a deposit of truth is a fundamental assumption of Christianity. Indeed, it is one of the two grand starting points of the Christian faith. We believe that God exists and that He has revealed Himself to us. Neither the existence of God nor the revelation of God are strictly provable if by that one means a demonstration that is non-falsifiable. However, such assumptions about God and His revelation are certainly warranted and reasonable based on a vast array of "proofs." In other words, an impressive case can be built to suggest that people are not blindly exercising religious faith when they believe in the existence of God and the truth of the revelation of God. Should we begin our study with the church's understanding of God or with revelation? It seems that we are caught in a dilemma, since God is known to us only through His revelation. God is certainly prior to His revelation, yet we cannot know God until He reveals Himself. I have chosen to begin our study of the history of Christian doctrine with a discussion of the revelation of God.

As a general overview of the subject of revelation, it may be argued that the issues relative to it are two: the number of books in the canonical Scriptures and the quality of those books. Briefly stated, the number of books in the canon was an issue that did not receive a definitive resolution until the creedal formulas of the Reformation in the sixteenth century from Orthodox, Roman Catholic, and Protestant perspectives. That is, church leaders differed in their lists of canonical books through the centuries, though there was general agreement relative to most of the books. Through the Reformation era, if a book was granted canonical status, it was viewed as having no errors in it of any kind, whether they be related to science, history, or morals. The accommodation of God to reveal Himself, it was understood, did not include mistakes; the Bible did not contain infallible truths in an errant shell. The words and the message were inseparable. Since the

36

Reformation, the reverse has often been the case: while discussions about the number of books in the canon are rare, the quality of the books has been repeatedly challenged by those who have imbibed Enlightenment ideals. Today many view the canonical books of their particular religious tradition as unauthoritative and error-prone, possessing a body of truth within an outer, replaceable shell.

The History of the Doctrine of Authority

The Ancient Church	The Medieval Church	The Reformation Church	The Modern Church

Formulation → Canonization → Re-evaluation

Irenaeus		Luther	Kant
Origen		Calvin	Schleiermacher
Athanasius		Zwingli	Strauss
Augustine		Beza	Barth
Gregory I		Bullinger	Bultmann

THE ANCIENT CHURCH AND AUTHORITY
(100–600)

The ancient church was committed to the Word of God. But exactly where was the Word of God to be found? Certainly in the Scriptures. But which Scriptures? Which of the Jewish and Christian writings were divinely inspired? And beyond such writings, where else might the Word of God be embodied?

We turn first for answers to these questions to the church fathers, those men and writings that directed the thinking of the Christian church in the immediate postapostolic period.[1]

THE CHURCH FATHERS AND AUTHORITY (100–150)

Three sources of authority seem to have been recognized in the early church, though it must be remembered that there was no universal opinion. While the church of our Lord can be referred to as a collective singularity, as in a passage like Philippians 3:6, conformity of practice and teaching among the churches at this time was lacking. The development of doctrine arises out of cultural and ecclesiastical circumstances, either questions put to the church by its members or threats posed to it by its adversaries. This insight is important in making the point that the church of the second century appears to have been without significant external or internal travail—a circumstance that would prove to be temporary. Perhaps this situation of relative comfort prevailed in the second century due to the insignificant size and influence of the church within the Roman Empire. At any rate, without a strong impulse propelling the church to defend and declare itself in the realm of authority, there is little evidence of reflection in these matters.

The documents from this period suggest several things. First, reflective of the Jewish heritage of the church, the writers of the period understood the Old Testament books to be authoritative, though the exact number of the books in that canon is unclear. This can be illustrated by the quotation formulas employed by the writers in the early-church period. Before Old Testament allusions or quotations, such prefaces as "For He [the Creator] says . . . ," "For the holy writings say . . . ," "For thus it is written . . . ," "For thus says God . . . ," and "For the Scripture says . . . " are common. Second, relative to the New Testament books, these earliest writers did not conceive of them as they did of the Old Testament ones. A concept of the presence of new authoritative books was grasped even in the late first century (2 Peter 3:15-16), but there seems to have been no idea of their equality with the Old Testament; on this issue there is complete silence. Certain of the writings of the apostles were highly regarded and used, as evidenced, for example, by Clement of Rome's view of Paul's letters to Corinth. Many of the apostolic books were circular letters to various churches, or were written to certain individuals, and thus may not have been known throughout the churches in the empire. Of the twenty-seven books that were later collected as the New Testament, the Fathers

38

allude to nineteen of them (the excepted ones being Luke, Colossians, Philemon, 2 Peter, 2 John, 3 John, Jude, and Revelation). These writers seem also to have had a high regard for certain writers or writings of their own era along with the apostolic writings. This is particularly true of *The Shepherd of Hermas* (which is referred to by its writer as a revelation), the *Epistle of Barnabas,* the *Didache,* and *1 Clement.* Perhaps the best judgment on this issue is that the earliest Fathers of the church did not have a precipitating cause that motivated them to reflect on the extent of authority; the issue was simply not raised.

Second, the earliest Fathers considered tradition to be authoritative. In the early church, tradition was understood to be the oral articulation of the gospel, just as the sacred books were the literary expression of it. In this sense tradition and Scripture, though in different forms of communication, are the same. Both the sacred writings and the word-of-mouth communication of the Christian message were the "Word of God." The authority was not the medium through which the message was communicated; the authority was the message communicated! Tradition is simply the oral presentation of the gospel. The means of understanding the gospel in a world of vast illiteracy was not the written word but the spoken word. However, the spoken word—tradition—was always in conformity with the Old Testament revelation and the teaching of the apostles; there was no oral tradition that stood in contrast with the written revelation of God.

Third, the earliest Fathers placed authority in the leadership of the church. Particularly is this evident with the rise of the bishop's office in the East and of apostolic succession in the West.

In the Eastern churches, as is clearly evident in the writings of Ignatius of Antioch (c.35–c.107), there was in many areas a shift from a plurality of leadership to the emergence of a single leader in each of the churches. The message spoken by the bishop was a bulwark against false teaching. Truth was not so much related to an ecclesiastical office or officeholder as it was related to the fact that the officeholder was standing in a line of succession with the apostles. Along with the written word and the oral word (tradition), the bishop was a faithful witness to the gospel. Those who did not have access to the sacred books, and yet embraced the message orally communicated to them, had a shelter of protection and comfort, their trusted pastor/bishop.

A similar line of authority arose in the West, articulated initially by Clement of Rome (d. 101?). Though he was not aware of the practice of having a single leader in each of the churches (the terms "elder" and "bishop" being conceived of as interchangeable terms; see Acts 20:28 and Titus 1:1,7), as was the emerging custom in the East, Clement did advocate the concept of an apostolic succession in the churches. That is, the plural leadership in the Roman church—the body of presbyters—was viewed as being in direct lineage from the apostles, who gained their authority through Christ. Apostolic succession was not so much the notion of an unbroken sequence of leaders in the churches as it was the continuation of the gospel message in the churches preserved by faithful leaders (2 Timothy 2:2). The theory can be rather simply expressed: God the Father sent Christ, His Son, into the world; Christ sent His apostles into the world; and the apostles have their successors as well. The lineal succession through the office of leadership was a proof that the presbyters were proclaiming the message of God; there was a seamless garment of truth throughout the decades in the churches. Thus, each church conceived of itself as being part of a genealogical tree whose root was God, whose trunk was Christ, whose major branches were the apostles, and whose lesser branches were the leaders of each of the churches in succession.

THE APOLOGISTS AND AUTHORITY (150–300)

The apologists were those men and writings that directed and defended the church during the period when it began to come under attack from persecutors on the outside and heretics on the inside.[2] It was because of the heretics, in particular, that the issue of authority rose in importance. If you were going to defend historic, apostolic Christianity, what exactly was that Christianity? Which Christian writings were "in" and which were "out"? The sifting process, leading toward the formation of the New Testament canon, went on.

The Apologists and the Structure of Authority

As the church expanded throughout the Roman Empire in the second century, and particularly after the dissolution of the Jewish state as a result of the Bar Kochba rebellion in the 130s, Christianity was no

 40

longer perceived as a Jewish sect. Increasingly, it was recognized as a powerful movement in its own right and so found itself facing the wrath of the state, the critique of false religions, and usurpers from within its own ranks (1 John 2:19). Each of these three hostile forces caused the church, as it rallied against them, to reflect on the issue of the nature of its authority. The brief period of the earliest fathers was over; it proved, in retrospect, to have been the calm before the storm.

The principal religious opponent from outside the church was Gnosticism, a blend of Eastern ideologies, Platonic philosophy, and some Christian principles. Gnostics claimed to possess unwritten apostolic traditions, as well as an array of written sources, to verify their teachings. The potent threat posed by Gnostic teachers forced the church to think through the issue of written and oral sources.

Two prominent teachings emerged at this time in the church that focused on many of the same issues: Marcionism and Montanism. Marcion (d. c.160), influenced by Gnostic dualism, believed the Old Testament and Paul's letters to be irreconcilable. He rejected the Jewish writings, including the whole Old Testament, and critically revised Luke's gospel while elevating the works of Paul. Montanus (2d c.) advocated a prophetic authority outside the Old Testament and the apostolic writings, an idea of a continuous or ongoing revelation from God.[3]

Added to these factors was the threat of the state that periodically confiscated the church's writings, making it costly and dangerous to possess unauthorized sacred books. This caused the church to think about the nature of authority, eliminate unworthy books, and preserve the true ones. In this process, a line of demarcation was drawn around the first-century writings; these alone were perceived to be authentic revelation.

The term "canon" is used in the New Testament writings (Galatians 6:16; Philippians 3:16) and in the early fathers (2 Clement 7:2) in the nontechnical sense of a standard, a measuring device. In the early church, the term came to be used with two different meanings, referring to those books that are the revelation of God as well as to those books that are merely useful for edification. Both Jerome and Augustine employed both the broad and the narrow usage of the term, though they recognized differences in quality and function among some of the books in question. (More will be said on the issue of the Old Testament apocryphal books below—an issue that divides Roman Catholics from Orthodox and Protestant believers to this day.)

To preserve the churches from errant teachings, bishops in the late second century began to assemble lists of the apostolic writings, recognizing that they alone should be read in church worship. While the letters of the emerging New Testament corpus were to be read throughout the churches (Colossians 4:16), the thought of the nearness of the Lord's return (John 21:21-22) perhaps blinded Christians to the necessity of gathering them together. Indeed, in the expansiveness of the empire, it is reasonable to assume that some early Christians were not even aware that some of the books existed! Gradually the concept of a "canon" emerged, although, as stated above, the term had both a narrow and a broad connotation. Also, while the canonical framework of the New Testament revelation was not precisely defined, the earliest churches followed the Hebrew canon that was the same as our thirty-nine Old Testament books arranged in a list of twenty-two books through various combinations to conform to the number of letters in the Hebrew alphabet. This canon did not include any of the Old Testament Apocryphal books, according to Josephus (c.37–c.100), the famed Jewish historian, and Philo (c.20 B.C.–c.A.D. 50), the prolific Jewish commentator. The first Christian writer to provide a list of Old Testament sources was Melito of Sardis. Other Christian writers, such as Origen, agreed with him. The earliest collection of books that we have is called the Muratorian Canon, named for the eighteenth-century Italian archaeologist who found the document in Milan. It is clear that by the time of its original composition (the late-second century), the writings of the apostles were elevated to the level of the Old Testament. However, this list did not include 1 and 2 Peter, 1 John, Hebrews, and James (the latter two books perhaps because of the influence of Marcionism). The third-century Syriac version of the apostolic writings does not contain the Revelation. Irenaeus (c.130–c.200), the bishop of Lyons in Gaul (France) and a prolific writer, alluded to all the apostolic writings except Philemon, James, 2 Peter, 2 and 3 John, and Revelation. In addition, he alluded to *1 Clement* and *The Shepherd of Hermas*, the most revered nonapostolic writings. Origen (c.185–c.254), one of the most renowned scholars in the early church, made a list of disputed

42

or uncertain books that included Hebrews (perhaps due to its uncertain authorship), James, 2 Peter, 2 and 3 John, Jude, the *Epistle of Barnabas, The Shepherd of Hermas,* the *Didache,* and the *Gospel of the Hebrews.* Thus, by the end of the second century and into the third century, a canon of Scripture began to emerge in the churches. The process was gradual and by no means uniform. The churches were widely scattered throughout the empire, making communication infrequent. The gathering of church leaders at this time was rare due to the alien status of the church in the empire. Each church experienced a degree of independence; customs varied from church to church.

In addition to the gradual recognition of authoritative books, the churches continued their appeal to tradition in order to preserve the faith. The term "tradition" came to have a variety of meanings in the early church, though it basically had reference to the oral presentation or creedal statement of the orthodox faith. Again, the validity of the gospel message, expressed orally or in a capsulized fashion, lay in its conformity to the Scriptures. The apostle Paul, for example, appears to have seen no difference between the Word of God written and that Word orally rehearsed (1 Corinthians 15:3,11; 2 Thessalonians 2:15). Thus, tradition and Scripture were equated because early church leaders saw a strict conformity between them; the former was valid because it was a faithful witness to the latter, though in a different form.

The Orthodox churches have argued that tradition, the oral gospel, preceded the written revelation of God and therefore has priority over it. One common expression of tradition was the creedal formulas that were used in the baptismal ritual. These were statements of orthodox faith confessed by individuals before the church prior to admission. The earliest of these was the Old Roman Symbol, which can be traced to the third century. The Apostle's Creed, which has been dated from the fifth century, appears to have been based on the earlier creed. The creeds possessed a derived authority in that their validity rested upon their being a faithful summary of the Scriptures.

The concepts of the bishop's office (which emerged early in the second century in the East, though with no uniformity throughout the churches in the empire) and apostolic succession were developed as a hedge against the forces pervasive to the gospel. Quite rapidly, the

43

churches accepted the idea of a single leader in each of the churches, perhaps due to the giftedness and learnedness of one in the church to refute heresy and console the afflicted. The shift to singularity of leadership, coupled with the idea that each church existed in an unbroken lineage of truth from the apostles, provided a bulwark against the heresies of the day. Tertullian (c.160–c.225), for example, argued that this genealogical derivation of doctrine and tradition from the apostles was the ground of orthodoxy. "Indeed," he wrote, "it is on this account only that they will be able to deem themselves apostolic, as being the offspring of apostolic churches. . . . Therefore the churches, although they are so many and so great, comprise but one primitive church, [founded] upon the apostles, from which they all [spring]" (*Prescription against Heretics* 20). In the emergence of the bishop's office, Irenaeus was important because he appears to have been the first to attribute to church leaders a special custodial relationship to the truth—a notion unknown to Ignatius, Tertullian, or Origen. A line in Irenaeus's writings, referring to the bishops, states, "Those who, together with the succession of the episcopate, have received the certain gift of truth . . . " (*Against Heresy* 4:26). By this time, the bishop was viewed not merely as the head of a local church but also as an incorrupt guardian of the truth, because he was a part of the single episcopate emanating from the apostles. It was neither the office of the bishop nor his historical lineage that conferred authority on the leadership in the churches at this time; rather, it was the message and its conformity to the teachings of the apostles. Irenaeus wrote, "True knowledge is [that which consists in] the doctrine of the apostles . . . according to the succession of the bishops . . . without any forging of Scriptures . . . a lawful and diligent exposition in harmony with the Scriptures" (*Against Heresy* 4:33).[4]

The Apologists and the Nature of Authority

The question before us is this: How did the early church leaders understand the intrinsic quality of the Scriptures? Is there evidence that they recognized that God's accommodation in revealing Himself to us through the medium of human language and fallen sense perception involved a willingness to speak the truth through error, an infallible message through human fallibility? Is there a separation of ideas from the words that convey them? How did the early church leaders understand God's ways of communicating His Word to us? Is there any evidence that they perceived errors in the Word of God?

The answer is simply that the apologists believed that the Scriptures were the Word of God in written form; there is no hint that they viewed the Bible critically. To them, the Bible, though written by an array of human authors, was God's Word. Justin Martyr (c.100–c.165), the first in the church to write on the subject, understood that God's superintendence was both verbal (extending to the exact words) and plenary (encompassing the totality of them). Writing about the Old Testament, he notes, "When you hear the utterances of the prophets spoken as it were personally, you must not suppose that they were spoken by the inspired themselves, but by the Divine Word who moves them" (*Apology* 36). In a rather eloquent passage, Clement of Alexandria (c.150–c.215) described the manner of inspiration as God "using righteous man as an instrument like a harp or lyre, [that he] might reveal to us the knowledge of things divine and heavenly" (*Exhortation to the Heathen* 8). Athenagoras (2d c.) expressed the same idea of divine inspiration as the ground for his polemic against false teachers. "The prophets [were] lifted in ecstasy above the natural operations of their minds by the impulse of the Divine Spirit, the Spirit making use of them as a flute player breathes into a flute" (*Apology* 9).

Some have sought to find justification for a broader view of inspiration in Origen, the Alexandrian scholar, who made use of an allegorical approach to Scripture. However, upon a scrutiny of the facts, it appears that Origen found in the allegorical method a justification for the defense of the literal meaning of obscure, difficult texts. For Origen, the literal meaning of the text was the point of departure for all other meanings. Bruce Vawter's conclusion about Origen's understanding of the text of Scripture is instructive.

It seems to be clear enough, that, in company with most of the other Christian commentators of the age, he most often acted on the unexpressed assumption that the Scripture is a divine composition through and through, and for this reason infallibly

45

true in all its parts. . . . He could therefore entertain the notion of verbal inspiration or of the literary authorship of God that could appear quite crass indeed, and it was this notion that he frequently carried with him when he examined the Scriptures.[5]

THE THEOLOGIANS AND AUTHORITY (300–600)

The acceptance of Christianity by Emperor Constantine in the fourth century led to a number of profound changes. For example, the era of persecution drew to a conclusion; the church triumphed over the pagan religions of its day, inaugurating a lengthy period of its supremacy; and Christianity was established as the official religion of the empire. Pagan temples were renovated into Christian worship centers; pagan festivals became Christianized celebrations; and emperors became interested in the prosperity of the church. New freedoms came to the church, and among these was the unprecedented privilege to gather together to discuss issues of importance and to prepare creedal summaries of their findings. It became a fertile period of doctrinal development.

The Theologians and the Structure of Authority

*B*ishops continued to stress the earlier structure of authority in the church, meaning the Scriptures, the bishop's office, and tradition. Tradition—as expressed in the oral message or creeds—continued to have an authority in the church, but only as it conformed to the witness of the apostles. However, in understanding the extent of the canon, the church made significant strides in this period, though the councils and their resultant pronouncements were regional, providing no consensus of opinion throughout the churches.

In the Eastern portion of the church, the Council of Laodicea (363) is instructive. The sixteenth canon listed the books to be read in the churches, while the fifty-ninth forbade the use of any other books in the liturgy of the church. (The word "canon" here refers to an article of conclusion of the council's findings.) In the list of Old Testament books, the council added Baruch and the "Letter" (a Greek

46

writing from the intertestamental period falsely attributed to Jeremiah or Baruch). The New Testament books included those currently recognized, with the exception of Revelation—a book of questionable apostolic authorship and uncertain meaning. Athanasius (c.296–373), the famed bishop of Alexandria, issued a list of books to be read in the churches in 366 or 367 in his "Easter Letter," which, among other things, brought uniformity to Christian celebrations throughout the empire. The occasion for Letter XXXIX was the mixture in the churches of apocryphal books with the divine Scriptures; he wrote to distinguish the two, forbidding the former to be read in the churches. Athanasius's Old Testament list did not include Esther, though Baruch was placed after Jeremiah; the New Testament list included all and only those that are recognized today in the Roman Catholic, Orthodox, and Protestant churches. He then speaks of "other books besides these not indeed included in the Canon" and lists them: the Wisdom of Solomon, the Wisdom of Ben Sirach, Esther, Judith, Tobit, the Teaching of the Twelve (the *Didache*), and *The Shepherd of Hermas*. These, he says, are the invention of heretics.

In the Western portion of the church, a degree of ambivalence is apparent on two counts: First, the term "canon" was used loosely to signify books that were to be read for the benefit of the church without differentiating the degree of edification they afforded (inspired books versus good general books). Second, there was no universal agreement on the books to be included as canonical.

In 394 Jerome (c.345–420) gave a list of books to be read in the worship of the church in a letter to Paulinus (366/67–431), bishop of Nola, that includes only those books that appear in our current canon. However, when Bishop Damascus of Rome (c.304–384) asked him to prepare a revision of the Latin text to standardize the Scriptures for the churches, the Latin Vulgate, he appended a second volume to the sixty-six inspired books. The writings contained in this second volume, though recognized as useful, were perceived as inferior in quality; they were to be read for edification, not for the establishment of doctrine.[6] Jerome accepted the Hebrew canon of Scriptures as earlier presented by Josephus and others, but he understood several pre-apostolic writings to be noncanonical (though edifying) works, namely, Judith, Tobit, the Maccabees, Susanna, and Bel and the Dragon. For

Jerome, the language of divine inspiration in the Old Testament era was Hebrew; in the New Testament era, Greek. The apocryphal books were preapostolic Greek texts and were therefore noncanonical.

Augustine of Hippo (354–430) was influential in calling the Synod of Carthage in 397. Canon thirty-six from this synod lists the "divine writings." While the synod affirmed the entire list of New Testament books as we have them today, it included several Old Testament books that Jerome had relegated to the inferior list of "canonical" books (such as Tobit, Judith, and 1 and 2 Maccabees). A later council in Carthage (418/419) reaffirmed the conclusions of the previous one. By this time, the New Testament revelation of God was agreed upon in the church, both in the East and West, though the specific extent of the Old Testament canon continued unresolved for centuries.

The Theologians and the Nature of Authority

The witness of the theologians is consistent with that of the pastors and scholars before and after them. These men viewed the Scriptures as being errorless, the literal words of God. For Augustine, whose views reflected those of the entire church of his day, the Scriptures were the words of the Holy Spirit dictated to human authors. He took comfort that this view was the unanimous witness of the church from the times of the apostles. For example, in the preface to his discussion of Psalm 33, he began by saying, "Let us then hear what the Holy Spirit by the mouth of his holy prophet says in the words of the Psalm" (8:71). A. D. R. Polman's summary of Augustine's view is magnificent.

> St. Augustine was fully convinced that the Scriptures were entirely the Word of God. Everything in the Old and New Testament was written by one Spirit and must be believed beyond all doubt. Any suggestion of partial inspiration was rejected out of hand. . . . In the Scriptures, even historical events are related by divine authority, and must therefore be believed absolutely.[7]

THE MEDIEVAL CHURCH AND AUTHORITY
(600–1500)

The issue of the number of books in the canon continued to be unresolved through the lengthy period of the Middle Ages, though the quality of the books continued to be understood in the tradition reflected in Augustine.[8] The dominance of Jerome's Vulgate, with its dual canon, is a partial explanation for the unresolved canon, as was the linguistic broadness of the term "canon" in the church. An example of the continued confusion is the findings of the Trullam Synod, which gathered in Constantinople in 692. In Article 2, referring to the number of books in the canon, an appeal was made to both the Council of Laodicea (363) and the Council of Carthage (397), though they contradicted each other on the issue.

There seems to have been no consensus among the church's leaders on the extent of the Old Testament canon. For example, Bishop Gregory I of Rome, called Gregory the Great (pope 590–604), rejected Maccabees as being apocryphal but embraced Tobit and Ecclesiasticus as Scripture. Isidore of Seville (c.560–636) placed Jerome's inferior books into the canon while expressing doubts about Hebrews, 2 Peter, James, and John's letters. John of Damascus (c.655–c.750), the great Eastern scholar, rejected the Old Testament apocryphal books but added Apostolic Constitutions and *1 and 2 Clement* to his list of New Testament ones. The issue was not the subject of a gathering of the church's bishops and so continued unresolved.

The first papal statement on the subject was issued by Eugenius IV at the Council of Florence (1438–1445). In this important gathering, aimed in part at conciliating the Eastern churches and healing the schism, Eugenius proposed that the books in the Latin Vulgate be regarded as universally inspired. That is, he obliterated Jerome's careful distinction between books to be read in the liturgy of the churches and books to be used for personal, private edification. He removed Jerome's dual distinction in the term "canon," merging the books of the two sections as equally authoritative.

In the early years of the Protestant Reformation, a synod was held in Paris, the Sens Synod (1528), which also issued a statement on

49

the question of the canon. It declared as authoritative the books decreed by the Council of Carthage (397), which included several books in Jerome's second "canon." Neither the Sens Synod nor the Council of Florence was a gathering of the entire church, so that their authority was only regional or personal in nature. Tommaso de Vio, Luther's opponent at the Leipzig debates, had reservations about the Old Testament apocrypha as well as James, 2 and 3 John, and Jude. Erasmus of Rotterdam, the leading humanist scholar of his day, questioned 2 Peter and the Apocalypse (Revelation). The point of this brief survey is that the issue of the canonical list was not resolved in the medieval period—it was not considered to be an issue that warranted an ecumenical declaration.

THE EARLY MODERN CHURCHES AND AUTHORITY (1500–1750)

Sources for authority became an issue in the late medieval period as the church was troubled by dispute and division.[9] Within the church, discussions on the nature and reception of the grace of God in the gospel created an increasingly sharp segmenting of opinion, of claim and counterclaim. By this time, most agreed that the church was in need of reform, but there was no consensus on the nature or extent of the changes required.

Out of this unsettled situation emerged two broadly cohesive and increasingly antithetical movements, each claiming to be the historic Catholic Church. One voice, the church at Rome, claimed historic continuity with the past through an impressive, unbroken lineage of bishops from the apostle Peter; the other came from the rising voices of priests and scholars who questioned Rome's truth claims and con-structed findings of their own. Thus, in the sixteenth century two reformations of the church emerged. (Actually, there were several others as well, but these two were the most enduring and influen-tial.) Since they were so much in opposition to each other, and shared much of the same past, a careful and distinctive declaration of authority was important.

THE ROMAN CATHOLIC CHURCH AND AUTHORITY

The structure of authority in the Roman Catholic Church was formally established at the Council of Trent (1545–1563). This council was a gathering of pope, cardinals, and bishops who collectively defined the emerging church in opposition to the simultaneously emerging Protestant movement. The findings of the council were expressed in the "Canons and Dogmatic Decrees," a lengthy document, and in the shorter Tridentine Profession of Faith.

The Roman Catholic Church and the Scriptures

The Council of Trent proposed that all the books found in the Old Latin Vulgate were to be received as having equal canonical and divine authority. Having discarded the dual nuance of the term "canon" and the distinction between the books Jerome had arranged in the Latin Vulgate, various intertestamental Greek books—those called apocryphal books by Protestants—were folded into the Old Testament Hebrew canonical books. Thus, this church has a larger list of canonical books than its counterparts, the Protestant and Orthodox churches. There is agreement on the New Testament list but not the Old Testament list, the difference being seven additional books (the Roman Church does not recognize all the apocryphal books as canonical, only seven of the fifteen). The Latin Vulgate became the official Bible in the church: "[The church] following the examples of the orthodox Fathers, receives and venerates with an equal affection of piety and reverence, all the books both of the Old and of the New Testament—seeing that one God is the author of both" (4.2). With reference to the enlarged canon, the decree of the council is specific: "If anyone does not accept as sacred and canonical the aforesaid books in their entirety and with all their parts, as they have been accustomed to be read in the Catholic Church and as they are contained in the Old Latin Edition, and knowingly and deliberately rejects the aforesaid traditions, let him be anathema" (4.2).

As regards the nature of the canonical books, the Canons and Dogmatic Decrees of Trent state a dictation theory of their authorship. The books composing both the written and unwritten tradition were "dictated either by Christ's own word of mouth, or by the Holy Ghost, and preserved in the Catholic Church by continuous succession" (4.2). Thus, the Scriptures are the infallible Word of God.

The Roman Catholic Church and Tradition

The early church leaders recognized the important role of tradition, defining it either as the oral articulation of the gospel or as creedal statements. Both were viewed as authoritative because of the perceived congruity of their teachings with Scripture. Tradition was Scripture-based. As the centuries passed, the word "tradition" took on the additional meaning of ecclesiastical customs or practices as well as the consensus of patristic interpretation. As time went on, the idea of tradition became less Word-based and tradition-as-authority was replaced by what Augustine referred to as "time-hallowed usage." Tradition came to possess an equal yet independent authority in the church. However, for Augustine, tradition did not have an independent status of authority; customs or ecclesiastical practices, however widespread or beneficial, were not a second source of authority distinct from the Scriptures. Can practices in the church that are not recorded in the Scriptures be considered apostolic? The first to posit this dual notion of authority in the church was Basil the Great, the fourth-century scholar in Asia Minor, in his work, *On the Holy Spirit*. He suggested that both written and unwritten traditions came from the apostles; the latter as binding as the former. Thus, the church appealed to the teachings of its pastors and scholars as authoritative ("... as also the said traditions, as well as, those appertaining to faith as to morals, as having been dictated, either by Christ's own mouth, or the Holy Ghost, and preserved in the Catholic Church by continuous succession," 4.2).

The Roman Catholic Church and Interpretative Authority

The Council of Trent also recognized that God had deposited in the church official teachers who were equipped to exclusively interpret the Holy Scriptures. The body of their interpretative insights was viewed by the church as authoritative. The third article of the Tridentine Profession states the point succinctly: "I also admit the Holy Scriptures, according to that sense which the Holy Mother Church has held and does hold, to which it belongs to judge of the true sense and interpre-

52

tation of the Scriptures; neither will I ever take and interpret them otherwise than according to the unanimous consent of the Fathers." The idea of tradition was not only greatly expanded over the centuries, but in addition it was invested with authority to define belief. The criteria for the authority of the church's teachers and teachings was threefold: authoritative truth is that which has been universally taught in the church; it is that which has been taught in the church over the centuries; and it is that which has been believed in the church. In the words of Vincent of Lérins, a scholar in the fifth century who first suggested the concept, true doctrine is what is believed "everywhere, always, by all." If a doctrine cannot claim universality, it must be rejected. The decrees of Trent stated the idea as follows:

> Furthermore, to check unbridled spirits, it decrees that one relying on his own judgments shall, in matters of faith and morals pertaining to the edification of Christian doctrine, distorting the Holy Scriptures in accordance with his own conceptions, presume to interpret them contrary to that sense which holy mother church, to whom it belongs to judge of their true sense and interpretation, has held and holds, or even contrary to the unanimous consent of the Fathers, even though such interpretations should never at any time be published. (4.2)

THE PROTESTANT CHURCHES AND AUTHORITY

In the early modern era, two movements sought to reform the legacy left by the late medieval church. Though their intents were similar, the reforms themselves were not. Being heirs of the same fifteen centuries of history, the polarized parties formed movements that each claimed to be the apostolic original.

Believing that an appeal to what was taught "everywhere, always, by all"—the unanimous consent of the teachers of the church—was a faulty foundation, the Protestant Reformers downplayed the role of tradition. They felt compelled to this conclusion for at least two reasons.

First, unanimity on several important issues of doctrine by the church's teachers simply does not nor has ever existed; many conflicting things have been taught by the church's teachers over the centuries. Thus, to select one teacher as opposed to another means the possible imposition of a third authority that is actually supreme over both the interpretation of history and the Bible—that is, the suffrage of the church. Since their opponents were believed to be teaching things possibly taught in the past but conflicting with the Bible, the Reformers rejected this method of truth verification. Standing before Emperor Charles V at the famous Diet of Worms in 1521, Martin Luther, recently excommunicated from the church and now about to be declared a criminal in the state, had a profound question addressed to him: "Who are you, Luther, to go against fifteen hundred years of the teaching of the church?" His reply was simply to deny the assumption; there was no unanimity of teaching in the church that stretched over the centuries. The teachers of the church had contradicted themselves.

Second, through the gradual acceptance of tradition over the centuries, the church had come to embrace doctrines that stood at variance with the apostles by either direct, contradictory teachings or by unwarranted additions. An example of a contradictory teaching would be the church's interpretation of the sacraments as mediums for the acquisition of justifying grace. An example of an unwarranted addition would be the embracing of five other sacraments in addition to baptism and the eucharist.

The Protestant Churches and the Structure of Authority

The Protestant Reformers accepted the Hebrew canon of the Old Testament Scriptures (the thirty-nine Old Testament books in our English Bibles) and the twenty-seven Greek New Testament books. They embraced the New Testament canon, differing not at all on this point with their Roman Catholic opponents. They claimed the same New Testament list given by Athanasius in 367 and by Jerome in the Latin Vulgate, though they were unwilling to base the assertion of the canonical books on tradition or (to use Augustine's term) "hallowed church usage." *The Gallican (French) Confession of Faith* (1559) lists each of the sixty-six books after referring to them as the "canonical

54

books" (Article III). The same list is repeated in *The Belgic Confession* (Article IV, 1561). The *Thirty-Nine Articles* of the church of England (Article VI, 1571) individually lists the Old Testament books and mentions the New Testament list without enumerating it. *The Westminster Confession of Faith* (Article I, 1647) lists the sixty-six books "under the name of Holy Scripture, or the Word of God written."

The Protestant confessions are explicit in rejecting the apocryphal books. For example, *The Belgic Confession,* after listing the books, notes, "All which the Church may read and take instruction from, so far as they agree with the canonical books; but they are far from having such power and efficacy as that we may from their testimony confirm any point of faith" (Article VI). *The Westminster Confession,* which states the same sentiment as the *Thirty-Nine Articles* of the Church of England (Article VI), notes, "The books commonly called the Apocrypha, not being of divine inspiration, are no part of the Canon of Scripture, and therefore are no authority in the Church of God, nor to be any otherwise approved, or made use of, than other human writings" (Chapter I.3).

For the Protestants, authority did not reside in the teaching ministry of pastors, scholars, and councils unless that which was taught by them was in conformity with the Word of God. Authority for the Reformers was derived for the churches through the Bible, the Word of God. The touchstone of correct teaching was conformity with the Scriptures, not with a particular office in the church or the declarations of any exalted gathering of church leaders. (The Reformers actually were following the practice of the ancient churches; all teachings and traditions were valid only in so far as they conformed to the Word of God, the gospel.) Speaking with the Roman Catholic concept of authority in view, *The Gallican Confession* states, "Whence it follows that no authority, whether of antiquity, or custom, or numbers, or human wisdom, or judgments, or proclamations, or edicts, or decrees, or councils, or visions, or miracles, should be opposed to these Holy Scriptures, but, on the contrary, all things should be regulated, and reformed according to them" (Article V). *The Westminster Confession* argues, "The Supreme Judge, by which all controversies of religion are to be determined, and all decrees of councils, opinions of ancient writers, doctrines of men, and private spirits, are to be examined, and in whose sentence we are to rest, can be no other but the Holy Spirit speaking in the Scripture" (Chapter I.1).

The Protestant Churches and the Nature of Authority

According to Protestants, the Bible is the very voice of God, and the Holy Spirit is the revealer of the content of the Word of God. *The Gallican Confession* reads, "We believe that the Word contained in these books has proceeded from God and receives its authority from him alone" (Article III). *The Belgic Confession* describes the manner of the Spirit's communicating the Bible by quoting 2 Peter 1:21 and stating, "God . . . , from a special care which he has for us and our salvation, commanded his servants, the Prophets and apostles, to commit his revealed Word to writing; and he himself wrote with his own finger the two tables of the law. Therefore we call such writings holy and divine Scriptures" (Article III). William Ames (1576–1633), the Puritan theologian, spoke for the Protestant tradition when he argued that the Holy Spirit superintended the writers of the Scriptures so that "they might not err in writing," though the Spirit performed His superintendence without annulling the particular literary character of each writer. The ultimate result of the Spirit's work through human authors is that the "Scripture is often attributed to the Holy Spirit."[10]

The Protestant Churches and the Assurance of Authority

For the Reformers, the Bible was the Word of God, it being the voice of the Holy Spirit to us. The Holy Spirit speaks in and through the Bible to the conscience of the godly. By the inner witness of the Spirit do the people of God know that the Bible is the Word of God. Echoing Anselm's dictum that in faith we seek understanding (not through understanding do we seek faith), Calvin writes: "Let it therefore be held as fixed, that those who are inwardly taught by the Holy Spirit acquiesce implicitly in Scripture; that Scripture, carrying its own evidence along with it, deigns not to submit to proofs and arguments, but owes the full conviction with which we ought to receive it to the testimony of the Spirit" (*Institutes of the Christian Religion* I.7.5). *The Gallican Confession* continues, "We know these books to be canonical, and the sure rule of our faith, not so much by the common accord and consent of the Church, as by the testimony and inward illumination of the Holy Spirit" (Article IV). *The Westminster Confession* simply says that "our full persuasion and assurance of the infallible truth, and divine authority thereof, is from the inward work of the Holy Spirit, bearing witness by and with the Word in our hearts" (Chapter I.5).

Jacob Arminius (1560–1609), the Dutch scholar, offered another proof of the Bible's authority. He stated that confidence in the Scriptures rests on the character of God, its author. His thought was that authority is only valid to the degree of the truthfulness of the claim maker. Therefore, since God is true, His claims must be true. He argued as follows:

> We conclude, then, that all things which have been, are now, or to the final consummation will be necessary for the salvation of the church, have been of old perfectly inspired, declared and written; and that no other revelation or tradition, than those which have been inspired, declared and contained in the Scriptures, is necessary to the salvation of the church. (*Disputation* II.24)

THE LATE MODERN CHURCHES AND AUTHORITY (1750–PRESENT)

In retrospect, it is now evident that the Renaissance — the so-called rebirth of learning, which occasioned significant advances in the arts and sciences — was a double-sided coin. The Reformers, having been enriched and challenged by their humanistic training, rejected many of the claims of the church. For them, the quest for a personal, though not individual, knowledge of the truth led, via a study of the ancient sources, to a discovery of the Bible. And this discovery of the Bible in part explains the Reformation. The Renaissance had another side that emerged in the seventeenth century and eroded many of the principles of the Reformation. For the Reformers, the quest for personal faith led to a rejection of "false" tradition and an embrace of the Bible, but learned scholars later rejected both the authority of tradition and the Bible. They viewed both the Roman Catholic Church with its tradition and the Protestants with their Bible as asking people to do basically the same thing—to trust an authority outside of themselves, to intellectually acquiesce and submit to someone or something other than themselves. In the seventeenth century, ravaged as it was by devastating wars, the imposition of an outward authority appeared precarious at best, utterly dangerous at most. The cry of the Enlightenment was to turn inward to find authority, something both personal and private though still corporate in nature.

The Enlightenment was an intellectual movement in Europe that sought to find a safe haven for the investment of authority; largely, the focus became the inner self. Though outwardly theistic, the philosophers of that day, who gradually transcended theologians as advice givers, attacked the notion that authority resided in either priest or pastor, either the church or the Bible. Rejecting notions of the utter sinfulness of mankind, they took a more optimistic view of humanity's potential to discover truth through the application of the scientific method. Karl Barth (1886–1968) defined the movement as "a system founded upon the presupposition of faith in the omnipotence of human ability."[11] Clyde L. Manschreck suggested that "man's rational powers in league with science made dependence on God seemingly unnecessary."

Men were confident that they had the tools with which to unlock the mysteries of the universe. Former distrust of human reason and human culture, as seen in the traditional emphases on depravity, original sin, predestination, and self-denial, gave way to confidence in reason, free will, and the ability of man to build a glorious future.[12]

The result was a growing movement that questioned the authority of the Bible, at least its central place in Western tradition.

It has been argued that on a wintry day in 1618 René Descartes (1596–1650) inaugurated the modern era when he sat in solemn contemplation about the nature of knowing in front of his stove.

58

The task that he set before himself was to discern truth that was beyond doubt (so-called "clear and distinct ideas"). His famous conclusion—"I think, therefore I am"—was a revolution in the quest for authority. He appealed neither to tradition nor to the Bible nor to the church. A new era dawned! Revelation was not so much derived from the traditional sources as through mental reflection on God-given information etched on the mind; knowledge of divine things, such as the existence of God, could be sustained through deduction, that is, through mental reflection. John Locke (1632–1704) argued quite the opposite. He suggested that the mind is not so much created with innate ideas as it is empty and waiting to be filled. That is, knowledge is the result of induction, of the gathering of information and the deriving of general truths from it. Though his theory of the acquisition of knowledge was quite opposite to that of Descartes, the "father of English Empiricism (or Sensationalism)" expanded the role of the mind in the quest for something to believe. While neither theory was an attack upon orthodoxy per se, the net result was often a denigration of revelation. Reason eventually judged the perimeters of knowledge in a manner hitherto unknown. It functioned not only in opposition to revelation but often in open hostility to it.

More influential than either Cartesian or Lockean theories of knowledge acquisition was that amalgam of the two approaches proposed by the Prussian theorist Immanuel Kant (1724–1804). Kant's theory was a cross between the Cartesian insistence on innate ideas and deduction and Lockean empiricism with its focus on induction. He argued that the mind contained distinct ideas implanted in it. Some facts can be known intuitively while other facts are acquired through fact gathering. Through these two venues, knowledge is obtained. This theory, he surmised, was the only buttress against the skepticism of David Hume (1711–1776), which so "woke him from his dogmatic slumbers." Religion was relegated to an innate "categorical imperative," a sense of God-given moral duty. Thus, theology was reduced to morality, and morality was elevated to theology. Though Kant's theory was, perhaps, superior to those of his opponents, knowledge for Kant was still very much experience-based and thus subjective, private, and personal. The place of revelation and the supernatural, as a consequence, was often marginalized. This can be seen most blatantly in Kant himself, who rejected the Bible as divinely authoritative and had little affection for the orthodox faith of his own Lutheran heritage. Locke, on the other hand, was more contrite in his application of the role of reason, retaining a belief in many of the miracles of the Bible, including the deity of Christ, though the title of his major work on religion seems now to have been a harbinger of trends to come: *The Reasonableness of Christianity.*

THE PROTESTANT TRADITIONS AND AUTHORITY

Reaction to the philosophical Enlightenment has been a dominant theme within Christianity in the last several centuries. Some spokesmen have stridently resisted it, marshaling elaborate polemics against any affront to the integrity of the Holy Scriptures. Other have found the best defense of the faith to be a refashioning or modification of traditional views and arguments. Generally, apart from a radical materialist approach to truth, scholars have sought to retain the Christian faith, though the recent centuries have been marked by a strident debate over the permanent, non-negotiable essence of the faith and the transient, disposable aspects of it.

The Protestant Liberal Tradition and Authority

Representative of an attempt to defend Christianity from the atheistic, materialistic tendencies of the Enlightenment, as well as from the supposed precritical naiveté of traditionalist views of the Bible, was the liberal movement of the nineteenth century. Liberals generally embraced the idea that traditional conceptions of the Bible and Christianity were as great a threat to true Christianity as the Enlightenment. The "father of modern liberalism" was Friedrich Schleiermacher (1768–1834), whom Barth argued "did not found a school, but an era."[13] He sought to defend Christian faith by establishing a foundation that was not liable to rational attack, a weakness in traditional conceptions of Christianity in his opinion. Following Kant, Schleiermacher declared the foundation of truth to be the conscious self. Defining religion as the feeling of dependence that we

60

have for God, he resolved to recover an authentic faith by beginning with the self. "I feel this or that way about Christ." That "feeling for God" was the place he began theology. Contrary to the Reformers, who argued that the Bible was self-authenticating, Schleiermacher suggested that the authority of the Bible was rooted in a faith that was antecedent to belief in Scripture. For him, personal feelings of faith determined the content of revelation; the Bible was an imperfect witness to Christ and the teachings of the apostles. It contains a mixture of truth and error. By placing the authority of Christianity in the inner self, he thought he had preserved Christianity from the attacks of skeptics and materialists. In fact, however, he tore authority from the witness of the Spirit through the Scriptures, plunging belief into an endless array of equally "true" subjective insights. In attempting to defend the faith, he placed its defense in the dark, depraved labyrinth of the inner self.

Schleiermacher's attempt to preserve Christianity by adopting Kantianism proved ineffective. The nineteenth century witnessed an ever-increasing attack upon the authority of the Bible and the viability of Christianity. For example, David Strauss (1808–1874), a theologian at Tübingen University, delivered a scathing attack upon the miracles of Christ in his widely read 1835 book, *Leben Jesu*. To Strauss, Christianity was a product of dream fabrication, the "miracles" of the Bible having a naturalistic explanation. He set in motion the much-heralded quest for the historical Jesus—the idea that, while the Bible was not an authentic guide to the knowledge of Christ and Christianity, a critical look at the documents of the Old and New Testaments through the lens of archaeology could recover the real, historic faith of Jesus, which stood in simplistic contrast to the complex perversions of traditional Christianity.

Turning away from Schleiermacher's radically subjective approach to preserve and defend Christianity, Albrecht Ritschl (1822–1889), among many others, sought to obtain an authentic portrait of Christ and Christianity through a more rigid application of the scientific method. That is, Ritschl sought to be more historically rooted and less subjective. Through source-discrimination methodology, such as that developed by Wilhelm Vatke and Julius Wellhausen in Old Testament studies and Strauss and F. C. Baur in New Testament studies, the

Ritschlian school attempted to recover an essential core of truth from the Bible. That is, the truth of Christianity should not be confused with the totality of the Bible, because the revelation of God is enmeshed in mythology. In the Bible somewhere is the revelation of God. To retrieve a respectable Christianity for the modern, critical world, they found a kernel theory, a Bible-within-a-Bible, to be a viable solution. The Bible is not the revelation of God; it contains the revelation of God surrounded by much that is bad history, science, and morals. This can readily be seen in Adolf von Harnack's *What Is Christianity?* (1899). Harnack found in the Bible a central, irreducible core of truth, the "real" message of Jesus—a present, emergent kingdom of God evident in a progressive moral righteousness, the fatherhood of God, and the brotherhood of mankind. To traditional Christians (now perceived as anti-intellectual), Harnack's "essential core" of Christianity was actually a tragic truncation of the Bible and the gospel.

The liberal movement in Protestant theology found a welcome reception in America in the late 1800s, particularly as the rise and predominance of science appeared to bring traditional interpretations of the Bible into question. Many believed that the Ritschlian approach to the Bible could preserve the essence of Christianity, avoid a cultural rejection of the faith, and allow Christians to remain intellectually honest at the same time. Liberalism emerged in America between 1880 and 1920, triumphed as the dominant interpretation of Christianity between 1930 and 1960, and subsequently has lost its forward momentum, disintegrated into partisan politics, and declined in influence. While the American liberal movement was never monolithic, its understanding of the Scriptures generally was consistent. Whether during the classic liberalism of the 1920s, the neo-liberalism in the 1930s through the 1950s, or the radical Bultmannian liberalism in the 1960s and 1970s, the kernel theory prevailed. The traditional approach to the Bible, involving belief in its universal integrity, was summarily rejected and the quest to recover the "real" Bible was relentlessly pursued.

Illustrative of this serious attempt to preserve the integrity of Christianity by finding the revelation of God in the Bible was the experience of William Newton Clarke (1841–1912), a Baptist theologian at Colgate Theological Seminary. Though Clarke was trained

OUR LEGACY

within the sphere of traditional interpretations of the Bible, the findings of science increasingly caused him problems. The intellectual crisis left him with only two options: leave Christianity entirely or find another way to be a Christian. His experience was much like that of his contemporary Harry Emerson Fosdick (1878–1969), perhaps the best-known figure in the liberal tradition in the early twentieth century. The solution both men discovered was to reject those parts of the Bible that they found either morally or intellectually questionable and embrace the "real" Bible. To find the "Bible," the solution was to look to Jesus. He was the window into God because His morals were divine, disclosing the essence of the character of God. The sermon that Jesus preached on the mount was the purest expression of God. Contrary material in the Bible could summarily (and, for some, thankfully) be dismissed. Gone were the days in the history of Christianity in America when the Bible was conceived as a lush, green meadow equally authoritative and true in all its parts. Now, for some, the more accurate metaphor for the Bible was a dung heap. In the manure and straw were gleaming nuggets of truth that had to be carefully extracted, the permanent separated from the transient, the eternal parted from the merely temporal.

A similar approach to authority was taken by Charles Augustus Briggs (1841–1913), a Presbyterian scholar at Union Theological Seminary, New York. Ironically, though liberal in his approach to authority, he was otherwise quite orthodox. He argued that in the history of Christianity there have been three sources of authority: tradition, the Bible, and reason. These sources are equal in authority. Briggs equated fallible tradition and fallen intelligence with the Bible!

At the height of classical liberalism, Shailer Mathews (1863–1941), a scholar at Chicago University, rose to prominence. Mathews sought to apply the insights of social development to the discovery of the kernel of truth within the Bible. He argued that liberals, not conservative Bible believers, were traditionalists; conservatives were inventors of novelty. By this approach, Mathews meant that true Christianity is defined by its ability to adjust to ever-changing needs; the conservatives, being static in their views of the Bible and Christ, failed the test. The essence of Christianity is not well-defined doctrinal beliefs but its social relevancy, which implied the ability to be constantly changing and adapting to ever-new social conditions. The difference between Mathews and his conservative critics is that what he called the permanent essence of Christianity (that is, morals) they perceived as secondary; what conservatives considered essential (that is, doctrine), he considered to be of little importance.

The British Protestant Conservative Tradition and Authority

The conservative British responses to liberal approaches to the Bible represent an interesting spectrum. For example, P. T. Forsyth (1848–1921), an English scholar who had rejected the liberal tradition in 1897 for a warm-hearted, Christ-centered evangelicalism, came to believe that the gospel of Christ was the inspired, infallible revelation of God. The message of redemption, which is available to us through religious experience, is the true Word of God. That is, Forsyth accepted an authoritative Bible, though not an inerrant one. In this way Forsyth could both criticize and accept Higher Criticism. Higher Criticism could be judged for rejecting the historic gospel, but, when guided by spiritual experience and subservient to the gospel, it could function to restore the true Bible. The proof of the Bible's inspiration for Forsyth was the personal experience of God's redemptive revelation in it. This "lonely prophet," being neither a classic liberal nor a traditional conservative, was the harbinger of the later neo-orthodox approach to the Bible. The message, not the context where it is discovered, is the Word of God.

A more conservative approach than Forsyth's was that of James Orr (1844–1913) of the United Free Church College of Glasgow, a critic of both Ritschlian theology and the Wellhausian reconstruction of the Old Testament. Orr rejected the doctrine of inerrancy, believing that textual errors in the sources used by some biblical writers were included in the Bible. The Bible possessed a high degree of accuracy, which he recognized as an argument for its ultimate supernatural origin. Though there were errors in the Bible, it remained the supernatural revelation of God. Orr did not interpret the Creation account literally, seeing it as having symbolic significance. He entertained the thought of a genetic linkage (though not a moral one) between lower species and humankind, and he understood the Fall to be merely descriptive of humanity's deviation from original purity. He was a conservative theistic evolutionist. At the heart of Orr's understanding of Christianity was the incarnation of Christ, the divine one becoming the God-man. Christianity was true because of its harmony with reason and moral experience. Thus, though he rejected the total integrity of Scripture, he wrote against the German Ritschlian school, which reduced Christ to mere humanness, as well as against the naturalism of Darwinian evolution. They both came up short because their radical naturalism did not take into account all available truth. Most particularly, they failed in denigrating personal experience.

An approach that has significant affinities with those of both Forsyth and Orr was that of W. H. Griffith Thomas (1861–1924), the Anglican scholar. Though he neither overtly (like Forsyth) nor tacitly (like Orr) rejected the inerrancy of Scripture—indeed, he defended it—his approach in the defense of the Bible was remarkably similar to theirs. Thomas's ultimate appeal in the defense of the faith and the historical accuracy of the Bible was not to empirical evidence, airtight rational arguments, and impassioned polemics but to spiritual experience. The work of the Holy Spirit upon the believer is itself the final authority, and spiritual experience is the subjective verification. The Word, the witness of the Spirit, reason, and the experience of the redeemed similarly testify to the truthfulness of the Bible. In his view, the Holy Spirit's work of revealing God in the Bible was a sufficient answer to modern rationalistic unbelief; the truth is verified by experiencing it. Thomas's stress was upon the exposition of the Bible, the proclamation of the Word, and a correct relationship to the Holy Spirit.

The German Protestant Conservative Tradition and Authority

Karl Barth (1886–1968), the famed professor of theology at Basel (1935–1961), had a thorough education in Ritschlian theology. Subsequently, however, he became increasingly dissatisfied, and eventually disillusioned, with its assertions. He emerged as a persistent critic of it following the initial 1919 edition of a brief commentary derived from his reflections on the book of Romans. The book proved so revolutionary that it took him from the pastorate and launched him into a career as a professor in several universities. In his doctrine of the Scriptures there are echoes of P. T. Forsyth, though likely no direct connection. The Bible is distinguished from the Word of God because, in Barth's mind, the revelation of God is Jesus Christ. The Word of God is not a thing; it is an event, an encounter with the living Christ. Christ is the Word of God and the Bible is a witness to Christ. Thus, the issue of inerrancy did not trouble Barth because the Bible was merely a means to revelation. Only the revelation (Christ) was infallible, not the means (the Bible). Further, the Bible becomes the revelation of God when Christ is revealed through the Word's witness in the text. The witness of the Spirit was not to the Bible as a whole but to its parts as Christ is revealed through particular texts. While Barth was a master of the Bible, quoting it voluminously, and while he revealed no specific errors in it, the thought of errors in the text would not trouble him because the real point of the Bible was not the words in it but the Christ in it.

The American Protestant Conservative Tradition and Authority

In America the answer to the question "What is the relationship between the inspiration of the Bible and accuracy of the Bible?" has been dominated by the explanation of Archibald A. Hodge (1823–1886) and B. B. Warfield (1851–1921) of Princeton Theological Seminary. Based upon the assumption that God is incapable of deception, Warfield argued that the Bible in the original manuscripts (which have been lost and therefore are not subject to verification) was without error. Thus, the Bible is the inerrant revelation of God. From this assumption, the Princetonians formulated detailed biblical and rational arguments to defend their view. The appeal was not so much to the inner witness of the Spirit to the experience of the believer, nor to the centrality of the gospel message; rather, the emphasis was upon polemics and apologetics. This approach became characteristic of both the evangelical and fundamentalist responses to the threats upon the Bible's integrity. This particular defense of inerrancy has been philosophically linked with Scottish Common Sense philosophy and Enlightenment Rationalism. It has recently received considerable criticism.

Within evangelical circles in recent decades there has been a philosophical shift back to the approach reminiscent of Forsyth and Orr (in which the Bible is seen as containing errors), though not the view reflective of Thomas. The argument has been that the message of the Bible is true but the contextual setting and certain historical, moral, or scientific data may not be. It is a conception of the Bible as containing revelation without being revelation, at least as a whole. The historical argument that has gone along with this theory of revelation is that the doctrine of inerrancy was actually a novel, recent view in the church, having emerged only after the Reformation. The historical view in the church, the really true one, was that God's accommodation to reveal Himself included error in inconsequential areas. What is striking about this particular teaching is that it has appeared in traditional schools and seminaries that once embraced the Princeton-Warfield theory of inerrancy, which reflects the historical opinion of the church. A considerable challenge to claims of its being the historical view of the church has been mounted.

THE ROMAN CATHOLIC TRADITION AND AUTHORITY

This church, much like the Protestant churches, has felt the disruptive influences of the liberal movement in theology, though its official response has been somewhat different. To preserve the claims of traditional orthodoxy, the church published *The Syllabus of Errors* (1864), which prohibited various teachings from being propagated in the church. Further, to preserve the teachings of the church from political, social, and theological trends, the famous Vatican I council (1869) buttressed the authority of the pontiff by declaring the doctrine of papal infallibility. That is, when acting in his official capacity as Christ's representative on the earth, the pope's declarations are *de fide,* or truths that must be believed. "When he speaks *ex cathedra,* that is, when in discharge of the office of pastor and doctor of all Christians, by virtue of his supreme Apostolic authority, he defines a doctrine regarding faith or morals to be held by the universal church . . . is possessed of that infallibility with which the divine Redeemer willed" (Session 4:4). Reiteration of papal infallibility can be found in the documents of Vatican II.

In recent years the Roman Catholic Church has published a new creedal statement, *Catechism of the Catholic Church* (1994). It is an attempt to respond to doctrinal latitudinalism on the one hand and growing religious ignorance in the church on the other hand by creating a positive affirmation of the church's teachings. The preface, signed by John Paul II, indicates that the document's purpose is to perpetuate church renewal and as such continues the work of Vatican II (1962–1965). Through its pages, the official views of the church can be gleaned. For example, the church recognizes that God has given a revelation of Himself through the Scriptures. The revelation of God is complete and inerrant, at least as to its purpose of revealing the salvation that is in Christ Jesus. It is found alone in forty-six Old Testament books (this in contrast to Protestants, who claim thirty-nine) and the twenty-seven New Testament books. Further, the church recognizes a second, equal source of authority to the Bible, and that is tradition. The Bible "is the speech of God as it is put down in writing under the breath of the Holy Spirit" (2.2.81), while tradition is the communication and application of those truths through apostolic succession from God through Christ to Peter and to all his successors. Scripture and tradition (what the church has taught the Bible teaches) are to be accepted with equal devotion, the two sources being noncontradictory in content. Connecting the Scriptures and tradition is the concept that through apostolic succession God has granted the exclusive privilege of interpreting the Scriptures to bishops of the church, who are understood to be in communication with the successors of St. Peter, the first pope of Rome. In a summary statement the catechism notes, "The task of interpreting the Word of God authentically has been entrusted solely to the Magisterium of the church. That is, to the pope and to the bishops in communion with him" (I.1.2.100).

THE ORTHODOX TRADITION AND AUTHORITY

Through a dispute in the Catholic Church over the authority of the Roman bishop in ecclesiastical affairs in the Eastern regions of the church, a schism occurred in 1054. The Orthodox churches came into being as a group distinct and separate from the Western Catholic Church. Unlike the Western Church, which claimed to be one (at least until the Reformation), the Eastern churches are several, currently numbering somewhere around fourteen ecclesiastical bodies, and are generally divided along ethnic lines. In each country, or in each ethnicity, the church is governed by a patriarch, archbishop, or metropolitan; there is no single head over the churches and no recognition of papal claims of primacy.

In Eastern Orthodoxy, authority resides in the unity of the church, not in papal primacy or the Scriptures; it is a function of the internal witness of the Spirit, not in any external authority or dogmatic statements. While Protestants have generally refused to grant equal authority to Scripture and tradition (a view the Roman Church embraces), the Orthodox Church rejects both coequality and inferiority. That is, tradition is generally received as subsuming Scripture. Scripture, the seven ecumenical councils and some later councils, patristic writings, liturgy, canon law, and icons are part of tradition. Tradition is authoritative within the church, and the church, which defines tradition, holds greater authority than the Scriptures.

The canon of the Scriptures number sixty-six books; there is no recognition of the apocryphal books of the Old Testament as canonical. Citing Cyril of Jerusalem, Athanasius, and John of Damascus for support, the Longer Cathechism of the Orthodox Catholic, Eastern Church (1839) lists the books individually. In rejecting the apocryphal books, the catechism states that they were not written in the Old Testament language of inspiration, Hebrew. In the catechism tradition precedes Scripture as a subject of discussion ("The most ancient and original instrument for spreading divine revelation is holy tradition"). Scripture is tradition preserved more exactly and unchangeably. Further, it is evident that the church, the collectivity of the faithful, is the sure repository of truth ("All true believers united by the holy tradition of the faith collectively is the sure repository of holy tradition"). Tradition must conform to Scripture to be valid, yet at the same time it is a guide to the right understanding of Scripture. From a conservative Protestant viewpoint, the concept of tradition has been enlarged over the centuries from what it meant in the early church. In the earliest centuries the word spoken (tradition) and the word written (the Scriptures) were the same in that each bore a faithful, noncontradictory witness to the gospel. However, the term "tradition"

has been enlarged so as to refer to a body of data that often conflicts with Scripture in both the Roman Catholic and Orthodox churches. For Protestants, this theory of authority is not so objectionable as the application and distortion of the theory over the centuries.

3

The Trinity: God as Three-in-One

It seems to occur when I'm the busiest—my well-planned schedule for the day is interrupted by two people who stand on the front porch with materials for me to read. With unease, I realize they are likely Jehovah's Witnesses who would want to engage me in religious conversation. I think, *These are dear people who deny the eternal deity of Christ. They will inevitably point to John 1:1, where the text can be translated "and the Word was a god." Ugh!* Though John 1:14 clearly refers to the same Word—the Lord Jesus—as "the God," the dialogue will likely continue as evidence is followed by counterevidence. Often the discussion will turn to the early church and the use of history. I have heard Jehovah's Witnesses assert that Trinity is not a biblical term, having been first used in the third century, and that the doctrine of the Trinity was not set forth until the fourth century; that is, church leaders invented the doctrine. What can I say? They are correct in asserting that the term is not found in the New Testament and that the formal doctrine was not spelled out until the fourth century. The error of the Jehovah's Witness teaching is rooted in at least one historical miscue. They assume that the early church invented the teaching on the Trinity, which conflicts with the Bible. That is, what the church wrote much later in a creed to describe the nature of God is a perversion of the original scriptural teachings. My reply is that the church did compose creeds but that these creeds were explanations of, not errant additions to, what the Bible teaches. The question, then, is this: Does the Bible suggest to us that Jesus Christ is truly God? While the word *Trinity* may have been invented later, the concept of the Trinity is present throughout the Holy Scriptures. Nowhere is the absolute deity of Christ denied in the Bible except by false teachers. Thus, theology is an explanation of what is in the Scriptures. A proper understanding of history greatly helps in porch evangelism!

The proclamation of the deity of Christ is integral to the gospel message. The Lord Jesus was born of the virgin Mary but was not created; He is God, a being without beginning or end. That simple message became a puzzlement that demanded serious explanation. Declaring before a polytheistic world that "the Lord is our God, the Lord is one" (Deuteronomy 6:4) and at the same time stating that Jesus Christ is God mandated some clarification. How could both statements be true? The implications of the doctrine of the absolute deity of Christ are as profound as they are difficult to explain. It took centuries for the church to fully delineate the relationship of the Father to the Son.

The History of the Doctrine of God

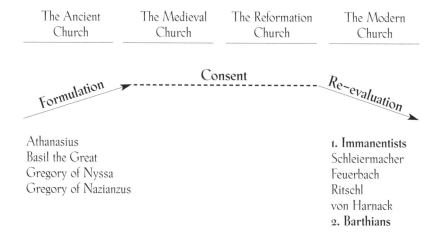

The Ancient Church	The Medieval Church	The Reformation Church	The Modern Church

Formulation → Consent → Re-evaluation

Athanasius
Basil the Great
Gregory of Nyssa
Gregory of Nazianzus

1. Immanentists
Schleiermacher
Feuerbach
Ritschl
von Harnack
2. Barthians

We turn now to the second of the two basic assumptions that undergird the Christian faith. The first was that God revealed Himself in that deposit of faith known as the Holy Scriptures. The second assumption is that there is a God—the God who revealed Himself through Jesus Christ. This single God is three in persons—the Father, the Son, and the Holy Spirit—yet one in glories. God is the triune one revealed in the baptismal formula of Matthew 28:19 and Paul's concluding statement in 2 Corinthians 13:14. The doctrine was formulated, developed,

72

or explained in the ancient church, reaching the apex of delineation at the Council of Constantinople in 381. And it was embraced by the church for well over a millennium afterward. But in recent centuries, since the rise of the Enlightenment, this doctrine, like most of the essential doctrines of historic Christianity, has been reevaluated in light of the rise of the sciences, philosophy, and the historical disciplines.

THE ANCIENT CHURCH AND THE TRINITY (100–600)

The development of the doctrine of the Trinity during the ancient church period provides a perfect case study for how the church develops doctrine according to need. As the church underwent its rapid growth and spread in the early centuries, it came up against diverse ideas about the nature of God. Church leaders had to hammer out a doctrine of God that would be faithful to the evidence of Scripture, and they did so.

THE CHURCH FATHERS AND THE TRINITY (100–150)

The evidence from the church fathers concerning the plurality of persons in the Godhead is neither systematic nor speculative. There is a certain naiveté in the writings. J. L. Neve summarized these writings as follows, "The early writers of the primitive church were not given to doctrinal speculation about the Baptismal Formula; they used the trinitarian formula, but this formula did not provoke them to a discussion of the relation of the three to each other."[1] In the same vein, J. N. D. Kelley concluded his discussion by saying, "The evidence to be collected from the Apostolic Fathers is meager, and tantalizingly inconclusive."[2]

The Church Fathers and the Relationship of the Father to the Son

In the Epistle a Letter to the Corinthians, often referred to as *1 Clement*, Clement of Rome (d. 101?) coordinated the three persons in a triadic formula: "As God lives, and the Lord Jesus Christ lives, and

73

the Holy Spirit . . . " (58:2). Elsewhere he wrote, "Have we not one God, and one Christ, and one Spirit of grace poured upon us?" (46:6). The preexistence of Christ seems to have been embraced by this early writer because Christ is viewed as having spoken through the Spirit in the Psalms (Psalms 16:2; 22:1). The writer of the *Epistle of Barnabas* stated that Christ cooperated with God in the creation (5:5; 6:12), that He received commands before the incarnation (14:3,6), and that He is the "Lord of the entire cosmos" (5:5; 12:7). Such statements indicate that he understood that Christ, though incarnate, existed before time. Ignatius (c.35–c.107), a disciple of the apostle John, repeated the baptismal formula three times in his letters (*To the Ephesians* 6:12 and *To the Magnesians* 13:2,2). Further, he referred to Jesus Christ as "our God," "God incarnate," and "God manifest as man" (*To the Ephesians* 7:2; 19:3). The writer of the homily *2 Clement* (actually a late-second-century writing) exhorted his readers to "think of Jesus as of God, as judge of the living and dead" (1:1).

There is no structured explanation of the plurality of persons in a single existence to be found in the earliest Fathers of the church. It is a doctrine that is complex and difficult; it required the development of distinct vocabulary and years of critical reflection undergirded by intense study in the Scriptures. The Fathers did not enter into the speculative aspects of theology. They were not called upon to explain the apparent contradiction in their proclamation that God is one and yet more than one.

The Church Fathers and the Relationship of the Spirit to the Father and the Son

The earliest Fathers in the church did not possess a developed understanding of the Holy Spirit. There is the repetition of the baptismal formula (Matthew 28:19) and the acknowledgment that the Spirit was operative in the world, but little else. It seems accurate to say that in the immediate postapostolic period the writers expressed confusion about the person of the Spirit and were generally silent about His work. Clement of Rome spoke of an outpouring of the Spirit upon the church (Pentecost inaugurated the Age of the Spirit). Ignatius spoke of the Spirit as one sent from God to preserve the church from error and direct its bishops in the truth (*To the Philadelphians* 7). Hermas

74

seems to have understood that the Spirit dwells in the believer (*The Shepherd*, "Mandate" 5.1-3). Further, the Fathers did grasp the truth that the Spirit was the inspiration behind the Old Testament and that He participated in Creation. Sadly, there are no indications in the Fathers of the vital distinction between the natural and supernatural operations of the Spirit.

Relative to the person of the Holy Spirit, the Fathers seem to have confused Him with the Son. The author of *2 Clement* states that the "spirit is Christ" (14.3). Hermas, in *The Shepherd*, says "that the Spirit is the Son of God" ("Similitude" 9.1). It should not be surprising that the full deity of the Spirit was not grasped. Actually, like the relationship of the Son to the Father, it was not a matter of discussion. The earliest focus of the church was upon the message of Christ's death and resurrection.

The Apologists and the Trinity (150–300)

The church emerged from embryonic beginnings in the events described in the book of Acts to become a formidable religious movement, a new expression of faith gradually understood to be distinct from Judaism. Perhaps due to its relatively small size in the Roman Empire by the century's end, it was not seen as a threat to the polytheistic beliefs that formed the majority expression of religion. That, however, gradually changed as Christianity became a force to be reckoned with in the subsequent centuries. Neglect was replaced by persecution and confrontation. Pagan scholars rose up to challenge the church's proclamation and denigrate its assertions. One of the serious attacks upon the church was relative to the doctrine of God. The attempt to formulate an adequate defense led some Christian teachers to inadequately state the deity of Christ. The attacks outside the church and the error perpetuated within it by those who explained it inappropriately provided the context for intense reflection and finally a clear explanation of the orthodox position in creedal form.

The Apologists and the Relationship of the Father to the Son

The discussion of the relationship of the persons of the Godhead was intrinsically related to the clarity of the church on the deity of the Lord

Jesus. That is, the person of our Lord and His redemptive work were the grids through which the apologists were able to see the more speculative aspects of the Trinity. Theology developed in the church as the need arose to answer critics who attacked the church's teachings; it emerged as the church was confronted with the need to defend and clarify its proclamation. For example, Marcion, a second-century teacher, imbibed and modified prevalent Gnostic teachings to assert two Gods and two Christs. He distinguished between an Old Testament Creator-God, who was wrathful, and the New Testament God, who was a loving Redeemer. He argued that Christians should shun the Old Testament God and the Old Testament books (some of the more recent ones as well) and embrace a more benevolent deity, namely, the God of Paul. Apologists such as Irenaeus (c.130–c.200) replied by arguing persuasively that the God of the Testaments is one, that the Creator is the Redeemer, and that there is one Christ. Marcion's heresy caused the church to reflect intensely on the relationship between the Father and the Son. Perhaps even more dangerous threats to orthodoxy came from a sect of Christian Judaizers, the Ebionites, and from the various Gnostics who firmly denied the deity of Christ, drawing the responses of Hippolytus (c.170–c.236) and Tertullian (c.160–c.225) in the defense of the truth.

Of a more lasting influence in the formulation of the doctrine of the triunity of God is the rise of both dynamic and Modalistic Monarchianism, each a response to heretical opinions. The term *Monarchianism* has to do with the unitary rule or being of God; it represents an attempt to preserve the unity of God while taking into account a diversity of persons. The Monarchians are best understood as seeking to confront the error of Marcion and the Gnostics, who viewed Christ as a subordinate, inferior emanation from God. Dynamic or Adoptionistic Monarchians explained the relationship of God to Christ as that of a power that came upon a man, infusing Him with the power of divinity. That is, advocates of this view denied the essential equality of the Father and the Son. Hippolytus described the teachings of one Theodotus, who came to Rome at the end of the third century, as follows: "[Theodotus asserted] that Jesus was a man, born of a virgin, according to the counsel of the father, and that after He lived in a way common to all men, and had become pre-eminently

76

religious, He afterwards at His baptism in Jordan received Christ, who came from above and descended upon Him" (*A Refutation of All Heresies* 7.35). Perhaps more influential among the Adoptionists was Paul of Samosata, a bishop of Antioch in Syria. Epiphanes wrote of his views "that the Logos came and dwelt in Jesus, who was a man; and thus, they say, God is one . . . one God the Father, and his Son in him, as the reason in a man" (*Heresies* 65.1). In essence, to maintain the singularity of God, the Adoptionists rejected Christ's deity; Christ through infusion became a God-empowered man. This particular view was not held widely in the churches, and Paul of Samosata was condemned by the Synod of Antioch in 269.

The influence of Modalism, or Patripassianism, was much more pervasive in the church. To preserve the unity of the Godhead, and fearing the danger of tritheism, a cluster of scholars argued that the names for God in the triadic formula were ways of explaining His single revelation. That is, to defend the singularity of God, they sacrificed the distinct, separate personalities or existences of God. Tertullian, speaking of the view of Praxeas (fl. c.200), noted, "He says that the Father himself came down into the virgin, was Himself born of her, Himself suffered, indeed, was Himself Jesus Christ" (*Against Praxeas* 1.2). Noetus, also a teacher in Rome, is described as asserting "that the Father is called the Son according to events at different times" (Hippolytus, *A Refutation of All Heresies* 10.27). The figure that is almost synonymous with Modalism in the church is Sabellius of Pentapolis (fl. c.220). Basil the Great (c.330–379) says he taught that "the same God, being one substance was metamorphized as the need of the moment required and spoke now as Father, now as the Son, and now as the Holy Spirit" (*Epistle* 210.3). This triumvirate of teachers— Praxeas, Noetus, and Sabellius—influenced the church at Rome, where several of the early bishops embraced the view. Whereas the Adoptionist explanation of Christ seemed to preserve the unity of the Godhead by denigrating the deity of Christ, the Modalist view preserved the unity of God at the expense of the plurality of the Godhead and the distinctive humanity of Christ. Modalism leaned toward the Gnostic and Marcionite positions in explaining Christ It dissolved the distinctiveness of God by overstating the unity of God, whereas Adoptionism attempted to define the distinctiveness of God by

THE TRINITY: GOD AS THREE-IN-ONE

understating the unity. While a very difficult issue to state, the doctrine of the Trinity is the cornerstone of Christianity. As the Orthodox tradition has so wonderfully stated, it is a mystery.

Though the early church leaders rejected Adoptionism and Modalism as well as set forth arguments for the deity of Christ, they were not able to articulate the Trinity of God without appearing to express the distinction between the Father and the Son in some form of Subordinationism. They struggled to adequately express the nature of God's unity, though they understood the distinctiveness of His persons. Justin Martyr (c.100–c.165), for example, argued for the preexistence of Christ from Old Testament theophanies, plural references that God makes of Himself (such as "Let Us"; Genesis 1:26), and the personification of God as Wisdom in creating and fashioning the world (Job 28). The relationship of the Son to the Father, according to Martyr, is expressed by the idea that He is God's Word, or Logos, as God's agent or representative in the world for His purposes.

Tertullian (c.160–c.225) of North Africa, more than any other early church leader, developed the distinctive terminology for the discussion of the doctrine of God. Among the numerous words that he coined, three are particularly important at this juncture. To describe the plurality of God, he used the term *trinitas,* or Trinity. In his polemic *Against Praxeas* (12), he wrote:

> Everywhere I hold one substance in three cohering. . . . All are of one, by unity of substance; while the mystery of the dispensation is still guarded, which distributes the Unity into a Trinity, placing in their order the three, the Father, the Son, and the Holy Spirit; three however . . . not in substance but in form, not in power but in appearance.

Second, he used the Latin word *persona,* translated as "person" in English for the Greek term *hypostasis.* He may have meant to imply that behind a mask (the term being from the stage) was one divine actor. Third, Tertullian used the term "substance," referring to that which the persons have in common. As later developed, it implied the

78

community of equally shared attributes in the Godhead. God, being spirit (John 4:24), is without body or parts, so that the word can be misleading. "Substance" implies not corporeality, but His divine character or attributes (God is known to us through the medium and manner of His dealing with us). With all this stated, however, scholars believe that Tertullian's explanation of the Trinity contained hues of Subordinationism. The language of analogy or illustration betrayed him as it does all those who seek to describe the infinite with finite words and illustrations. God has revealed Himself truly to His people, though not completely.

The difficulties of expressing the Trinity of God in the context of attempting to avoid the perils of Modalism (the view that stressed the unity of God so as to obscure His diversity) is seen in the Alexandrian school. Clement of Alexandria (c.150–c.215), for example, stressed the "eternal generation of the Son," the idea that the Son was begun in eternity by an eternal act of God with the result that He had no beginning. He thought that he had preserved the unity of God as well as the diversity of His persons. Origen (c.185–c.254) spoke of the eternal generation of the Son as well. He explained it by an appeal to his understanding of the eternal existence of the soul. He suggested that the Logos was in God eternally but was sent forth from God as an expression of will from mind. He was always the Word of the Father, but not always the spoken or revealed Word. The soul of the Son is eternally and equally with God, but in becoming revealed to us, He was not equal. In the *Fundamental Doctrines* Origen wrote:

> Therefore I think that we should be right in saying of the Saviour that he is the image of the goodness of God, but not that goodness itself. . . . We may say that the Son is good, but not absolutely good. And as he is the image of the invisible God he is by that token God, but not the God of whom Christ himself says "That they may know thee, the only true God." Thus he is the image of goodness but not unconditionally good, as is the Father. (1 2 13)

To precisely state the Trinity of God is difficult. Avoidance of one error has often pushed our scholars to embrace another. Philosophical grids proved inadequate and prone to understatement and over-emphases.

The Apologists and the Relationship
of the Spirit to the Father and the Son

The material found in the writings of the late-second- and third-century writers indicates that they progressed in their understanding of the work of the Spirit, though they still confused the Spirit with Christ. Justin Martyr called the Holy Spirit "the gift come down from heaven which was imparted to believers after Christ's resurrection and to the prophets before the incarnation" (*Address to the Greeks* 23). Irenaeus continued the insight of the Fathers that the Spirit was the inspiration behind the Old Testament. Novatian (c.200–c.258), the presbyter of Rome, had a rather developed understanding of the Spirit. In *On the Trinity*, he stated that the Spirit is the divine person and power that worked in the prophets and apostles in the past and now in the church. Chapter 29 is of particular importance because there he delineated the Spirit's work toward the believer. He grasped the relationship of the Spirit to the Joel 2 and Acts 2 passages and clearly taught a permanent indwelling ministry of the Spirit in the New Testament era and afterward. He recognized the Spirit as the Paraclete who was promised to abide in the saint in a lavish, unsparing manner; He is the Advocate and the "Spirit of Truth." The Spirit guards, guides, and indwells the church.

> It is He who in the apostles renders testimony to Christ, in the martyrs manifests the unwavering faith of religion, in virgins encloses the admirable continence of sealed chastity. In the rest of men, He keeps the laws of the Lord's teaching uncorrupted and untainted. He destroys heretics, corrects those in error, reproves unbelievers, reveals impostors, and also corrects the wicked. He keeps the Church uncorrupted and inviolate in the holiness of perpetual virginity and truth.

80

The relationship of the Spirit to the Godhead continued in a confused state while an understanding of His work gradually emerged. Justin Martyr, for example, seems to have identified the Spirit as Christ. "It is wrong, therefore," he said, "to understand the Spirit and the power of God as anything else than the Word" (*First Apology* 33). At other times, he placed the Spirit below angels in the order of priority (" . . . and the host of other good angels who follow and are made like Him, and the prophetic Spirit . . . " [*First Apology* 1.6]). The same confusion appears in the writings of Theophilus of Antioch. For him, Christ, the Word of God, is the Spirit of God (*To Autolycus* 2.10). Other writers distinguished the Spirit from Christ, according deity to both, but they did not attempt to explain the apparent difficulties in such a view; when the Spirit is seen as divine, shades of Subordinationism are apparent in the language of description. The persons of the godhead are distinguished, but the equality of the persons is not enunciated. Irenaeus identifies three distinct persons in the Godhead and refers to the "Let Us" statements in Genesis as proof (*Against Heresies* 1.2.1; 4.34.1).

THE THEOLOGIANS AND THE TRINITY (300–600)

The changes that came in the early fourth century in the church could hardly have been anticipated. Not only did the periodic, and sometimes devastating, persecutions end with Emperor Diocletian's reign, but Constantine emerged as tolerant and sympathetic of the Christian faith. Christianity became the official religion of the empire! The church not only triumphed in the empire of Rome in the fourth century; it outlasted it in the fifth century. This newly found freedom and importance of the church had significant implications. For example, the bishops of the church could gather and discuss troubling issues; they could delineate their findings through councils and creeds that had ecumenical and authoritative significance. The dominance of the church inaugurated the systematizing of theology.

The Theologians and the Relationship of the Father to the Son

The setting was thus prepared in an unprecedented way for the discussion of the relation of the Father to the Son when a presbyter in Alexandria set forth his views. Arius (d. 336) appears to have been a disciple of the Adoptionist Paul of Samosata via Lucan, a teacher in Antioch. Arius sought to avoid the perils of Modalism, a problem identified with the Alexandrian solution, by denying the equality of the persons in the Godhead. Arius and his bishop, Alexander (c.250–328), were on a collision course! Alexander's successor, Athanasius (c.296–373), quotes his opponent as saying, "The Son was not always; for since all things have come into existence from nothing, and all things are creatures and have been made, so also the Logos of God Himself came into existence from nothing and there was a time when He was not; and that before He came into existence He was not" (*Orations against Arius* 1.2.). Arius believed Christ to be an eternal being, having been created in eternity, but He did not share eternality with the Father. Arius accused the Alexandrian bishop of dissolving the distinctiveness of the persons of the Godhead by overstressing the divine unity. Athanasius charged Arius with destroying the equality of the persons in the Godhead by dismembering it. It appears that what each accused the other of embracing was not true of them. When Arius was expelled from Alexandria, he sought sympathy for his views in Eusebius of Nicomedia (d. c.342), an influential bishop in the imperial court at Constantinople. The controversy did not abate; on the contrary, it threatened the empire with schism!

After attempts at reconciling the parties in the dispute failed, Emperor Constantine called for a gathering of the bishops from throughout the empire. It was the first ecumenical (worldwide) gathering of church leaders. The year was 325 and the setting was in Nicaea in Bithynia, a town near the Eastern capital, Constantinople (by this time Rome was the capital in the West and Constantinople was the "new Rome" in the East). The council appears to have been attended by three factions: a minority who feared the error of Modalism, led by Eusebius of Nicomedia; a group of similar size that feared the Subordinationist error, directed by Athanasius; and a majority of bishops who did not understand the issues and longed for peace (see Acts 19:32). The outcome seems to have been predetermined as the Athanasian party had the backing of the emperor's adviser. The result was the great Nicene Creed, a document that all the parties

82

agreed to, though they interpreted it as meaning different things. There was agreement on the words but not on their meaning! They each appeared to take the creed as condemning their opponent's position. How are the phrases "begotten, not created" and "of the essence of the Father" to be interpreted?

Because of the confusion as to the actual meaning of the Creed of Nicaea, resolution was not in sight. What is the exact relationship of the Father to the Son? Is He of the same substance as the Father? Is He like the Father? Athanasius, acclaimed as one of the most remarkable bishops and theologians of his time, insisted upon the coequality of the Father and the Son. His approach to the problem of the Trinity stood in contrast to the philosophical heritage of the Alexandrian tradition of Origen and others. He looked at the issue through the lens of pastoral and redemptive concerns. He asked, "What kind of person must He have been to bring us the salvation that He alone could have and did bring to us?" His work *On the Incarnation* is a wonderful description of the deity of Christ and the connection of it to the gospel of Christ's satisfaction of the Father for our sin. One who is very and truly God could make atonement for sin if that sin was an infinite offense on the one hand and the offended God is always and forever righteous and just on the other hand. Justice requires either punishment of the offender or a substitute offense bearer. Righteousness and justice mandate that God be satisfied. Only God could offer up a sacrifice that could do this. Yet, who could qualify to be such a Redeemer? Athanasius found the solution in the absolute deity and incarnation of Jesus Christ. This insight informed his argument for the coequality of the Trinity of God.

As the years passed and the controversy continued unabated, the Arian party tended to become extreme, even asserting that the Son was unlike the Father. This, coupled with the scholarly work of the Athanasians, led to the triumph of the Athanasian party. The difficulty centered around the meaning of the terms "substance" and "persons." The Latin-speaking portion of the church (the West), following Tertullian, differentiated the terms. The Greek-speaking portion of the church did not. Thus, in the East, to speak of a single essence implied a single person, leading inevitably in their minds to the error of Modalism. In the West, to speak of two essences implied a new form of the Arian error. The work of unraveling the semantical dispute fell to the three Cappadocian scholars: Basil of Caesarea (c.330–379), Gregory of Nazianzus (329/30–389/90), and Gregory of Nyssa (c.330–c.395). They argued that the terms "essence" and "persons" were not to be understood as synonymous terms. In the singular essence of God exist three persons. Gregory of Nazianzus, in the *Oration on Holy Lights,* stated:

> When I speak of God you must be illuminated at once by one flash of light and by three. Three in Individualities or Hypostases, if you prefer so to call them, or persons, for we will not quarrel about names so long as the syllables amount to the same meaning; but One in respect of the Substance — that is, the Godhead. For they are divided without division, if I may so say, and they are united in division. (X)

The second ecumenical council of the church met at Constantinople, the empire's capital, in 381. Unlike at the Council of Nicaea, the issues were more clearly defined and the Arian party had declined in influence. The council reiterated the Nicene Creed, expanding its statement of the Trinity to include specific comments about the Holy Spirit while retaining the phraseology of Nicaea. The terms were now understood throughout the church. "Essence" or "substance" refers to the attributes or characteristics of deity equally shared by the three persons of the Godhead. God is truly one yet in an eternal triad of equal glories: God the Father, God the Son, and God the Holy Spirit. The differences in the Godhead, expressed by the term "persons," refer to functions within the Godhead related to the redemption of creation.

The Theologians and the Relationship of the Spirit to the Father and the Son

The discussion of the Trinity through the Council of Nicaea focused upon an attempt to accurately express the relationship of Christ to the Father. The relationship of the Holy Spirit to the Father and the Son was not an issue that provoked interest. Comparing the brief statement

84

in the Nicene Creed on the Spirit ("And [we believe] in the Holy Spirit") with that of the Creed of Constantinople suggests that the relationship of the Spirit to the Father and the Son emerged after the discussion of the Father and the Son. William Cunningham simply stated, "There is nothing said in the original Nicene Creed about the Holy Spirit, except the simple mention of His name, because, up to that time, the Scripture doctrine concerning Him had not been a matter of controversial discussion."[3] It's interesting that the church seemed little concerned about the Holy Spirit during its period of greatest Spirit-enabled growth and triumph.

Adolf von Harnack argued that the failure of the Council of Nicaea to focus upon the Holy Spirit is proof of the preoccupation of the gathering with the Son.[4] However, a heated debate emerged later (itself a logical development of the growing awareness of the full equality of the Father and the Son) concerning the Holy Spirit. Macedonius (d. c.362), a bishop in Constantinople and a semi-Arian, suggested that the Spirit was a creature, subordinate to the Son. Gregory of Nazianzus described the confusing medley of views that circulated about the Spirit in the following way:

> Of the wise among us some consider the Holy Spirit to be an energy, others a creature, others God, while others again cannot make up their minds to adopt any definite view out of reverence for Scripture on the point. On this account they neither accord to Him divine adoration nor refuse it to Him, and thus take a middle road, but which is really a very bad path. (*Theological Oration* 5.31)

Athanasius, the great African bishop, had Macedonius's view condemned at the Synod of Alexandria in 362. The logic of Athanasius's defense of the full deity of the Spirit paralleled his argument concerning Christ. Of the latter, he argued that He must be God because a creature cannot redeem creatures; only one who is God can save humanity. Relative to the Spirit, he stated that the one who conforms us to God cannot be a creature either. In both cases, one cannot make another into what He is not. In his first letter to bishop Serapion of Thmuis, Athanasius asked the question, how can the Holy Spirit belong to the same class of defiled creatures that are sanctified by Him? (*1 Serapion* 23). If the Holy Spirit is the source of the life, the one who unites the creature to God, how can He be a created being?

The fullest delineation of the Holy Spirit as consubstantial with the Father and the Son prior to the Council of Constantinople (381) is found in the work of the Cappadocian fathers. Basil of Caesarea stated, "One, moreover is the Holy Spirit, and we speak of Him simply conjoined as He is to the one Father through the one Son, and through Himself completing the adorable and blessed Trinity (*On the Holy Spirit* 45). Gregory of Nazianzus argued:

> For the Father is not the Son, and yet this is not due to either deficiency or subjection of Essence; but the very fact of being Unbegotten or Begotten, or Proceeding has given the name Father to the First, of the Son the Second, and of the third, Him of Whom we are speaking, of the Holy Ghost that the distinction of the Three Persons may be preserved in the one nature and dignity of the Godhead. (*Theological Orations* 5.4)

The Council of Constantinople, the so-called second ecumenical council, affirmed both the equality and the distinctiveness of the triune God. The important findings of this council, since the gathering of the church's leadership was largely restricted to the Eastern churches and not truly ecumenical, were reiterated by Hilary of Poitiers (c.315–367/8) and Augustine (354–430) in the West.

THE MEDIEVAL CHURCH AND THE TRINITY (600–1500)

What was argued by Athanasius, declared by the Nicene Council, clarified by the Cappadocians, restated at the Council of Constantinople, and reiterated in the West by Augustine was the unchallenged teaching in the church for over a millennium. Thus, the era that stretches from the time of the bishop of Hippo to the early modern period was one of consensus on this point. The truth expressed at Nicaea was simply recognized as the orthodox faith. John of Damascus (c.655–c.750), recognized as one of the few systematizers of Orthodox theology, expressed clearly the concept of a singularity of equalitarian characteristics shared by a plurality of distinct persons in the Godhead.

The period did witness strife in the Catholic Church over the doctrine of the Holy Spirit, though it only indirectly related to the doctrine of the Trinity. The issue appears to have been about the increasing tendency of the Roman bishops to seek supreme authority in the affairs of the churches throughout the Mediterranean world. In 589, at a provincial council in Toledo (now in Spain), church leaders added three words to the trinitarian creed of Constantinople (381), an ecumenical statement. Following the statement that the Spirit proceeds or is sent from the Father into the world, the council added the phrase "and the Son," being led in that direction by Augustine's understanding that God's essence is love, so that what any member of the divine triad is said to do toward another, the unspoken member would do also. The addition of the phrase did not cause strife in the church immediately because the council was not ecumenical. However, in 867, when Photius (c.810–c.895), patriarch of Constantinople, accused Nicholas I of Rome (c.819 to 822–867; pope 858–867) of introducing heresy by teaching two sources of the Spirit, that the Spirit proceeds from the Father and the Son (hence, the filioque controversy), dissension erupted. To Photius, this view destroyed the unity of God, though Augustine had insisted that the actions of the Father and the Son were one. In retrospect, it seems that the issue was much more than the meaning of John 14:26 or 15:26, which appear to have been accurately understood by Eastern church leaders. The conflict now seems to have been about two very important issues: theological accurateness and religious authority. First, does John 15:26 express ontological relationships in the Godhead or the temporal mission of the Spirit? If the former, as the Western churches generally insist, a hint of ontological Subordinationism can be detected relative to the Spirit. Second, what authority does an ecumenical creed possess in the church? Is such a creed alterable? Can the bishop of Rome dictate policy to other bishops in the one church? Is there a power in the Roman bishops that is not shared by the others? Could it be that an emphasis on the Son as the source of the Spirit increases the authority of the Vicar of Christ? The patriarchs in the East firmly resisted attempts to assert Roman authority, and at the same time they pressed the claim that an ecumenical creed is inviolable. Eastern church leaders rejected growing papal claims to supremacy while maintaining that tradition, particularly as expressed in the several ecumenical councils, was unalterable. This ecclesiological issue continued unresolved in the church and became a significant contributing cause of the schism of 1054, a formal division in the Catholic Church that created the Western Catholic Church and the Orthodox churches.

The late medieval period witnessed the development of two interrelated movements: the university and Scholasticism. The emergence of universities represented a shift from the monastic ideal of education, which focused on contemplation, to a less church-controlled environment where the commitment was to scholarship rather than to devotion, to the head rather than the heart. Though neither educational system excluded the priorities of the other, the emphases were clearly different. The goal in the university, though conducted by church leaders, was objective, intellectual knowledge derived by analysis and disputation rather than prayer and meditation.[5] Scholasticism has come to signify the theology, philosophy, and subsidiary disciplines within the universities that flourished in this era of medieval culture. Theology was not denigrated in this period, but it was subjected to the rigors of analysis rather than simply embraced by an unreflecting faith. Reinhold Seeberg defined the movement as follows: "The term scholasticism is used to designate the theology of the period from Anselm and Abelard to the Reformation, i.e., the theology of the later Middle Ages. Its peculiarity, briefly stated, consists in the logical and dialectical working over of the doctrine inherited from the earlier ages."[6]

The difficulty with the Scholastic approach to knowledge—that is, a distinct connectedness between rational understanding and truth— can be seen in the attempt to explain the Trinity. While the monastic approach easily led to compliant mysticism, a faith without foundation, this new way of understanding had the potential of limiting the role of faith. The Scholastic attempt to define the Trinity through heightened

88

rational reflection proved confusing. Fortunately, the results did not leave a permanent impact on our articulation of the doctrine of the Trinity. Anselm (c.1033–1109), who is perhaps most known for the ontological argument for the existence of God, clashed with Roscelin de Compiègne (c.1050–c.1125), who was condemned at the Synod of Soissons (1092) for teaching tritheism, that is, for denying the unity of the Godhead while stressing the three persons. While both men believed in the necessity of revelation to understand truth, they also were Scholastics embracing the ideas that such truth can be shown to be reasonable. Peter Abelard (1079–1142/3), a disciple of Roscelin, did not follow his mentor's error in explaining the Trinity, but he seems to have assigned a particular attribute to each member of the Trinity; that is, the Father is said to be all-powerful, the Son wise, and the Spirit good. Such discussions among the scholars assumed the orthodoxy of the Trinity; difficulties arose when one or another particular philosophical approach was used as a device to define and explain it.

The greatest of the Scholastics was Thomas Aquinas (c.1225–1274); his is the classic example of the university approach. Given Thomas's desire to equip Dominican missionaries in their confrontation with the Islamic faith, he employed the Aristotelian form of arguments. He believed in the Trinity because it was revealed by God in the Bible, yet he believed that the existence of God and the Trinity could be proved by rational argument. Admittedly, he did not dissolve special revelation into natural revelation, clearly maintaining the necessity of the distinction. For Aquinas, some things were beyond rational proofs and had to be accepted by faith. Colin Brown has summarized Aquinas's approach like this: "Thomas does not see philosophy as an alternative track to theology which enables him to prove rationally and intellectually items of faith which ordinary people have to accept simply by faith. Rather, it is a tool for clarifying issues."[7]

THE EARLY MODERN CHURCHES AND THE TRINITY (1500–1750)

The Catholic Church suffered a breakdown in the late medieval period. While many came to the opinion that the church was in need of renewal, church leaders were deeply divided over the nature of the needed restoration. Some, like Erasmus of Rotterdam (1466/9–1536), believed that correction in the areas of pastoral care, morals, and education was sufficient; others gradually came to see the problem as much deeper. The unrest in the church indicated to many the need for a renovation at more than external levels. As a result, the church's malaise led to a growing division of opinion as to the solution. Eventually the church in the West fractured into two broad movements, each claiming to be the heir of historic catholic orthodoxy: the Roman Catholic Church and the Protestant churches. While there were several areas of clear differences of opinion between the parties, there were enormous areas of doctrinal agreement, since both were heirs of the same rich centuries of tradition. The doctrine of the Trinity was one of them.

THE ROMAN CATHOLIC CHURCH AND THE TRINITY

*B*ecause the Roman Catholic Church shared with the Protestants the early ecumenical councils (in this instance those of Nicaea and Constantinople), it should not be surprising that the Council of Trent (1545–1563), the great defining moment in the birth of the Roman Catholic Church, would embrace the doctrine of the Trinity of God. Though the Canons and Dogmatic Decrees of the Council of Trent assume the doctrine of the Trinity, there were no sessions of the council devoted to this topic, because it was not a matter that separated the emerging church from their Protestant antagonists. Indeed, the third session of the council in 1546 began with the statement that it was meeting "In the name of the Holy and Undivided Trinity, Father, and Son, and Holy Ghost," followed by a reiteration of the Nicene Creed. As is true in the Protestant faith, the Trinity is a foundational doctrine. The Tridentine Profession of Faith was written after the Council of Trent had finished its work and functioned to summarize its salient conclusions. Ever since, it has been used as a confessional statement for those expressing their faith publicly. The first article begins with the phrase "I, ____, with a firm faith believe and profess all and every one of the things contained in the creed which the holy Roman church makes use of," and the Nicene Creed immediately follows.

THE PROTESTANT CHURCHES AND THE TRINITY

The Protestant churches, sharing so richly in the heritage of the Catholic Church, did not diverge from their Roman Catholic opponents in understanding the Trinity. Though Martin Luther (1483–1546) believed that trinitarian comprehension is beyond the grasp of natural, rational faculties, he wrote:

> Scriptures . . . cleverly prove that there are three persons and one God. For I would believe neither the writings of Augustine nor the teachers of the church unless the New and Old Testaments clearly show this doctrine of the Trinity. (*Works* 39.289)

The Augsburg Confession (1530), a marvelous expression of Lutheran orthodoxy, stated the Trinity beautifully: "The churches, with common consent among us, do teach that the decree of the Nicene Synod concerning the unity of the divine essence and the three persons is true, and without doubt to be believed" (Article I).

John Calvin and the Reformed traditions offer to the discussion of the Trinity neither uniqueness nor novelty but rather literary majesty, clarity, and brevity of statement. Book I of the *Institutes of the Christian Religion* is devotional as well as theologically overwhelming. Commenting on Paul's phrase that Christ is the "brightness of His glory," Calvin wrote:

> The fair inference from the Apostle's words is, that there is a proper subsistence of the Father which shines refulgent in the Son. From this, again, it is easy to infer that there is a subsistence of the Son which distinguishes him from the Father. The same holds in the case of the Holy Spirit; for we will immediately prove both that he is God, and that he has a separate substance from the Father. (I.13.2)

The Westminster Confession (1647), perhaps the grandest expression of confessional Calvinism, is beautiful in its description of God.

There is but one only living and true God, who is infinite in being and perfection, a most pure spirit, invisible, without body, parts, or passions, immutable, immense, eternal, incomprehensible, almighty, most wise, most holy, most free, most absolute, working all things according to the counsel of his own immutable and most righteous will, for his own glory; most loving, gracious, merciful, longsuffering, abundant in goodness and truth, forgiving iniquity, transgression, and sin; the rewarder of them that diligently seek him; and withal most just and terrible in his judgments; hating all sin, and who will by no means clear the guilty. . . . In the unity of the Godhead there be three persons of one substance, power, and eternity; God the Father, God the Son, and God the Holy Ghost. The Father is of none, neither begotten nor proceeding; the Son is eternally begotten of the Father; the Holy Ghost eternally proceeding from the Father and the Son. (Chapter II.1,3)

THE HETERODOX GROUPS AND THE TRINITY

Though the dispute between Roman Catholic and Protestant scholars was sharp and often acrimonious, there were nonetheless many areas of agreement in theology and practice. That is, in sharing a common heritage of several centuries of development, the two factions that emerged from the dissolution of the late medieval church in the West each claimed to be in the truest possession of the doctrines of the church, the other accordingly an example of perversion and deviation. One of the many areas of agreement among these strident proponents was the doctrine of the Trinity of God. Each side, for example, recognized the danger to Christianity posed by Michael Servetus (c.1511–1553), the Unitarian heretic. When a movement emerged in the churches that threatened the doctrine of the Trinity, Roman Catholics and Protestants recognized the danger to the Christian faith. One such movement emerged in the sixteenth century, a harbinger of centuries of attack after centuries of firm commitment.

The origins of Socinianism—a movement that became identified by its two most vocal advocates, Laelius Socinus (1525–1562) and his nephew Faustus Socinus (1539–1604)—appears to have been rooted in the liberal spirit of the Renaissance, Italian Rationalism. The Renaissance, spreading across Europe, found fertile soil for development in Spain, particularly in Michael Servetus. Servetus believed that Christianity, through centuries of development, had become disfigured from its original simplicity, and so he sought to return it to the original form. One such perversion of primitive Christianity was in the doctrine of God. Servetus believed a simplicity had evolved into a distorted complexity. Calvin stated: "The sum of his speculations was, that a threefold Deity is introduced wherever three Persons are said to exist in his essence, and that this Triad was imaginary, inasmuch as it was inconsistent with the unity of God" (*Institutes of the Christian Religion* I.13.22). Servetus's teachings attempted to restore the "real" essence of Christianity from centuries of accretions by priests, bishops, and popes. To the orthodox, it was an attack upon the very foundation of the Christian faith. Sadly, it was the beginning of the dissolution of the hegemony of trinitarian belief in the churches.

A cardinal feature of Socinian teaching was that singularity of essence mandates singularity of persons. That is, according to the Socinians, reason as well as Scripture demands if we believe in the unity of God we must deny a multiplicity of persons within the Godhead. Thus, in the one essence of God there is one person. The Racovian Catechism of 1562, an expression of Polish Socinianism, replied in answer to the demand "Prove to me that in the one essence of God, there is but one Person" by stating:

> This indeed may be seen from hence, that the essence of God is one, not in kind but in number. Wherefore it cannot, in any way, contain a plurality of persons, since a person is nothing else than an individual intelligent essence. Wherever, then, there exist three numerical persons, there must necessarily, in like manner, be reckoned three individual essences; for in the same sense in which it is affirmed that there is one numerical essence, it must be held that there is also one numerical person.

THE TRINITY: GOD AS THREE-IN-ONE

Complaining that the orthodox arrived at their views from "passages of Scripture ill understood" (*Racovian Catechism*, "Of the Knowledge of God" 3.1), Socinians rejected the Trinity of God. The doctrine of God was made subject to the emerging criteria of the Enlightenment, which subjected and reduced divine revelation to the standard of human reasonableness and private judgment. To the Socinians, as well as Unitarians and Rationalists in general, knowledge is obtained through reflection, analysis, analogy, and repetition; revelation is minimized, redefined, or rejected. By such a limitation, the supernatural claims of Christianity can be readily dismissed because miracles, by their very nature, are nonrepeatable, nonanalogical phenomena.

The importance of Socinianism, according to H. John McLachlan, is in being "part of the larger movement towards free inquiry, part of the breakaway from medieval scholasticism in the direction of modern empiricism."[8] This spirit of free inquiry, which now appears to have had a greater regard for the integrity and autonomy of humans than for the wisdom and revelation of God, spread rapidly across Europe, having a profound religious impact in Holland and England. Though James I had a copy of the Racovian Catechism publicly burned in 1614, Socinian ideas emerged at Oxford and Cambridge universities. Designated as Unitarianism, and closely aligned in belief with the English Deists, it was perpetuated by John Biddle (1615–1662) and Joseph Priestley (1733–1804), the latter known for his influential volume, *The Corruptions of Christianity*. James Orr has summarized the history of these movements, arguing that Socinianism, Unitarianism, and Deism are revivals of a fourth-century heresy.

Laelius and Faustus Socinus started the antitrinitarian movement known as Socinianism which spread widely and became especially strong in Poland. It resulted in seventeenth century England in a revival of the controversy over the doctrine of the Trinity. Many unitarians were not deists. But all deists had a unitarian conception of God and were sympathetic with the unitarians as against the trinitarians. Deism's spiritual ancestry leads back through unitarianism to Socinianism and back to Arianism.[9]

English Unitarianism and Deism fashioned their impact upon the British American colonies in the eighteenth century; it was part of the foreboding malaise that troubled Jonathan Edwards of Northampton, Massachusetts, as early as the 1730s. Called "Arminianism," the intruding rationalistic spirit had less to do with Jacob Arminius (1560–1609), the theologian from whom it derived its name, than it did with a rising mood expressed as confidence in human ability to parlay God's favor by human endeavor. Conrad Wright has argued:

> The Arminianism that Cotton Mather dismissed and Jonathan Edwards feared was the first phase of the liberal movement in theology which in the nineteenth century was named Unitarianism. It rejected the awful and inscrutable Deity of the Calvinists, and replaced him with a God of benevolence and law. It rejected the concept of human nature as totally corrupt and depraved, and supplanted it with one in which the ability of every man to strive for righteousness was admitted. It was, in a sense, the New England version of the theology of the Age of Reason, occupying a middle ground between orthodoxy on the one hand and infidelity on the other.[10]

Now, with some reflection, it is evident that it was the religious counterpart of the waves of popular, political sentiment that were blowing across a landscape in transition from a colonial dependent to a national identity.

The most prominent representative of Unitarianism in America was William Ellery Channing (1780–1842), pastor of the Federal Street Church in Boston. In 1819 he preached a sermon at the ordination of Jared Sparks in Baltimore, Maryland, that became something of the official creed of the movement. He began the celebrated "Unitarian Christianity" with an emphasis on the unity of God. "In the first place, we believe in the doctrine of God's UNITY, or that there is one, and only one" (*Works* 371). Channing then "protest[ed] the irrational and unscriptural doctrine of the Trinity" with three arguments. First, such a doctrine subverts the unity of God. Second, it makes no sense to think that any rational person, such as the apostle Paul, would have ever held to such a thought and not be called upon to defend it somewhere in his writings. Third, it denigrates from the worship of God by introducing pluralities. "We also think that the doctrine of the Trinity injures devotion, not only by joining to the Father other objects of worship, but by taking from the Father the supreme affection which is his due" (*Works* 373).

THE LATE MODERN CHURCHES AND THE TRINITY (1750–PRESENT)

It can be argued that Christianity since the Enlightenment has been profoundly shaped by the reductionistic, rationalistic spirit that informed and defined the Enlightenment. As has been stated,[11] the Enlightenment did not attempt to defile historic orthodoxy; it—like the Scholastic movement, with its deep church ties, and the Renaissance, which produced the Reformations—made a conscientious effort to defend the Christian faith. Though it may not have been the intent, the Reformations caused a breakdown of trust in tradition and a growing stress on the ability of the individual, as opposed to the declarations of either priest or cleric, to know truth. The rational faculties of men and women (as opposed to acquiescence to imposed, external authority) gradually emerged as equal to the authority of the church or the Bible. As the past centuries demonstrate, reason as a supreme source of authority has displaced revelation. Objective, external authority has been surrendered to privatized, subjective, inward authority. With the acceptance of the philosophical insights of Immanuel Kant (1724–1804), experience and reason came to define the structure of knowing; truth is experienced-based. Answering David Hume's devastating attack on the reasonability of the supernatural, Kant divorced religious verification from the realm of scientific and reflective thought, placing religion in the sphere of personal, moral sense, a God-given universal principle in all humankind. In doing so, Kant sought to save Christianity from criticism by putting it outside the realm of rational inquiry. The extreme of these insights bequeathed to the nineteenth century its characteristic features:

96

inward authority, moralism, and empty optimism expressed through politicization and "values clarification," the thought that there are no transcendent values. At its worst, it reduced Christianity to a "book of virtues."

Scholars in the Christian tradition, faced with the onslaught of philosophical and scientific advances, often felt disadvantaged by definitions of religion they inherited. Increasingly for many, the only option was to forge a new Christianity, undergirded by a new understanding of history, that would preserve the faith from the potent secularism of the Enlightenment on the one hand and the obscurantism of traditional Christianity on the other. The reshaping of Christianity has been a major theme in the history of the church in recent centuries.

THE PROTESTANT TRADITIONS AND THE TRINITY

*R*eaction to the Enlightenment among Protestants has been varied, to say the least. Some have felt the rationalistic impulses of the Enlightenment as well as the urge to preserve culture and the essential role of religion in it, and so they have modified or reshaped Christianity. Others have rejected such modifications as a threat to Christianity, perceiving revisionist attempts as hopelessly flawed, reductionistic, and dangerous. Protestants, like their Roman Catholic counterparts, felt that something had to be done to reverse the dangerous and destructive trends; however, they could not agree among themselves as to what was the wisest course of action.

The European Protestant Liberal Tradition and the Trinity

*A*t the beginning of the nineteenth century Friedrich Schleiermacher (1768–1834), a theologian and founder of the University of Berlin, sought to defend the Christian faith from the intrusion of the skeptical, rationalistic Enlightenment as well as the supposedly time-bound, archaic assertions of traditional orthodoxy. Though this "father of modern theology" rejected the Rationalist assumption that all knowledge is the sum of reflection (in this he agreed with Kant), he departed from Kant's definition of religion as a divine moral givenness, an internal principle imperiling orthodoxy, by suggesting that knowledge is rooted in the subjective and personal. That is, religion belongs neither

97

to the sphere of science nor to the sphere of ethics; it is a reality of its own. He began theology with people, not God; religion is the sense human beings have of an acute, profound dependence on God for life's significance. As Schleiermacher reflected upon the orthodox doctrine of the Trinity, discerning his depth of feeling or dependence on God, since affection preceded thought and was independent of it in his view, he began his discussion. Perhaps it is instructive of the importance of the doctrine in his thought that it was the last subject that he took up in *Christian Faith*; it was not God that was the focus of his discussion so much as it was people in their encounter with God. Schleiermacher retreated to the ancient heresy of Modalism as set forth by Sabellius: the Trinity is a triad of God-consciousness. He embraced the unity of God but rejected the equality of persons in the Godhead; the singular essence of God is of one person. "The designation of the First Person as Father, as well as the relations of the First Person to the other two Persons, seems rather to set forth the relation of the Persons to the unity of the essence than to be consistent with the equality of the three Persons" (*Christian Faith* II.751).

A devastating critic of experienced-based theology, such as that of Schleiermacher, was Ludwig Feuerbach (1804–1872), the disciple of Hegel's dialectical progressivism. He argued that a theology based on subjective feelings of dependence is really only personal theology and may not be a description of God at all; it may be people looking into a mirror and not knowing it. (This agrees with Karl Barth's later conclusion that nineteenth-century theology degenerated into a monologue of the soul with itself!) Feuerbach, carrying Hegel's theory of knowledge into the realm of New Testament studies, anticipated the modern materialist tradition by suggesting that God is a myth created to provide strength in the midst of human frailty. The discovery of anthrotheism, not theism, is the hope for humankind; God is the "fantastic projection of theology." Feuerbach revealed the fact that religious knowledge, when separated from divine revelation, ceases to exist; it becomes the knowledge of self! "The ego attains consciousness of the world through the consciousness of the Thou. Thus man is the God of man. That he exists at all he has to thank nature, that he is man, he has to thank man," wrote Feuerbach. Needless to say, this precursor of the modern positivist and agnostic tradition invested little time in his *Essence of Christianity* (1841) on the Trinity.

While Schleiermacher is said to have founded an epoch, Albrecht Ritschl (1822–1889) established a school of thought. Ritschl, the most dominant German theologian in the second half of the nineteenth century, was influenced by Schleiermacher, Kant, and the Hegelian approach of F. C. Baur in New Testament studies. He sought to avoid the subjectivism of Schleiermacher and the radicalism of Feuerbach by distinguishing between two types of knowledge, scientific and religious, the latter consisting of personal moral judgments. Accepting the insights of Higher Criticism, which attempted to retrieve truth from the Bible, and focusing on the life of Christ, he set out to write theology. However, the human element prevails in his theory of truth as it is grounded in "value judgments." Religion is subsumed under the category of ethics and morals. "God is love" is Ritschl's essential religious affirmation, and any other descriptions of God, such as His absoluteness, is "heathenish metaphysics." The Trinity of God would fit into this category for Ritschl. This essence of God is love; the substance of Christianity is moral ethics expressed in cultural-kingdom righteousness.

> Christianity, then, is the monotheistic, completely spiritual, and ethical religion, which, based on the life of its Author as Redeemer and Founder of the Kingdom of God, consists in the freedom of the children of God, involves the impulse to conduct from the motive of love, aims at the moral organization of mankind, and grounds blessedness on the relationship of sonship to God, as well as on the Kingdom of God.[12]

The European Protestant Conservative Tradition and the Trinity

Karl Barth (1886–1968), likely the greatest figure in Christian theology to appear in the twentieth century, rejected the liberal tradition of his training and earliest ministry, suggesting that "one cannot speak of

God simply by speaking of man in a loud voice." The place of God in Barth's theology is the opposite of what it is in Schleiermacher's teaching. While Schleiermacher took up the doctrine of God last in his work, Barth began his discussion of theology with God because He is prior to that which He reveals about Himself. Since we have the revelation of God, it is essential that we begin the task of talking about God by inquiring into the nature of the Being who gave it to us. Barth rejects the Adoptionistic tendencies of the later German liberal tradition, which suggested that Christ was only God in passion or vocation, not in His very being, as well as the Sabellianism rampant in Schleiermacher, the Modalistic denial of distinct persons in the Godhead. In a very lovely passage (one among many) in *Church Dogmatics,* he correlates the revelation of God with the nature of God.

> We mean by the doctrine of the Trinity . . . the proposition that He whom the Christian Church calls God and proclaims as God, therefore the God who has revealed Himself according to the witness of Scripture, is the same in unimpaired unity, yet also in unimpaired variety thrice in a different way. Or, in the phraseology of the dogma of the Trinity in the Church, the Father, the Son, and the Holy Spirit in the Bible's witness to revelation are the one God in the unity of their essence, and one God in the Bible's witness to revelation is in the variety of His Persons the Father, the Son, and the Holy Spirit. (I.1.353)

Barth did not prefer to speak of three persons or personalities in the Godhead because he felt it might impair thinking of God as one; he used the phrase "modes of existence" to explain the same idea. With Barth, interest in the Trinity became a part of the discussion of theology after a century of its absence among the German theologians, though it must be said that his viewpoint did not impact twentieth-century theology much, at least not in the sense of causing liberal theologians to embrace the Nicene Creed.[13] Clearly, he reintroduced the transcendence of God into the discussion of theology, though some have argued, and rightly so, that Barth's God is too distant.

The American Protestant Liberal Tradition and the Trinity

Latitudinal trends in American theology can be detected in the early eighteenth century in Jonathan Edwards's complaint about the rise of Arminianism, a movement rooted in the Enlightenment's stress on reasonability and the denial of the inability of people to impress God so as to move Him to benevolency on their behalf. These influences, perhaps seen in Charles Chauncy's rejection of the Awakening of the 1740s, proliferated in a broad context of ideas that, in part, fomented the revolutionary movement at the century's end. The birth of the new nation also witnessed the first liberal religious movement, Unitarianism, which polarized and divided the Congregational church in the nineteenth century. These liberal religious trends, coupled with the rise of the sciences, brought about a crisis in American theology by the late nineteenth century. Many felt that the only hope for preserving Christianity was to shed certain of its archaic, anti-intellectual, precritical teachings; separate the permanent from the transitory in the Bible; and create a new, more culturally sensitive version of the old product, the Christian faith. For this increasingly vocal group of writers, teachers, and clerics, this was the only way to save Christianity from secularism on the one hand and intellectual dishonesty on the other.

The result was a movement that took shape within several of the traditional denominations between 1880 and 1930 and emerged triumphantly from 1930 to 1960. Thereafter it began to disintegrate into competing ideologies, lost its central core of affirmations, and ceased to be a movement with definable goals, beliefs, and ethos. Representative of the "New Theology," as it was termed initially, is William Newton Clarke (1841–1912), a theologian at Colgate Theological Seminary. In 1894 Clarke wrote the first systematic theology for the emerging movement, *An Outline of Christian Theology,* and later he wrote another influential work, *The Christian Doctrine of God* (1909). Assuming a developmental concept of Christianity in which the deposit of theological truth is constantly shifting (though the moral attributes of God are unchanging), and assuming as well that our highest conceptions of God are derived from the noblest qualities of humanity, he suggests that the Trinity is a triad of the progressive revelation of God-consciousness. The Trinity is a moral unity, not a

101

metaphysical one. The triune God is one "person," not three persons in one; it is a trinity of moral manifestation. He rejected the notion that the Father, the Son, and the Spirit equally share in the divine characteristics while they differ functionally in the great plan of redemption. He said, "It is true that the name Son is not given in the Scriptures to the Second within the Godhead, but only to the Second in the manifested Trinity,—not to the Word, but to Christ. No 'eternal Son' is mentioned in the Scriptures."[14] It seems that Clarke advocated a form of ancient Modalism when he stated that "God is in some manner forever reproducing himself within himself" or that God exists in three modes of activity in the self-revelation through human consciousness, though the Modalists understood the nature of God to be far more than a moral essence. Hence, God is love (He is moral), and this essential of the one God is revealed in a trifold manner; the multiplicity of the revelation is the Trinity. Said Clarke:

> Here, we scarcely need to say, there are recalled three relations of God to men—revealing, revealed and abiding. The relations are not abstract but practical: in these three ways writer and readers were having to do with God. They had to do with Christ revealing God, with God as Christ revealed him, and with God as Christ had brought them home to him. These three were not only relations of one and the same God, but they were relations that concerned the saving of men.[15]

Clarke's understanding of God will be more evident in later discussions of the person of Christ and His atonement.

The most popular spokesman for the reconstruction of Christianity in America was Harry Emerson Fosdick (1878–1969), a disciple of Clarke who emerged through the controversies of the 1920s as the Jessup Professor of Homiletics at Union Theological Seminary and as pastor of Riverside Church in New York City. He combined oratorical skills with extensive publications to bring the new view of Christianity into the popular arena with zeal and courage. He was unabashed in his adherence to the New Theology, pivotally shaping it in the twentieth century. Like Clarke, Fosdick assumed a progressive, evolutionary concept of God, who gradually emerged, developed from pagan tribal deities to the later Hebraic idea of a God of righteousness; that is, the idea of God evolved from brutality to love and kindness. The Trinity was an attempt by Christians to express their enlarged knowledge of God—a knowledge so rich and full that it could no longer be described by traditional monotheism. Without intending to start a development that would issue in the classic creeds, they attempted to describe the divine in more than one way. What evolved into a metaphysical trinitarianism in the early centuries of the church was simply an attempt to express the unfathomable mystery of the one God. The "Trinity" is a repetition of singularity, a revelation of love, not three persons in one. He wrote: "In all this [his attempt to describe God] he was not metaphysically analyzing the divine nature but was indicating the manifoldness of the divine approach to man, and was endeavoring, in the spirit of his own words, to express the ineffable."[16]

While it is true that classic liberalism, or the New Theology, was modified in the 1930s by a host of theologians and scholars who, after the devastation of a world war, found it difficult to embrace the unqualified optimism often expressed in the movement (some finding Jonathan Edwards' more sober evaluation of humanity more to their sensibilities), the neo-liberal movement continued in the same stance relative to the doctrine of God. Though God was not conceived as starkly immanent (being identified with evolutionary social forces), as was the tendency in Europe and America before Karl Barth, the "Trinity" was viewed as a moral threeness-in-oneness, a trifold revelation of the moral character of God.

In the 1960s, the liberal movement evidenced increasing disintegration and diffusion. This could be seen in the increased and conflicting interpretations of the doctrine of God. The most radical expression of the so-called "fad theologies," a term indicative of the intensity and transitoriness of the view, was the Secularization-of-God movement. While the movement manifested a soft-core and a hard-core approach to the doctrine of God, Thomas J. J. Altizer was a spokesperson through *The Gospel of Christian Atheism*. He adopted a Hegelian, evolutionary theory, far outstripping Clarke or Fosdick to explain the Trinity as the emergence of human self-consciousness.

The three "persons" do not exist simultaneously but are stages of development. The idea of "Father" suggests universal being or wholeness; "God" ceased to exist in a dialectical process, becoming the Christ, the ideal of humanity; and the Spirit is a synthesis of the sacred God and profane humanity or self-consciousness. Altizer had no concept of either a God who is beyond us or of the Trinity.

Paul Tillich (1886–1965), a theologian at Union Theological Seminary in New York, developed an interior, psychological approach to the discussion of God. He believed that the doctrine of the Trinity was invented by human beings to supply a remedy for feelings of alienation and despair; it is a tool for coping with life's problems. God is not a being who possesses existence; He is a symbol of "our ultimate concern." "'Personal God' does not mean that God is a person. It means that God is the ground of everything personal and that he carries within himself the ontological power of personality. He is not a person, but he is no less than personal."[17] To Tillich, the term *Father* is a symbol of concern and care in an alienated world; the term *Son* is a symbol of self-giving; and the term *Spirit* is a synthesis of the two. Allan Killen has summarized his concept of God this way: "The purpose of Tillich's argument against the personality of God is not simply to express that there are three in the Godhead, and to correct the way the Godhead itself can be carelessly spoken of as a person, but rather to prove that there is not any 'person' in the Godhead let alone 'three persons.'"[18] All this should cheer us as we take courage and strength from ourselves to confront our problems; it is a self-help message. There is no objective being outside the universe who can come to our aid. It is no wonder that the lure of the liberal movement has lost its glitter and attractiveness to many.

In recent years, theologians have turned to process theism as a possibly fruitful way to understand the doctrine of God. Critical of the empty solutions offered by secular humanists, who reject transcendency entirely, as well as the arguments for classical theism, process theologians have found solace in the refinement of evolutionary philosophies and the emergence of new theories of mathematics and physics. From this perspective, God is not a timeless, all-powerful monarch (a concept they identify as rooted more in Greek thought than in the Bible); rather, He is love, sympathy, and compassion. He is

104

a God who is involved in our sufferings. God works in this world not so much by sovereign control and intervention as by persuasion through inspiring us. God works in our lives, process theologians claim, as we actualize His aims in the world. Christ is the collectivity of God's highest aims and aspirations. The traditional orthodox understanding of such terms as *eternity, omnipresence, immutability,* and *omniscience* are redefined; God is neither sovereignly active in this world nor all-knowing. The divine is a weak well-wisher whose knowledge of tomorrow depends on the fickleness of human perception and integrity. He is a contradictory being who is bipolar; He possesses a primordial nature, which is abstract and transcendent, and a consequent nature, which is concrete and relative. The Trinity is no more than a symbol; it is a combination of God's two natures, which are somehow united, and His subjective aim for the world.

Reminiscent of the liberal tradition both in Europe and in America in the past two centuries, Ewert H. Cousins stated: "The deepest reality of God is seen not in his detachment or in his power, but in his love. In contrast with the static Absolute and the All-powerful monarch, the process God is the God of persuasive love revealed in Jesus Christ."[19] The attempt of the liberal tradition within Christianity to redefine God, to fashion Him into a more culturally benign and socially responsive being, is reflective of the struggle of people in general to fashion God in our likeness. Isaiah speaks of the people of his day who cut down a tree and with some of the wood warmed themselves, but with other wood carved a god, only to fall down before it exclaiming, "My God!" (Isaiah 44:12-17). The liberal tradition reversed the Creation record. Instead of God declaring, "Let us make man in our image," man declares, "Let us make God in our image." Love without power is at best well-meaning ineptitude. A God who has no knowledge of the future is a poor guide. Theology has become a branch of science, sociology, and psychology.

The American Protestant Conservative Tradition and the Trinity

Some theologians within the classical tradition of Christian theism have offered what has been identified as a neo-classical view. While the view has been identified as "process theology in the evangelical camp," its defenders insist that, though similarities exist, the connection is invalid. For example, they argue that in their view, as opposed to process theism, God has willingly subjected Himself to the world and the submission is not due to some weakness on His part; He has willed to work through being made willing. Also, God's active role in the world is more than persuasion or hopeful desiring.[20] However, the "openness view of God" is a significant departure from the historic, orthodox interpretation of the nature and character of God. For example, the perfection of God's attributes is destroyed by the elevation of God's love to the denigration of His other attributes. Historically, at least, the church has held to the mystery of the equalitarian perfections of the attributes in the Godhead. This view, however, seems to suggest that God's love defines the divine reality. Neo-classicists suggest that traditional theism presents a God who is unkind, uncaring, uninvolved in human lives. This is an unwarranted charge. Traditional theism assuredly asserts that God simultaneously is righteous, just, holy, and wrathful as well as merciful and generous. Our God has revealed Himself to us truly, though not completely; our God is beyond the grasp of the finite. We refuse to reinterpret the Bible in such a way as to lose the wonder and awe of a being who is more complex than we may be. Further, the attribute of omniscience is redefined to mean that He can successfully handle immediate circumstances, not that He knows (and therefore controls) future events. God, in this view, has willed to limit His power by delegating some of it to creatures. What a frightening world it would be if the all-loving God put final authority into the hands of mere creatures! Love without power makes love merely an emotion; it offers no comfort that "God causes all things to work together for good to those who love God" (Romans 8:28). Of course, any discussion of God must admit mystery, yet this view is more akin to the liberal tradition of explaining the nature of God in that it surrenders transcendence to immanence, divine sovereignty to human freedom.

THE ROMAN CATHOLIC TRADITION AND THE TRINITY

Asked technically, the question might go something like this: Has the Roman Catholic community

106

changed its understanding of God as Trinity since the Council of Trent in the sixteenth century? Neither Vatican I in 1869 nor Vatican II in 1962–1965 reflected deeply on this particular issue, as the impact of the Enlightenment socially, scientifically, and theologically consumed the first council and the demise of the modern world, with the advent of postmodernism, was the focus of the second council. The question can be most fruitfully answered by studying the recent *Catechism of the Catholic Church* (1994), which was sanctioned by Pope John Paul. Officially, the Roman community, like the Orthodox churches and Protestant traditions, recognizes the correctness of the Nicene and Constantinople councils of the fourth century. Citing from the Second Council of Constantinople and the Council of Toledo, the catechism explains the Trinity like this: "We do not confess three Gods, but one God in three persons, the 'consubstantial Trinity.' The divine persons do not share the one divinity among themselves but each of them is God whole and entire: 'The Father is that which the Son is, the Son that which the Father is, the Father and Son that which the Holy Spirit is, i.e., by nature one God'" (253). The catechism states that the church devised a distinctive vocabulary to explain the doctrine and then defines each of those central terms. "The Church uses (I) the term 'substance' (rendered also at times by 'essence' or 'nature') to designate the divine being in its unity, (II) the term 'person' or 'hypostasis' to designate the Father, Son, and Holy Spirit in the real distinction among them, and (III) the term 'relation' to designate the fact that their distinction lies in the relationship of each to the other" (252). Thus, while significant differences exist between the major branches of Christendom, there is no fundamental discontinuity in teachings of the Trinity of God.

THE ORTHODOX TRADITION AND THE TRINITY

During worship services in the Orthodox community, whether it be in the Sunday or weekday liturgy, the faithful repeat the Nicene Creed. At the center of their confession is the triune God. For eleven centuries the Catholic Church, being undivided, embraced this creed as the essence of trinitarian faith. Though deeply challenged to defend the doctrine of the Trinity after being increasingly overwhelmed, after the seventh century, by the monotheistic Islamic faith, the church clung to the Shema: "Hear, O Israel! The LORD is our God, the LORD is one!" (Deuteronomy 6:4). When the Islamic apologists argued that proof of Christian polytheism was their adoration of Jesus Christ, the Orthodox responded by stating that Christianity was a monotheistic faith, yet their monotheism embraced the conviction that Jesus Christ must be spoken of as God. Demetrios J. Constantelos has written: "The essence of the faith can be rendered in a sentence: The Orthodox faith presents God revealed in Jesus Christ and man redeemed by Jesus Christ. . . . The Son of God Jesus Christ became manifest among men in order to regenerate man and make him a new creation through the Holy Spirit, the 'Giver of Life'."[21] Believing that the Western orthodoxies, Roman and Protestant, have been taken captive by the rationalistic spirit of the Enlightenment in stressing the intellectual content of the faith, the Orthodox Church emphasizes the mystery element in the Christian belief. Said Clendenin, "Eastern theology does not prescribe a leap into the irrational, but instead (1) a recognition of the radical limitations of human cognition and of conceptual language, and (2) celebration of the mystery so inherent in the story of Christianity."[22] Central of all mysteries is the absolutely transcendent, personal, triune God who became incarnate in the Lord Jesus Christ.

4

*T*he Person of Christ: Meet the God–Man

My all-time favorite Christmas card lacks the red, green, and white colors traditionally associated with the season. It does not depict the warmth of a Norman Rockwell painting or some wintry scene. As a matter of fact, it appears rather plain in black and white. On the front of the card are several of the great conquerors and despots of world history—Adolf Hitler, Julius Caesar, Alexander the Great, Napoléon, to name a few. Below their pictures is this statement: "Many men have sought to be God." Opening the card, one finds an impressionistic picture of the manger with the Christ child. The caption on the opposite side is stunning: "But only one God sought to be man." That really summarizes the meaning of Christmas and the Lord Jesus Christ. He alone is God's Son, the incarnate Lord. The central text from the Scriptures to explain Christ as the incarnation of God is John 1:14. "The Word became flesh, and dwelt among us, and we saw His glory, glory as of the only begotten from the Father, full of grace and truth."

The famous American Puritan Jonathan Edwards (1703–1758) pondered the place of this single, solitary life in a series of sermons for his Northampton parishioners in 1739. These sermons were posthumously published under the title *A History of the Work of Redemption.* Using as his basic thesis that "the Work of Redemption is a work that God carries on from the fall of man to the end of the world,"[1] Edwards presented a theory of world history from beginning to end. The focal point of history is the Lord Jesus Christ—just as it should be! The world was created by God but has become blighted by the Fall,

Edwards told his listeners. It is His divine purpose to redeem the creation, to cause human beings and the creation to experience recovery, which will occur in the consummation of this age. Edwards argued that "God created the world for to be Christ's spouse."[2] Using the Bible, both history and prophecy, as well as secular sources, he created a time line of events to the end of time. At the center of history is the Lord Jesus Christ. The period before Christ he named "Preparation for Redemption"; the period after Christ, "Accomplishment of Redemption." From the Incarnation to the resurrection of Christ is designated as the period of the "Purchase of Redemption"; at the center of Christ's life is Calvary. The world began in a created paradise and will end in a renewed garden with Christ, the Lamb of God, the exalted one present there. Edwards, as well as the Puritan tradition as a whole, was consumed with the wonder of God's salvation; Christ is the center of that redemption. In placing Christ preeminently in the role of the Savior, Edwards reflects the historic orthodoxy of the church.

The most intense discussion of the incarnate person of Christ emerged on the heels of the controversy in the church over the Trinity. At the Councils of Nicaea (325) and Constantinople (381), the bishops of the church were concerned to explain the mystery of the preincarnate relationship of the Father to the Son. Christ is God, the councils argued, in that He shares equality of attributes with the Father, the titles for Him (such as "Son of God") being functional descriptors. Once the church leaders firmly grasped the preincarnate relationship between the Father and Son, it did not take long for them to be consumed with another difficult question. How do you explain with finite words and a perfect but incomplete revelation the mystery of the incarnate person of Christ? How do you understand our Lord's deity and humanity, that is, the miracle of the Incarnation itself?

As we enter a discussion of this important teaching, it is imperative that we grasp a few things. First, the church never evidenced disbelief in the deity of the Savior until recent centuries. While church leaders could not explain the relationship of the two natures of Christ, nearly every one of them nonetheless held firmly to both natures. Contrast this with many of our current scholars, who have elevated the humanness of Christ to the exclusion or virtual exclusion of His deity. While

110

some have viewed Him as merely a human ideal, church leaders of an earlier time were willing to ascribe deity to Him. Second, the doctrine of the incarnate Christ was not invented in the fourth- and fifth-century councils; rather, it was explained there. Theology is no mere invention that evolves in its essence. It is the reflection by the church on the materials about God presented to us by God Himself in the Bible within a particular time frame or setting. The church from the beginning embraced the belief that Jesus is God; this is one of its several, central affirmations. It took centuries of circumstances to explain what had been embraced.

The History of the Doctrine of the Person of Christ

The Ancient Church	The Medieval Church	The Reformation Church	The Modern Church

Formulation → - - - - - Consent - - - - - → Re-evaluation

Tertullian	Schleiermacher
Athanasius	Hermann
Apollinarius	von Harnack
Nestorius	Ritschl
Cyril of Alexandria	Weiss
Eutyches	Barth
Leo III	Bultmann

THE ANCIENT CHURCH AND THE PERSON OF CHRIST (100–600)

Christianity was a Christ-centered faith right from the start. "Jesus is Lord" was the earliest, most basic confession. But that confession leaves unanswered some important questions, and so over time the church's thinkers worked out a sophisticated understanding of the divine and human natures of Jesus Christ. This was no mere abstract

111

philosophical endeavor: it was called for by crucial struggles going on within the church. The discussion about the person of Christ began slowly in the early church but picked up steam.

THE CHURCH FATHERS AND THE PERSON OF CHRIST (100–150)

*A*ccording to the testimony of Irenaeus, a third-century church leader, Clement of Rome (d. 101?) faithfully transmitted apostolic teaching in his letter to the Christian community at Corinth (*Against Heresies* III.3.3). Clement, then, may be seen as an important witness to New Testament belief. Having spoken of Christ as the preexistent Son of God (*1 Clement* 36), this writer spoke of Him as having been sent from God ["Christ is from God" (42)], being "established in the word of God with full assurance of the Holy Ghost" (42). In a rather moving passage, he wrote, "The scepter of the majesty of God, even our Lord Jesus Christ, came not in the pomp of arrogance or of pride, though He might have done so, but in lowliness of mind according as the Holy Spirit spake [Isaiah 52–53] concerning Him" (16.2). He also wrote of His resurrection and exaltation, at which time He was united with the Father in glory and received divine honor (32.4; 38.4; 43.6; 58.2; 63.3; 65.2). While Clement affirmed the deity and humanity of Christ, he did not speculate on the relationship between the two in His single being.

Among the most revered of the earliest Fathers was Ignatius of Antioch (c.35–c.107), a bishop and disciple of the apostle John. He was aware of the error that denied the fleshly incarnation of Christ—docetism (a term suggesting that Christ had the appearance of being human only)—and firmly denied it. There is an intriguing passage in *To the Ephesians* that suggests he understood Christ to be God and man. "There is only one physician, of flesh and of the spirit, generate and ingenerate, God in man, life in death, Son of Mary and Son of God, first passible [capable of suffering] and then impassible, Jesus Christ our Lord" (7.2). Ignatius joined the other Fathers in affirming that Jesus Christ is God and man, but he, as well as the others, did not attempt to present a rationale for the possibility. What Alois Grillmeier concluded from the writings of

112

Ignatius can be said of the earliest Fathers as a whole. "Despite this emphatic delineation of the God-man of Jesus Christ there is still no doctrine of two natures in a technical sense."[3] The Lord Jesus is viewed simply as both God and man; beyond this there is no speculation.

THE APOLOGISTS AND THE PERSON OF CHRIST (150–300)

There is a parallel between the development of the church's understanding of the preincarnate person of Christ and its understanding of the incarnate person of Christ. As the witness of the church spread into the Mediterranean world and beyond, the polytheistic culture was confused by the Christian proclamation that God is one and yet three. Similar consternation was felt over the declaration that Jesus was one and yet two. It seemed to nonChristian scholars that the new faith was easily refutable because it lacked rational coherency. The pagan philosopher Celsus, for example, attacked the teachings of the church by arguing that since Christ changed, He was not the immutable or changeless God whom Christians proclaimed. Also, he suggested that if Christ was God, then He only appeared to be human. Since Christians claimed that He was God, then either He or they were practicing deception. Origen (c.185–c.254) recorded the accuser's complaint: "Either God really changes his self, as they say, into a moral body . . . or he himself is not changed, but makes those who see him think that he is changed. But in that case he is a deceiver and a liar" (*Against Celsus* 4.18). Thus, the church was brought by external pressures to reflect on the person of the Lord and reply to its critics. The issue was not the invention of a teacher or something novel in the church; it was an explanation of its teaching. Seeking to defend the faith from those who would attack it is the essence of the task of the theologian; the finished product is systematic theology.

Irenaeus, bishop of Lyons in the West (c.130–c.200), understood that the central Christian proclamation had to do with the message of salvation; central to redemption is Christ. It is not unnatural that, with his great emphasis on salvation, he would be recognized as a Christocentric theologian. For Irenaeus, Christ is the God-man.

> There is therefore . . . one God the Father, and one Christ Jesus our Lord. . . . in every respect, too, he is man, the formation of God: and thus he took up man into himself, the invisible becoming visible, the impassible becoming capable of suffering, and the Word being made man, thus summing up all things in himself. (*Against Heresies* III.16)

The influence of Irenaeus's view of Christ was such that a phrase that he used of Him, "Jesus Christ the Son of God is one and the same," appears several times in the doctrinal formulation of the two natures within the one Christ in the fifth-century Creed of Chalcedon.

Another example of how the Western apologists understood the incarnate Christ—and among them there is consensus—is Hippolytus of Rome (c.170–c.236), a presbyter. He understood that Christ existed prior to His incarnation and so he spoke of His existence in two stages, preincarnate and incarnate. Hippolytus argued that Christ became the Son by virtue of His incarnation, the title being a functional one rather than an ontological one.

> And he has taken for humanity the new name of love by calling himself Son; for neither was the Logos before the incarnation and when by himself yet perfect Son, although he was perfect Logos, only begotten, nor could the flesh exist by itself apart from the Logos, as it had its existence in the Logos. Thus, then, was manifest one (single) perfect Son of God. (*A Refutation of All Heresies* 15)

The writings of the Eastern apologists concerning Christ are consistent with those of their Western counterparts. The little-known second-century apologist Melito of Sardis, whose writings are available only through quotations by other writers, may have been the first to speak of Christ as having two natures. In a fragment from Anastasius of Sinai (d. c.700), he wrote,

114

Being perfect God and likewise perfect man, He gave positive indications of His two natures: of His deity, by miracles during the three years following after His Baptism; of His humanity, in the thirty years which came before the Baptism, during which, by reason of His condition according to the flesh, He concealed the signs of His deity, although He was the true God existing before the ages. (*The Guide* 13)

Origen of Alexandria (c.185–c.254), one of the greatest biblical scholars in the early church, spoke of a twofold rule in the one Christ. Some specialists in his works believe that, while he saw Christ as the God-man, he so emphasized His deity that it overshadowed and diminished His true humanity (a tendency that often characterized Alexandrian theology as a whole, perhaps due to a Platonic philosophical approach to understanding reality). However, while his explanation of the relationship of the two natures in the one person may be flawed, he stood in the orthodox tradition of the church and embraced Christ as the God-man. In a somehow paradoxical expression of the point, he wrote:

Jesus, who died, is a man. Even in His own regard, He said: "But now you seek to kill me, a man who has spoken the truth" [John 7:19]. But while it is certainly a man who died, the Truth, Wisdom, Peace and Justice, of whom it is written, "The Word was God" [John 1:1], was not a man; and the God who is the Word, and the Truth, and Wisdom and Justice, is not dead. (*Commentaries on John* 28.14)

Taken as a whole, the early church leaders expressed the conviction that Christ was both God and man. Perhaps spurred by adversaries, such as Celsus, they embraced the Scriptures and proclaimed Christ, yet they did not speculate deeply so as to create a rational explanation of His two natures. Grillmeier is perhaps correct in his judgment that

115

"this unity [of the apologists concerning the incarnate Christ] is more intuitively seen than speculatively interpreted."[4]

THE THEOLOGIANS AND THE PERSON OF CHRIST (300–600)

Several events in the fourth century had a tremendous impact on the life of the church. First, the empire began to show signs of collapse following the Battle of Adrianople (376). Second, Christianity emerged from intolerance and persecution to triumph throughout the empire. The fruit of the latter, as has already been noted, is that the bishops of the church had the freedom to meet together and speak collectively to the issues that troubled it; indeed, such gatherings were politically sanctioned. As in the case of the discussion of the preincarnate relationship of the Son to the Father, so also is the case concerning the incarnate person of the Lord Jesus. To this point in the development of the understanding of Christ's person, the church grasped the idea that Jesus was both truly human and truly divine. Christians clearly conceived of Christ as possessing two natures, or sets of defining characteristics. The task before church leaders in this era was to explain that relationship. That people would be so consumed with questions of theology may seem strange to us only because the interests that consume our conversations are frequently on more temporary subjects!

The issue of the relationship of the two natures in Christ came to the forefront when a bishop from Laodicea, Apollinarius (c.310–c.390), proposed an explanation. While this bishop affirmed that Christ possessed two natures, he felt compelled to denigrate His full humanness to maintain His full deity. Christ was a less-than-human being who was overshadowed by divinity. Gregory of Nazianzus (329/30–389/90) described Apollinarius's view in the following way: "He assumes that man who came down from above is without a mind, but that the Godhead of the Only-begotten fulfills the function of mind, and is the third part of his human composite, inasmuch as soul and body are in it on its human side, but not mind, the place of which is taken by God the Word" (*Letter to Nectarius* 438).

Gregory's response to Apollinarius was at least twofold. First, his view, claimed Gregory, can only be sustained by playing tricks with the

116

meaning of the Scriptures. Here he points his audience to the meaning of the phrase "became man" in John 1:14 and the reference to possessing the attitude of Christ in Philippians 2:5. How could we be commanded to have the mind of Christ by the apostle when Christ did not have a mind? Second, Apollinarius's understanding appears to destroy the miracle of the redemption of humankind. If Christ was not truly human, how could He be the substitute for humans?

> If anyone has put his trust in Him as a Man without a human mind, he is really bereft of mind, and quite unworthy of salvation. For that which He has not assumed He has not healed; but that which is united to His Godhead is also saved. If only half Adam fell, then that which Christ assumes and saves may also be half also; but if the whole of his nature fell, it must be united to the whole of Him that was begotten, and so be saved as a whole. (*Epistle* 101)

At the second ecumenical gathering of the church, this time in Constantinople (381), Apollinarius's view was condemned. The revision of the Nicene Creed, the Nicene-Constantinopolitan Creed, which additionally addressed the issue of the deity of the Holy Spirit, thus formulated our doctrine of the Trinity. In the same creed is the sentence "[He] was incarnate by the Holy Spirit and the Virgin Mary and became human." The divine Christ is also human, the two in one!

The precise nature of the "two in one" was challenged again in the fifth century by Nestorius (b. after 351; d. after 451), the patriarch of Constantinople. In his attempt to explain the two natures in Christ, he appears to have understated the unity of the two natures by making the relationship between them merely moral, not organic. Consequently, Nestorius's view is often described as creating two Christs. He was willing to affirm that the virgin Mary bore Christ, but he refused to affirm that she bore God. The bishop of Alexandria, Cyril (c.375–444), called a council in his city and had his counterpart condemned (it appears that self-interest and quest for power did not escape the highest officeholders of the church!). The sixth anathema

117

hurled at Nestorius stated, "If anyone dare to say that the Word of God the Father is the God of Christ or the Lord of Christ, and shall not rather confess Him as at the same both God and man, since according to the Scriptures the Word became flesh; let him be anathema" (*The Twelve Anathemas*). The controversy took an unusual twist when both Cyril and Nestorius appealed to the bishop of Rome to adjudicate. Bishop Celestine (d. 432) supported Cyril and had Nestorius condemned in a regional synod in 430. The stage was thus set for another ecumenical gathering of the church, the Council of Ephesus in 431. Nestorius was condemned by the bishops of the church, though the issue was not completely resolved.[5] It was clear by this time that Christ possessed two perfect natures in one person, truly God and truly man!

Another advance toward the resolution of the issue of the person of Christ—and indeed, toward the division of the Catholic Church— occurred when a teacher in Constantinople, Eutyches (c.378–c.454), set forth his view and convulsed the church once again. Unlike the Appollinarians before him, he did not deny the humanity of Christ, and unlike the Nestorians, neither did he separate Christ into two beings. His error was that, in arguing strenuously for the unity of Christ, he dissolved the two natures into one. Eutyches was examined and condemned in a local synod under the direction of the patriarch of Constantinople, Flavian (d. 449), after he confessed that "our Lord was of two natures before the union [the unity of divinity and humanity in the Incarnation], but after the union one nature." At this point the bishop of Alexandria, Dioscorus (d. 454), appealed for the support of Leo I (c.400–461), bishop of Rome, and called for a council at Ephesus (449), thinking that he could secure the affirmation of Eutyches. Leo, however, dubbed the event "the Robbers Council," since his views were not read at the council, and sided with the patriarch of Constantinople in condemning both Dioscorus and Eutyches. With the support of the bishops of Rome and Constantinople, the fourth ecumenical council was called in 451 at Chalcedon. Five hundred twenty bishops gathered, the largest of the ecumenical councils, though Leo of Rome was not in attendance. The council condemned Eutyches, banished Dioscorus, and formulated the famous Chalcedonian Creed. The council decreed that the Lord Jesus Christ in the

Incarnation was truly God and truly man in one person without confusion of natures forever. "Our Lord Jesus Christ is one and the same, that He is perfect in godhead and perfect in manhood, truly God and truly man . . . in two natures, unconfusedly, immutably, indivisibly, inseparably, the distinction of the two natures being preserved and concurring in one person."

The pronouncements of the Council of Chalcedon did not end the controversy in the churches concerning the nature of the single person of Christ. Some of those who were disturbed by the Chalcedonian definition of Christology were really opposed, not so much to the doctrine the council had asserted, but to the words "in two natures." (While the Western portion of the church distinguished the terms "person" and "nature," the Greek East equated them, so that it seemed to some that Chalcedon advocated two Christs.) Eventually, these so-called Verbal Monophysites, single-nature Christologists, were reconciled by the findings of the fifth ecumenical council. Meeting in Constantinople in 553, and attended by about 150 bishops, the council consoled those with linguistic concerns but severed those who had more serious problems with the Chalcedonian Creed.

> If any one does not anathematize Arius, Eunomius, Macedonius, Apollinarius, Nestorius, Eutyches, and Origen, with their impious writings, as also all other heretics already condemned and anathematized by the holy Catholic and Apostolic Church, and by the aforesaid four holy councils, and all those who have been or are of the same mind with the heretics mentioned, and who remain to the end in their impiety, let him be anathema.

Following this ecumenical pronouncement, churches in Syria, Egypt, Ethiopia, and Armenia broke away from the "catholic" church. The result was the permanent shattering of the visible church into the Chalcedonian Catholic Church and the Monophysite Catholic Churches, the latter being represented by communities in the East. To this day, the Coptic churches of Egypt and Ethiopia, the Jacobite

THE PERSON OF CHRIST: MEET THE GOD-MAN

Church, and the Armenian Church remain Eutychian or Monophysite in Christology.[6]

THE MEDIEVAL CHURCH AND THE
PERSON OF CHRIST (600–1500)

A corollary to the ongoing discussion in the East was the rise of Monothelitism, a controversy about Christ's person relative to His will. In retrospect, however, it now seems that the underlying cause of the dispute was the military threat posed by the rising tide of Islamic militarism. The Eastern emperor at the time wanted to increase his armies to forestall intrusion from the East. Thus, he sought to reconcile the Monophysites. To do so, the patriarch of Constantinople proposed rapprochement with the notion that there was "one energy" in the two-natured Christ (later the phrase "one energy" was replaced with the words "one will"). This was a concession to Monophysitism by carrying the singularity from Christ's nature as a whole to a facet of that nature, the will. This approach to understanding Christ, like Apollinarianism and Monophysitism before it, denigrated the true humanity of Christ.

When the military situation in the East deteriorated with increasing Islamic conquests, particularly in areas of Monophysite concentration, the conciliatory measures became unnecessary. Further, considerable criticism for making such an attempt in the first place was mounting in the West. The final blow to Monothelitism came in 681 when the sixth ecumenical council gathered in Constantinople, the third ecumenical council in this city. The bishops decreed that Christ had two perfect wills, one pertaining to each of His perfect natures. Repeating much of the creed from the previous ecumenical council, the council added the following: "We likewise [teach] . . . two natural operations [wills]. . . . And these two natural wills are not contrary one to the other (which God forbid), as the impious heretics say, but His human will follows, not in resisting or reluctant, but rather therefore as subject to His divine and omnipotent will."

The council condemned both the former patriarch of Constantinople, Sergius (d. 638), and the "sometime Pope of Old Rome,"

120

Honorius (d. 638; pope 625–638), who had embraced the Mono-thelite error.[7]

Christological controversy was quite rare in the Western churches throughout the medieval period, though there was one irruption in eighth-century Spain; this, however, did not cause a schism in the church. In what came to be designated as "the Adoptionistic contro-versy," Elipandus of Toledo (717–802) and Felix of Urgel (d. 818) appeared to teach a form of Nestorianism. It seems that living under Arab rule caused many Christians to phrase their Christology so as not to unnecessarily cause problems. However, the Moors were being pushed from northern Spain by the Frankish kingdom and Charlemagne. Worlds of discourse were changing. As some theolo-gians heard these men teach, they accused them of asserting that Christ was truly the Son of God, even according to His human nature, by subordinating His humanity to His deity. He was the nat-ural Son of God according to His divinity but the adopted Son of God according to His humanity. The tendency of the teaching was to divide the person of Christ into two beings. This view was con-demned at a series of regional councils convened by the great Charlemagne. The supposed proponents repeatedly denied the teaching, and when they passed off the scene, few were willing to continue the discussion.

As has been rehearsed, the late medieval period in the West wit-nessed the rise of the universities (that is, the shift from the cathedral schools) and the emergence of the Scholastic method of inquiry. These occurred during a time of renewed interest in the writings of Aristotle, which precipitated discussions of the relationship of faith and reason. The place of reason in the defense of faith increasingly took center stage in Western theological activity (this in marked contrast to the churches in the East). In general, the Scholastics reproduced the Christology of the traditional, ecumenical creeds and thus remained catholic and Chalcedonian, though at times their particular way of stating and arguing it suggests that their tendency was to stress the divinity of Christ and slight His humanity in the one person. This par-ticular tendency is evident in Peter Abelard (1079–1142/3), Peter Lombard (c.1100–1160), Thomas Aquinas (c.1225–1274), and Duns Scotus (c.1265–1308).

THE EARLY MODERN CHURCHES AND THE PERSON OF CHRIST (1500–1750)

The church in the late medieval period was rent by dissension, which lead to division in the sixteenth century. While the causes were numerous, the great effect was that the Western Chalcedonian Catholic Church polarized into two warring factions, coalescing into the Roman Catholic Church and the Protestant churches. Though the issues were profoundly significant, in retrospect it's plain that there were broad areas of agreement, reflective of the fact that both factions shared a common theological heritage. As has been stated already, Roman Catholics and Protestants agreed on the importance of the Holy Scriptures in formulating faith and the doctrine of the Trinity. To illustrate the point, the Canons and Dogmatic Decrees of the Council of Trent—the great defining moment in Roman Catholic history—enunciated only those areas of disagreement with their antagonists; there is no grand section on the person of the Lord Jesus Christ. The person of Christ was not an issue that rent the unity of the Chalcedonian Catholic Churches.

THE ROMAN CATHOLIC CHURCH AND THE PERSON OF CHRIST

As noted above, the documents of the Council of Trent do not enunciate the doctrine of the person of Christ. It, like the Protestant orthodoxies and the Orthodox churches, share in the findings of Chalcedon (451) and the two subsequent ecumenical councils held in Constantinople (553, 681), which embraced the findings of Chalcedon. The Tridentine Profession of Faith (1564), a confessional summary of the Council of Trent, makes reference to the Nicene-Constantinopolitan Creed of 325/381, which does contain a refutation of Apollinarianism. The second article would likely be interpreted as referring to the other Christological councils. "I most steadfastly admit and embrace apostolic and ecclesiastic traditions, and all other observances and constitution of the same church."

THE PROTESTANT CHURCHES AND THE PERSON OF CHRIST

One of the curious arguments that

 Roman Catholic Church leaders made to their antagonists was that without the central, governing authority of the teaching magisterium, the church could not be preserved from endless divisions. Protestants replied that, given the priesthood of every believer, the inner witness of the Spirit was a sufficient guide to preserve the church, and that the tyranny of imposed, human authority was more dangerous than the risk of individualist interpretation. A look at the landscape of Protestantism should at least give some preliminary credence to the Catholics' complaint. For whatever reasons, Protestants subdivided into a variety of traditions and sects. Thus, as one approaches the Protestant Reformation, it is necessary to speak of a spectrum of traditions.

Martin Luther (1483–1546) had no difficulty embracing the traditional creeds of the church concerning Christology, affirming the full deity and humanity in the one person. What makes Luther hard to grasp is his explanation of the dual natures in Christ. It seems that he stated the divinity of Christ so as to downplay His humanity. Paul Althaus stated,

> How is it possible for Luther to maintain the true humanity of Christ under these circumstances? He teaches that Jesus Christ, according to his human nature, also possessed the attributes of the divine majesty, that is, that even the child Jesus was omniscient, omnipotent, and omnipresent.[8]

Althaus perhaps correctly suggests that Luther's confession of Christ is orthodox but that his dogmatic theory is confused and confusing. Lutheran orthodoxy did progress beyond Luther on this point. *The Augsburg Confession* (1530) has wonderfully summarized the historic, orthodox affirmation of Christology. "Also, they teach that the Word, that is, the son of God, took unto him man's nature in the womb of the blessed Virgin Mary, so that there are two natures, the divine and the human, inseparably joined together in unity of person; one Christ, true God and true man" (Article III)

The Genevan Reformer, John Calvin (1509–1564), dealt at length with the incarnate person of Christ in book two of the *Institutes of the*

THE PERSON OF CHRIST: MEET THE GOD-MAN

Christian Religion. In a chapter entitled "How the Two Natures Constitute the Person of the Mediator," Calvin stated:

> When it is said that the Word was made flesh, we must not understand it as if he were either changed into flesh, or confusedly intermingled with flesh, but that he made choice of the Virgin's womb as a temple in which he might dwell. He who was the Son of God became the Son of man, not by confusion of substance, but by unity of person. For we maintain, that the divinity was so conjoined and united with the humanity, that the entire properties of each nature remain entire, and yet the two natures constitute only one Christ. (2.14.1)

Thus, Calvin stood within the historic, ecumenical creeds of the church both in faith and explanation (this in contrast to Luther and some of the Anabaptists).

The influence of Calvin was far more extensive than that of any other Reformer of the time, as is evidenced by the large number of Reformed creeds that were subsequently published, some twenty-one representing many national expressions of his understanding of the Scriptures. For example, *The Gallican Confession* (1536), an expression of French Reformed thought, succinctly summarized the essence of the Incarnation with these words: "We believe that in one person, that is, Jesus Christ, the two natures are actually and inseparably joined and united, and yet each remains in its proper character" (Article XV). In the *Thirty-Nine Articles* of the Church of England (1571), a document that is less Calvinistic in character than others, Christ is described in the following manner:

> The Son, which is the Word of the Father, the very and eternal God, and of one substance with the Father, took on Man's nature in the womb of the blessed Virgin, of her substance: so that two whole and perfect Natures, that is to say, the

124

OUR LEGACY

Godhead and the Manhead were joined together in one Person, never to be divided, whereof is one Christ (Article II).

The Westminster Confession (1647), the grandest expression of English Puritan Reformed thought, after describing Christ's two natures, concluded with these words:

So that two whole, perfect, and distinct natures, the Godhead and the manhood, were inseparably joined together in one person, without conversion, composition, or confusion. Which person is very God and very man, yet one Christ, the only mediator between God and man. (Article VIII.2)

Scholars of the Protestant Reformation have noted two broad methods employed to bring about religious change. The "Magisterial Reformations," such as the Lutheran and Reformed movements, stressed the necessity of the role of the state. In so doing, the Reformers, such as Luther and Calvin, placed an emphasis on the interconnectedness of the church and state, perceiving their separate roles as vital for bringing about a lasting reformation of the church. The "Radical Reformations," such as the numerous Anabaptist groups, viewed the state from less positive perspectives, often assigning a negative, adversarial role to it. It is difficult to generalize about the Anabaptists because they represented wide-ranging perspectives. The Magisterial Reformers frequently attacked them, in print and otherwise, as dangerous subversives. Some of the Anabaptists, particularly in the Netherlands, departed from orthodox doctrine in the matter of the Incarnation. Menno Simons (1496–1561), for example, denied that Christ had human flesh, asserting that His "flesh" descended from heaven in the Incarnation. In other words, he taught a view of Christ that was docetic. The Anabaptists who followed the teachings of Simons, thus known today as Mennonites, did not embrace this particular teaching of their mentor and instead identified with the more conservative elements of the tradition, such as the Zürich Brethren.

125

THE HETERODOX GROUPS AND THE PERSON OF CHRIST

*W*ithin the discussion of the "radical tradition" of the Reformation belongs a delineation of the views of Michael Servetus (c.1511–1553) and Laelius (1525–1562) and Faustus (1539–1604) Socinus. Their views are indicative more of the enormous variety of movements and opinions under the designation of the term than of affinity among them. Unlike the aberration of Menno Simons, who sought to be intensely biblical (that is why he refused to use the term *Trinity,* though he clearly embraced the teaching), Servetus and the Socinians reflected an attachment to humanistic and rationalistic interests in their attempt to understand the Bible. Servetus appears to have perceived that the intellect was less liable to error, contrasting with the traditionally orthodox description of the intellect. In his understanding of the sources of knowledge, reason, and Scripture, the former judged the latter (interpretation was subjected to reason rather than to tradition). Escaping the Inquisition in Spain only to be burned as a heretic in Calvin's Geneva, Servetus denied the doctrine of the Trinity and the Chalcedonian interpretation of the God-man in Christ; he asserted that Christ was neither God nor man. Calvin's description of his view is characteristically graphic.

> In our age, also, has arisen not a less fatal monster, Michael Servetus, who for the Son of God has substituted a figment composed of the essence of God spirit, flesh, and three uncreated elements. First, indeed, he denies that Christ is the Son of God, for any other reason than because he was begotten in the womb of the Virgin by the Holy Spirit. The tendency of this crafty device is to make out, by destroying the distinction of the two natures, that Christ is somewhat composed of God and man, and yet is not to be deemed God and man. (*Institutes of the Christian Religion* 2.14.18)

Christ is neither God nor man; "no kind of Godhead exists in the Mediator" and "a phantom is substituted instead of man" (2.14.18).

In retrospect, it can be seen that Servetus was part of a movement rooted in a growing rationalistic, historically nontraditional approach to the Christian faith. It may be termed the emergence of the Protestant Enlightenment tradition, whose spirit was fashioned by the Italian Renaissance and found an increasing number of advocates in Europe. The influence of Servetus was felt, as previously noted, in the Socinian movement, which found increasing acceptance among the upper classes in Poland. The movement in 1562 produced the Racovian Catechism (so called after the city of Racow, a Socinian/ Unitarian center), which stated and defended their understanding of the Scriptures. While affirming that Christ was "the only begotten Son of God," literally born through a virgin's supernatural conception, the catechism argues that the divinity in Him was the presence of the Holy Spirit or the power of God. Thus, Christ was an empowered man; He did not share ontological unity with God the Father. Speaking of Christ, the catechism noted:

> If by the terms divine nature or substance I am to understand the very essence of God, I do not acknowledge such a divine nature in Christ; for this is repugnant to right reason and Holy Scripture. But if, on the other hand, you intend by a divine nature the Holy Spirit which dwelt in Christ . . . I certainly do . . . acknowledge such a nature in Christ as to believe that next after God it belongs to no one in a higher degree.[9]

Christ, then, is a spiritually astute, inspired, and inspiring man. However, while He may be like God in profound measure, identifying with God's purposes and visions, He shares no equality of being with God.

Unitarian conceptions of Christ spread into England in the seventeenth century and to America in the eighteenth. The spirit of the Enlightenment, which rejected external authority for personal choice, evidenced itself in a two-pronged impact in the new nation. First, the attraction of English and Scottish entitlement theories for creating government were felt in the political discussions that led to the Declaration of Independence and the Constitution. Second, the same theories of private entitlement in the sphere of religion, the rejection of state religion and priestcraft, led to a free market of religious ideas. In that general context, Unitarianism emerged through Ebenezer Gay (1696–1787), Charles Chauncy (1705–1787), and Jonathan Mayhew (1720–1766), Boston-area clergymen. It was through William Ellery Channing (1780–1842) that the movement moved out of the shadowy arena of attacks upon Calvinism to set forth its teachings. Channing's ordination address in 1819 for Jared Sparks became the creedal expression of American Unitarianism. Speaking of Christ, he noted:

> We believe Jesus is one mind, one soul, one being, as truly one as we are, and equally distinct from the one God. We complain of the doctrine of the Trinity, that, not satisfied with making God three beings, it makes Jesus Christ two beings, and thus introduces infinite confusion into our conception of his character. This corruption of Christianity, alike repugnant to common sense and to the general strain of Scripture, is a remarkable proof of the power of a false philosophy in disfiguring the simple truth of Jesus.[10]

The insights of Servetus, the Socinians, and the Unitarians concerning Christ, the attempt to reject His deity while clinging to His humanity, have dominated theology in the last two centuries even in those traditions that would have vigorously rejected the teachings of their seventeenth-century heirs.

THE LATE MODERN CHURCHES AND THE PERSON OF CHRIST (1750–PRESENT)

While heterodox groups in the early modern period introduced a threat to orthodox beliefs in the person of Christ, it was in the late modern period that views on this matter really became diverse. Conservatives continued to hold up Chalcedonian Christology, but liberals experimented with all sorts of ideas of Christ's person that fell short of a God-man dual nature.

PROTESTANT TRADITIONS AND THE PERSON OF CHRIST

It was among the Protestant traditions, specifically the Protestant liberal traditions, that doctrines of Christ's person most diverged from orthodoxy. Liberal theologians often had good intentions in reshaping theology; they generally wanted to make Christianity palatable in the new context of the late modern period. Conservative Protestants nevertheless detected a serious danger in liberal doctrines of Christ, and they did their best to defend against it.

The European Protestant Liberal Tradition and the Person of Christ

The liberal tradition emerged as an attempt to rescue Christianity from the threat of extinction. It originated from two sources: first, the Enlightenment stress on the power of the human intellect to understand the universe and humankind apart from the traditional sources of authority, whether it be kings, pope, priests, creeds, or Scripture; and second, the rise of the sciences, which seemed to indicate that the Bible might speak about religion, if reduced to the private, individual, symbolic sphere, but did not offer a worldview that explained existence. The weight of the sciences, coupled with heightened respect for the mental processes, caused many to seek a new way of maintaining the centrality of religion. Liberals viewed their task as that of preserving the faith by accommodating and modifying it to prevailing social and scientific conditions. We would suggest that their motive may have been commendable, but their endeavor was flawed by giving too much away and retaining far too little of Christianity. In fact, as the American J. Gresham Machen (1881–1937) argued in the 1920s, what was retained after the transfiguring process was complete was not biblical Christianity at all; it was an intellectually deficient, retrograde movement, the very antithesis of true religion.

The attempt to save Christianity from traditional interpretations, which were increasingly under intellectual scrutiny because of devel-

129

opments in a wide range of the scientific disciplines, was embodied at the beginning of the nineteenth century in Friedrich Schleiermacher (1768–1834). Scholars have recognized him as the "father of modern theology," a trailblazer and trendsetter. Rejecting the possibility of an objective revelation from God in the Bible and fearing the destruction of transcendent religion through the rationalist attacks of the philosophers, he placed the ground of authority on inward experience, making Christianity a private, personal value judgment. By putting Christianity outside the realm of objective verification, he thought he could avoid the troubling issues raised by the sciences. In so doing, he turned away from objective criteria for verification to the inward self or feelings. Christianity is true because it is personally meaningful; it solicits profound feelings of dependence on God. The Bible is a record of religious experiences, not unique to those of anyone at any time; its authority rests in its ability to verify current experience by giving an assurance through illustration that people in the past felt the same wonderful things.

As Schleiermacher probed his inner feelings concerning Christ, he rejected as illogical the Chalcedonian confession, which viewed Christ as the incarnate God-man. Instead, Christ was merely a man, though distinguished from humanity by the constant potency of His dependence on God. Christ is the ideal of humanity, a model; He was what we should strive to be. He is divine, though not deity (meaning that He is simply a wonderful person), because of a certain elevated God-consciousness that He possessed. Schleiermacher could speak of Christ's virgin birth and sinlessness, but he did not mean that Christ was supernaturally conceived; instead, he reinterpreted such traditional terms to mean that Christ was infused from His natural conception with an awareness of God's presence ("virgin born") and that He was always aware of it ("sinless").

The beginning of His life was also a new implanting of the God-consciousness which creates receptivity in human nature. . . . The beginning must have transcended every detrimental influence of His immediate circle; and because it was

130

OUR LEGACY

> such an original and sin-free act of nature, a filling of His
> nature with God-consciousness became possible as a result.[11]

In essence, the traditional, orthodox notion of Christ as the God-man was an "imperfect representation of God," which the heathen sages corrected but early Christianity embraced. "Christ is everywhere distinguished from God, for He appears only as a deputy with full power, and hence His power is represented as resting in the Father."[12] Christ, when all is said by Schleiermacher, is really only a better person than we are because God was more active in His life than in ours.

The rise of "classic liberalism" is identified with Albrecht Ritschl (1822–1889) and a coterie of his disciples, such as Wilhelm von Hermann and Adolf von Harnack. The Ritschlian school was the dominant form of Christian revisionism until the arrival of the post–World War I era. Though perhaps more influential for his method of doing theology than for his particular doctrines, Ritschl sought to ground Christianity on a more historical foundation than either the "mythology" of the traditional approach to the Bible or the subjectivism of his mentor, Friedrich Schleiermacher. That is, he sought a more scientific approach to Christianity. Accepting the assumptions of the Higher Critical school of New Testament interpretation, that the Bible contains the revelation of God only and is not in its entirety revelation, Ritschl combined them with the authority of the religious community to determine who Christ actually was. Ritschl followed the lead of Immanuel Kant (1724–1804), who believed that his approach of segmenting knowledge into two types, scientific and religious, would put Christianity beyond the attacks of its critics. What he suggested was that religion must be separated from the realm of scientific knowledge; that is, religion belongs to the ethical, personal realm, not the objective realm. The structure of religion, thus, is a subjective value judgment asserted by the believing community; it is what the believers confess, not what science qualifies or what the Bible says if read at face value.

Because Ritschl believed that the Chalcedonian formula was a scientific judgment made in the sphere of religion, there was a fatal error in it. It was not a real expression of Christianity, since Christian faith speaks only in the realm of ethics, not science. Instead, the value of Jesus was in the church's perception that He could bring salvation, which meant that Christ was God's ambassador to cause an ethical righteousness to prevail on the earth. Christ is divine (not deity) because He alone of all humanity understood God's purposes and sought to effect them. That is, His identification with God is vocational in nature, not in unity of being. Christ's uniqueness is that He models God's ethical ideals for humankind. "He [is] himself the prototype of that life of love and elevation above worldly motive which forms the distinguishing characteristic of the kingdom of God."[13] It is difficult to understand how Ritschl could escape the charge that his Christ, like Schleiermacher's, was merely a human being.

A coterie of scholars in the late nineteenth century rejected the historical approach in understanding Christ employed by Ritschl and the Ritschlian tradition. In their judgment, any attempt to reconstruct Christianity through historical documentation, even following critical methodology, was doomed to failure. Designated as the History-of-Religions School, such scholars as Wilhelm Bousset (1865–1920) and Ernst Troeltsch (1865–1923) sought to find the essence of religion, a true and authentic kernel, through the study of comparative religions. The assumption they embraced was that certain commonalities can be found among all religions and these are the essence of true religion. (This teaching is reminiscent of such Deists as Benjamin Franklin, and such Unitarians as Thomas Jefferson, of the eighteenth century.) Also, several religious belief systems in the first century grow out of the same environment and were mutually dependent for their basic ideas, except for some elements found in the apostle Paul's teachings. Thus, Christianity is not superior to any other contemporary religion; all of them share a common community of ideas. Though the school generally embraced the historicity of Jesus, they were unified in believing that the New Testament presents a distorted and untrustworthy view of Him.

The European Protestant Conservative Tradition and the Person of Christ

The Christology of the nineteenth century neglected, if not destroyed, the Chalcedonian insight that Jesus Christ is truly God and truly man. The thrust of the century was to disregard His transcendence, leaving Him merely human, though somewhat more enlightened or insightful than the average person. As it turned out, so claimed one of its greatest critics, a century of research was conducted by a group of brilliant scholars and serious church leaders who undervalued Christ and overestimated themselves; the endeavor was characterized as a monologue of the soul impressed with its own divinity. That giant of a critic was Karl Barth (1886–1968). Though often challenged by more conservative theologians for leaving the philosophical insights of Hegelianism only to embrace the equally destructive philosophy of Søren Kierkegaard, Barth struggled against the immanentist theology of his teachers and contemporaries.

In retrospect, it now seems apparent that the Swiss theologian may have corrected the error of the nineteenth century in overemphasizing humankind, and thereby confusing God with humankind, by so stressing the transcendence of God that historical events do not receive a balanced accounting. For Barth, the Bible was not so much the Word of God as it was a medium of the disclosure of Jesus Christ. The focus for Barth in doing theology was Christ, the revelation of God; the Bible is a witness of that revelation. When approaching the question of Christ, Barth felt constrained to find the answer in the Scriptures.

> We understand this statement as the answer to the question: Who is Jesus Christ; and we understand it as a description of the central New Testament statement, John 1:14: "The Word was made flesh". Therefore this New Testament verse must guide us in our discussion of the dogmatic statement that Jesus Christ is very God and very Man.[14]

His understanding of Christ was that He is truly ontological deity and real humanity in one person; he is neither a human with an unusual sense of God's presence nor one who merely possessed deep insight into His designs for the world. In a very lovely passage that merits repeating, Barth stated his Chalcedonian understanding of Christ succinctly.

133

> If we paraphrase the statement "the Word became flesh" by "the Word assumed flesh," we guard against the misinterpretation already mentioned, that in the incarnation the Word ceases to be entirely Himself and equal to Himself, i.e., in the full sense of the Word of God. God cannot cease to be God. The incarnation is inconceivable, but it is not absurd, and must not be explained as an absurdity. . . . Jesus is the Mediator, the God-Man, in such a way that He is God and Man. This "and" is the inconceivable act of the "becoming" in the incarnation.[15]

While there are many that appreciated Barth's insights, at least in comparison to the destructive trends in the previous century, he seems to have had few followers and many opponents. It is difficult to understand how twentieth-century theology in Europe was restrained by Barth's insights; indeed, the better view is that theology tended to return to the human-centeredness of the previous century in the hands of Barth's successors. As Barth found it possible to embrace the objective Christ with only a witness to Him, the Bible, he discovered rational and philosophical support in Søren Kierkegaard's insight that the historical method is lineal in nature (it tells us only what we can know from below, not from God), not vertical (a knowledge of God requires a personal self-revelation to us). Barth's method, like that of those in the nineteenth century he scorned, proved to be more lasting than his own particular beliefs about God that he derived from it.

The return of twentieth-century theology in Germany to roots in the previous century can be seen in Rudolf Bultmann (1884–1976). Finding philosophical inspiration in Martin Heidegger (1889–1976), and using a profoundly critical approach to the New Testament writings, Bultmann constructed a nineteenth-century Christ. In his judgment, He was a synthesis between a radical, moral rabbi, and an apocalypticist preaching an imminent era of righteousness. Jesus was a real Jewish man, but the historical events that highlighted his life according to the New Testament, such as the cross and the resurrection, are nonhistorical, mythological occasions for the discovery

134

of meaning through a personal quest to find our own authentic existence twenty centuries later. Little of the true Christ is available to us, nor is it important to find the true Christ, according to Bultmann, since he divorced facts from relevance, denigrating the former and personifying the latter. To separate relevance from historical fact is to destroy hope; hope that has no basis except for personal myth is only self-adulation and disillusion.

Thus, while Barth was able to deliver a welcome broadside of criticism to nineteenth-century religious liberalism, crippling and discrediting decades of an "intellectually" enlightened redefinition of Christianity, his work was short-lived in effect. Emil Brunner (1889–1966) of the University of Zürich, for example, agreed with Barth in much of his criticism of liberalism but differed from him by advocating an incoherent theory of the integrity of Scripture. He seemed to suggest that revelation was somehow apart from the written Word of God. The Bible is inspired of God and it is not.

The reformulations of the liberal tradition in the twentieth century, which took Barth's criticisms of old liberalism seriously, have sadly returned to the mere humanness of God that were so clearly evident in the previous century. The transcendence of God dissolves into an identification of Christ with cultural or other-cultural hopes. Jürgen Moltmann (b. 1926), like so many disillusioned by war, found in the Bible a nonpropositional promise of a future hope as the integrating focus of "revelation." The significance of Christ was not His identity with deity but His power to transform the world into a better place. While rejecting the "intellectuality" of the nineteenth-century liberal approach, twentieth-century liberalism replaced the quest for authority with nonobjective, personal experience. The penchant to view Christ as a symbol of hope or myth, while rejecting the Bible's witness to Christ as the God-man, continued.

The American Protestant Liberal Tradition and the Person of Christ

The revisionist liberal movement, often dubbed the "New Theology," emerged in the waning decades of the nineteenth century and became the dominant expression of Christianity in America after 1930.

American theologians followed the lead of the Ritschlian school in forging their new view, particularly the insights of Rudolf H. Lotze (1817–1881) in philosophy, Albrecht Ritschl (1822–1889) in theology, and Adolf von Harnack (1851–1930) in church history. Liberalism was composed of three closely linked ideas: the immanence of God, the adaptation of religious ideas to culture, and a progressive understanding of the kingdom of God.

The estimate of Christ within the liberal movement was to view Him as a man, clearly a great human figure. While claiming to have a historical understanding of Christ, liberal church leaders discounted the transcendental features of Christ and were enamored with His human character. Lyman Abbott (1835–1922), the pastor of Plymouth Church, Brooklyn, New York, spoke of Christ as "the Son of God" and "begotten of God in the flesh," but his understanding was quite untraditional. He viewed Christ as the product of the evolution of the divine spirit in humanity spiraling forward and upward in manifestation until it apexed in Christ. He was a man profoundly possessed of the life of God. "Does this divinity in Christ differ in kind, or only in degree, from the divinity in men? . . . The divinity in man is not different in kind from the divinity in Christ, because it is not different in kind from the divinity of God."[16] In his autobiography, he noted: "Those who are familiar with my writings will recognize that it was from the teachings of my father that I evolved my own conception of Jesus Christ, not as God and man mysteriously joined together in a being who represents neither what God is nor what man can become, but God in man."[17]

Arthur C. McGiffert (1861–1933) was a scholar in the emerging liberal tradition, having trained in Germany under Harnack. From his mentor he imbibed a modernist interpretation of Christianity. He distinguished himself in America as a church historian at Union Theological Seminary, New York. There he also served as president prior to retirement in 1927. In a rather controversial book, *The God of the Early Christians,* he argued that the conception of who Jesus was changed in the early centuries from a simplistic original to a disfigured complexity as Christianity emerged and its influence spread. The underlying assumption was that theology emerges from and is defined by an ever-changing social context. Jesus' self-understanding was that

136

he was a naive Jewish peasant, a preacher of moral righteousness. "There is no reason to suppose that the early Jewish disciples deified Jesus, or thought of him as anything more than God's servant and anointed."[18] It was the apostle Paul, in preaching Christ to the Gentile world, who redefined Christ by applying the thought of deity to Him for the first time. McGiffert viewed the apostle Paul's understanding of Christ as a modification of Jesus' own perception of Himself by referring to Him as the agent or representative of God. Paul originated the title "the Son of God" to refer to Him. "Christ is not the supreme God himself, but the Son of God."[19] It was only in subsequent centuries, with a further change in social setting, that Christians spoke of Christ as God.

"Have done with your theological Christ and give us back Jesus the ethical teacher" was the cry of the most popular preacher of the tradition, Harry Emerson Fosdick (1878–1969).[20] Following the Ritschlian school, Fosdick separated scientific and historical knowledge from religious knowledge; doctrine was cold and lacked the warmth that experience supplied to the soul. The Scriptures were for him a nonfactual book that was the fountain of valid experiences. He repeatedly ridiculed the notion that "Jesus is God," saying, "That statement alone is not orthodoxy; it is heresy."[21] For Fosdick, Christ was a mere man inspired by God who became an ethical ideal for all humanity. "The God who was in Jesus is the same God who is in us."[22]

A branch within the growing liberal movement in America in the nineteenth century was the social gospel movement. While most in the liberal tradition sought to bring a more intellectually relevant message to the pulpits in the midst of the routine of pastoral concerns and duties, a minority in the movement took the more aggressive approach of identifying social ills and seeking their resolution, often urging governmental intervention. Societal improvement was identified as the essence of the gospel. Social progress was viewed as a millennialistic activity. Its most prominent formulators in America were the Columbus, Ohio pastor Washington Gladden (1836–1918) and the Rochester Theological Seminary professor Walter Rauschenbusch (1861–1918). Rauschenbusch's works reflect the movement in its maturity, particularly his later works, Christianity and the Social Crisis (1907) and A Theology of the Social Gospel (1917).

The tendency of social gospel advocates to reduce Christ to merely heroic proportions can be seen through their understanding that Jesus sought to bring about an ethical kingdom on the earth, not a church. The disciples, Rauschenbusch supposed, lost Jesus' ethical vision, and that has been the cause of subsequent political and social turmoil. Jesus is an archtypical model of piety, having deep concerns about moral injustice and ethical righteousness. His "divinity," a driving personal idealism, was the same spirit that was incarnated in the prophets, though perhaps more wonderfully complete in Christ. It was his moral vision for humanity that not only caused him to rise above his contemporaries but has made him a model for all time.[23] With this said, however, the ancient teaching of the transcendence of Christ as the God-man is brushed away as a distortion or perversion that was invented as the disciples carried Christianity outside its Jewish setting into a Gentile culture.

A series of factors coalesced at the beginning of this century, the World War being just one of them, that caused some in the liberal movement to become uncomfortable. The central assumption in the movement of moral progress, with its undergirding notion of human improvability, was rendered improbable. Preaching to his Riverside Church congregation in 1935, Harry Fosdick announced the triumph of liberalism over fundamentalism but sounded the warning that "The Church Must Go beyond Liberalism," a reformulation of the liberal movement that would carry it to even greater heights. The result of his concern, and that of several others, was a movement that purposefully disregarded the airs of triumphalism and easygoing, unending progressivism for a more serious understanding of the human heart and life.

Representative of neo-liberalism or neo-orthodoxy, a movement that was the dominant form of liberalism from 1930 to 1960, were the insights of Reinhold Niebuhr (1892-1971), the most influential theologian in the first half of the twentieth century. For all the positive directions in his theology, such as a more serious regard for the human dilemma, he did not reject the reductionistic view of God inherent in the assumptions of old liberalism. The Bible remained an occasion of revelation, called myth, that takes place in the sphere of subjective, personal experience; it was not historical or objective. It merely

138

pointed to a truth and was not the truth itself. Immanence in theology overshadowed the "myth" of divine transcendence.

American liberalism survived as a cohesive movement in the neo-liberal reformulations of theology until the 1960s. However, at that time liberalism as a movement disintegrated into factions. The most radical expression of the demise of liberalism into liberalisms, each theologian having his or her personal encounter with the biblical "myths," each denying the possibility of an objective word from God, was the God-is-dead movement, or "Christian atheism," which gained faddist notoriety in the 1960s under Thomas J. J. Altizer and William Hamilton. The notions of God and Christ were completely secularized. In the human Christ, God became identical with humanity in the loss of His own existence.

The person identified as having the most influence upon American theology in the last half of the twentieth century was Paul Tillich (1886–1965), who left Germany in the 1930s and taught for many years at Union Theological Seminary, New York. Tillich's description of God as the ground of everything personal, rejecting the idea that He is a person, caused him to verge into a radical immanence view of God. Further, he was unwilling to speak of Christ as divine, preferring to think of Him as God's anointed. He simply employed the oft-confusing notions of ontological philosophy to embrace a finite being as the Christ, a "God"-adopted man. Alexander McKelway, commenting on Tillich's understanding that the phrase "God-man" is nonsensical, stated: "Tillich has not said, nor will he say with the 'incarnational' Christologies of Nicaea and Chalcedon, that Jesus was 'truly God and truly man'. No, it is the adoptionist position to which he holds with greater consistency. God chose Jesus, Jesus became the Christ."[24] Using philosophical insights and psychological terminology, Tillich returned to a nineteenth-century liberal Christ, but in new dress!

Immensely popular in the 1980s among many in the liberal tradition was process theology, an evolutionary theory of Christianity rooted in the insights of Alfred Whitehead's (1861–1947) understanding of reality or metaphysics as "becoming" rather than being, in Teilhard de Chardin's (1881–1955) evolutionary scientific insights, and in Charles Hartshorne's (b. 1897) radical immanentism. In the hands of John Cobb Jr., perhaps its most prominent advocate, process theology portrayed Christ as the one who, to a degree unmatched by any other, manifested the objective character of God. Christ is the present incarnation of the past purposes of God. Like Tillich's theology, though expressed through a different formula of assumptions, process theism understands Christ to be a human being who has deep insight into God's nature.

Theology in the 1990s was shaped by the motif of social oppression as expressed in quite a variety of "liberation theologies." The tendency to denigrate the transcendence of God and Christ continued, as did the secularization and socialization of theology. Christ remained the embodiment of the central concerns of the particular theologian's interests and passions, which were assumed to be the incarnation of God's interests. Christ was merely a human window into the desires of God; He was not the transcendent God who became flesh to reveal God to us, bear our judgment before God for us, rise bodily for us to vindicate His divine mission, and reign forever over us. Instead, today there are at least three prominent manifestations of the theology of the relief of the oppressed: black liberation theology, which is rooted in the civil rights movement of the 1960s; Latin American liberation theology, the rejection of much of Western capitalism for the promise of a social utopia; and feminist theology, the rejection of gender inequality. In each of these theologies, Christ is the ultimate symbol of the oppressed spirit.

The American Protestant Conservative Tradition and the Person of Christ

Theological traditionalists, sometimes referred to as evangelicals or fundamentalists, have reacted strongly to the reinterpretation of historic orthodoxy by their liberal counterparts. Two of the most articulate in this endeavor were J. Greshem Machen (1881–1937) and Carl F. H. Henry (b. 1913). Henry strove to maintain the intellectual credibility of the conservative movement, which in his day sought to distance itself from the growing liberal movement. He saw the emerging separatist movement as possessing profound potential, though in danger of falling into isolationism and irrelevancy. Machen, on the other hand, represented the intense strife with liberalism in the 1920s and 1930s, the fundamentalist-modernist controversy. He was an unre-

140

lenting critic of the liberal tradition, claiming that it evidenced an "intellectual decadence."[25] In his judgment it represented a retrogression of the intellect and moral ineptitude because it was nonChristian and unscientific. "The movement designated as 'liberalism' is regarded as liberal only by its friends; to its opponents it seems to involve a narrow ignoring of many relevant facts."[26] He stated that the liberal movement had sacrificed the Bible on the altar of science. It had determined to find the shape of Christianity by the supposed shape of the hard sciences, rejecting a literal interpretation of the Bible in order to make it fit with the "more sure word" of the scientific community. "In trying to remove from Christianity everything that could possibly be objected to in the name of science, in trying to bribe off the enemy by those concessions which the enemy most desires, the apologist has really abandoned what he started out to defend."[27] In a passage that could apply to any decade of the struggle with liberalism in the twentieth century, Machen described the issues clearly.

> What is the relationship between Christianity and modern culture: may Christianity be maintained in a scientific age? It is this problem which modern liberalism attempts to solve. Admitting that scientific objections may arise against the particularities of the Christian faith — against the doctrine of the person of Christ, and of redemption through His death and resurrection — the liberal theologian seeks to rescue certain of the eternal principles of religion, of which these particularities are thought to be mere temporary symbols, and these general principles he regards as constituting "the essence of Christianity."[28]

Machen was adamant that the liberal tradition reduced Christ to being a mere example for faith, while historic Christianity had regarded Him as the object of faith. In several striking contrasts, he compared the liberal reconstruction of Christ with the biblical one. "Liberalism regards Him as an Example and Guide; Christianity, as a Saviour: liberalism makes Him an example for faith; Christianity, the object of faith. . . . Liberalism regards Jesus as the fairest flower of

141

humanity; Christianity regards Him as a supernatural person."[29] Commenting on the prologue to John's gospel ("the Word was God") relative to the liberal tradition, Machen is classic.

> These things have been despised as idle speculation, but in reality they are the very breath of our Christian lives. They are, indeed, the battle ground of theologians; the church hurled anathemas at those who held that Christ, though great, was less than God. But those anathemas were beneficent and right. That difference of opinion was no trifle; there is no such thing as "almost God." The thought is blasphemy; the next less thing than infinite is infinitely less. If Christ be the greatest of finite creatures, then still our hearts are restless, still we are mere seekers after God.[30]

THE ROMAN CATHOLIC TRADITION AND THE PERSON OF CHRIST

The Roman Catholic Church, as do both the Orthodox churches and the Protestant churches, claims confessional affinity with the so-called ecumenical or universal councils of the early church, that is, those gatherings of the church's bishops before the schism of the twelfth century and the division of the church in the fifteenth. The specific councils dealing with the person of Christ are four in number, culminating in the Council of Chalcedon in 451 and its findings, which were reaffirmed in the Council of Constantinople in 553. At least by historic profession, the Roman Catholic Church confesses that Jesus Christ is all that conservative Protestants claim of Him: He is the God-man witnessed of in John 1:14.

The crucially defining moment in Roman Catholic history was in the sixteenth century at the Council of Trent. Indeed, there the church was created, from a dogmatic and definitional point of view. The doctrinal findings and affirmations of the council affirmed historical conformity with the councils of Chalcedon (451) and Constantinople (553). Today the question becomes this: Has the Roman Catholic Church altered its teachings since the Council of Trent? The answer

142

appears to be twofold, paralleling the answer of the Protestant churches. Officially, the *Catechism of the Catholic Church* (1994) suggests that the church still embraces a warm connection to the past in dogmatic affirmation. In a section entitled "True God and True Man," the catechism rehearses the ancient errors of the church concerning Christ's incarnate person, initiating the discussion with the affirmation that

> the unique and altogether singular event of the Incarnation of the Son of God does not mean that Jesus Christ is part God and part man, nor does it imply that he is the result of a confused mixture of the divine and the human. He became truly man while remaining truly God. Jesus Christ is true God and true man. During the first centuries, the church had to defend and clarify this truth of faith against the heresies that falsified it. (464)

The truth that Jesus Christ is God and man remains the dogmatic statement of the faith that every loyal son and daughter of the church is required to confess.

There is, however, another answer to the question of historic congruity in the Roman Catholic community. The liberal tradition has made its inroads into the Roman Catholic Church much as it has into the Protestant churches. By adopting a progressive view of historical development, which allows for the affirmation of past creeds without the necessity of truly embracing them, a liberal spirit has found a place in the community among the church's teachers, who function in a nondogmatic, unauthoritative fashion. (There is a striking parallel within the mainline Protestant denominational circles in America today; ancient creeds are recognized but are seen as archival witnesses to a regressive past. The amazing difference is that most of the mainline churches openly confess that they have changed their confession of faith, the past being archaic; the Catholic Church instead holds firmly to the past but remains silent about the teachers in its community who flagrantly reject their doctrinal heritage as literally valid.)

THE PERSON OF CHRIST: MEET THE GOD-MAN

Some teachers have either left or been forced out of the church (an example being Hans Küng of Germany) yet many remain at their posts, perhaps sequestered in the silence of nonpublication.

Hans Küng (b. 1928) is illustrative of the church's deep embrace of Chalcedonian orthodoxy, an unwillingness to redefine the terms through the use of literary criticism. He emerged as a critic of his church, particularly of its view of authority and the retreat to dogmatism in order to preserve continuity with the past. Küng viewed the Vatican Council II in the 1960s as a hope of change in the church, but he saw the subsequent actions of John Paul II as frustrating the council's intent by mandating an unreflective orthodoxy. However, it was largely the area of Christology, not authority, that brought about his excommunication. Küng's understanding of Christ caused fellow theologian Karl Rahner to call him a "Protestant liberal." In his view, Christ was the representative of God; He did not share ontological unity with God. Küng advocated an adoptionist view of Jesus Christ; He was a valiant leader, a man who pointed others to God.

Karl Rahner (1904–1984), perhaps the most influential Roman Catholic theologian in the twentieth century as well as the most powerful person at the Vatican II Council, can best be described as a mediating theologian in the church. Clearly he was ambiguous and difficult to understand, though he affirmed the theanthropic identity of Christ as truly God and truly man. Rahner is representative of one solution to the currents of change troubling the church.

John Paul II has sought to resolve the struggles by asserting the historic faith of the church (that is, dogmaticism); Küng has done the same by rejecting imposed authority for a critical approach to the sources of doctrine and accommodation to modern culture; Rahner sought to mediate the two extremes. He seems to have been a modern Thomas Aquinas in methodological approach. As Thomas adopted Aristotelian methodology in his Dominican apologetics against the Islamic faith, Rahner adopted the tools of modern philosophy to defend and preserve Roman Catholic orthodoxy. While one may wonder if the venture was fruitful, it cannot be doubted that, in an array of confusing terminological distinctions, he thought he had established a means of sustaining historic orthodoxy in the modern world.

144

THE ORTHODOX TRADITION AND THE PERSON OF CHRIST

The Orthodox churches embrace "Holy Tradition" as the source of faith. As generally defined, *tradition* means those beliefs and practices that are passed down. In a Christian context, it signifies what Christ communicated to His apostles and has been subsequently handed down from generation to generation (2 Timothy 2:2). The Bible, the Nicene Creed, and the other decrees of the ecumenical councils are part of the tradition of the church. These are considered inviolate, noncontradictory, and absolute, though other parts of tradition, such as the teachings of a particular scholar, an icon, or a local synod, are not accorded the same status.

Thus, the Orthodox churches adhere to the findings of the seven ecumenical councils, from Nicaea (325) to the second Nicaea Council in 787. The relationship of the natures of Christ in His singular being was addressed in the councils held at Constantinople I (381), Ephesus (431), Chalcedon (451), Constantinople II (553), and Constantinople III (681). While the Council of Chalcedon stated the doctrine of the theanthropic Christ most definitively, it was the first Constantinople council that affirmed His true humanity unequivocally. In the *Longer Catechism of the Eastern Church* (1839), an exposition of the Nicene-Constantinopolitan Creed, in answer to the question "What do we understand by the word incarnation?" the reply is "that the Son of God took to himself human flesh without sin, and was made man without ceasing to be God" (Article Three, 178). In reply to the inquiry about the addition of the words "was made man," the creed answered, "to the end that none should imagine that the Son of God took only flesh or a body, but should acknowledge in him a perfect man consisting of body and soul" (Article Three, 180). A contemporary writer seeking to articulate the Orthodox faith for those perhaps unfamiliar with it described Christ as follows:

> Our God is an incarnate God. God has come down to man, not only through His energies, but in His own person. The second Person of the Trinity "true God from true God", was made man: "The Word became flesh and dwelt among us"

145

(John 1:14). A closer union than this between God and His creation there could not be. God Himself became one of His creatures.[31]

5

The Work of Christ: What the Cross Means for Us

Anne Lamott, in her book *Bird by Bird,* tells the story of a girl and her younger brother. The girl comes down with a potentially life-threatening disease and needs a blood transfusion. After testing each member of the family, the doctors determine that her brother's blood is the best match for her. The boy's parents sit down with him and try to explain blood transfusion in a way they think such a young child can understand. They say the doctors want to take the blood out of his body and put it into his sister's body so that she can get better. The boy looks solemn and asks if he can think about it for a while. The next morning he says that he's willing to give his blood for his sister. So, before long, he's lying on a gurney next to his sister and blood is flowing through the tube in his arm. After a bit, the boy grabs the sleeve of a passing doctor and asks, "Doctor, when do I start to die?"

That boy had tragically misunderstood what a blood transfusion would do to him, yet he was willing to give his life for his sister, whom he loved. There's been even greater misunderstanding surrounding the life-giving death of Jesus Christ. Why did Jesus Christ, the Lamb of God, suffer such an ignominious end? The charges against Him amounted to fabricated maliciousness, unworthy of the end that He suffered. Pilate repeatedly claimed Him to be innocent, yet He was publicly executed on an instrument of Roman justice. Accusers were paid to lie about both His claims and the promise of His resurrection after death. Why did such a death have to occur? Whatever the answer may be (and there have been many in the annals of the church), the apostle Paul made it abundantly clear that Christ's death is integral to the gospel. "I delivered to you as of first importance what I also received, that Christ died for our sins according to the Scriptures" (1 Corinthians 15:3).

It is precisely at this point that the malaise of today's church becomes all too apparent. Far too many of our churches have been taken captive by the cultural values of personal self-interest and advancement. The psychological self has replaced the centrality of the gospel in what the church offers to an increasingly secularized world. The how-to's of personal happiness have been substituted for the preaching of Calvary, cultural accommodation substituting for the shame of the cross. It is amazing to think that the cross in the ancient world was a symbol of disgust; today it has been commercialized and trivialized by a wide variety of fashionable religious jewelry. Christ has not been run out of this world in which we find ourselves. In fact, He appears to be much spoken of in the public media sources. However, all too often He has been carefully refashioned, even by professing Christians, in such a way as to justify whatever our needs and wants may be. The meaning of the death of Christ, however, strikes at the very core of the identity of the church; it is the church's proclamation. Is Christ's self-giving a symbol for political aspirants or societal reformers? Is it a myth with some inner psychological meaning of hope to remedy feelings of alienation? Did Christ come to make us better in our business life or even better lovers? Why did He come to us?

The question of the meaning of the death of Christ cannot be divorced from the discussion of the person of the Savior and the sinful nature of humankind. The sin that is in humankind is tied to the grace that comes to us in Christ. *Who* and *what* are integral to *why*. Who is the Lord Jesus Christ? He is God who became man—the miracle of the Incarnation (John 1:14). For what purpose did He come to us? Because we are in profound need of Him. But why does our need require such a remedy? We are sinners who have violated the righteousness of God and stand under judgment. If that is our need, then the solution could only be a Savior—a Savior who is able to solve our dilemma. Christ is that Savior. But how does He save? That is the question before us.

OUR LEGACY

Views of the Atonement

	Purpose:	Fact:	Focus:	Result:
Abelardian	Unnecessary	Optional	Exemplary of a virtuous life	Encouragement of imitation
Socinian	Unnecesary	Optional	Necessity of repentance	Encouragement to repentance and eternal life
Ransom-to-Satan	Liberation	Necessary	Payment to Satan	Release from bondage
Grotian	Demonstrate the government of God	Optional	Exemplary	To prevent future sin
Arminian	Demonstrate the government of God and save the creature	Necessary	Retributive (substitute for a penalty)	To deal with past sin
Anselmic	Demonstrate the government of God and save the creature	Necessary	Retributive (substitute for a penalty)	To deal with past, present, and future sin

Discussions of the atonement, or the meaning of the death of Christ, have generally involved four questions. The answers to them are the bases for various views that have been set forth in the history of the church. First, was the death of Christ necessary or was it the option God arbitrarily chose to reclaim lost humanity? Second, from the divine perspective, was the death of Christ grounded in the love of God or the justice of God? The third question is this: from humanity's perspective, was the atonement the remedy for the guilt of sin or for the acts of sin? Fourth, did Christ suffer for the crimes of humanity or did He die as a moral object lesson of some sort? The way the issue of Christ's death is framed by the questions that are posed of it leads to the answers we give. If the death of Christ is of "first importance," as the apostle indicated, it is crucial in the church's essential message before a lost world that we understand what it means that "Christ died for our sins" (1 Corinthians 15:3).

To gain some insight into this subject, we turn to the pages of our history. While the story is not uniform (sadly, there is often evidence of the neglect of the Holy Scriptures), the discussion is a timely one and will remain so as long as we have the command to "go into all the world and preach the gospel to all creation" (Mark 16:15).

THE ANCIENT CHURCH AND THE WORK OF CHRIST (100–600)

The Passion narratives in the Gospels take up disproportionately large parts of those biblical books. Likewise, the cross of Christ loomed large in the thinking of the early Christians. As was the pattern with every other major doctrine, though, not all Christian thinkers understood the meaning of Christ's death in the same way, and over time their conception of it expanded and became more sophisticated.

THE CHURCH FATHERS AND THE WORK OF CHRIST (100–150)

The Fathers were unspeculative; they appear to have been deeply concerned with the proclamation of the gospel by word and life, but they were short on the necessity of explaining the faith. What you have in them, therefore, is the repetition of biblical phrases with no detailed discourses on their meaning. It is as though the audiences of these writings understood them, being much closer than later generations to the apostles and their world. James Orr summarized the point by saying, "The Apostolic Fathers are profuse in their allusions to redemption through the blood of Christ, though it cannot be said that they do much to aid us in the theological apprehension of this language."[1]

Clement of Rome (d. 101?), an elder in the assembly whom Irenaeus claimed faithfully passed on apostolic instruction to the church in Corinth, spoke of the death of Christ in his epistle. From his epistle, it appears clear that Christ was conceived of as the one who had procured redemption for humankind, that Christ's redemptive work had to do with His death, that the death of Christ related to the disposition of the Father, and that His work is the basis for our repentance and forgiveness. Clement wrote, "Let us fix our gaze on the blood of Christ and know how precious it is to His Father because it was poured out for our salvation and brought the grace of repentance to the whole world" (*1 Clement* 7.4). Elsewhere he exhorted the Corinthians in tones reminiscent of the Epistle to the Hebrews, "This is the way, beloved, in which we found our salvation, Jesus Christ, the High Priest of our offering, the defender and helper of our weakness" (36.1). In a passage that seems to hint at Christ's substitution, Clement noted, "For the sake of love which he [God] had for us did Jesus Christ our Lord, by the will of God, give His blood for us, His flesh for our flesh, and His life for our lives" (49.6).

The letter (actually a treatise) attributed to Barnabas, the companion of Paul, contains the notion that the death of Christ brought life to sinners through a substitution for them. Perhaps more likely written in the early second century than the late first century, the unknown writer of this work connected forgiveness with Christ's death, quoting from Isaiah 53, the great Suffering Servant passage. "For to this end the Lord endured to deliver His flesh unto corruption that by the remission of sins we might be cleansed which cleansing is through the blood of His sprinkling" (5.1). In a subsequent passage he wrote: "If, then, the Son of God ... suffered so that His being wounded might make us alive, let us believe that the Son of God could not suffer, except for our sake. . . . The Lord commanded this because He Himself was about to offer the vessel of His spirit as a sacrifice for our sins, so that the type established in Isaac, who was offered on the altar, might be fulfilled" (7.2).

Ignatius (c.35–c.107), the bishop of Antioch, wrote a series of letters, mostly to churches on his journey to Rome, where he was martyred about the year 110. In a personal word to the Ephesian church, he cried out, "My spirit is devoted to the cross" (*To the Ephesians* 18.1). To the Trallians he wrote, speaking of Christ, "who died for us, that through faith in his death you might escape dying" (*To the Trallians* 2.1).

Within the corpus of these early Fathers is the anonymous *Epistle*

to Diognetus. While there is considerable debate about the dating of the work, it clearly is later in composition than the other writings in the collection. Most place it in the late second century. For the purpose of the discussion before us, it is important because it contains a rather wonderful description of the atonement of Christ. It is evident that the writer understood the death of Christ to be a divine substitution, a casting of humanity's sin upon Christ, who paid the debt of our iniquity. It contains such a majestic passage that it echoes the way Martin Luther would write of Christ centuries later.

> And when our iniquity had been fully accomplished, and it has been perfectly manifest that punishment and death were expected as its recompense, and the season came which God had ordained, when henceforth He should manifest His goodness and power (O the exceeding great kindness and love of God), He hated us not, neither rejected us, nor bore us malice, but was long-suffering and patient, and in pity for us took upon himself our sins, and Himself parted with His Son as a ransom for us, the holy for the lawless, the guileless for the evil, the just for the unjust, the immortal for the mortal. For what else but His righteousness would have covered our sins? .... O the sweet exchange, O the inscrutable creation, O the unexpected benefits; that the iniquity of many should be concealed in One Righteous Man, and the righteousness of One should justify that are iniquitous! (*Epistle to Diognetus* 1.2,9)

THE APOLOGISTS AND THE WORK OF CHRIST (150–300)

The early church leaders, deriving their understanding of the atonement from the New Testament (Romans 3:25), which was deeply informed by the Old Testament Scriptures, understood the meaning of the death of Christ to have been a sacrifice. This theme is particularly evident in the writings of the Western apologists. For example, the North African Tertullian (c.160–c.225), who was the first church father to write in Latin as

152

Greek gradually ceased to be the common language in the West, carried his training in law into the defense of Christianity. Understanding that an offense mandated a recompense, he argued that Christ lived and died for the sinner, satisfying God for wrongs done. In doing so, he became the first church leader to use the term "satisfaction" in reference to our Lord's death. Though his understanding of the death of Christ was not as developed as it would later become in the church (for example, the concept of substitution can only be inferred in his writings), he did not regard Christ's death as either an object lesson or as self-sacrifice. He summarized his understanding of Christ and His work like this:

> By remitting sins, He did indeed heal man, while He also manifested Himself who He was. For if no one can forgive sins but God alone, while the Lord remitted them and healed men, it is plain that He was Himself the Word of God made the Son of man, receiving from the Father the power of remissions of sins: since He was man, and since He was God, in order that since as man He suffered for us, so as God He might have compassion on us, and forgive us our debts, in which we were made debtors to God our creator. And therefore David said beforehand, "Blessed are they whose iniquities are forgiven, and whose sins are covered. Blessed is the man to whom the Lord has not imputed sin"; pointing out thus that remission of sins followed upon His advent, and "fastened it to the cross"; as that as by means of a tree we were made debtors to God [so also] by means of a tree we may obtain the remission of our debt. (*Prescription against Heretics* 18.3)
>
> We believe that there is but one God, who is none other than the creator of the world, who produced everything from nothing through his Word, sent forth before all things; that this Word is called the Son, and in the name of God was seen in divers ways by the patriarchs, was ever heard in the prophets and finally brought down by the spirit and Power of God the Father into the Virgin Mary, was made flesh in her womb, was

153

born of her and lived as Jesus Christ; who thereafter proclaimed a new law and a new promise of the kingdom of heaven, worked miracles, was crucified, on the third day rose again, was caught up into heaven and sat at the right hand of the Father; that he sent in his place the power of the Holy Spirit to guide believers; that he will come with glory to take the saints up into the fruition of the life eternal and the heavenly promises and to judge the wicked to everlasting fire, after the resurrection of both good and evil with the restoration of their flesh. (18.13)

Irenaeus (c.130–c.200), the second bishop of Lyons, further clarified the meaning of Christ's death. Like his counterpart Tertullian, Irenaeus understood that the death of Christ was mandated because God's justice demands that wrongs be requited. While people sinned and should pay God for the evils done, they cannot. Therefore, someone else must pay if they are to have any hope. "Indeed, through the first Adam, we offended God by not observing His command. Through the second Adam, however, we are reconciled, and are made obedient even unto death. For we were debtors to none other except to Him, whose commandment we transgressed at the beginning" (*Against Heresies* 5.16.3). In the same passage Irenaeus refers to Christ as "reconciling us to God by His passion." Thus, Christ's death as the second Adam is conceived of as having destroyed sin's grip over the descendants of the first Adam.

Redeeming us by His own blood in a manner consonant to reason, [He] gave Himself as a redemption for those who have been led into captivity. . . . The Word of God, powerful in all things, and not defective with regard to His own justice, did righteously turn against that apostasy, and redeem from it His own property. . . . Since the Lord thus has redeemed us through His own blood, giving His soul for our souls, and His flesh for our flesh . . . all the doctrines of the heretics fall to ruin. (*Against Heresies* 5.1.1)

Irenaeus's unique contribution to the understanding of the atonement was in his explanation of the means of its accomplishment by Christ, commonly called the recapitulation theory. The substance of his idea is that what we lost in our identity with the actions of the first Adam we regained through the actions of the second Adam. "He summed up in Himself the long roll of the human race, bringing to us a compendious salvation, that what we lost in Adam, being in the image and likeness of God, we regained in Christ Jesus" (*Against Heresies* 3.18.1). Thus, Irenaeus made an advance in the delineation of the atonement by putting forth its first synthetic explanation. He stressed the sacrificial nature of Christ's death, the necessity of His death being connected to the character of God (the justice of God as demanding payment for evil), and the fact that atonement was accomplished through the life and death of Christ.

The tendency of apologists in the Eastern portion of the church—in contrast to the emphasis in Tertullian on the meaning of Christ's death as a sacrifice—was to view the death of Christ from the perspective of its accomplishment (victory, identity with Christ). Irenaeus, though living in the West, evidenced this emphasis and thereby exhibited his tutelage in Asia Minor under Polycarp (c.69–c.155), a disciple of the apostle John. In the East, church leaders stressed the concept of the death of Christ as a ransom for sinners (themes clearly seen in Mark 10:45 and 1 Timothy 2:6) and the resultant defeat of evil and oppression. The idea of a redemptive ransom implied that freedom from bondage was achieved through the offering of a payment to the captor. This image of Christ's death became a central motif in the Greek writers; Christ is the victor![2]

Clement of Alexandria (c.150–c.215), a teacher and prolific writer, has been criticized for viewing Christ as a teacher who imparts true knowledge and brings forth the duties of love unfailingly. However, he spoke of Christ's death as a ransom, a purchase from the bondage of sin of sinners. "But hear the Saviour: 'I regenerated thee, who were ill born by the world to death. I emancipated, healed, ransomed thee. I will show thee the face of the good Father God. Call no man thy Father on earth. For thee I contended with Death, and paid thy death, which thou owest for thy former sins and thy unbelief towards God'" (*Who Is the Rich Man That Shall Be Saved?* 23). Later in the same

155

work he wrote, " . . . about to be offered up and giving himself a ransom . . . for each of us he gave his life" (37).

Perhaps more important, and certainly more controversial, is the view of our Lord's death held by Origen (c.185–c.254), called by not a few the greatest scholar of Christian antiquity. Some have argued that he taught a fully developed ransom-to-Satan theory; others, such as John Mozley, suggest that we cannot be sure.[3] Adolf von Harnack, the German church historian, stated that Origen gave more detailed attention to the significance of the death of Christ than any before him in the church. Harnack summarized Origen's view with four points. First, Christ's death was a victory over demonic authorities (Colossians 2:14-15). Second, His death was a satisfaction for sin offered to God. Third, Christ's death was vicarious (substitutionary). Fourth, His death was a ransom paid to the devil (Hebrews 2:14).[4] The fact that the second and fourth of these views appear to be mutually contradictory has led some to argue that Origen interpreted the texts of the Bible as he came to them individually and did not attempt to synthesize diverse elements.

THE THEOLOGIANS AND THE WORK OF CHRIST (300–600)

After centuries in which the church existed without official status in the empire, often being treated with hostility and grievous persecution, a new era dawned under Constantine. Not only did the times of rigorous confrontation with a hostile state end, but in addition the church emerged as the religion of the empire. In this setting the church's scholars—its bishops—could more freely express their views in writing. Though not one of the dominating concerns of the church in this era, the death of Christ was a vital doctrine in the churches.

One of the outstanding leaders of the church in this period was Athanasius (c.296–373), bishop of Alexandria. Though more readily identified with the trinitarian controversy, this remarkable North African church leader wrote a treatise on the work of Christ, *On the Incarnation*. The point of the work is to demonstrate that the incarnation of Christ is the only remedy for humanity's fallen condition. By this, Athanasius provides insight into his understanding of the gospel. Two elements are evident in the work as it relates to his understand-

156

ing of the atonement. First, much in the tradition of Irenaeus, he understood that Christ restored to humanity what was lost through Adam's disobedience (a restitutional view). Second, he viewed the essence of Christ's work to be substitutionary. Athanasius based the need for the work of Christ on the fallen condition of the human race. The judgment is judicial in nature and God requires that He be appeased or else eternal condemnation will be the just result. In a particularly profound passage Athanasius noted:

> So, as the rational creatures were wasting and such works in course of ruin, what was God in his goodness to do? Suffer corruption to prevail against them and death to hold them fast? And where were the profit of their having been made to begin with? For better were they not made, than once made, left to neglect and ruin. For neglect reveals weakness, and not goodness on God's part—if, that is, He allows His work to be ruined when once He had made it—more so than if he had never made man at all. . . . It was, then, out of the question to leave men to the current of corruption; because this would be unseemly, and unworthy of God's goodness. (6)

Athanasius's answer is the God-man: the incarnate Savior who came as humankind's substitute, dying in our place to satisfy God's just judgment.

> And thus taking from our bodies one of like nature, because all were under penalty of the corruption of death he gave it over to death in the stead of all, and offered it to the Father—doing this, moreover, of His lovingkindness, to the end that, firstly, all being held to have died in Him, the law involving the ruin of men might be undone . . . and that, secondly, whereas men had turned toward corruption and quicken them from death by the appropriation of his body. (8)

In the subsequent chapter he wrote: "He surrendered it [His body] to death instead of all, and offered it to the Father . . . in order that by dying in Him the law with respect to the corruption of mankind might be abolished. . . . The logos of God, being above all, by offering His own temple and bodily instrument as a substitution for the life of all, satisfied all that was required by His death" (9).

Cyril (c.315–387), bishop of Jerusalem, provides clear evidence that the church of his day understood that the death of Christ was expiatory (it satisfied God's just wrath) and substitutionary (it was in our place) in nature. His writings are eloquent and clear. For example, he wrote:

> Do not wonder that the whole world was redeemed, for it was no mere man, but the Only-begotten son of God who died for it. The sin of one man, Adam, availed to bring death to the world; if by one man's offense death reigned for the world, why should not life reign all the more "from the justice of one"? If Adam and Eve were cast out of paradise because of the tree from which they ate, should not believers more easily enter into paradise because of the Tree of Jesus? If the first man, fashioned out of the earth, brought universal death, shall not He who fashioned him, being the Life, bring everlasting life? If Phinees [Phineas] by his zeal in slaying the evildoer appeased the wrath of God, shall not Jesus, who slew no other, but "gave himself a ransom for all," take away God's wrath against man? (*Catechetical Lectures* 13.2)

In the East, the trio of Cappadocian scholars, Basil the Great (c.330–379), Gregory of Nazianzus (329/30–389/90), and Gregory of Nyssa (c.330–c.395), were of immense influence. The last-named seems to have interpreted the atonement in the fashion of Origen, evidencing hues of a ransom-to-Satan theory. That is, he interpreted the atonement by focusing on its fruit. However, his contemporary and friend Gregory of Nazianzus called his view "fire upon outrage" (*Orations* 45.22). Gregory of Nazianzus set forth the death of Christ in the tradition of Athanasius and Cyril; it was an expiatory substitution offered to God to satisfy His righteous demands. "For my sake He was made a curse, who destroyed my curse; and sin, who taketh away the sin of the world and became a new Adam to take the place of the old just so he makes my obedience His own as Head of the whole body" (*Orations* 30.5).

In the West, the influence of Augustine of Hippo (354–430) has continued to be overwhelming. Though he did not make the death of Christ a focus of study in any particular work, he did explain his understanding of the death of Christ as a sacrifice. In this way, Augustine reflects continuity with the centuries of gospel proclamation that preceded him in the church and safeguarded the same message for centuries thereafter. In his treatise *The Trinity* he wrote,

> Four things are to be considered in every sacrifice,—to whom it is offered, by whom it is offered, what is offered, for whom it is offered,—the same one and true Mediator Himself, reconciling us to God by the sacrifice of peace, might remain one with Him to whom He offered, might make those one in Himself for whom He offered, Himself might be in one both the offer and the offering. (4, 14)

After quoting 2 Corinthians 5:21, he commented:

> He does not say, as some incorrect copies read, "He who knew no sin died for us," as if Christ Himself sinned for our sakes; but he said, "Him who knew no sin," that is, Christ, God, to whom we are to be reconciled, "hath made to be sin for us," that is, hath made Him a sacrifice for our sins, by which we might be reconciled to God. He, then, being made sin, just as we are made righteousness . . . He being made sin, not His own, but ours, not in Himself, but in us. (*Enchiridion* 33)

159

While there were traces of a ransom-to-Satan theory in the writings of Origen and Gregory of Nyssa, the preponderance of the works in the ancient church expressed a belief in the death of Christ as a sacrifice and ransom—"sacrifice" defining the meaning of His death, "ransom" explaining the benefits of it. Christ died, they understood, as a sacrifice to God for sinners. His work was that of an offering to appease the wrath of God. It was a sacrifice that merited the release of humankind from the bondage of sin.

THE MEDIEVAL CHURCH AND THE WORK OF CHRIST (600–1500)

The early medieval period—that period of time stretching from the dissolution of the Roman Empire to the emergence of the scholastic movement—did not evidence any detailed or controversial discussions of the work of Christ. Instead, there is a continuation of previous themes.

Exemplifying this in the West were the writings of Gregory the Great, bishop of Rome in the late sixth century. Recognized as the first pope in the church by later Protestants—a view embraced by neither the Roman Catholic community nor the Orthodox churches, though for different reasons—he argued that the atonement of Christ was a sacrifice offered to God to appease His wrath against sinners; it was a substitutionary offering. He summarized the essence of the death of Christ in his understanding when he wrote, "Guilt can be extinguished only by a penal offering to justice." He elucidated his understanding of the atonement by connecting it to Chalcedonian Christology.

> It would contradict the idea of justice, if for the sin of a rational being like man, the death of an irrational animal should be accepted as a sufficient atonement. Hence, a man must be offered as the sacrifice for man; so that a rational victim may be slain for a rational criminal. But how could a man, himself

stained with sin, be an offering for sin? Hence a sinless man must be offered. But what man descending in the ordinary course would be free from sin? Hence, the Son of God must be born of a virgin, and become man for us. He assumed our nature without our corruption. He made himself a sacrifice for us, and set forth for sinners his own body, a victim without sin, and able both to die by virtue of his humanity, and to cleanse the guilty upon the grounds of justice. (*Moralia* 17)

In the Eastern, or Byzantine, portion of the still-united church, John of Damascus (c.655–c.750) is recognized as a Greek theologian, writer of liturgy, and church father. He synthesized Greek patristic thought before him and gained recognition as an exponent of orthodoxy. In his major work, *Font of Wisdom,* in the third part of the standard textbook on philosophy and theology, he commented upon the meaning of the death of Christ. Contrary to Origen or Gregory of Nyssa, he spoke against the atonement as being a ransom to Satan. It was, in his judgment, an offering to God.

Since our Lord Jesus Christ was without sin, "because he hath done no iniquity, he who taketh away the sin of the world, neither was there deceit in his mouth," He was not subject to death, even though death had by sin entered the world. And so for our sake He submits to death and dies and offers Himself to the Father as a sacrifice for us. For we had offended Him and it was necessary for Him to take upon Himself our redemption that we might be loosed from the condemnation—for God forbid that the Lord's blood should have been offered to the tyrant! (*The Orthodox Faith* III.27)

Cur Deus Homo by Anselm of Canterbury (c.1033–1109), the greatest theologian of his time, has been heralded as both the worst and greatest book ever written. Opinions about its worth have broken along party lines: those who oppose the theory he set forth find it horrible, and those who embrace the theory as reflective of the Scriptures applaud it. Justo Gonzalez's judgment is nonetheless true: "With Anselm a new era began in the history of Christian thought."[5] Anselm, using the fictitious Boso as a literary foil to pose questions and render affirming judgments, set about to present a rationalization of the person of Christ and the atonement, the first grand synthesis of the doctrine in the history of the church. He began his argument by asserting that the atonement can only be understood in light of the human dilemma. Man, created to have fellowship with God, suffered disgrace and alienation in the Fall, having gravely offended God. The race of humankind, henceforth, has deprived God of the honor due Him and therefore must either reparate God for the wrong done or suffer punishment for having done it; there must be a satisfaction or a just judgment. God could not simply forgive people without just grounds, because His righteous character demands that a compensation be made. But people, being incapable of rendering to God the honor due Him, could not appease God and therefore remain hopelessly condemned. Anselm, then, found the solution to the dilemma in the God-man — classic Chalcedonian Christology.

> The God-man whom we are seeking cannot be made either by the conversion of one into the other [here he refers to the two natures], or by the commixture of both into a third, defacing both — for either result would be useless for the object of our search. But in whatever way these two natures be said to enjoin, it is still so that God is not the same as man, it is impossible that both should do what is necessary to be done. For God will not do it, because He ought not, and man, because he cannot; therefore that God and man may do this, it is needful that the same person shall be perfect God and perfect man, who shall make this satisfaction; since he cannot do it unless he be very God, nor ought, unless he be very man. Thence, since it is necessary, preserving the entirety of either nature, that a God-man should be found, no less needful is it that these two natures should meet in one being: which can

be done in no other way but that the same person should be perfect God and perfect man. (II.7)

Anselm's interpretation of the death of Christ has been predominant among Christian thinkers, particularly among late medievalists, the Reformers, and the Protestant conservative tradition as a whole. Sixteenth-century Reformers, such as Luther and Calvin, sought to clarify Anselm's view in light of their own biblical studies in at least two areas. First, while Anselm, following a feudalistic framework, wrote that humankind is under God's just wrath for offending His honor, the Reformers, following the particular insight of the book of Romans, argued that it is God's righteousness that was violated. Second, while Anselm argued that God must be satisfied for offenses against Him or else wrath awaits us, the Reformers stressed the satisfaction of God through punishment. That is, Anselm stressed the alternatives of payment or judgment; the Reformers saw clearly the biblical concept that a penal judgment had to be rendered. Would God render the payment, being the only one who was really qualified to do so (though never obligated to do so), or would each person assume the payment of it? The ones who assumed the obligation themselves in difference to Christ will endure an endless judgment and never requite the debt. That is why the godless face an eternity apart from God.

The works of Peter Abelard (1079–1142/3) stand in marked contrast, in spirit and content, to those of Anselm. Indeed, it may be argued that, apart from the persistent though infrequent embrace of a ransom-to-Satan theory in the early centuries and modifications of them in subsequent times, the opinions of these two church leaders represent a general division of interpretive opinion. Abelard understood the atonement of Christ ethically (the essence being love), while Anselm focused upon judicial aspects.

Abelard appears to have removed the tension between the love and the justice of God, dividing and thereby denigrating the character of God. He was willing to put aside God's absolute justice, rejecting the idea that a payment for sin is the ground of divine forgiveness. Further, he not only deemphasized the role of God's justice but he also redefined righteousness, suggesting that righteousness is not so much what God is as it is what He does. The righteousness of God and the manifestation of love by God are equated. Using an argument that would be often repeated, Abelard suggested that freeness of salvation is a contradiction if it required the payment of a price (this sounds very much like the argument of later Socinians and Unitarians). Christ's death is not so much a satisfaction of God's wrath by a proxy as it is an act of devotion that has the result of melting our hearts to relinquish our selfish, unloving behavior; it is an overpowering moral example. Humanity's essential problem is neither Satan's dominion nor God's justice; it is a lack of love. Such love, when stimulated in us by the example of Christ's love as seen in His selfless death, is the ground of God's reception of us back into fellowship with Him.

The difficulties with the Abelardian understanding of the atonement, as well as those many modifications of it in the same tradition, are several. First, it bases the atonement on an emotional attitude in people rather than upon a satisfaction of God's character. Consistent with most attacks upon an Anselmic view of the atonement is the denial of the justice and righteousness of God. It is these attributes of God that necessitate a substitutionary satisfaction of God's wrath. Second, any theory that subordinates or eliminates one or another of the attributes of God destroys the perfection of God's person. It represents a denial of God's true being (here is the ground for objecting to recent attempts at redefining classic theism, whether they be liberalism's process theism or evangelicalism's "openness" theism). Third, such a view renders the death of Christ unnecessary. Since the focus of the death of Christ was to move the creature to an emotional response and in no way to move God, the sufferings of Christ are needless. The sufferings were a solicitation of us, not a satisfaction of God. Fourth, this view is based upon a weak view of sin. Sin is not seen as an offense against all that God is in His perfection; it is a mere lack of being all that we should be. It is only the Anselmic view that embraces the biblical notion of God's inviolable justice and righteousness as well as the absolute helplessness of humanity's plight. Finally, it is a view that offers no hope for the hardened sinner. It requires a melting brought about by an emotional turning from lovelessness. It mandates a change of behavior without a change of human nature. Beyond all of this, it is contrary to Paul's exposition of Christ's death

164

in the Romans epistle. Christ's sacrifice, as well as the Old Testament sacrificial system, suggest an objective, not merely a subjective, result.

Peter Lombard (c.1100–1160) was the second most influential medieval scholar in the church, taking a backseat only to Thomas Aquinas. Lombard's doctrine of the atonement appears to have been a medley of the various views (the contrasts among them not being resolved) that were in the church before him, including those of Origen (ransom-to-Satan), Anselm (satisfaction), and Abelard (moral influence). Following Abelard, the death of Christ was conceived of as a revelation of the love of Christ for us that was designed to cause in us a corresponding love for God whereby we are justified. On the other hand, Christ was viewed as redeeming us from eternal punishment and infusing progressive grace in us through the sacraments (more on this issue will be said later).

It is beyond dispute that Thomas Aquinas (c.1225–1274), the Dominican scholar, was one of the greatest theologians of the medieval period. This is true not merely due to the range and volume of his work, as well as his polemics against the Islamic faith through the use of Aristotelian categories, but because of his enormous influence, which stretches through the centuries. So important are his writings that scholars of diverse interpretations validate their claims by appealing to him. Thomas's interpretation of the death of Christ identifies him with Anselm. Like so many theologians before him, Thomas rejected the notion that humankind is in bondage to the devil. "The devil never had power over men; hence we are not delivered from his power through Christ's passion" (*Summa Theologica* Q. 49, art. 2, pt. III). In a sense, humanity is in bondage to Satan, but it is a result of the judicial judgment of God in casting us out of His presence. Christ's death is a penal offering to the just God procuring humankind's release from wrath and forgiveness. It is the payment of a debt through a substitute.

> Since, then, Christ's passion was a sufficient and a superabundant atonement for the sin and the debt of the human race, it was a price at the cost of which we were freed from both obligations. For the atonement by which one satisfies for self or

another is called the price, by which he ransoms himself or someone else from sin and its penalty, according to Daniel 4:24; "Redeem thou thy sins with alms." Now Christ made satisfaction, not by giving money or anything of the sort, but by bestowing what was of greatest price—Himself—for us. And therefore Christ's Passion is called our redemption. (*Summa Theologica* Q. 48, art. 5, pt. III)

Thus, Thomas, like Bernard of Clairvaux (1090–1153), opposed Abelard's understanding of the death of Christ. However, unlike Anselm, Thomas denied the absolute necessity of Christ's death as the ground of satisfaction, though he believed that His death was how forgiveness was secured; the stress is upon the quality of the person that rendered the forgiveness of sins a possibility. Christ's death provided a superabundant treasury of forgiving grace.

An interesting blend of the views of Anselm and Abelard is evident in John Duns Scotus (c.1265–1308). For this Franciscan scholar, Christ's death was an act of benevolence that ends humanity's separation from God as well as an action of substitutionary satisfaction rendered by Christ while on the cross to God the Father. What makes Scotus unique in his Anselmic emphasis is that he rejected the claim that forgiveness could have only been procured through the death of the God-man. That is, while this is how forgiveness actually was obtained for us, redemption did not necessitate Christ's death. God could have chosen another way to secure humanity's forgiveness. God decided on this method, among several possible others, out of no necessity in Himself (such as justice or righteousness); it was His free choice to do it this way. Theologians often refer to this view of God's actions, being rooted in His freedom rather than His attributes, as a "relaxation" theory because it involves a relaxation of God's standards. God merely chose to redeem through the death of Christ, with no intrinsic necessity to do so, for God's freedom overrides His attributes of justice and righteousness. In essence, Scotus argued that the events of redemption need not be rooted and defended along the lines of rational necessity. However, he opposed the rational necessity of the supposed

166

demands of justice in favor of those of "free will" (this argument can be seen in American evangelicalism today, as will be noted).

Is God's freedom in opposition to the demands of His righteousness? Can freedom transcend His justice? Is it possible for God to act contrary to His own character and Word? Martin Luther's response to this view is worth repeating.

> Among the distinguished teachers there are some who say that forgiveness of sins and the justification by grace consists entirely of divine imputation [that is, a divine declaration or reckoning], that is in God's accounting it sufficient that he whom he reckons or does not reckon sin is justified or not justified for his sins by this. . . . If this were true, the whole New Testament would be nothing and in vain. And Christ would have labored foolishly and uselessly by suffering for sin. (*Works* 10, 465)

THE EARLY MODERN CHURCHES AND THE WORK OF CHRIST (1500–1750)

As has been previously noted, the Catholic Church experienced several divisions that have thus far been a permanent rending of the professing visible body of Christ. The first of these came in the context of a discussion of the nature of the incarnate Christ in the sixth century and resulted in the formation of the Chalcedonian Catholic Church (embracing dual-nature Christology) and the Monophysite Catholic Church (embracing single-nature Christology). A second schism occurred in the Chalcedonian Catholic Church in the eleventh century over the authority of the bishop of Rome in Eastern affairs; this resulted in the Eastern Chalcedonian Orthodox churches and the Western Chalcedonian Catholic Church. (Obviously, I am writing from the perspective of a Protestant and have a preconditioned bias in gathering facts and presenting them; those in other traditions would demonstrate a similar bias in describing their tradition's historic rootage and unique originality. While no historian can lay a claim to complete objectivity, he or she should be fair!)

A third major division in the church came about in the sixteenth century within the Western Chalcedonian Catholic Church. From the disintegration of the Western church in the late medieval period (1350–1500) came two movements, each claiming to be the true heir of ancient Catholicism: the Roman Catholic Church and the Protestant churches. As in any division within a single movement that shares the same, rich history, there are areas of vast agreement between the two parties. However, such a division is also an indication of the presence of areas of significant disagreement as well.

THE ROMAN CATHOLIC CHURCH AND THE WORK OF CHRIST

The Council of Trent (1545–1563), a gathering of Roman Catholic bishops and other high officials under the directive of Paul III, articulated an authorized statement of the church's teachings, more detailed than that of any previous council. The findings of the council, both in the Canons and Dogmatic Decrees as well as in the Tridentine Profession of Faith, reflect the issues that divided the church; the former was not a creed in the classic sense. These statements indicate, by the absence of certain definitive articles, that the issues troubling the church in the sixteenth century did not directly relate to the doctrine of the atonement. Both sides in the dispute were essentially Anselmic in structure, though there were significant differences. A number of these can be gleaned from the two documents. First, there was no controversy between the antagonists about the historic facts of the gospel, that is, about the incarnation, death, and resurrection of Christ. The Tridentine Profession of Faith begins by quoting the Nicene-Constantinopolitan Creed with the crucial phrase " . . . who, for us men and for our salvation, came down from heaven, and was incarnate by the Holy Ghost of the virgin Mary, and was made man; and was crucified also for us under Pontius Pilate; he suffered and was buried; and the third day he rose again, according to the Scriptures." Second, the Canons and Dogmatic Decrees connect forgiveness to the death of Christ. As

168

corruption through Adamic unity is inherited at birth, so righteousness comes through the passion of Christ.

> Since by the propagation they contract through him [Adam], when they are conceived, injustice as their own, so if they are not born again in Christ, they would never be justified, since in that new birth there is bestowed upon them, through the merit of his passion, the grace by which they are made just. (*Decree concerning Justification* 3)

Third, the benefits of the death of Christ are progressively infused, not instantaneously granted. This is the grand point of dispute between Roman Catholics and Protestants! That is, the fundamental issue was not so much the crucial role of Christ's death but rather the manner of the procurement of His benefits.

The Canons and Dogmatic Decrees assign the basis of justification to the work of Christ.

> The efficient cause is a merciful God who washes and sanctifies gratuitously, signing and anointing with the Holy Spirit of promise, who is the pledge of our inheritance; but the meritorious cause is his most beloved, only-begotten, our Lord Jesus Christ, who when we were enemies, for the exceeding charity wherewith he loved us, merited justification for us by His holy passion on the wood of the cross. (7)

However, the document connects the means of justifying grace to the sacramental system, most particularly baptism and the Eucharist (more will be said on this point in a later discussion of the Roman Catholic view of salvation). Christ's death procured a bounteous wealth of forgiveness, which is then apportioned through the grace-induced repetition of the sacraments. Speaking of the Eucharist, for example, the creed states,

> The holy council teaches that this is truly propitiatory. . . . For appeased by this sacrifice, the Lord grants the grace and gift of penitence and pardons even the gravest of crimes and sins. . . . It is rightly offered not only for sins, punishments, satisfactions, and other necessities of the faithful who are living, but also for those departed in Christ but not yet fully purified. (2)

While the church teaches the atoning death of Christ, His death procures for the faithful the potential of salvation, not salvation itself. Christ died, therefore, to make salvation possible and grants the benefits of His redemptive grace to those who attend for themselves and for others to the divine means of its acquisition, grace-accumulated merit through grace-caused obedience. The death of Christ is the basis of a life of progressive justification (the sacraments being the means of manifesting faith and acquiring merit) that culminates in a final justification in heaven. Justification is, therefore, a form of progressive sanctification based upon the merit that Christ obtained in the atonement and granted to the church to graciously dispense to the faithful.

THE PROTESTANT CHURCHES AND THE WORK OF CHRIST

The nature and implications of the death of Christ were among the major issues that divided the Western Catholic Church in the sixteenth century. The Protestant concept of *sola Christus* ("Christ alone") captured the point of contention. Protestants proclaimed that God was propitiated through the death of Christ and that Christ did not merely make salvation possible but rather obtained forever a complete and full salvation. The Roman Catholics said no to all this. Christ, indeed, did die for us, but His death procured merit, which is initially granted and progressively increased, bearing fruit to eternal life. Integrally related to *sola Christus* is the insistence upon *sola gratia* ("grace alone") and *sola fides* ("faith alone"). It is by grace alone through the completed work of Christ that salvation is possible; it is not something that people can do. The sacramental system appeared to them to suggest that to

170

Christ's grace was added works for its attainment, denigrating Christ's accomplishment. Both *sola gratia* and *sola fides* are based upon the truth of *sola Christus*. These doctrines are at the very heart of the meaning of the good news, which was the seminal issue of controversy in the church at that time. The Reformers interpreted the death of Christ as a penal offering to justice, a substitutionary atonement. By so doing, they agreed with the insights of Anselm of Canterbury, though making some refinements in the earlier theologian's work.

For Martin Luther (1483–1546), the atonement rested in the character of God. God, being just and righteous, demands that His well-placed wrath be appeased or else judgment will be the result. His very character demands that reparation be made and salvation be purchased. The only one who could do that was humankind's righteous representative, the Lord Jesus Christ. Christ died to purchase a complete and full redemption on the cross, where He was judged by God Himself in our place. Salvation, for Luther, was based not on an emotional appeal by the sinner but solely on the work of the Redeemer. "Christ, the son of God stands in our place and has taken our sins upon his shoulders. . . . He is the eternal satisfaction for our sin and reconciles us with God, the Father" (*Works* X.49). In comparing Anselm's understanding of the atonement with Luther's, Paul Althaus wrote:

> For Anselm, there were only two possibilities, either punishment or satisfaction. For Luther, the satisfaction takes place through punishment, not of the sinner but of Christ. The punishment of sin consists in God's wrath together with all that this wrath brings upon men. So Christ stands under God's wrath. He suffers it in his passion. He dies the death of the sinner. But, unlike us sinners, he suffers and dies an "innocent and pure death." Thereby he has "paid God" and brought it about that God takes his wrath and his punishment away from us.[6]

Luther elsewhere speaks of this understanding of the death of Christ as "the real holy gospel" (*Works* 40.3.352). *The Augsburg Confession* (1530), one of the grand statements of Lutheran orthodoxy, states:

It is also taught among us that we cannot obtain forgiveness of sin and righteousness before God by our own merit, works, or satisfactions, but that we receive forgiveness of sin and become righteous before God by grace, for Christ's sake, through faith, when we believe that Christ suffered for us and that for his sake our sin is forgiven and righteousness and eternal life are given to us. (Article 4)

John Calvin (1509–1564), the Genevan Reformer and fountain-head of the tradition that bears his name, understood that the death of Christ effected an appeasement of the wrathful God for humanity's sins. In this, like Luther and other Reformers, he embraced penal substitutionary atonement as a foundational affirmation. Calvin wrote:

The very form of the death embodies a striking truth. The cross was cursed not only in the opinion of men, but by the enactment of the Divine Law. Hence, Christ, while suspended on it, subjects himself to the curse. And thus it behooved to be done, in order that the whole curse, which on account our iniquities awaited us, or rather lay upon us, might be taken from us by being transferred to him. . . . For the Son of God, though spotlessly pure, took upon him the disgrace and ignominy of our iniquities, and in return clothed us with his purity. . . . This term ["condemned sin in the flesh," Romans 8:3], therefore, indicates that Christ, in his death, was offered to the Father as a propitiatory victim; that, expiation being made by his sacrifice, we might cease to tremble at the divine wrath. (*Institutes of the Christian Religion* II.16.6)

Repetitions of Calvin's understanding are replete through the confessional statements of the Reformed tradition. Often the phraseology is inspiring. *The Scots Confession of Faith* (1560) has a lovely section on Christ's death:

172

That our Lord Jesus offered Himself a voluntary sacrifice unto His Father for us, that He suffered contradiction of sinners, that He was wounded and plagued for our transgressions, that He, the clean innocent Lamb of God, was condemned in the presence of an earthly judge, that we should be absolved before the judgment seat of our God; that He suffered not only the cruel death of the cross, which was accursed by the sentence of God; but also that He suffered for a season the wrath of His Father which sinners had deserved. (Article 9)

The Belgic Confession of Faith (1561) speaks of Christ, "who hath presented himself in our behalf before his Father, to appease his wrath by his full satisfaction, by offering himself on the tree of the cross, and pouring out his precious blood to purge away our sins" (Article 21). *The Heidelberg Catechism* (1563) answered the question of the meaning of Christ's suffering this way: "That throughout his life on earth, but especially at the end of it, he bore in body and soul the wrath of God against the sin of the whole human race, so that by his suffering, as the only expiatory sacrifice, he might redeem our body and soul from everlasting damnation" (Q. 37).

An amalgamation of nuances of both the Lutheran and Reformed traditions can be seen in the *Thirty-Nine Articles* of the Church of England (1571), the creedal affirmation of the Anglican/Episcopalian community worldwide. The confession does not contain a particular section delineating the meaning of Christ's death, yet its continuity with the sixteenth-century Protestant Reformation is clear by scattered references to Christ's death and its interpretation of the doctrine of salvation as a whole, justification in particular. Article 2 states in reference to Christ: "[He] truly suffered, was crucified, dead, and buried, to reconcile his Father to us, and to be a sacrifice, not only for original guilt, but also for all actual sins of men." Article 11 notes that "we are accounted righteous before God, only for the merit of our Lord and Savior Jesus Christ, by faith, and not for our own works or deservings." The fifteenth article speaks of Christ like this: "Christ in the truth of our nature was made like unto us in all things (sin excepted) from which he was clearly void, both in his flesh, and in his spirit. He came to be the Lamb without spot, who by the sacrifice of Himself once made, should take away the sins of the world."

Among the Calvinists in Holland, a division of opinion emerged at the end of the sixteenth century that would create a separate tradition within the Protestant Reformation. Deriving its name from a theologian in the church, Jacob Arminius (1560–1609), the Arminians felt that Reformed theology should be amended for greater conformity to the Scriptures and to increase the viability of defense from rationalistic attacks, particularly those of the Socinians and Grotians (see below for a discussion). In the process of formulation, particularly as expressed in the Five Remonstrances (1610), the Arminian party took shape.

Among the several issues that mark out the Arminian party, one was a unique nuancing of the doctrine of the death of Christ that showed them to be at variance not only with the Calvinists but also with the Lutherans. The most immediate context for the modification was the controversy that was raging at the time with Hugo Grotius, who defined the atonement as a moral demonstration of Christ's repudiation of sin. In the skillful hands of three theologians—Simon Episcopius (1583–1643), Stephanus Curcellaeus (1586–1659), and Philip van Limborch (1633–1712)—a view emerged that refuted Grotianism while moving away from the Calvinist-Lutheran explanation. In contrast to the Grotians, who denied the judicial aspects of Christ's death, they affirmed that Christ died as a sacrifice for sin, an offering of Himself to the Father. Curcellaeus noted, for example, "That God might show how much he hates sin and might hereafter effectually deter us from it, he willed not to forgive us, except upon the intervention of that sacrifice by which Christ offered his own slain body to him" (*Opera Theologica* 25.300). Limborch wrote:

Our own view is that the Lord Jesus Christ was a sacrifice for our sins, truly and properly so called; by sustaining the most grievous tortures and the cursed death of the cross . . . presenting himself there [in heaven] before the Father, he appeased him angry with our sins, and reconciled us to him. Thus he bore for us and in our place the most grievous affliction, and so turned away from us deserved punishment. (*Theologia Christiana* 26.262)

Having stated all of this, which implies essential agreement in such matters with the reformers, they distinguished themselves from the Calvinist tradition by denying that Christ's atonement was a payment for the particular sins of sinners. Nor would they agree that it was a complete satisfaction of God's justice for sin. Limborch taught that the satisfaction was not for all sin forever but merely for past sin in the believer's life. Curcellaeus is blunt in stating, "Christ did not make satisfaction by enduring the punishment which sinners merited. This does not belong to the nature of a sacrifice, and has nothing in common with it" (*Institutes of the Christian Religion* 5.19.15). In short, the death of Christ was not a substitution whereby Christ died in the place of the sin of specific sinners; it was a generalized substitute penalty for humankind. In the doctrine of substitution, as understood in the Reformed tradition, Christ's death was a strict equivalent in the place of the sinner's sin; there was no concept that Christ died for the idea of sin only. Curcellaeus noted: "And it may be said that our Lord satisfied the Father for us by his death, and earned righteousness for us, in so far as he satisfied, not the rigor and exactitude of the divine justice, but the just and compassionate will of God" (*Institutes of the Christian Religion* 3.22.2).

Asked to revise the doctrine of the church by the Remonstrant or Arminian party, as expressed in the Five Remonstrances (1610), a formal investigation resulted in the Synod of Dordt in 1618. The synod rejected the Remonstrances and condemned the Arminians, issuing the Canons of the Synod of Dordt. The second article of the canons addressed the death of Christ and the redemption of humankind. The Dutch church affirmed that Christ's death was specifically a satisfaction of God for the evil actions of individuals, not for the generic idea of sin. It was an appeasement of God through the substitution of Christ for specific people once, forever, and absolutely complete.

> It was the will of God, that Christ by the blood of the cross, whereby he confirmed the new covenant, should effectually redeem out of every people . . . all those, and only those, who were from all eternity chosen to salvation, and given to him by the Father . . . [that he] should purge them from all sin, both original and actual, whether committed before or after believing. (Article 2.8)

Each section of the pronouncements of the canons of the synod contains corresponding articles that denounce Remonstrant assertions. This portion of the creed notes that it rejects the teaching of those "who teach that God the Father appointed his Son to death on the cross without a fixed and definite plan to see anyone saved by name" (Article I) and "who teach that all people have been received into the state of reconciliation and into the grace of the covenant, so that no one on account of original sin is liable to condemnation" (Article 5).

The School of Saumur, a French Reformed school in the city that bears its name, emerged in the seventeenth century as the leading Huguenot academy in the country. Established by Philippe du Plessis-Mornay in 1598, the school rose to prominence under John Cameron (c.1579–1625) and became dominant under Moïse Amyraut (1596–1644). Amyraut, a voluminous writer, can rightly be called the theological father of modified Calvinism due to the fact that his teachings formalized a theological methodology that effected another lasting division among Calvinists. He, unlike Jacob Arminius, remained within the confines of the Reformed faith, though with ever-increasing difficulty. While Amyraut did clearly affirm the substitutionary death of Christ and shunned the Arminian explanation of the atonement, he did believe in a hypothetical universalism, a belief that God willed all humankind to be saved through the exercise of faith in Christ. Christ, therefore, died for all humankind without exception (unlimited atonement). However, knowing that none would repent and believe, having no ability to do so, God chose some to be saved. Some Amyraldians who stressed hypothetical universalism tended to verge into the Arminian camp; others did not because of their understanding of the inability of humankind to embrace the gospel. Amyraut remained within the Calvinist tradition. Though his views were clearly modifications of traditional Calvinistic thinking on the subject of the atonement, his stress on human inability and divine election kept him in the Reformed camp.

THE HETERODOX GROUPS AND THE WORK OF CHRIST

The Reformers and their Roman Catholic counterparts represented alternatives, quite distinct in nature and implication, to the general direction of the church as a whole in the late medieval period. Though certainly divergent in opinion on basic issues, they sought to relate revelation, reason, and tradition together in the construction of doctrine. While the Roman Catholics, some protested, elevated the role of the church and tradition over the Holy Scriptures, the Protestants sought to give priority to the Scriptures, taking a lesser view of the role of the church and tradition. There were others in the Reformation era who took an elevated view of the role of reason in theological development, a sort of biblistic rationalism in which the meaning of Scripture was defined by reasonability to a greater degree than in either the Roman Catholic Church or the Protestant churches. This can be readily seen in the Socinian movement, a precursor of the modern Unitarian movement.

The Socinians of the sixteenth and seventeenth centuries emerged under the leadership of Laelius (1525–1562) and Faustus (1539–1604) Socinus. As noted earlier, the Socinians denied the triunity of God, rejecting the deity of Christ and Chalcedonian Christology. For them, Christ was an elevated ideal of humanity. In their rejection of the death of Christ as an appeasing substitution offered to God for sinners, Socinians began by denying the fundamental assumption of both Protestant and Roman Catholic theology: the idea that God's justice needed to be satisfied. Faustus Socinus said, "If we could get rid of this justice, even if we had no other proof, that fiction of Christ's satisfaction would be thoroughly exposed and would vanish" (*Works* III.1). The

Socinian understanding of God's character was that justice and mercy are not indispensably connected; they are part of His optional will. This means that without the satisfaction of justice, God can exercise mercy. Indeed, this is how they understood that grace is free! The Racovian Catechism is quite clear: "Since I have shown that the mercy and justice which our adversaries conceive to pertain to God by nature, certainly do not belong to him, there was no need of that plan whereby he might satisfy such mercy and justice" (Chapter 8).

The essence of the Socinian argument is twofold: First, the satisfaction view is opposed to free grace. If we are saved freely by God, it is a contradiction to suggest that it was not free at all, Christ being required to die to obtain it.

> To a free forgiveness nothing is more opposite than such a satisfaction as they [Catholics and Protestants] contend for, and the payment for an equivalent price. For where a creditor is satisfied by the debtor himself, or by another person on the debtor's behalf, it cannot with truth be said of him that he freely forgives the debt. (Chapter 8)

The second argument juxtaposes not only justice and mercy but also complete forgiveness and moral rectitude. That is, a free and complete forgiveness destroys the motive for obedience.

> If full payment has been made to God by Christ for all our sins, even those which are future, we are absolutely freed from all liability to punishment, and therefore no further condition can by right be exacted from us to deliver us from the penalties of sin. What necessity then would there be for living righteously? (Chapter 8)

Socinians defined the atonement of Christ as an inspiring object lesson; it is a moral encouragement and stern warning for all who would aspire to eternal life. In reply to the question of the necessity of Christ's death, the catechism noted:

> There are two reasons for this, as there are two methods whereby Christ saves us: for, first, he inspires us with hope of salvation, and also incites us both to enter upon the way of salvation and to persevere in it. In the next place, he is with us in every struggle of temptation, suffering, or danger, affords us assistance, and at length delivers us from eternal death. (Chapter 8)

The Socinians, who embraced several ancient heresies, distorted and destroyed the unity of God's character in juxtaposing justice and mercy, denying the necessity of satisfying the former in order to receive the latter. In this they followed a teaching found earlier in John Duns Scotus and Thomas Aquinas that God's redemption was only arbitrarily through Christ's penalty-bearing death. Further, they followed Peter Abelard in defining the atonement as a moral influence. This understanding of the atonement sees no connection between the death of Christ and the forgiveness of sin; Christ's death neither appeases God nor moves Him to pardon sinners.

The denial of substitutionary atonement arose from two sources. The first was a failure or an unwillingness to perceive the attributes of God as being in perfect harmony. For example, the justice of God was often denigrated for the sake of mercy (also freedom and sovereignty); the two were seen as opposites. Second, in downplaying the justice of God in the atonement, Socinians saw Christ's death on Calvary as one of the possible ways that salvation could have been procured. Hence, this particular means of redemption was arbitrary, not necessary. Historically, scholars have begun the discussion of the atonement with humankind's fall and God's justifiable wrath. Here, however, the atonement is explained as a nonnecessary, though useful, example for humankind. This was true not only of Abelardians and Socinians; it was also the posture of the Grotians.

The Grotian theory of the death of Christ derives its name from its formulator, Hugo Grotius (1583–1645). Grotius was a Dutch jurist and statesman who became enmeshed in the religious struggles that troubled the church following the Synod of Dordt (1618). His view represents a middle way between the Reformers and the Socinians. Like the Socinians, Grotius rejected the idea that Christ's death was a payment for the sins of sinners. In accord with the Reformers, however, he denounced the notion that the atonement was a moral example. To Grotius, whatever the atonement meant, it was a "real" atonement. Grotius explained his view by beginning with the moral law of God, though he argued that since the law is an effect of God's will, not God's will itself, God was free to relax its demands and not require punishment for its disobedience. With such an assumption, Grotius denied that disobedience demands retribution.

Upon this premise, Grotius claimed that God simply relaxed the claims of the law, with no real satisfaction, and saved the sinner. God deemed it unwise and unsafe to remit sin without some satisfaction, so he grounded the necessity of the atonement in the creature, not in the unchanging attributes of the Creator. Therefore, to show His hatred for sin, Christ's sufferings are important as a preventative to creaturely libertinism. Forgiveness is based on an emotional attitude toward the law of God, a person simply repents of past failures and promises future amendment. In essence, Christ died to reveal how seriously God takes the violation of His laws. This stout warning, when taken seriously, is the basis of forgiveness.

Of this theory, generally called the governmental theory, Gonzalez noted:

> Grotius developed an interesting theory of the atonement, affirming that the reason that Christ had to suffer was not to pay for the sins of humankind or to give us an example, but rather to show that, although God was willing to forgive us, he still considered the transgression of the law a serious offense that could not go without consequences.[7]

180

THE LATE MODERN CHURCHES AND THE WORK OF CHRIST (1750–PRESENT)

The emergence of the rationalistic spirit in the seventeenth century, generally termed the Enlightenment, caused in subsequent centuries a reposturing of the Christian faith or at worst a redefinition of it. Regardless of one's evaluation of the Enlightenment, it continues to have extensive influence. Philosophical and scientific advances brought into question the viability of Christianity, at least as it had been traditionally defined. The scientific method appeared to stage an assault upon the supernaturalistic assumptions of traditional religion, such as the existence of God, the nature of revelation, and the deity of Christ. The understanding of the work of Christ endured a similar reevaluation.

THE PROTESTANT TRADITIONS AND THE WORK OF CHRIST

The reevaluation of the work of Christ was greatest in the liberal wing of Protestantism. Here theologians, influenced by the ideas of their time, developed teachings on the atonement that seemed more defensible to them than the orthodox viewpoint. Meanwhile, conservative Protestants fought for the tradition of a redemptive death of Christ.

The European Protestant Liberal Tradition and the Work of Christ

Friedrich Schleiermacher (1768–1834) reflects the attempt of an increasing number of theologians to do theology within the sphere of the assumptions of the Enlightenment, particularly in the wake of the insights of the philosopher Immanuel Kant (1724–1804). Like many, Kant separated the knowledge of God from the realm of scientific verification, making religious knowledge a subjective, personal value judgment. Embracing this insight, Schleiermacher thought that Christianity could be preserved from its critics. In the skilled hands of this sympathetic "defender," the Christian faith lost its historical dimension, becoming a vague feeling of dependence on God. The Trinity, at least in the Nicene sense, was lost. Christ became an

181

inspired and inspiring archetype of humanity at its ideal best. Without a divine Christ and a God who is unwaveringly righteous and just, the work of Christ was refashioned; when the idea of God's justice is set aside, the necessity of His appeasement is also.

Schleiermacher spoke of errors that had crept into Christian theology. These he identified as an emphasis on the sensual details of Christ's death, which he spoke of as the "triviality of wounds theology," on the concept of a penalty-bearing substitution on Christ's behalf for the sinner, and on the idea that Christ fulfilled the divine will in our place or for our advantage in the sense that we are thereby no longer obligated to fulfill it ourselves.[8] When he defined the atonement of Christ, he echoed the Abelardian-Socinian notion of a moral influence theory. Christ—being quite the valiant, selfless person He was—died to rally us to similar noble thoughts and actions. Claiming that "no Christian mind could possibly desire this [a penal sin-bearer], nor has sound doctrine ever asserted it," he stated: "Christ's highest achievement consists in this, that He so animates us that we ourselves are led to an ever more perfect fulfillment of the divine law."[9] For Schleiermacher, Christ's work as our great High Priest was in His role as a sympathetic, inspiring man and not as the priest who became for us both the offerer and the sacrifice. Otto Pfleiderer summarized the theologian's view this way:

> Schleiermacher rejects the idea of a transcendental reconciliation through the atoning sufferings of Christ as the representative of mankind before God, and puts in its place the historical view of the matter, according to which Christ by the total impression of his personality had such a strengthening and beatifying influence on men's religious consciousness that they felt themselves saved and reconciled, that is, delivered, or gradually being delivered, from the hindering and miserable contradiction of higher and lower consciousness.[10]

 In the shaping of modern religious liberalism, Albrecht Ritschl (1822–1889) was second only to Schleiermacher in influence. Indeed,

American liberal thought has often been denominated as Ritschlianism. The thoughts of this highly acclaimed theologian concerning Christ's work are instructive. Like Schleiermacher, Ritschl embraced a moral influence view of Christ's death, yet with a certain uniqueness. Schleiermacher's focus was upon Christ's inspiration of an increasingly God-conscious life in the community of the church; Ritschl stressed His moral benefit to society or the kingdom of God. Christ's mission, according to Ritschl, was not so much to establish a redeeming community called the church but to bring about a cosmic ethical righteousness among men. Said Ritschl,

> It is unbiblical, then, to assume that between God's grace and His righteousness there is an opposition, which in its bearing upon the sinful race of men would lead to a contradiction, only to be solved through the interference of Christ. . . . It is unbiblical to assume that the sacrificial offering includes in itself a penal act, executed not upon the guilty person, but upon the victim who takes his place.[11]

Christ's death is an inspiring illustration of forbearance, patience, and love for humanity. As in Schleiermacher's view, Christ's role as a priest was that of compassion and sympathy for people, not an offering of Himself for the people's sin.

The European Protestant Conservative Tradition and the Work of Christ

The most penetrating and unrelenting intellectual response to nineteenth-century liberalism is found in the work of Karl Barth (1886–1968), clearly the greatest theologian of the twentieth century. He was an unrelenting critic of Schleiermacher and the Enlightenment attempt to refashion Christianity, to humanize the supernaturalism of God, Christ, and the Bible. While he strenuously opposed these trends, it seems that in regard to his understanding of Christ's work on the cross, as in the case of his understanding of revelation, he did not go far enough to rid himself of his nineteenth-century heritage. In his view of the atonement, Barth was simply baffling, though it must be confessed that he offered us no systematic treatment of it in his *Church Dogmatics*. There are places in his writings where he seemed to speak favorably of the notion of penal substitution. He noted, for example, "But what did take place? At this point we can and must make this decisive statement: What took place is that the Son of God fulfilled the righteous judgment on us men by Himself taking our place as man and in our place undergoing the judgment under which we had passed."[12] However, in other places he is clear that the cardinal feature of Christ's death is not substitution.

> The concept of punishment has come into the answer given by Christian theology to the question of Isaiah 53. In the New Testament it does not occur in this connection. . . . We must not make this a main concept as in some of the older presentations of the doctrine of the atonement (especially those that follow Anselm of Canterbury), either in the sense that by suffering our punishment we are spared from suffering ourselves, or that in so doing He "satisfied" or offered satisfaction to the wrath of God. The latter thought is quite foreign to the New Testament.[13]

Barth saw the atonement from the vantage point of what it accomplished rather than what took place in it. His emphasis, like that of nineteenth-century liberalism, was upon reconciliation. Donald Bloesch summarized Barth's view as follows: First, the cross is not a revelation of God's wrath for the sinner, a place where His justice is requited for any number of unrighteous acts by sinners. It is the moment of the triumph of God's love. Second, His death on the cross is a revelation of God's forgiveness accomplished outside of time; what happened at the cross is not the ground of God's forgiveness. That Christ went to Calvary is proof of God's forgiveness having already been accomplished. What took place at Calvary was that God revealed through Christ that He had already forgiven us. Christ is the proclaimer of our victory and reconciliation. Bloesch wrote, "[Barth]

184

depicts reconciliation as having been accomplished in the act of humiliation and incarnation. The cross and resurrection simply confirm and reveal what has already taken place. He also speaks of these events as the climactic unfolding of the eternal decision of the Son of God to unite himself with human flesh for the sake of our salvation."[14]

The cross is the revelation of the moral conquest of the world's evil by the victor. It is the disclosure by God in Christ that He has reconciled us to Himself. The death was not to accomplish reconciliation through appeasement; it was to reveal that God had already forgiven us. This apparently without a satisfaction of His own righteousness. So Barth left us with some questions. How could God be just and yet forgive sinners without a payment?[15] How does the forgiveness of God relate to His unalterable divine character?

The American Protestant Liberal Tradition and the Work of Christ

The liberal tradition has roots in America that precede the late nineteenth century, when the impact of European thought began to capture the colleges, universities, and seminaries. Indeed, it can be argued that the Enlightenment spirit was bred in the soil of America through movements that can be discerned as early as the eighteenth century. Though German scholarship (especially the thought structures of Albrecht Ritschl and the Ritschlians) may have provided Americans with the philosophical and methodological insights that characterized it, it was very much native-spun and would have emerged inevitably even without them.

The clash in the 1740s between the Northampton pastor Jonathan Edwards (1703–1758) and the Boston cleric Charles Chauncy (1705–1787) over the validity of the Great Awakening was a harbinger of change on the theological horizon. As early as the 1730s, Edwards complained of evidence of "Arminianism" (a term expressive of the Enlightenment's emphasis on the ability of humanity to impress God favorably and its downplaying of traditional notions of depravity) in New England. Chauncy's emphasis on religious life as being largely cognitive, urbane, and means-oriented struck Edwards as a danger that was only slightly less disturbing than that posed by the wild-eyed enthusiasts who turned to inward states of ecstasy to verify religious claims.

Edwards' insights proved to be accurate. He had detected a religious change that, having become the vogue in educated circles in England and Scotland, was beginning to penetrate the British colonies in North America. Conrad Wright commented:

> The Arminianism that Cotton Mather dismissed and Jonathan Edwards feared was the first phase of the liberal movement in theology which in the nineteenth century was named Unitarianism. It rejected the awful and inscrutable God of the Calvinists, and replaced him with a God of benevolence and law. It rejected the concept of human nature as totally corrupt and depraved, and supplanted it with one in which the ability of every man to strive for righteousness was admitted. It was, in a sense, the New England version of the theology of the Age of Reason, occupying a middle ground between orthodoxy on the one hand and infidelity on the other.[16]

As a result of these trends, New England Congregationalism was fractured into competing religious ideologies. A liberal-conservative division occurred among the churches.

The most prominent spokesman of the Unitarian movement in America was William Ellery Channing (1780–1842), a Boston pastor. Following the trends set by Charles Chauncy, Jonathan Mayhew (1720–1766), and Ebenezer Gay (1696–1787), Channing showed himself to be the theological heir of the European Socinians. He considered Christ to be the ideal of humanity, sin to be the mistakes that come with imitating bad examples, and the atonement to be a moral impetus to personal resolve. Such attributes of God as righteousness and justice he rejected, preferring instead to emphasize God's benevolent attributes; that is, those aspects in which the now-blighted image of God can still be seen in the creature were defined as God. The standard for defining God became an idealization of humanity!

As the eighteenth century passed into the nineteenth, the winds of the democratic Enlightenment birthed a new nation, an unprecedented political experiment of qualified self-rule. A nation was born that rested on a rather weak view of human nature combined, as it often does, with profound millennialistic optimism. Richard Mosier summarized the implications of political liberalism on religion when he wrote,

> The Revolutionary could no more admit a sovereign God than he could a sovereign king. . . . Rulers henceforth rule only by the consent of the governed. The God of the Puritans, stripped of His antique powers, had no recourse but to enter as a weakened prince into the temple of individualism and there to seek refuge.[17]

It is in this context of the democratization of religion that Unitarianism posed such a potent threat because, with its easygoing optimism of human nature, it seemed to be in alignment with the spirit of the age.

It was within New England Calvinism that a concerted effort was mounted to respond to the threat of the Unitarian/Socinian movement, which had divided Congregationalists into Unitarian and Trinitarian factions following the hiring of a Unitarian, Henry Ware (1764–1845), to be a theologian at the traditionally Calvinist Harvard College in 1805. Calvinists (sometimes referred to as "New England divines" or "new divinity men") struggled to defend their heritage against the threats of the popular Unitarians. However, in the context of that admirable task, Calvinism in New England underwent significant changes that unwittingly laid the foundation for the rise of classic American liberal thought at the end of the century. An illustration of this is the experience of Andover Theological Seminary, America's first major seminary. Though founded in the wake of the defection of Harvard to Unitarianism, Andover by the 1890s became a major center for the defense of the "New Theology." The attempt to defend Calvinism brought about such modification of its own theology that it became the seedbed for a new theological system. This can be seen in the doctrine of the death of Christ as it was interpreted by the New England teachers and pastors. Turning from a penal substitution theory, the tendency was to listen more to the societal virtues of fairness and social equity for explanations of biblical concepts than to the Bible itself. Sadly, the theory of Grotius, a governmental or moral persuasiveness theory, was revived and became increasingly dominant within the Calvinist tradition. Jonathan Edwards Jr. (1745–1801), the son of the Puritan of Northampton fame, defined the atonement as a demonstration that disobedience brings moral judgment. "The fact is, that Christ has not, in the literal and proper sense, paid the debt for us. . . . The proper sense of this is, that since the atonement consists, not in the payment of a debt, but in the vindication of the divine law and character; therefore it is not opposed to free grace in pardon."[18] The arguments for this revisionist theory sound very much like those of Hugo Grotius. If salvation is free, then it could not have been purchased. If we are freely forgiven, it would lead to a waywardness of living. Speaking of this modification, Robert Ferm is particularly insightful.

> The Christian life is obedience to the moral law, fitting in with divine government. The death of Christ is [clear and unmistakable evidence] that God will punish wrongdoing. Divine government must be upheld at any cost, and fear of vindictive justice becomes the weapon to enforce obedience. Paradoxically, however many other items of New Divinity dogma offended the spirit of the time, this theory blended well with the current political temper.[19]

The popularizer of New England theological attempts to create a theology that could defend itself against Unitarianism was the great antebellum evangelist Charles Grandison Finney (1792–1875). Finney felt that the Unitarian menace, coupled with the deficiencies of traditional Calvinism, called for a theological revision that would have mass appeal and, therefore, restore the vote for Christianity. In several areas of theology, Finney found the insights of the New England innovators much to his liking. This enormously successful proclaimer of the Christian faith denied the penal substitution of Christ and embraced a moralistic, governmental understanding. Christ did not die in the sinner's place, bearing his burdens against a just and righteous God. His death instead serves as a stern warning for the necessity of personal rectitude. Finney was blunt when he noted: "I must say that the atonement was not a commercial transaction. Some have regarded the atonement simply in the light of the payment of a debt; and have represented Christ as purchasing the elect of the Father, and paying down the same amount in his own person that justice would have exacted to them."[20] In the rejection of penal substitution, and in the presentation of his own explanation, Finney suggested that he was a man who was not to be interpreted apart from his social context.

> It is a common practice in human governments, and one that is founded in the nature and laws of the mind, to reward distinguished public service by conferring favors on the children of those who have rendered this service, and treating them as if they had rendered it themselves. This is both benevolent and wise. . . . The public service which he has rendered to the universe, by laying down his life for the support of the divine government, has rendered it eminently wise, that all who are united to him by faith should be treated as religious for his sake.[21]

The transitional link between New England theology and classic liberalism, as it relates to the doctrine of the atonement, was Horace Bushnell (1802–1876). This heir of Nathaniel Taylor's theology (often called Taylorism or New Haven theology) departed from a Grotian governmental theory to embrace a moral example or Abelardian view, which became dominant in classic American liberalism at the end of the nineteenth century.

As has been stated earlier, the New Theology emerged on the American scene in the waning decades of the previous century, with deep roots in both America and Europe. The cardinal tenets of this revisionist theology were a stress on the immanence of God to the exclusion of His transcendental qualities, a belief that religion is and must be a culturally relevant phenomena, and the identification of

Christianity with moral progress and the emergence of the kingdom of God with a merely spiritualized coming of Christ to inaugurate it. This form of liberalism emerged in the 1880s and remained the dominant expression of the tradition until the late 1920s, when a neo-liberalism displaced it.

Lyman Abbott (1835–1922), the pastor of the Plymouth Congregational Church, Brooklyn, New York, found Charles Finney's stress on freedom of the will, Horace Bushnell's emphasis on the spiritual nature of faith, and Henry Ward Beecher's focus on love to be the inspiration for his ministry as he used the insights of evolutionary science to refashion Christianity.[22] For Abbott, the meaning of the atonement was rooted in two fundamental foci of the evolutionary process, the struggle for self and the struggle for others. Christ's struggle for humanity is not unlike our own; He is simply the model for our self-giving, self-sacrificing spirit. It is His example of giving that, when emulated, gives life. "There is no authority in Scripture for the doctrine that God puts the penalty due to a guilty person upon an innocent one. We are saved by the blood of Christ because we are saved by the life of Christ poured into our life."[23]

Another illustration of the New Theology's approach to the death of Christ is that of the Baptist pioneer at Colgate Theological Seminary, William Newton Clarke (1841–1912). He clearly rejected the idea that Christ died as a penal, vicarious Sin-bearer. "It was not in any technical sense 'in our stead,' but it was for our sake," said Clarke of Christ's death.[24] Christ, who is the "revelation" of God, died to reveal in a spiritual sense the Father's hatred of sin and of His great love and forgiveness of humanity.

> We must not think that he endured the same evils that sin naturally brings upon the sinner, for it is impossible: no one but a sinner could do that. Bearing sin does not mean that. To say that his death was a substitute for our death, and that he died that we might not die, is to use the words, "die" and "death," in two senses, and to speak misleadingly. He died for us; his "feet were nailed for our advantage on the bitter cross"; and

190

we do not need a closer definition than this of the sense in which he died "for us."[25]

Harry Emerson Fosdick (1878–1969), the popularist apostle of American liberalism, spoke from his pulpit in much the same manner. Like his mentor, Fosdick interpreted the atonement within the Abelardian framework as a morally inspiring event offering a thrilling illustration of personal self-giving. After referring to the Anselmic theory as warped and distorted, he explained his understanding of it this way:

> He has given us so perfect and convincing an illustration of the power of boundless love expressing itself through utter sacrifice that he has become the unique representative on earth. . . . To multitudes it has meant alike a revelation of the divine nature and a challenge to sacrificial living of their own which they could in no wise escape.[26]

In the 1920s the most concise statement of classic liberalism came through the writings of Shailer Mathews (1863–1941), who taught at both the University of Chicago and the University of Chicago Divinity School. Using the interpretative grid of social progress as the cause of the emergence of new concepts of religion, he suggested that recent changes in the social sciences mandated a new look at old theological perspectives ("Christian experience as interpreted by successive social minds"). He was blunt when he rejected the notion of the penal, vicarious, substitutionary work of Christ, saying, "It is a travesty of Orthodoxy to say that God has been bought off by the death of a perfect man."[27] Christ's death was interpreted as a symbol that God is concerned for people in their struggles for moral progress and His encouragement of us in the long and difficult task of persevering with a thankless humanity. "Only by living personally, that is, with the sacrificial social-mindedness of Jesus does one come into unity with men and God."[28]

As ironic as it may seem at first glance, the seeds that caused a revision of liberalism in the 1930s were sown decades before World War I, which had so much to do with dispelling the notions of an enlightened humanity and inevitable social progress. Victorian moralism (which unfortunately was identified as authentic Christianity, even though it was only a product of the silly idealism of the Enlightenment) began to be seriously questioned at the end of the nineteenth century. It was, however, Harry Emerson Fosdick, the unwavering advocate of liberal religious thought, who warned of a needed change in his important 1935 sermon, "The Church Must Go beyond Liberalism." He assured his audience that liberalism had won its battle with theological obscurantism and then issued a challenge to create a "new liberalism." In the hands of a coterie of scholars, such as Walter Marshall Horton (1895–1966) of Oberlin College, John C. Bennett (1902–1995) of Union Theological Seminary, New York, and H. P. Van Dusen (1897–1975), also of Union Seminary, neo-liberalism emerged and dominated the American scene from the 1930s to the 1960s. Neo-liberalism was often designated "realistic theology" because it treated theology with less of an optimistic penchant than the older brand, viewing sin as a grave manner in the human condition. (At this point, at least, some found the insights of Jonathan Edwards more credible than the easygoing platitudes of the mere "not yet" of human imperfection.) Yet while the rhetoric seemed to imply a more biblical attitude toward traditional notions of sin and grace, such was hardly the case. Using the linguistic insights of neo-orthodoxy (language is largely symbolic), neo-liberalism was able to use evangelical terminology but give it an entirely different meaning. While neo-liberals spoke of sin in more realistic terms, the anthropology of neo-liberalism was a truncated and twisted perversion of orthodoxy. Its doctrine of the atonement bore more affinity with the moral example tradition than with the scriptural picture of Christ's death. In a collection of essays by several neo-liberals, George Thomas rehearsed the predominant interpretations of the atonement, being careful to speak favorably of each one, claiming that the truth is to be found in parts (not the whole) of each. He stated that the apostle Paul taught a "vicarious satisfaction" view, which to the rationalist represents a "profoundly immoral concept of justice," and then he added:

"Would it not be more intelligible to say . . . that his death was . . . the culmination of his sacrificial life of love?"[29]

In the 1960s the liberal movement began to disintegrate. Though liberalism continued, it ceased to be a cohesive movement with a definable purpose, goal, and enveloping ethos. American liberalism, much like its counterpart American evangelicalism, fractured into competing theologies and ideologies (black theology, feminist theology, and liberation theology). The most influential theologian in the liberal tradition during the post–World War II era, a man representative of the diffusion of theology, was Paul Tillich (1886–1965). Tillich came to prominence at Union Theological Seminary, New York, through a reformulation of liberal thought generally known as the "theology of being." At times, Tillich appeared amazingly orthodox, such as when he argued that a forgiveness based on the love of God without taking into account His justice is false.[30] However, for Tillich, justice was not an attribute of God; it was a natural law that issued from God in the form of separation or estrangement. Justice was not a perfection of His character; it was His moral quest for love (love and justice never conflict because they are the same thing). Justice needs no requiting for wrongs done, because God is always love. Humankind exists in existential estrangement from God. The Christ symbol is the manifestation of God's love wooing humankind to Himself, ending our psychological alienation. The cross of Christ is not the ground of divine forgiveness but the manifestation that God Himself has dwelt with the consequences of guilt. God fully participates in our alienation, not desiring it to continue. The death of Christ is not atoning; it should remind us that God has already done all that is needed to end our alienated feelings toward Him. Tillich argued that the biblical phraseology concerning the death of Christ is highly symbolic; it simply should not be taken literally. Thinking that a term like "substitutional suffering" is unfortunate and confusing, he wrote: "God participates in the suffering of existential estrangement, but his suffering is not a substitute for the suffering of the creature. Neither is the suffering of Christ a substitute for the suffering of man. . . . No substitution, but free participation, is the character of divine suffering."[31] Thus, Tillich's explanation of the death of Christ is a divine sympathetic view. The realization of God's care about our awful psychological isolation should cause us to consider ending it by believing that God was never far from us in the first place.

A more recent form of liberal theology is process theism. Through a number of books written by Norman Pittenger, Daniel Day Williams, Schubert Ogden, John Cobb Jr., and Lewis S. Ford (to name only a few), process theologians have adopted the methodology of liberal theology in understanding the nature of Scripture and have employed it to reinterpret the religious symbols of the Bible within an evolutionary mold. Unlike the classic liberal tradition, which was rooted in the assumptions of Newtonian science, process theism is an epistemological adaptation of the newer insights of the scientific community, particularly quantum physics.

To understand how process theism conceives the death of Christ, the view of Norman Pittenger is illustrative. Beginning with a rejection of the ideas that God is immutable, omnipotent, and impassible as "sub-Christian concepts" (a view embraced by the Bible itself and those who "take the biblical idiom as final and inerrant"), Pittenger finds the ideas of Abelard instructive.[32] The atonement is a revelation of love that not only issues from Christ in Jesus, a spirit of care and self-giving, but it changes God in the sense that He participates in suffering, knowing what it will bring about in the creature. God is love, says Pittenger, and through the death of Christ the love of God is disclosed and released. The impact on the creature should be a motive to love; the impact on God is that it provides a new and more genuine outlet for Him to love. It has enlarged the vistas of God's love for His creatures and capacity for identity with their sufferings, though He has never been otherwise than loving.

The process view of the atonement represents both a radical alternative in understanding the character of God as well as something of a return to an Abelardian view. In this latter sense, process theism has shown itself to be in the lineage of traditional liberal religious thought in Europe and America.

The American Protestant Conservative Tradition and the Work of Christ

Without doubt, the most acute defense of traditional orthodoxy against the assertions of the liberal tradition came from the pen of

J. Greshem Machen (1881–1937), a professor at Princeton Theological Seminary and the founder of Westminster Theological Seminary in Philadelphia in 1929. In *Christianity & Liberalism* (1923) and *What Is Faith?* (1925), Machen answered his liberal opponents. He began his reply in both books with the matter of the use of history. He accused his opponents of hiding their true position by distinguishing the term "theory" from the term "fact." According to Machen, the liberals used "theory" to indicate what is only hearsay. Machen replied that we may speak of substitution as a theory, but what we really mean is that it is a fact. He refused to disjoin the two words, though it may be often done in popular speech. The very statement that an atonement took place is a statement of fact.[33]

A second objection of the liberals goes something like this: Is it not enough to believe in the fact of the atonement without the necessity of ascribing a particular meaning to it? Machen's answer is that such a view of words without meaning is a complete break with the teachings of the church historically. Words and meaning have traditionally been inseparably connected. He stated, "With regard to this objection it should be observed that if religion be made independent of history there is no such thing as a gospel. For 'gospel' means 'good news', tidings, information about something that happened."[34]

Another liberal objection is that the traditional view is too narrow, restricting the doctrine of salvation to the name of Jesus, thus eliminating many who have never heard His name. Machen's reply is that Christianity is an exclusive religion; its central proclamation is that salvation is only in and through Jesus. However, it is a derelict church that restricts the hearing of the gospel by its failure in proclamation; God does not restrict the hearing of the gospel.

A further liberal line of argument against the traditional interpretation is that it is unreasonable to think that one person should suffer for the evil of another. In the realm of human analogies this would be true, said Machen, but the Christian doctrine of the atonement is rooted in the doctrine of the deity of Christ. The majesty of Christ answers the objection.

Yet another objection is that the traditional view degrades the character of God by making Him unwilling to forgive sin unless He be requited. His love is thus diminished. Machen's reply was that the liberal takes sin far too lightly, being "totally at variance with the teachings of the whole New Testament and of Jesus Himself." The atonement through Christ does not denigrate His love to elevate His justice. Such a view of justice, he asserted, "is based upon the most abysmal misunderstanding of the doctrine itself."

THE ROMAN CATHOLIC TRADITION AND THE WORK OF CHRIST

The Roman Catholic Church is a confessional community; it is bound by a variety of official creeds that define its orthodoxy. These include the ecumenical councils of the church from the first Nicene (325) to the second Nicene (787) council—those several gatherings of the bishops who collectively spoke on issues troubling the church. In addition, the Roman Catholic Church has had three major councils after the division of the Western Catholic Church in the sixteenth century: the Council of Trent (1545–1563), Vatican I (1869), and Vatican II (1962–1965). Of these several later councils, Trent is the definitive statement of the church's orthodoxy.

The earliest creeds do not specifically define the atonement of Christ but rather simply repeat the phrase that He was "crucified also for us." Further, neither the Council of Trent nor the two Vatican councils delineate the meaning of Christ's death. It would appear that the issues that divided the Catholic Church in the West in the late medieval period did not include the meaning of the atonement (the points of contention being the nature of sin in humanity, humanity's relationship to the reception of grace, and the role of faith and works, among others). The meaning of confessional statements can be gleaned from catechisms that are designed to teach the meaning of the creeds to the laity. The recent *Catechism of the Catholic Church* (1994), which was commended to the churches by Pope John Paul II, provides insight into the position of the church on matters of faith. The catechism in part follows the order of the Nicene-Constantinopolitan Creed and comes to the phrase that Christ was crucified under Pontius Pilate. The catechism defines the atonement in explicitly Anselmic terms: Christ died as a substitutionary penal offering to God for sinners. For example, the catechism notes:

196

> Jesus did not experience reprobation as if he himself had sinned. But in the redeeming love that always united him to the Father, he assumed us in the state of our waywardness of sin, to the point that he could say in our name on the cross: "My God, My God. why have you forsaken me?" Having thus established him in solidarity with us sinners, "God did not spare his own Son but gave him up for us all," so that we might be "reconciled to God by the death of his Son." (603)

Elsewhere in the catechism we read:

> The Scriptures had foretold this divine plan of salvation through the putting to death of "the righteous one, my servant" as a mystery of universal redemption, that is, as the ransom that would free men from the slavery of sin. Citing a confession of faith that he himself had "received," St. Paul professes that "Christ died for our sins in accordance with the scriptures." In particular Jesus' redemptive death fulfills Isaiah's prophecy of the suffering Servant. (601)

However, official confessions are one thing and the interpretation of them by the teachers of the church is another, particularly in the light of the theological liberalism and hermeneutical promiscuousness that have been permitted to spread within the Roman Church. Because of new linguistic insights, the past has been treated as having little bearing on current discussions of the meaning of truth. A wide and disparate variety of doctrine is taught in Roman Catholicism these days under the banner of orthodoxy.

THE ORTHODOX TRADITION AND THE WORK OF CHRIST

The Orthodox Church, like the Roman Catholic and the Protestant churches, is a confessional community.

197

Indeed, a distinguishing feature of this particular community is the elevation of the ancient creeds to an inviolate status. As the Scriptures are part of tradition as an authority source, so are the creedal formulations and the church's scholars. As to the meaning of the death of Christ, the *Acts and Decrees of the Synod of Jerusalem,* under Dositheus (1641–1707), patriarch of Jerusalem, in 1672, states: "We believe our Lord Jesus Christ to be the only mediator, and that in giving Himself a ransom for all He hath through His own blood made a reconciliation between God and man, and that Himself having a care for His own is advocate and propitiation for our sins" (VIII). *The Longer Catechism of the Orthodox Catholic, Eastern Church* (1839), an exposition of the Nicene-Constantinopolitan Creed, in answer to the question "How does the death of Jesus Christ upon the cross deliver us from sin, the curse, and death?" states:

> As in Adam we had fallen under sin, the curse, and death, so we are delivered from sin, the curse, and death in Jesus Christ. His voluntary suffering and death on the cross for us, being of infinite value and merit, as the death of one sinless, God and man in one person, is both perfect satisfaction to the justice of God, which had condemned us for sin to death, and a fund of infinite merit, which has obtained him the right, without prejudice to justice, to give us sinners pardon of our sins, and grace to have victory over sin and death. (208)

The language employed in the description of the atonement of Christ is such that it might lead the inquirer away from an important distinction between the Orthodox churches and the Western churches. Eastern scholars complain that the Roman Catholic Church and the Protestant churches have been unduly influenced by the legal and judicial terminology used by Augustine and Anselm of Canterbury. Whereas the Catholic Church, for example, has stressed the legal proceedings between the sinner, the sin-bearing Christ, and a forgiving and justifying Father, the Eastern churches feel that such an emphasis has disjointed the unity of the death and resurrection—

death occurred, yes, but so did the victory in and through it. The Eastern churches do not stress the death of Christ so much as they do the result of that death. The characteristic emphasis is, therefore, upon our union with Christ and the deification of humanity as the believer, through Christ's victory, becomes more conformed to His image (this is referred to as "theosis," Godlikeness). Daniel Clendenin came to the crux of the issue when he wrote, "This accent on legal concepts, in contrast to the idea of mystical union perpetuated in the East, is seen by Orthodoxy as the real issue that unites the West theologically [that is, both Catholics and Protestants] and divides it from the East."[35] Instead of seeing Christ as victim, the Eastern churches prefer to see Him as the victor—a theme seen in the early church writers as well as more recently in Karl Barth, among others.

With all of this said concerning this essential distinction of perspectives on the atonement between the Eastern and Western churches, the comments of Daniel Clendenin and Timothy Ware[36] are confusing when they end their discussion by minimizing the differences. They suggest that each of the ancient orthodoxies actually believe the same things, but the difference is in emphases. If the Eastern churches do not deny legal aspects in the death of Christ, as are clearly evident in Athanasius, for example, and traces of "theosis" or union and conformity to God are evident in the Western church leaders, and if each actually embraces what the other is accused of seriously denigrating, one wonders why these issues cannot be resolved by teaching what has been neglected in each tradition.

199

6

Salvation: A Story of Sin and Grace

There are a few hymns that seem to have a nearly universal attraction to the people of the Lord. These are songs sung by believers near and far, several centuries ago and today. Each has somehow poetically captured the heartfelt wonder of Christians for the beauty of God, the gift of the Lord Jesus Christ, and the forgiveness of sin through the work of the Holy Spirit. One of these is Reginald Heber's "Holy, Holy, Holy," a majestic description of God's being. Then there is "Amazing Grace," John Newton's grand testimonial to God's mercy in granting forgiveness to sinners. Another is "Rock of Ages" by Augustus Toplady, a poem that extols the unmerited grace of God and the helplessness of human endeavor. Those who know of true Christianity have experienced the content of these songs. They are aware of the blinding, rapturous vision of God's holy character and the sweet sense of divine release following the knowledge of condemnation. They know that it is only through fleeing from the dark labyrinth of the inner self to find a refuge in Christ that there is any hope for the troubled soul.

We come in our study of the history of doctrine to the very core of the gospel in its applicational sense. Here the discussion concerns the acquisition of the mercies of Christ made possible through God's gracious gift of His Son. In the mystery of the wisdom of God from eternity, He willed to bring glory to Himself through the redemption of sinners. How could God be anything but wrathful toward the rebellious? The answer lies in humankind's healing and restoration. What humankind could not do, being separated from the righteousness of God, God Himself did in granting to us His Son, who became for us both judgment and righteousness. It is Christ's penalty-paying sacrifice that appeased God so that He could freely and justly forgive us. Christ merited for us forgiveness and righteousness.

The issue before us in this chapter is that of what the sinner is to do, or can do, to receive this gracious forgiveness. It's all about sin and grace — the sin that is in humankind and the grace that flows from Christ. These are profoundly interrelated doctrines. In fact, as many have argued, the character of the salvation that is in Christ can never be comprehended apart from the sin that is in humankind. George Fisher summarized the point well: "The one word which expresses both the nature and end or aim of Christianity is Redemption. The correlate of Redemption is sin. Parallel, therefore, in importance with the doctrine of Redemption in the Christian system is the doctrine of sin. The two doctrines, like the facts which they represent, are mutually inseparable."[1] A teaching that does not take into account the biblical data of the devastating impact of sin will inevitably result in a heightened view of human ability to effect needed change and will correspondingly denigrate the centrality of Christ and His atonement. If one has the ability to right wrongs, a divine intervention is unnecessary; the degree that he or she does not have that strength is the degree that assistance or rescue is necessary.

The History of the Doctrine of Salvation

The Ancient Church	The Medieval Church	The Reformation Church	The Modern Church
Formulation ↗	*Sacramentalized* ↘	*Rediscovered* ↗	*Re-evaluation* ↘
Origen	Gregory I	1. **Stated**	Kant
Tertullian	Anselm	Calvin	Schleiermacher
Cyprian	Aquinas	Luther	Ritschl
Ambrose		2. **Reactions**	Bushnell
Augustine		Socinus	
		Arminius	
		School of Saumur	

202

Thus, in the human saga of redemption, we come to the place where anthropologists, sociologists, psychologists, and theologians differ. It is no small matter to decide. Is Christ a helper or a gratuitous Savior? Did He come to show us the way or to be the Way?

Answers to such important questions can be provided through the pages of our past. Though stained by human bias and ignorance, history nevertheless provides a lens to look at any subject. It alerts us to how people before us have sought to answer certain questions, and it records for us how they used Scripture to formulate their opinions. This imperfect volume of knowledge, called the history of the church, remains a valuable tool in our search for an understanding of the Holy Scriptures.

THE ANCIENT CHURCH AND SALVATION
(100–600)

In the ancient period most of the issues that later generations of Christian theologians would discuss in relation to salvation were already being raised. The doctrine of salvation remained largely undeveloped in the earliest period, but by the time of Pelagius and Augustine, Christians were wrestling with such weighty issues as the human ability to believe in God and the necessity of grace in the regeneration of a sinner.

THE CHURCH FATHERS AND SALVATION (100–150)

To look upon a previous time through the lens of a later period renders, at best, a certain distorting and twisting of the facts. That in a prior time the church was not consumed with a necessity to reflect on questions that are subsequently compelling is not abnormal. However, to allow the data from an early period to be authoritative in later discussions calls for caution because contexts influence how truth is presented. What this insight implies for a discussion of the doctrine of salvation is that the church fathers, as has been the case in every doctrine we have surveyed, were not preoccupied with untangling the paradoxes in the proclamation of the gospel that would occupy church leaders in the later centuries. The

203

issue among these fathers was not so much a reasoned defense and explanation of the hope of the church as it was the proclamation of that hope through witness of life and word. This is not to suggest that one particular activity of the church in its ever-changing situations is superior to that of another. While the issues that attracted the interest of church leaders changed, bringing with them a needed alteration of approach or tactics, the continuity through all the centuries has been the inspiring drive to proclaim the forgiveness of God in Christ. Issues that create a volcanic upheaval of rhetoric may be passed over in silence by others because the discussion was never raised as pertinent. This is certainly the case with the church fathers. As Kelley has noted,

> For the most part . . . they are rehearsing the clichés of cate-chetical instruction, so that what they say smacks more of affirmation than explanation. While taking it for granted that men are sinful, ignorant and in need of true life, they never attempt to account for their wretched plight.[2]

The church fathers understood that humanity was in need of the Savior and that human sin was the cause of our distance from God. Clement of Rome (d. 101?), an early elder, stated in his Letter to the Corinthians that redemption is through the Lord Jesus Christ and not by our works. "We, therefore, who have been called by His will in Christ Jesus, are not justified by ourselves, neither by our wisdom or understanding or piety, nor by the works we have wrought in holiness of heart, but by the faith by which almighty God has justified all men from the beginning" (32). The so-called *Letter of Barnabas*, which is actually a theological treatise by an anonymous writer in the second century, manifests the same themes. "Before we believed in God the habitation of our heart was corrupt and weak. . . . When we received the remission of sins and set our hope in the Name, we were made anew and created again from the beginning. Now God truly dwells in us, in the habitation which we are" (16). The writer of the *Epistle to Diognetus*, a work addressed to a political official, describes a salvation that is only in Christ.

204

> When our iniquity was complete, and it had become perfectly clear that punishment and death were its expected recompense, and the time came which God had appointed to show forth His kindness and power . . . He did not hate or reject us. . . . Indeed what else could cover over our sins except His righteousness? In whom was it possible for us, in view of our wickedness and impiety, to be justified, except in the Son of God alone. . . . That the righteousness of the One should justify the wicked many! (9)

Beyond these scattered statements by writers whose focus was upon the implications of being a Christian in a hostile culture, there is no synthesis of the teaching of the relationship of humankind's sin to the reception of God's unmerited favor in Christ.

THE APOLOGISTS AND SALVATION (150–300)

The universality of human sinfulness and the need for divine grace in Christ was acknowledged in a general form by the church. The apologists, who were the first to synthesize the teachings of the church and thus may be called our first theologians, frequently grappled with the issues of sin and grace in their polemics, the church being called upon to defend itself from different quarters as it advanced in the empire. To bring the discussion into sharper focus, the questions before us are two: Is humanity's power to do good diminished by sin, and if so, to what extent? What is the precise relationship between human will and the workings of God in granting salvation?

The Eastern Apologists and Salvation

Justin Martyr (c.100–c.165) had a fairly developed understanding of sin and grace, which he expressed in his defenses of the Christian faith. As with the apologists as a whole, Martyr had no conception of any debilitating connection or inheritance from the fall of Adam. He treated the sin of Adam as a yielding to the devil's devices, a happening that is replicated in our experience. Sinfulness is a matter of having

205

been conditioned to make bad choices. "We were totally unaware of our first birth . . . and were trained in wicked and sinful customs. In order that we do not continue as children of necessity and ignorance, but of deliberate choice and knowledge . . . " (*Apology* I.61). While redemption is only through Christ, sin is more a behavior or habit of moral life than it is an obstacle to salvation. Martyr would say that sin has not affected the ability of humankind to freely choose Christ, which they may do.

> We have been taught, are convinced, and do believe that He approves of only those who imitate His inherent virtues, namely, temperance, justice, love of man, and any other virtue proper to God who is called by no given name. . . . If men by their actions prove themselves worthy of His plan, they shall, we are told, be found worthy to make their abode with Him. . . . Our Creation was not in our own power. . . . But this—to engage in those things that please Him and which we choose by means of the intellectual faculties He has bestowed to— this makes our conviction and leads to faith." (*Apology* I.28)

Such statements about the ability of humankind, which seem to minimize the effect of sin on moral choices, can be understood in light of the polemic of the church leaders against the Gnostic sects which asserted that the Christian faith denied moral responsibility. In defending themselves, the apologists affirmed freedom of the will. William Shedd summarized the point succinctly:

> At a time when the truth that man is a responsible agent was being denied by the most subtle opponents which the Christian theologians of the first century were called to meet, it was not to be expected that very much reflection would be expended upon the side of the subject of sin which relates to weakness and bondage of the apostate will.[3]

Two other apologists in the East are worthy of particular attention, Clement of Alexandria (c.150–c.215) and Origen (c.185–c.254). Both men, being identified with the prominent church of Alexandria, Egypt, defined Alexandrian theology as it took shape in the struggle against the Gnostic heretics of the day. As is normally the case, the bulwark erected to defend the church shaped the expression of its faith—for both good and bad. Clement understood that Adam was created with the potential of an increase of virtue but wasted the possibility through the indulgence of the will in sinful practice. Through humankind's physical descent from Adam, we have inherited a warped sensuality whereby we are subject to irrationality. He insisted upon the necessity of divine grace to assist in the process of moral improvement, teaching that the initiative in the renewal and change of the sinful heart is taken by the person; the first motion toward holiness is the work of the individual, with the assistance of God following.

> A man by himself, working and toiling from passion, achieves nothing. But if he plainly shows his great desire and complete sincerity in this, he will attain by the addition of the power of God. Indeed, God conspires with willing souls. But if they abandon their eagerness, the spirit which is bestowed by God is also restrained. To save the unwilling is to exercise compulsion; but to save the willing belongs to Him who bestows grace. Nor does the kingdom of heaven belong to the sleeping and the lazy; rather, the violent take it by force." (*Who Is the Rich Man That Is Saved?* 21)

Origen was unique among early church leaders because he denied the historicity of the fall of Adam, treating it as an allegory of a precosmic disordering of humanity. He felt that the best way to defend the church against the Gnostic assertion of Christian fatalism was to suggest a pretemporal existence of the soul and a voluntary, individualized corrupted state (such as that which befell some angels). Many pure spirits or souls participated in varying degrees in the archangels' rebellion. Those less criminally indicted were confined to mortal bodies;

others became demons. Hence, humans come into the world in a state of rational and moral disorientation, the body being a form of judgment (*The Fundamental Doctrines* 2.9.6). Thus, "every rational soul has free will and choice; also, that it has a struggle against the devil and his angels and opposing powers, in which they strive to burden it with sin, while we if we live rightly and properly, should endeavor to shake ourselves free from any disgrace" (1.Preface.5). To defend free will as he defined it, he denied the devastating impact of sin on humankind's moral abilities and made salvation appear to be a morality contest brought about by a causative cooperative endeavor between the creature and the Creator. "The human will is not enough for the obtaining of the end. . . . For these things are accomplished by God's assistance. . . . Thus, our own perfection is accomplished neither by our doing nothing, nor yet is it complete by us; but God does the greater part of it" (3.1.18).

The Western Apologists and Salvation

For whatever reasons—perhaps the absence of a strident Gnostic threat or the lack of attachment to Platonic thought, which laid an emphasis on the spiritual and mystical dimensions of life to the neglect of the physical and earthly—Western apologists took a different tack in explaining the fall of Adam and its effects. Tertullian (c.160–c.225), unlike Origen, viewed Adam as a historical figure and the human soul as having been created by God in him and passed, along with the body, from parent to child (a view called traducianism). "We acknowledge, therefore, that life begins with conception, because we contend that the soul begins at conception. Life begins when the soul begins" (*The Soul* 27). Further, he argued that every soul, though possessed of free will, is innately stained with the result of Adam's error. However, he did not set forth a clear doctrine of Adamic solidarity by explaining the manner of our participation in Adam's first sin, nor did he hint that guilt was passed on to Adam's progeny. Instead, our inheritance from Adam is a disordered sensuality, a proneness to irrationality. In the matter of inability and freedom, Tertullian was inconsistent. He waffled between the two views, first asserting one and then the other without seeking to explain how both might be valid. "Some things are by virtue of the divine compassion,

208

and some things are by virtue of our agency" (21). However, he stated that as the branch of a wicked tree cannot bear good fruit unless it be grafted into a good tree, and as branches are not self-grafting agents, so God's grace is greater than our free wills.

Irenaeus (c.130–c.200) expressed the same general view as his North African counterpart. Adam was created by God in His image, possessing rationality and free will, but voluntarily disobeyed, leading the race to ruin. "Through the disobedience of that one man . . . the many were made sinners and lost life" (*Against Heresies* 3.18.7). The fall of humanity in Adam did not entail a loss of human liberty. People are free to choose life or death.

> In man as well as in angels, he has placed the power of choice . . . so much so that those who had yielded obedience might justly possess what is good, given indeed by God, but preserved by themselves. On the other hand, they who have not obeyed . . . judgment: for God did kindly bestow on them what was good; but they themselves did not diligently keep it. . . . Rejecting therefore the good . . . they shall all incur the just judgment of God. (4.37.1)

THE THEOLOGIANS AND SALVATION (300–600)

In the centuries that preceded the concentrated work of Augustine to delineate the relationship of sin and grace in the confrontation with the Pelagians, the church's understanding of the nature of fallen humanity, as it relates to the call of God to salvation, only gradually emerged. The lack of discussion of such issues at the very core of Christian confession can be accounted for by several factors. First, the general outline of Christian orthodoxy was present in the earliest Christian writers. Salvation was viewed as a gift graciously given by God through the provision of Christ's death for undeserving people. The church was Christ-centered and cross-centered in proclamation and ritual. Second, as arguments are shaped by opponents, causing a perpetual imbalance, and as doctrine is formulated only at points of conflict and not holistically, the Gnostic and Manichaean accusation of Christian fatalism led to a counterdenial that resulted in an unbiblical stress on freedom. Third, it was only when an influential person in the church seriously denigrated the necessity of God's grace while exalting human ability that the church was compelled to define the issues more clearly. That is, the issues of sin and grace were not the definitive tension points in the earliest centuries of the church. This occurred through the Augustinian-Pelagian controversy of the fifth and sixth centuries. Fourth, Calvin suggested that early church leaders not only stressed freedom because "a frank confession of man's powerlessness would have brought upon them the jeers of the philosophers with whom they were in conflict" but also because "they wished to avoid giving fresh occasion for slothfulness to a flesh already indifferent toward good."[4] The fear of promoting moral laxity led to a stress on the moral imperatives and personal responsibility.

The Pre-Augustinian Eastern Theologians and Salvation
Prior to the defining discussion in the West in Augustine's day, church leaders in the East embraced doctrines resembling those of the earlier apologists, though there were discernible advances. For example, the doctrine of original sin was given greater emphasis, though people (through free will) were seen as causatively cooperating with God in salvation. Faith was perceived as the means of salvation. Athanasius (c.296–373), the influential Alexandrian bishop, perceived a unity between Adam's first sin and the race of humankind, but he did not understand that humankind participates in Adam's guilt. Gregory of Nazianzus (329/30–389/90) is an example of the times; he embraced an Adamic unity, noting the parallels between the second Adam and humankind, and stressed the voluntary power of the individual will. "When you hear, 'To whom it is given,' add, to those who incline that way. For when you hear, 'Not of him that willeth, nor of him that runneth, but of God that sheweth mercy,' I counsel you to think the same. . . . Even to wish well needs help from God" (*Oration* 37.13).

The Pre-Augustinian Western Theologians and Salvation

The Western portion of the Catholic Church was less impressed with the potency of Gnostic infiltration; accordingly, church leaders stressed to a greater degree than elsewhere the effects of sin on the will. The tendency was to place less emphasis on human ability and more upon divine grace, though a causative cooperationism crept into their language. Ambrose (c.339–397), the celebrated bishop of Milan, is a case in point. At times he spoke of Adamic solidarity and human guilt. "Adam existed and in him we all existed; Adam perished and in him all perished" (*Commentary on Luke* 7.234). Yet he stated, "In everything the Lord's power cooperates with man's efforts; our free will gives us either a propensity to virtue or an inclination to sin" (2.84). Hilary of Poitiers (c.315–367/8), called the "Athanasius of the West" for his strident defense of Nicene orthodoxy, illustrates the same inconsistency. He argued for identity in Adam's condemned state, but he also argued for causative cooperative ability to effect personal salvation.

> In preserving our righteousness, unless we are guided by God, we shall be inferior through our own nature. Wherefore, we need to be assisted and directed by his grace in order to attain the righteousness of obedience. The persevering in faith is of God, but the origin and commencement of faith is from ourselves. It is part of divine mercy to assist the willing, to confirm those who are making a beginning, to receive those who are approaching. But the commencement is from ourselves, that God may finish and perfect. (*Commentaries on the Psalms* 119)

The Augustinian-Pelagian Controversy

Equipped with an impressive intellect, cultural refinement, and high moral qualities, Pelagius (c.354–after 418), a British monk, arrived in Rome around 380 and quickly emerged as a spiritual leader of both clergy and laity. Controversy over his religious views emerged through his teaching and writing (*Exposition of Paul's Epistles* 405) as well as an

-increasing body of convinced followers, principally Rufinus, Paulinus of Nola, Sulpicius Severus, and Celestius. The essence of his teaching had to do with the nature of humankind as it relates to the sin of Adam; only by implication is the argument about the freedom of the will. Does humankind have the ability to do what divine justice demands of us? This question ultimately hinges on an understanding of the nature of any liability inherited through Adam. The sum of Pelagius's teachings can be summarized in three basic postulates.

First, Pelagius and his followers taught that there was no connection between what Adam did and the state wherein we are born into the world. He opposed the doctrine of Adamic unity and guilt by birth inheritance. The state of birth, as it relates to Adam, is merely that of a tendency to follow bad examples, which, for some reason, we voluntarily emulate. There is no identity in Adam's fall, each person being born into the same state as Adam before the Fall and voluntarily falling from grace. Our condition is a voluntary one.

Second, with the doctrine of inherited inability disregarded, the corollary emerged — the freedom of humanity's will. By this, Pelagians taught that people have the ability to choose between good and evil. They possess a will inhibited only by a tendency to follow bad examples. The will is defined as a determining power, not as a selecting agent of the available options presented to it.

Third, grace is an assisting gift from God if one chooses to avail oneself of it. This "illuminating grace" influences humankind toward voluntary cooperation with God; it is a resistible grace.

A corollary of Pelagius's denial of human inability was the assertion that God's election of humankind to salvation was dependent upon His knowledge of the actions of the sinner if given a view of God's grace. The doctrine of inability and God's merciful intervention for humankind in determining the objects of His redeeming grace is the opposite of another corollary — the doctrine of human ability and the dependency of God upon the will of the creature to carry out His purposes.

When Augustine (354–430), the bishop of Hippo in North Africa, became aware of Pelagius's views, he perceived them as a threat to the life of the church. He responded with a barrage of polemical writings against his opponents. In contrast to Pelagius, Augustine argued that by Adam's first sin, in which the entire human race participated, sin came

212

into the world, corrupting every person both physically and morally. Everyone, being of Adam, is born into the world with a nature that is so corrupted that they can do nothing but sin. "Thence, after his sin, he was driven into exile, and by his sin the whole race of which he was the root was corrupted in him, and thereby subjected to the penalty of death" (*Enchiridon* 26). Humankind, according to Augustine, did not lose the ability to exercise the freedom of will; however, the exercise of the will was limited to only evil choices (freedom being defined as the capacity to make choices in conformity with one's desires).

Therefore, for Augustine, the need for grace was central. Our disfigured condition is not so much that we are unable to choose Christ; rather, it is that humanity does not have a desire to know Christ because we are unaware of His beauty. The effect of the unmerited favor of God is twofold: first, God reveals the wonder of His Son's redeeming mercies; and second, He strengthens the will so that humankind can freely embrace Christ as the sinner's only hope of forgiveness. This grace is irresistible. God, through grace, boasts the will, strengthens and stimulates it, so that the will itself, without any coercion, desires to love Christ. People do not save themselves, because they cannot, nor are they saved against their will, because they will not. The will is made compliant. "Neither the grace of God alone, nor he alone, but the grace of God with him . . . " (*On Nature and Free Will* 10).

Absolute inability on the sinner's part necessitates a divine initiative and drawing mercies. Further, since humankind is unable to be aware of God's grace, God could not have determined to save based upon a foreseen response of the sinner. Hence, God's mercies must be unconditional; His grace alone, not anything the creature could be foreseen to do (since, according to Augustine, he could do nothing), is the basis of God's choices. Thus, instead of basing redemption of the creature's "known" response, Augustine understood the salvation of humankind to be rooted in God's eternal predestination, or choice, to save whom He pleases.

Between grace and predestination there is only this difference, that predestination is the preparation for grace, while grace is the donation itself. When, therefore, the apostle says,

213

> "Not of works, lest any man should boast. For we are His workmanship, created in Christ Jesus unto good works," it is grace; but what follows— "which God hath prepared that we should walk in them"—is predestination, which cannot exist without foreknowledge. (*Predestination of the Saints* 19)

As the city of Rome was threatened by the ravages of Alaric, king of the Goths, in 409, Pelagius left with Celestius for North Africa and a hopeful confrontation with Augustine in Hippo. Shortly thereafter, he departed for the East, leaving his counterpart to explain his views. Augustine pushed for the condemnation of his opponent's views in two provincial councils in Carthage (412, 418). Emperor Honorius issued an edict against them; and Bishop Zosimus of Rome, who had formerly offered support, spoke against their views as well. To offset Pelagius's growing influence in the East, Augustine sent a Spanish presbyter, Orosius, to make his case, though Pelagius was acquitted in two synods there. In 431, at the third of the so-called ecumenical councils, this one held in Ephesus, Pelagius's views were universally condemned by the church. It appears, however, that Eastern bishops were more concerned with Christological issues as they related to the condemnation of Nestorianism than with Western interests in the doctrines of sin and grace. They were willing to raise their collective voice against Pelagius to secure Western support, essentially that of Bishop Celestine of Rome, against Nestorius. As important as Christological issues were in the East, that's how important anthropological issues were in the West. Actually, error in both areas of the church's teaching represented a threat to the life and health of the church.

The Cassian Controversy and the Synod of Orange (529)

Though Pelagius's view of human ability was condemned by the Council of Ephesus, and though the church, at least in the West, embraced Augustine's understanding of sin and grace, Augustine's doctrine of predestination was vigorously opposed by many who would otherwise oppose Pelagius. The controversy, therefore, continued not in North Africa, where the Vandals destroyed a once-vibrant Christianity, but in Gaul (France), the new intellectual center in the West. The tendency among the church leaders was to separate the doctrine of predestination from the doctrine of the necessity of God's unmerited favor.

John Cassian (c.360–after 430) appeared in the West in the early fifth century, having been educated in the East, and was a friend of John Chrysostom, the famous bishop of Constantinople. Having established himself as a prominent monk in Marseilles, and being largely responsible for the spread of monastic ideals in the West, Cassian entered the controversy between Augustine and Pelagius by proposing a mediating view.

Cassian argued that while death and the corruption of human nature passed from Adam to all his progeny, it merely weakened humankind's powers for good. Whereas Augustine argued that Adamic unity involved complete human impotence, and whereas Pelagius suggested that humankind came into the world healthy, Cassian proposed that we are partially disabled. Therefore, grace is needed to save us, but the nature of the required help is only that of the assistance and strengthening of natural abilities. In teaching causative cooperative ability, he asserted that God does most of what is needed to save the sinner, though not all. Each person often, though not always, does a part to earn salvation. Thus, he rejected the concept of unconditional election and based predestination on foresight rather than foreknowledge. Those who perish do so against God's will. Said Cassian, "When His [God's] kindness sees in us even the very smallest spark of good-will shining forth or which He Himself has, as it were, struck out from the hard flint of our hearts, He fans it and nurses it with His breath, as 'He will have all men to be saved'" (*Spiritual Discourse* 13).

Others joined in mounting an attack on Augustine's views, principally Vincent of Lérins (d. c.450) and Faustus of Riez (d. c.490). The approach of Vincent of Lérins was to suggest that his opponents' views were new to the church; that is, usage determines validity (*Commonitorium* 26). Faustus argued that faith is not real without free will. Without the power of contrary choice, humankind cannot be said to be truly free. Since we are free, and Christ having died for everyone, he argued that God has restored to us a free will. Election and predestination, accordingly, are based on what God foresaw the creature would do when presented with a choice (*On Grace and Free Will* 1.11).

215

Opposing the Cassians was Prosper of Aquitine (c.390–c.463) and Hilary of Arles (c.401–449). In the growing controversy, a series of synods were called that culminated in the Synod of Orange (529). The bishops of Rome, who generally held Augustine's views in high esteem, rejected Cassian's semi-Pelagian opinions while ignoring the doctrine of predestination. As a result of this synod, a moderate Augustinianism prevailed through the insistence of Felix IV and Boniface II of Rome. The canons affirmed Adamic solidarity in guilt and spiritual death, embraced the concept of human inability to cooperate with God in causing salvation, denied freedom of the will, and affirmed that salvation is a gift from God through Christ without any human merit. "Whoever says that the grace of God can be bestowed in reply to human petition, but not that grace brings it about so that it is asked for by us contradicts Isaiah the prophet and the Apostle [Isaiah 65:1; Romans 10:20]" (Canon 3). Though the synod's findings were Augustinian in tone, they were only moderately so. While election was recognized, unconditional election was not mentioned (though it was implied), grace was not seen as irresistible, and predestination was expressly anathematized. The synod advocated cooperative salvation from an Augustinian perspective.[5] The synod's findings were referred to the bishop of Rome, who approved the resolutions, thus setting the pattern for Catholic theology in the medieval period, a semi-Augustinianism.

THE MEDIEVAL CHURCH AND SALVATION (600–1500)

Three distinct periods of development in the doctrine of salvation are detectable during the medieval era. So we will look at this subject using the following breakdown: early medieval church (600–950), middle medieval church (950–1300), and late medieval church (1300–1500).

THE EARLY MEDIEVAL CHURCH (600–950)

*A*s the church progressed through the centuries after the Synod of Orange, Augustine's views on the cor-

216

ruption of human nature and the necessity of the Holy Spirit in regeneration continued to be affirmed. That is, the teaching of the enslavement of the will to evil and the need for the unmerited grace of God to redeem was affirmed. What gradually receded in importance were the teachings of divine predestination and unmerited election. These "harsher doctrines," which seem to flow consistently from the doctrine of inability, were rejected. An example of this tendency in theology was Gregory I of Rome (c.540–604), who affirmed Augustine's views generally but rejected Augustine's views of predestination and irresistible grace. A sort of divine-human causative cooperationism seems to be in view when Gregory writes, "The good we do is both of God and of ourselves. It is God's prevenient grace, ours through obedient free will. And again, if it is not ours, why do we hope that a reward will be given us? . . . And again, it is not improper that we seek a reward, because we know that by obedient free will we chose to do what is good" (*Moralia* 33.21.40).

In the ninth century, the Western church was disturbed by a renewal of Augustine's views in the teachings of Gottschalk of Orbais (c.804–c.869). Though harsher than Augustine in his advocacy of predestination, this monk's opinions were a reiteration of those of his mentor. In his case, at least, the church evidenced that it had progressed beyond the views of Augustine. Gottschalk was opposed by Rabanus Maurus (c.780–856), abbot of Fulda, and Hincmar (c.806–882), bishop of Reims, and silenced by imprisonment. The actions taken against this monk indicate that Augustine's views were less consistently revered in the church. Predestination was seen by fewer church leaders as the answer to human inability, irresistible grace was displaced with cooperative grace, and foresight replaced the foreknowledge of God as the determinate of salvation.

THE MIDDLE MEDIEVAL CHURCH AND THE SCHOLASTICS (950–1300)

Scholasticism denotes the theology and philosophy of the period between Anselm and the Reformation. It suggests an educational shift from a monastic educational theory (which emphasized the passivity of the intellect, inner submissiveness of heart, and the contemplative life) to a cathedral and university educational model (which stressed the use of the mind and the rational nature Christianity). This shift can be explained in part by apologetical needs arising in the church from its confrontation with Islam.

Anselm of Canterbury (c.1033–1109) seems to have embraced the theological ideas of Augustine in a less abrasive but inconsistent manner. He taught that humankind owes to God "justice or rectitude of will, which makes persons upright or right of heart" (*Cur Deus Homo* 11). This, however, was lost through the actions of Adam, and humankind comes into the world condemned for their lack of righteousness. "In regard to these infants, I cannot understand this sin I am calling 'original' to be anything else than that same deprivation of the required justice, which I described before as a result of the disobedience of Adam, by which all are children of wrath" (*The Virgin Conception* 27). Like Augustine, Anselm defined the freedom of the will as an ability to make choices. The Fall did not destroy the freedom of the will, but it did limit the choices one can make; that is, humanity is free only to choose evil (choices being a reflection of human nature). Freedom, according to Anselm, is the ability to continue in an upright will. This was lost in Adam, though the will was not. We are free, but having lost uprightness, we are only free to sin. Salvation is a gift from God to humanity, yet humanity has the ability to resist God's grace. Salvation grace is a free and unmerited gift from God, not in any human merit. Jasper Hopkins summarizes the point in this way: "Thus Anselm can speak of faith as coming through grace; and like Augustine, he can silently leave it a mystery why this grace, which cooperates with the act of faith by being its necessary precondition, should be given to some men and not to others."[6]

A gradual shift occurred in the medieval period in the perception of grace in salvation; that is, grace came to be seen as given to the professing Christian gradually, not instantaneously. With this insight, redemption was perceived as a process that culminated in salvation at the time of death or, more likely, after some period of time in purgatory. The acquisition of degrees of grace was through the sacramental system. Christ's death was understood to have procured forgiving grace, but that grace was merely made available. Reception of grace was tied increasingly to the sacraments.

On the subject of salvation as a sacramental process, perhaps no writer outshone Peter Lombard (c.1100–1160), a teacher in the Cathedral School of Notre Dame in Paris and writer of the most influential book of the medieval period, *The Four Sentences,* prior to the works of Thomas Aquinas. The book became immensely popular in academic circles, with students writing innumerable summaries of it. However, the difficulty with the book was that its conclusions were often vague. The teachings of Lombard became crucial in the development of what would become classic Roman Catholic theology in the Reformation era.

Lombard, like Anselm, defined the inheritance from Adam as the absence of righteousness as well as a propensity to wrong actions. Further, though salvation begins with an initial infusion of grace, grace must be increased if it is to bear fruit in eternal life. The means of the increase of grace are the sacraments. Justification is not an instantaneous act of imputation but the result of gradual infusion. Salvation is through the grace purchased by Christ alone in His appeasement of God the Father. The means of obtaining the grace of Christ is the gracious provision of the sacraments. While Lombard was not the first in the church to posit seven sacraments (Bernard had several more), his popular textbook promoted that number and articulated their function.

Of greater importance than Lombard was the Dominican scholar Thomas Aquinas (c.1225–1274). The place accorded this great teacher in the formulation of Roman Catholic theology was stated by Pope Leo XIII on August 4, 1879, when he suggested that the "greatest and most special honor was given to the Angelic Doctor at the Council of Trent, when, during its sessions, together with the Bible and the formal decrees of the Sovereign Pontiffs, the Fathers of the Council had the open *Summa* [his most important work] placed upon the altar so that thence they might draw counsels, arguments, and oracles." In the tradition of Augustine, through the Synod of Orange, Aquinas argued that humankind is an absolute debtor to God and cannot merit salvation. "It is impossible that any creature should cause grace" (*Summa Theologica* Q. 112.1). People can and ought prepare themselves for God's grace, but it is no guarantee that God will extend mercy. "Hence, however much a man prepares himself, he does not necessarily receive grace from God" (Q. 112.3). Thomas seems to have been confused when it came to the doctrine of justification, because he clearly affirmed that it is an instantaneous act, on God's part, of declaring the sinner righteous, and yet he spoke of justification as a process. "The justification of the ungodly consists as to its origin in the infusion of grace. . . . Now the infusion of grace takes place in an instant and without succession" (Q. 113.7). However, he spoke of justification as a process and grace as capable of being lost. Thomas followed Augustine's confusion of justification and sanctification, the essence of justification being an infusion of sanctifying grace that can be increased through the means of the sacraments, possibly culminating in final grace. "Sacraments are necessary for man's salvation, in so far as they are sensible signs of invisible things whereby man is made holy" (Q. 61.3). Elsewhere he wrote, "And it is thus that the sacraments of the New Law cause grace: for they are instituted by God to be employed for the purpose of conferring grace" (Q. 62.1).

THE LATE MEDIEVAL CHURCH AND THE SCHOOLMEN (1300–1500)

The church after Aquinas entered a confusing period. On the eve of the Reformations, the church had drifted from semi-Augustinianism to semi-Pelagianism and, at times, even to Pelagianism. It was the opinion of many that the church was in need of moral and theological reform. A Roman Catholic scholar summarized the distortion of teaching this way:

> The church's spiritual wealth was thought to consist in the "merits" which Jesus had accrued through obedience during his life and death. This capital, though it was limitless, was to be spent judiciously in return for the proper performance of certain tasks. Clerics earned quantities of it by carrying out the eucharistic ritual, and could apply what they earned where they wished; for example, to cancel out the eschatological punishment which some sinner was facing. Even lay

220

> people could earn shares of the merits of Christ by saying words and doing deeds to which ecclesiastical authorities had attached "indulgences." How did it happen that Christians came to construe their relationship with God as a kind of invisible ledger sheet?[7]

The most prominent voices in the *via moderna*, the modern way, as it came to be called, were William of Ockham (c.1285–1347), a Franciscan friar who taught at Oxford and Munich; Robert Holcot (d. 1349), a Dominican friar who taught at Oxford and Cambridge; and Gabriel Biel (c.1420–1495), who is associated with the founding of the University of Tübingen. The essence of their teaching was that the grace of God is granted on the basis that we do the best we can. Said Holcot, "According to God's established law the pilgrim who does what he can to dispose himself for grace always receives grace."[8] Gregory of Rimini (d. 1358) described the state of the church's teaching this way: "It is the opinion of many moderns that man, by his natural powers alone, with the general concurrence of God, can perform a morally good act in the present state of fallen nature, as for example to love God above all things, to be sorry for and to detest one's sins. . . . They depart from the definitions of the church and favor the condemned error of Pelagius." The popular teaching by many in the church has been summarized by a contemporary today: "Many in the medieval church believed that God saved by grace, but they also believed that their own free will and cooperation was 'their part' in salvation. The popular medieval phrase was, 'God will not deny his grace to those who do what they can.' Today's version, of course, is 'God helps those who help themselves.'"[9]

THE EARLY MODERN CHURCHES AND SALVATION (1500–1750)

It is not too much to suggest that the church of the fourteenth and fifteenth centuries was in need of repair. While the common people

221

blended an oft-distorted version of Christian teachings with magic and superstition, the church's leadership often evidenced avarice, ignorance, and neglect. From Giovanni Boccaccio, Dante, and Erasmus, social criticism and ridicule was heaped upon the clergy of the day. The complaints of John Wycliffe, John Huss, and Girolamo Savonarola about the life of the church had a ring of reality to them. The time had come for change. Indeed, change was in the air; it was the era of the Renaissance and the discoveries of Columbus.

While many shared a belief that the church was in need of reformation, there was no uniform agreement as to the depth of the problem or the solution. It was in this era that the church suffered schism; there was no general consensus as to the nature of the correction of the church. As a result, two major traditions, neither disjoined from a selected past, were formed: the Protestant churches and the Roman Catholic Church. They disagreed on the nature of the changes that were needed and, more importantly, on the nature of theology that would support those changes. It is in the areas of sin and grace, as well as several ancillary teachings, that the essence of the differences between the two traditions are found.

THE ROMAN CATHOLIC CHURCH AND SALVATION

While Roman Catholics and Protestants have made use of the history of the church to sustain the validity of their claims, both have used the past selectively, emphasizing those writings that support their cause. By neglect as well as selection, the past is brought into "court," where a less than impartial jury renders a verdict. This gets to the heart of a difference between these traditions that has been noted earlier. Protestants certainly use the past, though they often neglect to treat it fairly, but they are adamant that creeds and councils are secondary. In other words, they embrace a notion of discontinuity between apostolic instruction and the church's teachers. The Bible is infallible, say conservative Protestants; interpretation gains its validity only by approximation to the Bible. Roman Catholics, however, see a greater unity between later teachings in the church and those of the apostolic age. That is, to sustain its truth claim, the Roman Catholic tradition has an authority source at least equal to

222

the Bible—namely, the teaching magisterium of the church—that selectively uses the past to sustain its claims. Historically, the crux for Protestants in approaching religious truth is conformity to the Bible, or at least a lack of conflict with it.

The great defining moment of the Roman Catholic tradition was the Council of Trent (1545–1563). Meeting to consider the reform of the church, Roman Catholic leaders defined themselves in such a fashion as to clearly separate themselves from the emerging Protestant movements on the European continent and England. It seems that what the scholars did at Trent was to gather together favorable teachings from selected sources through the centuries, claiming to be setting forth only what the church had everywhere and exclusively taught for all time.

The Council of Trent and Sin

The Canons and Dogmatic Decrees of the Council of Trent explicitly affirm the doctrine of the Adamic unity of humankind and a real participation in Adam in his first sin. Sin, death, and divine wrath were occasioned by Adam so that all are born into the world spiritually separated from God—"the death of the soul" (5.2). Thus, infants, though they do so without any actual sins, come into the world in need of divine cleansing. This cleansing from the vile implications of Adam's disobedience is effected through the sacrament of baptism. "For, by reason of this rule of faith [that children are born in need of cleansing], from the tradition of the apostles, even infants, who could not as yet commit any sin of themselves, are for this cause truly baptized for the remission of sins, that in them that may be cleansed away by regeneration, which they have contacted by generation" (5.4). Baptism, having removed the guilt of Adam's sin, leaves the child in a state of innocence with a free will that may or may not choose to sin (though, for some unexplained reason, all people do choose sin). The Roman Catholic Church is quite clear on this point. "If any one denies, that, by the grace of our Lord Jesus Christ, which is conferred in baptism, the guilt of original sin is remitted; or even asserts that the whole of that which has the true and proper nature of sin is not taken away . . . let him be anathema" (5.5). In the instance of baptism, a child is saved in the same manner as the repenting thief upon the cross next to Christ—apart from any works and merely through the grace of God.

Unlike the infant, the thief had both original sin and actions of sin that required cleansing; unlike the infant, the thief expressed heartfelt faith in the person of the Savior. A proper inability and uncooperative disposition is removed by the grace of baptism so that continuance in that state and increase of that grace are all that are needed to come to a final salvation. Unlike the Reformers, Roman Catholic scholars viewed sin only as evil actions, not as the very nature of our being that remains with us until a final glorification. The issue is not so much about the birth defect of original sin as it is about when the effects of it are purged. Does the purging occur at the time of baptism or at glorification?

The Council of Trent and Grace

Within the official Roman Catholic community, salvation is by grace. However, Catholics view the granting of grace differently from how their Protestant counterparts view it. Roman Catholic scholars limit forgiveness to those sins already committed, not to future sins. Thus, justification is the gradual, experiential infusion of righteousness, not an instantaneous nonexperiential imputation. For Roman Catholics, justification has the idea of purging or removal of sin, a making of one right in thoughts and actions. For the Reformers, one is simultaneously a saint and a sinner, freely forgiven and laden with sin. Initial grace, which is granted through baptism, produces unformed, though complete, faith and gradually takes on the characteristics of a maturing faith. "The instrumental cause is the sacrament of baptism, which is the sacrament of faith, without which [faith] no man can ever be justified" (*Canons and Decrees* 6.7). While the gifts of grace are infused at once, they are capable of increase and decrease, leading to life or death. Justification is a process of becoming or being made more righteous.

> They, through the observance of the commandments of God and of the church, faith co-operating with good works, increase in that justice which they have received through the grace of Christ, and are still further justified. . . . And this increase of justification [the] holy church begs, when she prays. "Give unto us, O Lord, increase of faith, hope, and charity." (6.10)

Justification is thus the gradual infusion of Christ's virtues into the one claiming to be justified (6.16). While works and merit are grace-caused, there can be no salvation without merits; grace and work are integrally related to the obtaining of salvation. "And, for this cause, life eternal is to be proposed to those working well unto the end, and hoping in God, both as a grace mercifully promised to the sons of God through Jesus Christ, and as a reward which is according to the promise of God himself, to be faithfully rendered to their works and merits" (6.16). The conflict over the meaning of the Scriptures between the Roman Catholic teachers and the Reformers is evident in the canons that follow the delineation of the doctrine of justification.

> If any one saith, that men are justified, either by the sole imputation of the justice of Christ, or the exclusion of the grace and the charity which is poured forth in their hearts by the Holy Ghost and is inherent in them; or even that the grace, whereby we are justified, is only the favor of God: let him be anathema. (II)

> If any one saith, that the good works of the one that is justified are in such manner the gifts of God, that they are not also the good merits which he performs through the grace of God and the merit of Jesus Christ, whose living member he is, does not truly merit increase of grace, eternal life, and the attainment of that eternal life, is so be, however, that he depart in grace,— also an increase of glory: let him be anathema. (XXXII)

The Council of Trent and the Sacraments

The function of the sacraments is monumentally important in the Roman Catholic view of the gradual infusion of justifying grace. Indeed, the sacraments are the means whereby the merit of Christ is accredited to the account of the faithful. In introducing the discussion of the sacraments in the seventh session at the Council of Trent, the

225

scholars noted, "For the completion of the salutary doctrine on Justification . . . it hath seemed suitable to treat of the most holy Sacraments of the church, through which all true justice either begins, or being begun is increased, or being lost is repaired." The council assigned anathemas to any who failed to see the sacraments as the instruments through which grace is accumulated from the treasury of Christ's merit (Canon IV, VII).

THE PROTESTANT CHURCHES AND SALVATION

For most Protestants today, the beginning of the reform of the church is identified with the protest of Martin Luther (1483–1546) when he complained of the perversion of the indulgence system in the posting of the Ninety-Five Theses on the Castle Church door in Wittenberg. Through a complexity of issues, not the least of which was his own nationalistic spirit and the costly endeavor of church renovation in Rome, Luther called for a debate among the scholars. This was made poignant to him when Johann Tetzel sold such "forgivenesses" to his parishioners. The assumptions of the indulgence system were several: first, sins have penalties that are exacted following contrition either in this life or in purgatory; second, an infinite treasury of Christ's forgiving merits is available through the church; and third, the church can dispense Christ's merits as is deemed wise. Doubting the validity of such church claims, Luther's uncertainty led to a growing confidence that such teachings were alien to the true teachings of the Bible. Thus began the storm that would change forever the Western Catholic Chalcedonian Church. From a Protestant viewpoint, Alister McGrath explains this great event in religious history. "You must never think of the Reformation solely as a negative thing, as a response to weakness. It was also about our rediscovery of the Gospel. . . . But in part, the Reformation was this glorious rediscovery of what God had already done for his people and would continue to do for them."[10]

The Lutheran Churches and Salvation

The Lutheran churches followed their founder closely in the subjects so close to his heart: sin and grace.

Lutheranism and sin. In his preface to the reply to Erasmus's *Diatribe of the Freedom of the Will,* Luther applauded his opponent for recognizing that he, among very few, had put his finger on the real issue that divided them. "I praise and commend you highly for this also, that unlike all the rest you alone have attacked the real issue, the essence of the matter in dispute." The essential point of contention was the degree of effect that Adam's sin has had upon the race. Erasmus's and Luther's differences of opinion did not lie in the understanding of the Adamic fall so much as upon the lasting nature of the effects of the fall on humankind, and especially on the role of the sacrament of baptism. Within Roman Catholic teachings, baptism is a laver of washing that cleanses from the guilt of Adamic identity; for Luther, the sacrament does not have this objective function because humankind's nature does not change as a result of a washing with water.

For Luther, water baptism does not cleanse the guilt and inability inherited through original sin. Humanity's will is in bondage and not free to act in any other way than in accord with its vain perpetual nature. Thus, any notion of causative cooperation, even a gracious cooperation, is impossible because humankind has no merit to commend itself to God. "Next: when Christ says in John 6: 'No man can come to me, except My Father which hath sent me draw him' (v.44), what does he leave to 'free-will'?"[11] *The Formula of Concord* (1560), a document that sought to define and clarify issues troubling the Lutheran churches, spoke of the ability of the unregenerate in this way:

> We believe, teach, and confess, moreover, that the yet unregenerate will of man is not only averse from God, but has become even hostile to God. . . . Therefore we believe that by much is it impossible that a dead body should vivify itself and restore corporal life to itself, even so impossible is it that man, who by reason of sin is spiritually dead, should have any faculty of recalling himself into spiritual life. (II.Aff.2)

To Luther, then, as to his followers, the very essence of the controversy of his day was grounded upon the belief that humankind's state was such before the holy and righteous God that there was nothing that people can do. If there is salvation, it must be of grace alone!

Lutheranism and grace. Flowing from the assumption that salvation must be of grace alone, a second issue emerged: justification by faith alone. Justification is a declarative act by God based solely on the meritorious work of Christ to appease God's wrath and grasped by simple, heartfelt faith. After quoting Romans 4:2-3 concerning Abraham's righteousness before God, Luther noted:

> Here, too, please take note of Paul's distinction as he recounts Abraham's twofold righteousness. The one is of work; that is, moral and civil. But Paul says that this did not justify Abraham in the sight of God, even though it made him righteous in the sight of men. . . . The other righteousness is that of faith, and consists, not in any works, but in the gracious favour and reckoning of God. See how Paul stresses the word "reckoned;" now he insists on it, and repeats it, and enforces it.[12]

Justification is not a process of becoming; that is the doctrine of sanctification. (Luther would argue that the principal error of Roman Catholic doctrine was a failure to define sin properly, thereby turning justification into a progressive sanctification that may or may not culminate in true righteousness.) Justification is an absolute divine decree.

The Augsburg Confession (1530) states this cardinal concept as follows:

> Also they [the Lutheran churches] teach that men can not be justified (obtain forgiveness of sins and righteousness) before God by their own powers, merits, or works; but are justified freely (of grace) for Christ's sake through faith, when they believe that they are received into favor, and their sins forgiven for Christ's sake, who by his death hath satisfied for our sins. This faith doth God impute for righteousness before God. (I.VI)

228

Lutheranism and the sacraments. The sacraments, baptism and the Eucharist, are seen as signs of God's goodwill and pleasure; they are testimonies or "a picture or seal" of God's grace already given and received in the Word of God. Behind the symbol or sacrament is the Word of God. The symbol has no efficacy; it is the Word of God that causes to happen what the symbol merely signifies. While stating that baptism "works forgiveness of sins, delivers from death and the devil" (IV.2), Luther then says in the *Small Catechism* in answer to the question "How can water do such great things?": "It is not water, indeed, that does it, but the Word of God which is with and in the water, and faith, which trusts in the Word of God in the water. For without the Word of God the water is nothing but water, and no baptism; but with the Word of God; it is a baptism — that is, a gracious water of life and a washing of regeneration" (IV.3). The sacraments, then, have a subjective function as a witness to faith in God's generosity; they do not have an objective function of being the actual means of acquiring God's grace. *The Augsburg Confession* makes this careful distinction.[13] "Wherefore they condemn those that teach that the sacraments do justify by the work done, and do not teach that faith which believes the remission of sins is requisite in the use of Sacraments" (I, XIII).

The Calvinist Churches

Generally the Protestant Reformers did not differ in their understanding of human inability, though Ulrich Zwingli (1484–1531) of Zürich and Philipp Melanchthon (1497–1560), Luther's successor, were qualified exceptions. They all began their discussion of salvation with the utter helplessness of humankind. From this insight came their understanding of salvation by grace alone and by Christ alone through faith alone. J. I. Packer has noted this point:

> Historically, it is a simple matter of fact that Martin Luther and John Calvin . . . and all the leading Protestant theologians of the first epoch of the Reformation, stood on precisely the same ground here. On other points they had their differences; but in asserting the helplessness of man and the sovereignty of God in grace, they were entirely at one.[14]

229

Calvinism and sin. Like Luther, the Genevan Reformer embraced the notion of Adamic solidarity. For Calvin, humankind participated in the disobedience of Adam and, therefore, everyone is born into the world without righteousness and under the wrath of God. Unlike the Roman Catholic scholars, Calvin believed that this state is not altered by the sacrament of baptism; humankind is lost apart from a heartfelt faith in Christ. *The Heidelberg Catechism* (1563) asks the question "Canst thou keep this [the law] perfectly?" The reply is brief: "No; for I am by nature prone to hate God and my neighbor" (I.5). Thus for Calvin, like Luther, the will is in bondage to evil; it is incapable of meriting salvation. *The Westminster Confession of Faith* (1647) notes: "Man, by his fall into a state of sin, hath wholly lost all ability of will to any spiritual good accompanying salvation; so as a natural man, being altogether adverse from that good, and dead in sin, is not able, by his own strength, to convert himself, or to prepare himself thereunto" (IX.3).

Calvinism and grace. Because of humankind's desperate condition, salvation has to be a work of God alone. Since it is from God, it must be based solely on the unmerited favor of God for the simple fact that, if God was caused to be moved to mercy by any thing other than Himself, it would not be of grace but of reward and merit. Salvation is by grace alone and by Christ alone through faith alone. Justification before God means a complete absolution of sin because of Christ's intermediary redemptive work. "'To justify' means nothing else than to acquit of guilt him who was accused, as if his innocence were confirmed. Therefore, since God justifies us by the intercession of Christ, he absolves us not by confirmation of our innocence, but by the imputation of righteousness, so that we who are not righteous in ourselves may be reckoned as such in Christ," wrote Calvin.[15] Whereas the Roman Catholic scholars joined inward personal righteousness with the righteousness of God, the Reformers despaired of any possibility of personal goodness and fled to Christ and His righteousness for refuge. In another place he concluded, "Thus the Lord helps us, not by leaving us a part of righteousness in our works and by supplying part out of his loving-kindness, but by appointing Christ alone as the fulfillment of righteousness."[16] This righteousness is through faith, a hearty trust in the promises of God. *The Westminster Confession*

230

summarized the point as follows: "Those whom God effectually cal-leth he also freely justifieth; not by infusing righteousness into them, but by pardoning their sins, and by accounting and accepting their persons as righteous: not for any thing wrought in them, or done by them, but for Christ's sake alone" (XI.1). Subsequently the writers of the confession added, "Faith, thus receiving and resting on Christ and his righteousness, is the alone instrument of justification" (XI.2).

Calvinism and the sacraments. Like the Lutherans, the Calvinists see the sacraments as having a confirming function as opposed to a redemptive force. They are symbols and signs of the invisible work-ings of God described in the Word of God. *The Westminster Shorter Catechism* defines a sacrament as a "sensible sign" whereby "the ben-efits of the new covenant are represented, sealed, and applied to believers" (Q. 92). Baptism, then, is an outward sign and seal "of his ingrafting into Christ, of regeneration, of remission of sins" (XXVIII.1). The function of the sacrament is declarative; it is a witness to the invisible workings of God in the soul through grace. It is not a means of the acquisition of redeeming grace.

Calvinism and Arminianism. In the ongoing defense of the Protestant faith, the Reformers struggled with the Roman Catholic party in the sixteenth century. In the seventeenth century they each encountered a common threat in the rising tide of rationalistic, reli-gious inquiry most poignantly expressed, among many voices, by the Socinians. One effect of the confrontation with these adverse senti-ments was dispute and division among Protestants themselves. Jacob Arminius (1560–1609), a Calvinist scholar, came to the conclusion that Calvinism should be altered for biblical as well as polemical rea-sons to adequately answer the attacks being hurled at the Christian faith. As Arminius was joined in the fray by others, a party emerged— the Arminians—that sought to remain firmly Protestant but at the same time release itself from poorly conceived defenses of the Christian faith. When compromise was not forthcoming among the antagonists, a third major theological tradition emerged, joining the Lutheran and Calvinists, as expressions of Protestant orthodoxy.

The essential disagreement between the Calvinists of Holland— sometimes called the Gomarists, borrowing from the name of Arminius's opponent Franciscus Gomarus (1563–1641)—and the

231

Arminian or Remonstrant party focused on the issues of the relationship of Adam's sin to the human race, including the degree of human inability, and the relationship between sovereignty and the human will. The Arminian party asserted that, while humankind has certainly fallen from grace, the inheritance from Adam includes neither guilt nor a sinful inclination of will. They confessed a corruptive influence in the realm of the moral and intellectual nature of humankind but argued that it did not affect the ability to make choices. The imputation of Adam's first sin, for which all humankind is born liable, does not entail an absolute inability to respond to God as Lutherans and Calvinists have affirmed. Arminius noted:

> It may admit of discussion, whether God could be angry on account of original sin which was born with us, since it seems to be inflicted upon us by God as a punishment for actual which had been by Adam, and by us in him. . . . I do not deny that it is sin, but it is not actual sin. . . . We must distinguish between actual sin and that which is the cause of other sins, and which on this very account may be denominated "sin."[17]

Thus, according to Arminius, humankind is punishable only for sins each has committed, having received no inherited corruption from Adam but merely disordered sensibilities. By such an assertion, the Remonstrant party felt it could counteract the charges that God is unfair and humankind is not free. God extends the same manner of grace to all; humankind is free to accept or reject it.

The second point has to do with the abilities of humanity as it relates to salvation. While the Arminians spoke of the impotency of the will in much the same phraseology as the Lutherans and Calvinists, they defined it differently. Though the will is viewed as unable to obey without the work of the Holy Spirit, the relationship between divine and human agency is that of cooperative assistance. Regeneration is explained not so much as the Holy Spirit overcoming a hostile will, melting it into compliance, as it is a work of God assisting and increasing the power of natural faculties to respond to God.

232

The influence of the Holy Spirit succeeds only to the degree that the human will concurs. Salvation is by the grace of God alone, but humanity can prevent the grace of God from becoming effective by refusing to receive it.

> That this grace of God is the beginning, continuance, and accomplishment of all good, even to this extent, that the regenerate man himself, without prevenient or assisting, awakening, following and co-operative grace, can neither think, will, nor do good . . . so that all good deeds or movements, that can be conceived, must be ascribed to the grace of God in Christ. (*The Five Remonstrants*, Article IV)

The Arminian view of human ability allows humanity to resist God's distribution of saving grace as well as to lose the grace cooperatively received.[18]

Calvinism, Saumurianism, and modified Calvinism. The further you are away from an object, the easier it is to generalize; greater proximity brings with it nuance and a need to qualify. While scholars debate whether or not Calvin was a Calvinist (at least as the term became defined by some of its later advocates), the unmistakable point is that the movement identified with the Genevan Reformer has been altered in the hands of its friends as the system advanced through different social and cultural settings. This can be argued for the Calvinism of Holland, the Arminians of Holland, and the Calvinism of the academy at Saumur, France.

Perhaps for many of the same reasons that the Remonstrant party sought a revision of Calvinism, though not in the same way, the Calvinist Moïse Amyraut (1596–1644) shaped a vibrant Calvinism in the school of Saumur. However, his publication of a *Brief Treatise on Predestination,* as well as other writings, divided the ranks of Reformed Protestantism once more. In his teaching, justification took precedence over predestination as a cardinal teaching (a shift from an emphasis on the work of God to Christ). Further, he advocated a hypothetical universalist view of the death of Christ—Christ's death

233

was for all humankind, not merely the elect. Josue de la Place (1596–1655), a disciple of Amyraut's, went so far as to attack the Calvinistic doctrine of the immediate imputation of Adam's sin to the race (that humankind is born with the guilt of Adam and sinful actions only verify it) for a mediate view (guilt, being rooted in personal actions, follows hereditary sin). The Reformed churches rejected this view in 1644. Claude Pajon (1626–1685) drifted further from Calvinism by arguing that God's persuasive influence is universal and that salvation is strictly humanity's choice. Such teaching allowed his students to pass beyond him into Arminianism and Romanism; the emphasis on natural revelation and human ability opened the door for Deist and Unitarian teachings in the churches. With all this stated, it is the less severe teachings of Amyraut that some suggest are more in accord with Calvin's than are later Reformed thought. By such an assertion, it is claimed that Calvin is the fountainhead of modified Calvinism.

Calvinism and Wesleyanism. John Wesley (1703–1791), the Anglican Reformer and unwitting founder of Methodism, explained the manner of redemption in such a way that his views defy categorization. He is a blend of Calvinism and Arminianism, being not quite either (conservative expressions of Methodism generally adhere to the tenets of Arminianism in these issues rather than to Wesley's position). As to the nature of humanity, he was explicitly Calvinistic in affirming Adamic solidarity and imputed guilt. "Original sin is conceived as inbred sin, as an evil root in man from which all other sin springs, both inward and outward sins" (*Sermons* I.11.534). In another place, he explained the imputation of Adam's first sin this way: "In Adam all die; that is, (1) Our bodies then became mortal. (2) Our souls died; that is, were disunited from God. And hence (3) We are all born with a sinful, devilish nature" (*Works* 7.277). However, he was a clear advocate of cooperative grace and causative ability. He wrote: "Wherein may we come to the very edge of Calvinism? In ascribing all good to the free grace of God. In denying all natural free-will, and all power antecedent to grace. And in excluding all merit from man; even for what he has or does by the grace of God" (*Works* 7.285).

Wesley was able to hold these two contradictory concepts—inability and ability—together by suggesting that the evil effects of Adamic unity are ameliorated prior to a work of saving grace through the application of the universal atonement of Christ. Through an initial witness to the gospel, called preventing grace, God begins the process of opening the darkened eye and creating a thirst for divine things. It is a work that leads to repentance if the person desires. Repentance leads to convincing or saving grace. Of repentance he noted:

> These works are not the effective cause of his acceptance with God. Yet God expects them, and looks upon them with favour, because they are the necessary token that the profession of penitence is indeed sincere. Thus good works meet for repentance, e.g., a sincere attempt to make amends for wrongs done to one's neighbor, are in a sense a previous condition of justification. (*Sermons* 2.451)

By defining sin in the believer as only acts of cognitive commission, not duties left undone or unknown misdeeds, Wesley was able to propound a doctrine of gradual perfectionism.

The Heterodox Groups and Salvation

The era of the Reformations must be seen in the larger context of the rise and progress of the Renaissance, an intellectual and cultural movement that spread across Western Europe. This so-called "rebirth of knowledge" through the emergent universities brought about a look to the past to find direction for the church. The recovery of the church meant a renewal of its message that was brought about by the study of the ancient sources upon which it is based. As the quest for renewal unfolded, it became clear that polarized divergent opinion would lead to a schism in the Catholic Church. Thus, the Roman Catholic Church and the Protestant churches emerged in the sixteenth century, each claiming validity from the Bible and the scholars of the previous centuries (each appears to have used the past selectively). While that debate raged between combatants, another movement emerged with roots in the Renaissance, one that stressed the use of reasonability as the criteria of biblical teachings. Though devoted to a belief in the integrity and authority of the Bible (very much the opposite of the later Enlightenment in this regard), its proponents grounded authority in the ability of the mind to define and discover truth. Such a theory of the origin of truth implies an understanding of the rational processes as not having been severely affected by the fall of Adam. One example of this secondary thread of the Renaissance was the Socinian movement.

The Socinians, led by Laelius Socinus (1525–1562) and his nephew Faustus (1539–1604), attempted to frame a Christianity that was rational. In doing so, they deprived the faith of many of its supernatural claims (the triunity of God, the deity of Christ, and substitutionary atonement), creating a naturalism that denied the claim to be Christian at all. At the heart of Socinianism, as well as that of every other expression of "Christian" naturalism, is the denial of the utter and complete sinfulness of humankind. *The Racovian Catechism* explains the relationship of Adam to the race as real but defines the implications in terms of disoriented sensibilities, not guilt and punishment. Original sin is merely "the habit of sinning" and "a very strong disposition to wickedness," and the more strident descriptions of humanity's plight, such as that in Psalm 51:5, are defined as "a certain hyperbolic exaggeration" (10.5). Humanity's plight, then, is that of a voluntary propensity to follow bad examples. The Socinians provide no rationale as to why this observable phenomena exists or why it is universal. One could reasonably expect that if humankind's problems stem from a tendency to follow bad advice, there should be one or two in all human history who did not do so. If everyone without exception does the same thing, a better explanation may be a deep-seated, involuntary principle.

What humankind lacks, according to the Socinians, is a moral stimulus sufficient to overcome some bad habits. This is the work of the Holy Spirit in regeneration; it is a work of inspiration to duty. "It is certain that the first man was so created by God as to be endowed with free will; and there was no reason why God should deprive him of it after his fall" (5.10). Salvation is moral in nature; it is a life lived in obedience to the moral principles of the Bible. "Faith renders our obedience more estimable and more acceptable in the sight of God; and, provided it be real and sincere, supplies the deficiency of our obedience, and causes us to be justified by God" (9.9). Without the doctrine of the utter sinful-

236

ness of humankind, Christianity is reduced to sentimental do-goodism. Here are loud echoes of Pelagius in the fifth century and the harbinger of modern religious liberalism in the nineteenth!

Because Christianity has traditionally conceived of God as just and righteous, of humankind as sinful and under God's deserved wrath, and of salvation as the gift of God that is of grace alone through Christ's death on the cross, the doctrines of the eternal initiative of God have been central. The predestinating and electing mercies of God tell us how God would be merciful to undeserving people; that is, He simply willed to do so without explaining to anyone why He did it. These doctrines are the comforting answer, though admittedly they have been misapplied and ill-defined, to humankind's dreadful plight in judgment and sinfulness. It is not surprising that the Socinians, and many after them of the same mindset, believed that humankind is really not so bad after all, and then created a God without incontrovertible wrath. God is viewed as a benevolent being who waits for us to reply to Him as we should. Predestination is denied because it is believed that the net result would be a moral lackadaisicalness among Christians. If God did it all for us, gratitude would not be sufficient to bring about obedience.

> This is evident from hence, that all things relating to piety and religion would be in us from necessity: and if this were the case, there would be no need of our efforts and labor in order to be pious. For all exertion and application is wholly superfluous where all things are done through necessity, as reason itself shows. But if exertion and application be taken away from piety and religion, piety and religion must perish. (5.10)

Heirs of Socinian Rationalism were the Deist and Unitarian movements that flowered in England in the late sixteenth and early seventeenth centuries as well as in America in the late eighteenth and early nineteenth centuries. Unitarianism was particularly influential in America, providing late-nineteenth-century liberalism with its understanding of human nature and progressive optimism.

SALVATION: A STORY OF SIN AND GRACE

THE LATE MODERN CHURCHES AND SALVATION
(1750–PRESENT)

The emergence of the Enlightenment, sometimes called the Age of Reason, has had a tremendous influence upon Christianity. The very essence of its intellectual mindset has proven adverse to the Christian teaching of the sinfulness of humankind and the need for a divine Savior to rescue us from despair and hopelessness. Instead of embracing a belief in humankind's inability to fashion earthly utopias, Enlightenment philosophers and theologians promised hope through cultural engineering and social progress, substituting the "not yet" of a future utopia for human imperfection, education for salvation, and the promise of earthly perfection for a heavenly one. Such euphoria seems silly now for most people; apathy and despair have replaced any corporate hope as culture, using the very principles of the Enlightenment, has degenerated to new and frightening levels of individualism, privatism, and anarchy. Yet at one time the Enlightenment was a potent foe to everything denominated as Christian. One has defined it this way: "The Enlightenment represents man's emergence from a self-inflicted state of minority. A minor is one who is incapable of making use of his understanding without guidance from someone else. . . . Have the courage to make use of your own understanding is, therefore, the watchword of the Enlightenment."[19] The turn to an inward authority, whether it be the mind or common sense, has characterized the past several centuries and shaped much of professing Christianity in the West.

THE PROTESTANT TRADITIONS AND SALVATION

Protestantism, with its tradition of diversity and freedom, was a laboratory for its more liberal members to experiment with different ideas about salvation. Some of these experiments diverged rather far from orthodoxy as it had been defined in earlier centuries, though conservatives attempted to preserve a more biblical picture of sin and grace.

The European Protestant Liberal Tradition and Salvation

The fountainhead of the liberal tradition of interpreting Christianity was Friedrich Schleiermacher (1768–1834). Most scholars in retrospect would agree with Karl Barth's evaluation of his importance when he indicated that Schleiermacher did not merely found a school of thought — he started an era! Schleiermacher's era found the starting point in defining Christianity in subjective experience rather than in an objective revelation of God. This was a view that Schleiermacher hoped would provide a safe refuge for Christianity from the onslaught of the scientific, philosophical, and literary communities.

The questions that the nineteenth-century religious community pondered were two. First, what is the nature of God? The answer involved the severance of the traditional embrace of transcendence and immanence for an overemphasis upon the latter and a denial of the former. Second, what is the relationship of the Bible to revelation? Again, the liberal tradition rejected the identity of the two as one and the same for the view that the Bible merely *contains* the revelation of God. The primary religious emphases of the century became inward authority, moralism, optimism, and Pelagianism. In retrospect, Christianity in the hands of these cultural accommodators became little more than a personal struggle for self-identity in an alienating world. It gradually lost its distinctiveness, becoming another branch of the social sciences.

However, the fountainhead of the movement exuded a conflicting message; he was a medley of antithetical sources. From a Pietistic heritage, Schleiermacher stressed Christianity as a private, subjective experience of God; the philosophical inheritance of Kant led him to reject traditional approaches to religious knowledge; and his parental attachment to Calvinism led him to embrace elements of that tradition. His approach to Christianity was unique. However, more important for the development of the liberal tradition was his theological method than his particular views. He, like many, was a steppingstone to the encroachment of the Enlightenment, which he opposed, and to a greater divergence from orthodoxy.

The inconsistency in his teachings is apparent in the doctrine of redemption. As previously noted, Schleiermacher rejected the Nicene Creed as an accurate witness to the teachings of Scripture concerning Christ. For Schleiermacher, Christ was merely an expression of God, who is evident in everyone to a lesser degree. Further, Christ's death was only a moral exhibition and exhortation; it was not meant to placate

239

divine wrath. Sin was merely incomplete moral comprehension without any penalty. It needed no remedy, only a strong whisper of divine love. Christianity was not so much about purging from the divine accusation against us as sinners as it was a morally uplifting, self-help movement. However, the work of bringing the distrustful and prideful to dependence on God (this being salvation) was a work of God alone. In the work of regeneration, people are passive; they receive a gift from God.

> But as regards what happens after the Word has made its impression on the soul, in the attainment of its aim for men, here we cannot concede man's natural co-operation. Even the consent accompanying the reception of the Divine Word, as far as it is directed to what is essentially and characteristic in it, can be ascribed only to the antecedent work of grace.[20]

Rejecting the widely held notion that faith is a work that causes God to embrace the sinner, Schleiermacher defined the will as a receptive organ that responds to stimulants; it is not a causal agent. In these areas of belief, Schleiermacher reflects the Reformed tradition of orthodoxy.

The communication of the liberal tradition into American theological circles came through the influence of Albrecht Ritschl (1822–1889). He appears to have had a greater influence in theological method and content than Schleiermacher. Ritschl, unlike Schleiermacher, viewed religion in its corporate, moral aspect rather than in its private, subjective encouragements. Hence, salvation is viewed as kingdom-oriented, a moral and political reign of righteousness on the earth. Though his brand of Christianity was more "scientific," he rejected the Trinity, denied the absolute deity of Christ, and viewed the atonement as a moral impetus. To Schleiermacher, Christ was the "Son of God" because of His profound affinity for God; for Ritschl, Christ was divine because He alone shared in God's desire to make the world a better place. Theological terms were defined by Ritschl through the concept of an earthly kingdom.

Ritschl defined the human dilemma as sinful; however, he viewed sin as the relative absence of the Good (the "Good" being kingdom virtues). Concepts such as an inherited sinful propensity and inability are cast aside. In the place of original sin as an explanation of human behavior, Ritschl proposed a universal moral law. Guilt arises from the misuse of freedom in breaking this moral, kingdom idealism. Though sinful, the consequences of behavior are only temporal in nature; God is viewed as a wishful grandparent, rather than an offended judge demanding reparation, having been stripped of His powers to act on His own behalf.

Justification, like sin, was defined by Ritschl within a kingdom framework. To be justified is to change one's attitude toward Christ and to live in light of His kingdom aspirations.

> To believe in Christ implies that we accept the value of the Divine law, which is manifest in His word, for our reconciliation with God. . . . Faith in Christ is neither belief in the truth of His history nor assent to a scientific judgment of knowledge such as the presentation of the Chalcedonian formula. It is not a recognition of His Divine nature of such a kind that, in affirming it, we disregard His life-work and His action for the salvation of those who have to reckon themselves as belonging to His community.[21]

An influential coterie of scholars emerged in Germany between 1880 and 1920 reacting to their mentor, Albrecht Ritschl, and founding a new approach to doing theology. Such theologians as William Wrede (1859–1906), Wilhelm Bousset (1865–1920), Ernst Troeltsch (1865–1923), and Herman Gunkel (1862–1932) rejected any attempt to build theology on a historical or scientific foundation, turning instead to comparative religions. Though different in method from Ritschl, the History-of-Religions School arrived at many of the naturalistic, humanistic conclusions concerning the meaning of Christianity. The essence of "true" religion is moral. Truth is discovered at the points where all religions converge in agreement, such as

241

in certain areas of ethics. Each is in error at points of dispute and divergence. Christianity is a human religion as are all the others. Jesus was a historical figure, but Paul perverted His truth claims by borrowing heavily from Gnosticism and ancient pagan mystery religions. Salvation is a moral sentiment.

The European Protestant Conservative Tradition and Salvation

The greatest critic of the nineteenth-century liberal tradition was Karl Barth (1886–1968), the most influential theologian of the twentieth century. Unlike his liberal opponents, Barth tenaciously affirmed the necessity and integrity of revelation. For him, the knowledge of God was only possible to us through a disclosure that was greater than natural revelation. Barth not only believed in the historicity of Adam and the biblical Fall as described in Genesis 3, but he believed that the root error of the Enlightenment was to be found in its rejection of it. "Its starting-point in the 'rational orthodoxy' . . . was a readoption on the Humanistic, Arminian, Socinian and finally the acknowledged Roman Catholic rejection of what were supposed to be the too stringent assertions of the Reformers concerning the fall of man—the indissolubility of human guilt, the radical enslavement of man to sin."[22] Justification is an act of God freely declaring the sinner to be forgiven in Christ. In a wonderful passage Barth described the divine act of forgiveness:

> The man who receives forgiveness does not cease to be the man whose past . . . bears the stain of his sins. The act of divine forgiveness is that God sees and knows this stain infinitely better than the man himself, and abhors it infinitely more than he does even in his deepest penitence—yet He does not take it into consideration, He overlooks it, He covers it, He passes it by, He puts it behind Him. He does not charge it to man; He does not "impute" it.[23]

This justification of a sinner by God is through faith alone, never on account of faith or because of works. Barth's understanding of the

242

meaning of Christianity is remarkably different from that of his teachers and quite in keeping with the Reformers.[24]

The American Protestant Liberal Tradition and Salvation

The roots of this tradition are found in the religious reaction to the Enlightenment that progressively impacted America in the eighteenth century and flowered in the context of the birth of the nation. The political assertion of rule through political entitlement by an informed electorate, the freedom of rule without a monarch, had a corollary. The vogue of political rights brought with it an optimistic view of human abilities that made the older orthodox claims about human inability appear passé. In this politically charged social environment of individual rights and personal freedom, Unitarianism and Deism became popular among the intellectual elites of the emergent nation, such as Franklin, Jefferson, Adams, and Madison. With their stress on Christianity as essentially moral, Unitarianism and Deism denied the doctrines of humankind's innate inability and moral ineptitude for optimistic views of human nature.

While many threads combined to weave the fabric of classic American liberalism, Unitarianism supplied it with a practical moral optimism concerning the possibility of human progress as well as the denial of divine wrath and human inability. The liberal tradition has certain common doctrinal characteristics through its many manifestations. Among these are a denial of human inability to perfect one's own righteousness, the assertion of the divine being as primarily benevolence, and the defining of true religion as essentially composed of human altruism.

An example of these several postulates is Lyman Abbott (1835–1922), pastor of the Plymouth Congregational Church, Brooklyn, New York, and an outstanding proponent of liberal values. Abbott was convinced that evolution had provided the key to understanding humankind. He argued that humanity evolved from a lower animal and had progressed so far as to acquire a spiritual sense. The key to further development is the positive use of temptation. One can either fall back into an animal state because of temptation, or one can use it to advance in virtue. Salvation from animalism is within the power of everyone. "Redemption is wrought for man by the spirit of God in man, making a man of him and giving him power to be master over himself. The control wrought by redemption is self control."[25] According to Abbott, the race finds itself in the vortex of conflict: to use our powers as we ought means progress; to use them otherwise leads to brutishness. "Every man is two men, — a divine man and a human man, an earthly man and a super-earthly man; he is linked to the lower, out of which he is emerging; he is linked to the upper, toward which he is tending."[26] Sin is the tolerance of our primate past; redemption is a present force within.

In the 1920s the most prominent, scholarly spokesman for liberal Christianity was Shailer Mathews (1863–1941), a professor at the University of Chicago and the Divinity School. Describing sin as "the domination of his lower inheritance," "a violation of those personal forces both of God and human society," Mathews defined salvation as obedience to an immanent divine law of goodwill. It "results from new adjustments with God, the nature of which, thanks to science, we are understanding better."[27] Sin is rooted in two sources: first, the backward pull of a primitive state from which we are being progressively delivered by the ascending evolutionary process; and second, societal primitiveness, which similarly is being overcome by advances in society. Terms such as *guilt* and *hell* were simply symbols used in a much less advanced society to arouse feelings of spiritual discontent in people's lives. Mathews argued that in his century, since barbarism had significantly declined, it was better to put aside medieval pictures of punishment and speak of the love of God as revealed in the spirit of Jesus. Thus, religious terms are reduced to the role of culturally limited symbols that have only an abiding psychological element in them. Advancement in the sciences has rendered the older way of interpreting those symbols as harmful to progress. Said Mathews, "Our theological inheritance is not false, but for many persons, outgrown."[28] Redemption is the state of resolutely living by higher evolutionary principles while rejecting the primitivism within ourselves and society of moral injustice. It is following the example of Jesus, that remarkable Jewish peasant. "The Christian salvation centers about God in a man, not a man made into a God."[29]

The criticism of classic liberalism, primarily due to its overt idealism expressed in social progress, reached a crescendo in the 1930s. Many within the movement, religious conservatives as well as secular humanists outside it, saw the movement as hopelessly tied to nineteenth-century Victorian moralism and reformist triumphalism that blinded itself to the harsh realities of a world that showed few indications that human nature was improving. The mandate for a change of direction came from within the movement, from the popularist Harry Emerson Fosdick when he preached in 1935, "The Church Must Go beyond Liberalism" from his Riverside pulpit. The result was the rise of neo-liberalism, which dominated the liberal tradition in America until the 1960s. Sometimes designated as "realistic theology," its approach to traditional interpretations of theology, such as the concepts of sin and social progress, showed constraint. This is evident by the renewal of interest in the American theologian Jonathan Edwards and Puritanism, which had been treated with little serious interest by the progressive historians and theologians previously. However, in the matter of a heartfelt return to historic orthodoxy, there was no progress. The absolute inability of humanity, the divine quelling of God's wrath by the divine-human Christ, a salvation from a literal hell through a divine intervention, and salvation through grace alone remained part of a scorned and irrelevant past within the movement.

As the liberal movement lost its intellectual cohesiveness in the 1960s, it lost its defining core of beliefs and fractured into numerous competing ideologies. Today, the most prominent of those are the various liberation theologies, which focus on restoring victims' rights and overcoming the suppression of minority privileges.

The most influential theologian in the liberal tradition in the latter half of the twentieth century was Paul Tillich (1886–1965), a prominent professor at Union Theological Seminary, New York. For Tillich, the essential nature of humanity involved the ambiguous concept of finitude, which finds expression in anxiety. Anxiety is humanity's self-awareness that limitation tends to lead to emptiness and meaninglessness. Humanity must decide to actualize their potential, not live on past dreams of innocence. That is, humanity's basic problem is internal and psychological. We have a drive for meaning that is frustrated by a fear of retrogression; it is the state of estrangement. Humankind—having

 245

come from nothing, according to Tillich—fears returning to nothing. The biblical Fall is a myth; it is merely a symbol of this human condition.[30] Sin is estrangement from God (essence), which is manifested in the psychological perception of personal insignificance, uncertainty, and vague past memory. Salvation is the personal acceptance of the "New Being." Christ is a person in whom the qualities of the "New Being" adhered. The power seen in Christ, who accepted his estrangement yet dared to hope and dream, is also in everyone, and it is up to us to follow Christ, emulating his example of appropriating this freedom and power from within. "Regeneration is the state of having been drawn into the new reality manifest in Jesus as the Christ. . . . Faith which accepts Jesus as the bearer of the New Being is this basis."[31]

While Tillich's definitions of terms appear profound at times, they are also misleading. He revealed himself as a true heir of the liberal tradition, however he may have interpreted Christianity through contemporary philosophical and psychological insights, by treating language as subjectively symbolic. The Bible is merely a book of ever-changing symbolic images; however, what never has changed in the liberal tradition is the affirmation that historic Christian interpretation of God, Christ, humanity, sin, and salvation is hopelessly archaic and meaningless, if not damaging, for those who have a sense of estrangement in the "modern" world.

The most potent answer to the American liberal tradition in the twentieth century came from the pen of J. Greshem Machen (1881–1937), the former professor at Princeton Theological Seminary and founder of Westminster Theological Seminary. Among the many faults that Machen saw manifest in the liberal tradition of his day was that sin had been defined away.

> Modern liberalism has lost all sense of the gulf that separates the creature from the creator; its doctrine of man follows naturally from its doctrine of God. . . . According to the Bible, man is a sinner under the just condemnation of God; according to modern liberalism, there is really no such thing as sin. At the very root of the modern liberal movement is the loss of the consciousness of sin.[32]

Because liberalism set forth a faulty view of humankind's dilemma, it proclaimed a superficial solution to humankind's needs. While sin is not in us, the solution is. It is all a matter of correct thought-process training and emotional resolve to trust in ourselves; we must all rise above our conscience. "Liberalism finds salvation (so far as it is willing to speak at all of 'salvation') in man; Christianity finds it in an act of God. . . . According to Christian belief, Jesus is our Saviour, not because He has inspired us to live the same kind of life that He lived, but because He took upon Himself the dreadful guilt of our sins and bore it instead of us on the cross."[33] Thus, to Machen, the liberal movement was a failed enterprise, a huge disaster, because its hope was only in making this fallen world a little better, its joys the mere disillusions of temporal happiness, and its god a weakling of powerless love and willful ineptitude. Machen eloquently argued the point this way:

> The search for joy in religion seems to have ended in disaster. God is found to be enveloped in impenetrable mystery, and in awful righteousness; man is confined in the prison of the world, trying to make the best of his condition, beautifying the prison with tinsel, yet secretly dissatisfied with his bondage, dissatisfied with a merely relative goodness which is no goodness at all, dissatisfied with the companionship of his sinful fellows, unable to forget his heavenly destiny and his heavenly duty, longing for communion with the Holy One.[34]

The American Protestant Conservative Tradition and Salvation

Voices were raised as early as the 1720s that the spirit of *Arminianism*—a term used broadly for many forms of religious rationalism—was poking up its ugly head in the British colonies. However, it was not until the 1760s that the threat materialized with the emergence of Deism and Unitarianism among the intellectual elites of Eastern Massachusetts, the merchants of Philadelphia, and the

Virginia gentry. As the nineteenth century opened, the emphasis on rationalism had become an imposing enemy to traditional orthodoxy when Harvard College openly embraced Unitarianism, as did a considerable number of the Congregational churches in New England. What made it worse was that the Unitarians advanced a popular preaching style that appealed to the masses in offering a new theology sterilized of such "harmful" doctrines as the absolute depravity of humanity and the discriminatory grace of God. Adamic solidarity, the belief that humankind comes into the world already condemned for what another had done, seemed foreign to a nation of people who took pride in the ability of humanity to govern without king or priest and who found blame as well as blessing in voluntary moral choices.

In response to Unitarianism, the first manifestation of the liberal tradition in America, conservative scholars mounted a defense for the churches. The Congregationalists in New England responded with a strong polemic as well as the establishment of the first of the major denominational seminaries in the country, Andover Theological Seminary. They, however, fractured into two competing camps. Traditional Calvinists generally defended orthodoxy by appealing to the past and rehearsing the same time-worn arguments. The other camp modified their Calvinism so as to have a more cogent, relevant defense. The system of doctrine that emerged from this second approach is often referred to as New England theology, as New Haven theology (since it was promulgated at Yale Divinity School), or as Taylorism (since its major systematizer was Nathaniel W. Taylor of Yale). While embracing the sinfulness of humanity, these scholars rejected the doctrine of original sin, feeling the sting that a personal nonparticipatory view of sin might cause in the defense of the faith in a democratic mindset. Samuel Hopkins (1721–1803), a prominent pastor and former student of Jonathan Edwards, boldly asserted: "Sin does not take place in the posterity of Adam in consequence of his sin, or that they are not constituted sinners by his disobedience."[35] Nathaniel Emmons (1745–1840) argued the same point in saying, "Nothing can be more repugnant to Scripture, reason, and experience, than the notion of our deriving a corrupt heart from our first parents."[36] What these and other writers sought to affirm is that human

248 sinfulness is the result of personal, individual choices. However, if

humanity has the ability to determine their state, it would appear consistent to say that they have the ability to cause their righteousness, just as they are the cause of their sin.

The trend among the New England divines was most clearly evidenced in the antebellum evangelist Charles Grandison Finney (1792–1875), an ardent opponent of Unitarianism and Deism as well as Calvinism. Although Finney was orthodox in most areas, he denied the doctrines of original sin, inherent sin, and total depravity because he felt they were incompatible with human freedom—an assumption central to his theology. Rather than speak of inability, Finney embraced moral depravity, a voluntary state of unwillingness. "Moral depravity, as I use the term, consists in selfishness; in a state of voluntary committal of the will to self-gratification."[37] This lead Finney to argue that people have the ability to turn to God and cause their own regeneration based on natural ability. He noted:

> The sinner has all the faculties and natural abilities requisite to render perfect obedience to God. All he needs is to be induced to use these powers and attributes as he ought. . . . Regeneration then is a radical change of the ultimate intention, and of course, of the end or object of life. . . . Regeneration . . . must consist in a change in the attitude of the will, or a change in its ultimate choice . . . to the interests of His kingdom.[38]

This doctrine consistently aligned with his rejection of a substitutionary view of Christ's death. Indeed, according to Finney, Christ died to assure us by illustration the importance of obeying His moral laws. Thus, in the teachings of Finney is born the notion that conversion is only a choice that people make to align their lives with the interests of God.

New England theology proved to be an insufficient bulwark against the inroads of the liberal tradition in America. In fact, it may be argued that the concessions of orthodoxy that it made in the defense of Christianity actually opened the door for the more destructive influence of classic liberal theology at the end of the century.

THE ROMAN CATHOLIC CHURCH AND SALVATION

The Roman Catholic community has endured many of the same pressures from the Enlightenment that have been felt in the Protestant communities. The Church responded to such threats upon its authority as those posed by political socialism and higher criticism with the publication of the *Syllabus of Errors* (1864), which seems in retrospect to have driven dissent underground, and the assembling of Vatican I (1869), which asserted papal infallibility. The official, confessional doctrine of the church has not changed since it was set forth at the Council of Trent in the sixteenth century, though issues concerning the relationship of language as symbol and myth have allowed for a greater breadth of teaching by some of the institution's scholars and writers, such as Karl Rahner. However, in 1994 the extensive *Catechism of the Catholic Church* appeared as part of the agenda by the current hierarchy of the church to affirm traditional Catholic doctrine. A comparison of this document with the Council of Trent will indicate whether the official doctrine of the Roman Catholic Church has changed, though it must be affirmed that there have been some significant additions to it (for example, the recognition of papal infallibility, the immaculate conception of Mary, and her immaculate assumption into heaven).

The Catechism and Sin

The document affirms the biblical account of the Fall and the transmission of guilt through Adam to the entirety of humanity. Further, the church recognizes that a denial of humanity's fallen condition affects the central message concerning Christ. "The Church, which has the mind of Christ, knows very well that we cannot tamper with the revelation of original sin without undermining the mystery of Christ" (389). (This insight the liberal tradition has not valued.) As a result of Adam's sin, he lost the grace of original holiness and has communicated to all his progeny a state or condition of spiritual cursing and death. However, while sin has had a terrible effect upon humankind, the nature of the defect is far less than argued by the church's opponents, the Reformers, in the sixteenth century. "Human nature has not been totally corrupted: it is wounded in the natural powers proper to it; subject to ignorance, suffering, and the dominion

250

of death—an inclination to evil that is called 'concupiscence'" (405). In the summary statement of the doctrine, the catechism states that "human nature is weakened in its powers" (418). Whereas Luther and Calvin, as well as the Protestant traditions that are rooted in their teachings, argued that Adam's sin brought to humankind the wrath of God, spiritual alienation, and a corruption of all the human faculties, the Roman Catholic Church insists that the ravages of Adam's fall did not have such a monumental effect. Differences on these issues are the foundation stone of disputes about the nature of redeeming grace and salvation between traditional Roman Catholics and Protestants.

The Catechism, the Sacraments, and Grace

The measure of the defect inherited from Adam is directly correspondent to the sinner's ability to cooperate with God in salvation; this appears to be an uncontestable thesis. Defining the result of Adam's sin as the loss of original righteousness, as well as a perversion of human nature (yet not a total corruption), the catechism argues that all humankind comes into the world devoid of righteousness. The sacrament of baptism has the function of ameliorating the loss of righteousness, leaving only a twisted nature. "Baptism, by imparting the life of Christ's grace, erases original sin and turns a man back toward God, but the consequences for nature, weakened and inclined to evil, persist in man and summon him to spiritual battle" (405). The catechism goes on to say, "Justification has been merited for us by the Passion of Christ. It is granted through Baptism" (2021).

Because baptism does not cleanse from human frailty, a twisted human nature remains that must be cleansed before one can obtain a final absolution. Therefore, other sacraments are necessary. The progressive infusion of righteousness, the renewal of humanity's still-twisted nature, is first and foremost through the unmerited grace of God in a progressive justification and conversion. Interpreted as a process rather than a declarative act by God, "justification establishes cooperation between God's grace and man's freedom" (1993). However, God provides additional grace, as long as there is a willing cooperation, leading to eternal life. The way God has worked out salvation is through a gracious merit system. "Merit is to be ascribed in the first place to the grace of God, and secondly to man's collaboration.

Man's merit is due to God" (2025). God graciously works to produce charity, which He in turn rewards in merits. These grace-caused acquisitions of human endeavor result in works pleasing to God, who grants rewards based upon merit. "We can merit for ourselves and for others all the grace needed to attain eternal life" (2027). Final salvation depends on the process of a gradual sanctification through grace-caused merit.

The means through which God graciously causes the increase of charity is through merit, and this merit comes through the sacraments of the church. "The church affirms that for the believer the sacraments of the New Covenant are necessary for salvation. . . . The fruit of the sacramental life is that the Spirit of Adoption makes the faithful partakers in the divine nature by uniting them in a living union with the only Son, the Savior" (1129). Additional grace is necessary for at least two reasons: first, the initial act of God does not cleanse humanity's corrupted nature; and second, grace can be lost through disobedience, even to eternal death. "Christ instituted the sacrament of Penance for all sinful members of his church: above all for those who, since Baptism, have fallen into grave sin, and have lost their baptismal grace and wounded ecclesial communion. It is to them that the sacrament of Penance offers a new possibility to convert and to recover the grace of justification" (1446). The catechism seems confusing when it asserts that the fruit of the sacraments—merit and an increase of eternal life—are not dependent on the priest who officiates or the righteousness of the recipient, because it adds, "Nevertheless, the fruit of the sacraments also depend on the disposition of the one who receives them" (1128).

The Catechism and Mary

Decrees and pronouncements by the church in the last two centuries regarding the immaculate conception of Mary (her perpetual sinlessness) and her ascension into heaven without death (the Assumption) have brought about a lively discussion of Mary's role in the church. The formal conclusions of Vatican II (1962–1965) referred to her continual intercession to secure eternal life for the faithful by stating, "The Blessed Virgin is invoked by the Church under the titles of Advocate, Auxiliatrix, and Mediatrix."[39] Has Mary been elevated to the position of a co-redeemer with Christ? The latest catechism indicates that the answer is no, though there is considerable controversy over the matter currently for at least two reasons. First, while devotion to Mary is prescribed, adoration is forbidden (971). Second, the source of the merits of Christ, according to the church's beliefs, rest solely in Him. The officials of the church and Mary share the role of diffusing His merits. It would seem that Mary's role, given her elevated state in heaven, is the same as that of the church on the earth in its sacramental system. Mary may have more ability to effect the distribution of grace than the priestly functions of the church on earth, but they together share the role of distribution, not origination.

THE ORTHODOX TRADITION AND SALVATION

The Orthodox churches approach the doctrine of salvation from a different perspective than either the Roman Catholic Church or the Protestant churches. The emphasis in the Western churches is generally upon sin and grace from a legal perspective. Eastern theologians suggest that such an emphasis on Christ as purchasing redemption, while true, is a distortion, being too negative in outlook. Whereas Western churches focus on the need and means of procuring salvation, the Eastern Orthodoxies stress the fruit of it, a mystical union and identity with Christ as the very essence of Christianity. From a Western perspective, it is shocking that the doctrine of justification by faith has received little attention with Eastern Orthodoxy. Daniel Clendenin has written, "In the history of Orthodox theology . . . it is startling to observe the near total absence of any mention of the idea of justification by faith. Justification by faith has received 'short shrift' in Orthodoxy; in fact, the most important text of Orthodox theology, John of *Damascus's Orthodox Faith*, never even mentions the idea."[40] However, it is unfair to conclude that the Eastern churches do not recognize the validity of legal aspects in the gospel. Indeed, they have, as is evidenced in the works of Athanasius of Alexandria. It is simply that their emphasis is upon the effects of the work of Christ.

In seeking to describe the miracle of salvation as it relates to human ability, the Eastern churches argue for some form of divine-human causative, cooperative relationship. "Orthodoxy uses the term

253

cooperation or synergy . . . 'we are fellow workers with God'. . . . If man is to achieve full fellowship with God, he cannot do so without God's help, yet he must also play his own part: man as well as God must make his contribution to the common work, although what God does is of immeasurably greater importance than what man does."[41] Thus, the Eastern tendency is to view the effects of the fall of Adam in the manner of the Roman Catholic Church; it has caused a loss of righteousness and a disordering of the senses but not a total corruption of the human nature and an inability to obey God. *The Confession of Dositheus* (1672) states: "A man, therefore, when he is regenerated, is able by nature to incline to what is good, and to choose and work moral good. . . . He is not able of himself to do any work worthy of a Christian life, although he hath in his own power to will, or not to will, to co-operate with grace" (Decree XIV). God has predetermined to give all humanity sufficient grace to obtain life. Those who use the grace properly are those whom God knew beforehand would so use it and, therefore, chose them to live. It is no wonder that Ware has noted, "The Orthodox picture of fallen humanity is far less somber than the Augustinian or Calvinist view."[42] Humanity can cooperate with God to become like God, "partakers of the divine nature." Salvation is viewed as a process effected by the Scriptures, the sacraments, and the religious community of increased mystical union with God, not an identification with His essential being, but one of practical holiness. Whereas Western Christians would likely use the term "sanctification" to describe this process, the Eastern churches speak of "deification" or "divinization."

The means of salvation in Eastern Orthodoxy bears a remarkable similarity to Roman Catholic views; that is, grace is apportioned through the sacraments. Described as "a holy act, through which grace, or, in other words, the saving power of God, works mysteriously upon man" (*Longer Catechism* Q. 284), the sacrament of baptism causes "a man who believes . . . [to die] to the carnal life of sin, and . . . [be] born again of the Holy Spirit to a life spiritual and holy" (Q. 288). Baptism has the function of cleansing away the hereditary effects of Adam's transgression and bestowing immortality (*Confession of Dositheus* Decree XVI). Postbaptismal sin, which causes the loss of holiness and life, is more grave than prebaptismal sin because the hopeful are viewed as having a greater ability to resist evil but have refused to do so. Cleansing and renewal of life, however, is possible through the sacrament of penance. Upon death, the morally fallen and unrepentant, though at one time baptized and possessing spiritual life, are cast into Hades, where there is hope of deliverance "by the Supreme Goodness, through the prayers of the Priests, and the good works which relatives of each do for their Departed" (*Confession of Dositheus* Decree XVIII).[43]

SALVATION: A STORY OF SIN AND GRACE

7

The Church: God's Gathered Community

Geoffrey had always been fascinated by India—its cultural diversity, Kipling's stories, Gandhi's heroism. So when he retired, the first major trip he and his wife, Eleanor, took was to the great subcontinent. But it wasn't long before he began to wonder why he had been so eager to come here. True, the train ride through the foothills of the Himalayas had provided spectacular views. And few sights are so romantic as the Taj Mahal gleaming in the moonlight. But everything was so different from what he was used to. The spicy food began to bother him. The poverty of so many of the people was depressing. And scenes of misplaced religious fervor disturbed him. It all seemed so . . . foreign. But then, one Sunday, Eleanor found a Christian church and they entered with the other worshipers. Though the service was not conducted in English, they somehow felt that they were participating in it. The people they met smiled and seemed genuinely glad to see them. Suddenly Geoffrey felt at ease; he felt . . . at home. On the other side of the world he had found family.

That's what being a part of Christ's church is like—having family members nearby and around the world. God has willed to gather a people from among the nations and mold them into a new unity. The means for this accomplishment, and the cornerstone of the new edifice, is God's own Son, who purchased the church through His incarnation, life, and death and who continues to gather the community together through the work of the Spirit and the Word of God. The unity of the church comes from its one Lord and from teachings that have remained unchanged and inviolate throughout the centuries. The church is nourished by its living Lord and sustained by a living hope. Though beset by many troubles in the world, the church awaits the coming of the Lord. It is only when the last saint is gathered into the church that the church militant will complete its task and be lifted in triumph at the glorious appearing of Christ. The purchased bride will experience the consummation of divine love in the marriage feast of the Lamb!

It is to this theme—the church—that we now turn. Because the subject is large, it is necessary to limit the scope of the discussion. Accordingly, the focus of this chapter will be upon the meaning and structure of the church as well as upon the sacraments of the church.

The History of the Doctrine of the Church

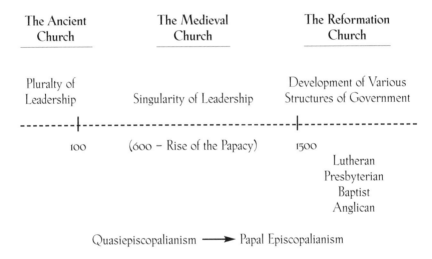

The Ancient Church	The Medieval Church	The Reformation Church
Plurality of Leadership	Singularity of Leadership	Development of Various Structures of Government

100   (600 – Rise of the Papacy)   1500

Lutheran
Presbyterian
Baptist
Anglican

Quasiepiscopalianism ⟶ Papal Episcopalianism

THE ANCIENT CHURCH AND THE DOCTRINE OF THE CHURCH (100–600)

The doctrine of the church is one doctrine that began developing rapidly right from the start. People were being added to the church in great numbers; how was the church to be set up to take care of them? Meanwhile, the church was moving into regions with differing

258

cultures and was facing periodic persecution and false teaching; just what was the church supposed to be? Practical and immediate concerns forced church leaders to begin defining the church and its sacraments.

THE CHURCH FATHERS AND THE DOCTRINE OF THE CHURCH (100–150)

The New Testament, which was brand-new at that time, provided the church fathers with clues about how to set up the church. It seems the Fathers focused on the church offices as providing the key to understanding the structure and nature of the church.

The Church Fathers and the Nature of the Church

There are frequent references to the church in these earliest witnesses after the first century. Clement of Rome (d. 101?) spoke of the church at Corinth as an "elect portion" (*1 Clement* 29). Ignatius (c.35–c.107), whose views on polity and authority in the church are seminal, was the first to speak of the church as catholic, or universal, and defined the church using the head/body analogy (*Letter to the Ephesians* 17). Writing to the Smyrneans, he stated, "Wherever the bishop appears, let the people be there; just as wherever Jesus Christ is, there is the Catholic Church" (8). The writer of the *Epistle of Barnabas* refers to the church as "the new people" (5). Hermas, in *The Shepherd,* refers to the church as drawing its members from the world being gathered into one body.

> "Because," saith he, "all the nations that dwell under heaven, when they heard and believed, were called by the one name of [the Son of] God. So having received the seal, they had one understanding and one mind, and one faith became theirs and [one] love. . . . Therefore the building of the tower became of one color even bright as the sun . . . after they entered in together, and became one body." ("Similitude" 9.17)

259

The Church Fathers and the Structure of the Church

The biblical data indicates that four primary offices were present in the primitive church: apostles, prophets, evangelists, and pastor-teachers (Ephesians 4:11). Of these, the first three appear to have been nonresidential; that is, those who were confirmed to have these gifts and were called to use them in an official function traveled among the churches. The pastor-teacher gift, on the other hand, was exercised in the churches by men who resided permanently with their flocks. The terms designating the pastors in the churches were two: "bishop" and "elder." The former is from the Greek word *episcopos,* meaning an overseer, which describes the duty of the officeholder. The latter term is the Greek word *presbyteros,* suggesting the dignity of the office-holder. It is clear from the Scriptures that the terms were used interchangeably (Acts 20:17,28; 1 Timothy 3:1-2; Titus 1:5,7) and appear in plurality (Acts 20:17; Hebrews 13:7; Titus 1:5). The direction of the local assemblies was to be under the leadership of several elder-bishops who performed their function in parity; the elders-bishops were collectively called a "presbytery" (1 Timothy 4:14). Along with the elders were deacons (Philippians 1:1; 1 Timothy 3:8-13)—and perhaps also deaconesses (Roman 16:1; 1 Timothy 3:11), though this is a matter of dispute.

In subsequent centuries, church structure evolved toward a greater complexity and specificity. While some scholars have argued for continuity of later churches with the primitive church, it is clear that, at best, this is only partly the case. With altering experiences and times, the management of the church has changed in ways not envisioned by the circumstances of the first century. Several distinct governmental forms (for example, episcopalian, congregational, and presbyterian) have emerged, each claiming biblical precedent. This has raised some interesting questions of the New Testament data. Is there a single biblical pattern of church government? This seems hardly the case since advocates of various systems selectively use supportive texts, neglecting the evidence of texts that suggest other structures. Does the New Testament present us with diverse and irreconcilable ecclesiologies? Or does the Bible provide broad principles and patterns only, so that the church would be maximally adaptable to any variety of diverse cultures and circumstances? This view would suggest that no single

260

ecclesiological structure appears in the Bible beyond a few basic offices, their qualifications, and their functions. History cannot resolve this issue, though it does lend credence to the last view.

As churches emerged throughout the Roman Empire, they did so with a degree of independence, though they all were bound together by a common faith, read various apostolic writings passed among the churches, and heard itinerants (apostles, prophets, and evangelists), some bearing direct witness to events of the Bible. Churches in the West appear to have retained a plurality of leaders in the churches—elders-bishops and deacons—longer than churches in the East. In Asia Minor, for example, the synonymous terms for church officers, "elder" and "bishop," were separated, creating two separate offices. Church leaders made the latter term singular, while the former remained plural. That is, some of the churches in the East shifted to a single leader in each of the churches, the bishop. However, this was not a universal practice in the early second century.

The *Didache* (c.140), a manual of Syrian origin, recognized the work of itinerant apostles and prophets but stipulated two plural offices in the churches. "Elect for yourselves . . . bishops and deacons worthy of the Lord" (14). Insight into the manner of selecting the church's officeholders is seen in the words "Elect for yourselves"; at this time the gathered church appears to have chosen its leaders. The manner of the worship service is as follows: "On the Lord's day gather together, break bread and give thanks" (15).

Two writings from the West (both associated with the church at Rome) suggest that the leadership in the church was directed by a plurality of officers, bishops-elders and deacons. Clement of Rome, in his *Letter to the Corinthians*, noted that church leaders in his day were appointed by the apostles: "As for these . . . who were afterwards appointed by them . . . " (44). Elsewhere he noted, "Through the countryside and city they [the apostles] preached; and they appointed their earliest converts, testing them by the spirit, to be bishops and deacons of future believers. Nor was this a novelty for bishops and deacons had been written about a long time earlier" (42). The appointment of leaders was to be "with the consent of the church." Hermas, in *The Shepherd*, about 140 to 155, spoke of a writing that "you shall read . . . in this city along with the presbyters who are in charge of the church" ("Vision" 2.4). Apparently, the Roman church was led at this time by a plurality of leaders, the presbytery; no single leader had emerged.

The influential writings of Ignatius of Antioch in Asia Minor evidence a shift from the New Testament pattern. The office of bishop was separated from that of elder and was made singular, though the office of elder remained plural. Presiding over each church, as he envisioned it, was a single bishop. In the *Letter to the Trallians* he exhorted his readers "that you do nothing without the bishop, and that you be subject also to the presbytery [elders]" (2). In the same letter he made the point that there are three offices in the church. "In like manner let everyone respect the deacons as they would respect Jesus Christ, and just as they would the bishop as a type of the Father, and the presbyters [elders] as the council of God and the College of apostles" (3). In his *Letter to the Ephesians* he noted, "Anyone who acts without the bishop and the presbytery and the deacons does not have a clean conscience" (7).

While Clement of Rome does not appear to have embraced a single leader in the churches during his time, he seems to have been the first to buttress the authority of the church's teaching by advocating a form of apostolic succession within the bishops-elders office. He argued that the church's message is true because of an unbroken heritage of succession from God through Christ to the apostles, who passed the message to the bishops (remember that at this time a concept of collected apostolic writings was not envisioned). That is, each church could be certain of its orthodoxy because it had a "genealogical tree" revealing its lineage from the apostles.

> The apostles received the gospel for us from the Lord Jesus; and Jesus Christ was sent from God. Christ, therefore, is from God, and the Apostles are from Christ. . . . They went forth in complete assurance of the Holy Spirit, preaching the good news that the Kingdom of God is coming. . . . They appointed their earliest converts . . . to be bishops and deacons. (*Letter to the Corinthians* 42)

The succession envisioned by Clement of Rome appears to have been a system assuring that truth would remain in the churches; it was not about a succession of men in an office. The emphasis was upon the passing on of truth (2 Timothy 2:2). Gradually, the combination of Ignatius of Antioch's emphasis on a single bishop in each church and Clement of Rome's teaching on succession caused a quasiepiscopal form of government to prevail in the churches by the middle of the second century, although the churches retained their autonomy and the bishops throughout the empire viewed themselves as a confederation of equals.

The Church Fathers and the Sacraments of the Church

The earliest Fathers of the church were aware of only two sacraments: the Lord's Table, or the Eucharist (the thanksgiving feast), and baptism. The order of the two was first baptism, performed once, and then the Lord's Table, a repeated ritual. The *Didache* specifically states: "Let no one eat or drink of the Eucharist with you except those who have been baptized in the name of the Lord" (9).

Baptism. Baptism was seen as the sign of entrance into the church, the redeemed community, because it conveys the washing accompanied with the forgiveness of sins. Whereas in subsequent centuries the church has separated the meaning of the sacrament from the symbol, the washing from the water (that is, they either placed the symbol in anticipation of the sign or after it), the earliest Fathers put them together in one inseparable moment. This is why J. N. D. Kelley was able to make the assertion that from the beginning baptism was universally accepted as the rite of admission to the church, and "it was always held to convey the remission of sins."[1] The *Epistle of Barnabas* described the fruit of water baptism in these graphic terms: "We go down into the water laden with sins and filth, and rise up from it bearing fruit in the heart, rest our fear and hope on Jesus in the spirit" (11). *The Shepherd of Hermas* refers to baptism as a seal—an assurance—of the forgiveness of sins. "The seal, therefore, is the water. They go down into the water dead, and come out of it alive" (Parable 9.16). It is, however, certain that the sacrament did not have the ability to cleanse unless it was appropriated in faith, the Word of God's promise and the water having an inseparable bond. That is, after a

263

person was instructed in the faith and fasted in preparation, then he or she received the outward sign of rebirth, the water, which signified the inward presence of spiritual life. The *Epistle of Barnabas* connects the benefits of the sacrament with hearing and believing (11). The *Didache* states that a person should be baptized "after . . . foregoing instructions" (7). The efficacy of baptism was connected with a prior awareness and devoted confession of the thing signified, forgiveness of sins through Christ. The prerequisite of receiving instructions appears to exclude the practice of infant baptism at this time in the church.[2] From the earliest of our instruction manuals, the *Didache*, a person would be baptized in running or still water, cold or warm water, by immersion or pouring (if pouring, it was to be done three times on the head), and done in the names of the Trinity, preceded with a period of fasting by both administrator and recipient (7).

The Eucharist. The earliest Fathers in the church held an ambivalency concerning the Lord's Table. They saw it in terms of a physical reality and a thanksgiving with what has been described as a natural and unconcerned realism. The *Didache* makes this comment on the structure of church worship: "On the Lord's Day gather together, break bread and give thanks" (11). The Eucharist was a thanksgiving remembrance. It is the worship of God through symbol and a rehearsal of the redemption brought through Christ. As bread and wine bring needed physical nourishment to the body, these symbolize the giving of spiritual life through Christ. "Upon us, however, you have bestowed spiritual food and drink, and eternal life through your Servant" (10).

THE APOLOGISTS AND THE DOCTRINE OF THE CHURCH (150–300)

The understanding of the church among the apologists did not substantially differ from that of their predecessors, though they explained its meaning more fully. Again, they were concerned about the nature, structure, and sacraments of the church.

264

The Apologists and the Nature of the Church

Justin Martyr (c.100–c.165) referred to the church with at least two new insights. First, the church is where those who are called brethren gather. Second, in seeking to explain the new faith to a Jewish man, he referred to the church as under a new covenant, as distinguished from the Old Covenant, or Law. The church is composed of New Covenant believers, the old promises having been superseded by the greater ones the old foreshadowed. "Now, law placed against law has abrogated that which is before it, and a covenant which comes after in like manner has put an end to the previous one; and an eternal and final law—namely Christ" (*Dialogue to Trypho* 11). Aristides (2d c.), perhaps a philosopher in Athens, is known to us only by his writing. He spoke of the church as "a third race" and "a new race." Whereas the world had previously been composed of Jews and pagans, it was now composed of a third category gathered from the two, that is, Christians (*Apology* 2). Irenaeus (c.130–c.200) understood the church to be the "children of Abraham." While ancient Israel did not receive the promises made to Abraham of a land, it meant that the promises were not given to them. They were to be fulfilled in Abraham's true seed—the church—in a future, literal fulfillment (*Against Heresies* 5.34.1; see also 5.32.2). Clement of Alexandria (c.150–c.215) thought of the church as the gathering of the saints to receive instruction through the hearing of the Scriptures ("I call a church not a place, but the collection, congregation, of the elect"). Origen (c.185–c.254) suggested that the church has both a universal and a localized aspect, the totality of the saints and a single gathering of them (*Against Celsus* 6.48).

The Apologists and the Structure of the Church

As previously indicated, there was a dramatic, though gradual, change of leadership structure in the second century, from a plurality of leadership in the churches to a single administrative head, a bishop, with elders and deacons under him. This has been explained as the rise of the monarchical bishop, an incipient episcopal form of local governance that appears to have arisen as the church sought to preserve its message from attack by erecting a succession theory of truth. By this, they argued that those churches could be assured of standing in the truth proclaimed by the apostles because a genealogical tree of truth succession could be demonstrated from the apostles to the bishops.

This approach to assurance of orthodoxy was continued and developed by the apologists. Tertullian (c.160–c.225), attempting to preserve the churches from false teaching, stated the point succinctly: "All doctrine which agrees with the apostolic churches, those nurseries and original depositories of the faith, must be regarded as truth, and as undoubtedly constituting what the churches received from the Apostles, what the Apostles received from Christ, and what Christ received from God" (*Prescription against Heretics* 21). Generally, the church was viewed as the sole depository of truth because it had a monopoly on the apostolic writings, the apostolic oral tradition, and the apostolic faith. Each individual church was assured of sharing in this variegated wealth by its connection through succession to the apostles.

Irenaeus illustrates this principle by citing the church at Rome, which had been founded by two apostles, Peter and Paul. Indeed, the Roman church was given a primacy for this reason. "For with this Church, because of its superior origin, all churches must agree, that is, all the faithful in the whole world, and it is in her that the faithful everywhere have maintained the Apostolic Tradition" (*Against Heresies* 3.3.2). Irenaeus listed the twelve bishops from Peter to Eleutherius in Rome and then commented, "In this order, and by the teaching of the Apostles handed down in the Church, the preaching of the truth has come down to us" (3.3.3). While Irenaeus continued the emphasis in the churches on a single leader, a practice that in his day appears to have become universal, he seems to have been among the first to view the bishop's office with a special power, as a custodianship of the apostolic truth ("the certain gift of truth"). In his writings the bishop appears to have been more than the head of a local gathering of Christians; he was conceived of as having a relationship to the church universal. He was part of an episcopate that was one.[3]

Cyprian of Carthage (d. 258), the first African bishop to endure a martyr's death, advanced the doctrine of the church. Like Irenaeus and others, he argued that the bishops were the successors of the apostles in the church and that the unity of the church resided in the bishop's office. He seems to have developed this argument to silence the claims

266

of his opponents, who insisted that he was holding to ideas (in regard to the readmission of those who temporarily had lapsed from the faith in the persecutions) that were nonapostolic. The reply to his opponents, the Novatians, was that the church is one and the bishops are also. Therefore, he, being a bishop in the one church, was in the orthodox, apostolic faith. "The episcopate is one, each part of which is held by each one for the whole. The church also is one. . . . Her head is one, her source is one, and she is one mother" (*Unity of the Church* 5). While the church is one and the bishops, though many, are one, each bishop is part of a federation of coequals. No bishop (in Cyprian's judgment) had the right to impose his authority upon another. Thus, he envisioned a parity among the bishops. Cyprian recognized the priority of Rome among the churches, though he refused to assent to the primacy of Peter's successors. When Bishop Stephen, who was martyred shortly before Cyprian, attempted to impose his opinions on the bishopric of Carthage, Cyprian reminded the Roman bishop about the chastisement of Peter by Paul, who "furnished thus an illustration to us both of concord and of patience, that we should not obstinately love our own opinions" (*Epistle* 70).[4] Another evidence bishops did not exercise jurisdictional authority in the matter of the selection of bishops over other churches was that a bishop was chosen in the presence of his people and not by a distant decree. "The bishop should be chosen in the presence of the people, who are thoroughly familiar with the life of each one, and who has looked into the doings of each one in respect to his habitual conduct" (*Epistle* 67). This is corroborated by Hippolytus of Rome (c.170–c.236), who wrote, "Let the bishop be ordained after he has been chosen by all the people" (*Apostolic Tradition* 2).

Cyprian was adamant that salvation is only in the church, that is, in the apostolic truth of which the church was the singular depository. For him, as well as for the church in general, there was no salvation outside the church. That was so because the church alone had the gospel. The church, the bishop, and the gospel were inseparable. "He can no longer have God for his Father, who has not the church for his mother" (*Unity of the Church* 6). This argument seems to have emerged as a useful weapon against the schismatics of the day, such as the Novatians, who threatened the unity of the church.

The Apologists and the Sacraments of the Church

The apologists wrote a good deal about baptism and the Eucharist, though one might argue that they didn't carry the doctrines of the sacraments much further than did the Fathers.

Baptism. The apologists, like the earliest Fathers in the church, believed that baptism was the sign of entrance into the family of God, the church. Combining the significance of baptism (the rebirth) with the sign of it (water) as one single event, it was interpreted as the entrance into eternal life and church identity. Justin Martyr, for example, connected the washing with water with Jesus' comment to Nicodemus in John 3, "Except you be born again, you cannot see the kingdom of God" (verse 3), preceding it with his own words that "they are brought by us where there is water, and are regenerated in the same manner in which we were ourselves regenerated" (*First Apology* 61). Clement of Alexandria spoke in a similar way. "When we are baptized, we are enlightened. Being enlightened, we are as adopted sons. Adopted as sons we are made perfect. . . . It is a washing by which we are cleansed of sins" (*The Instructor* I.6.26). Water was conceived to have the function of cleansing from past sins.

With this stated (which may seem heretical to some), it must be remembered that the early church leaders did not separate the significance of baptism—an invisible cleansing—from its external symbol. These two occurred simultaneously. This took place in the context of faith in Christ; that is, faith in Christ was expressed in coming to the water to receive salvation. Justin Martyr expressed the church's view with these words:

> Whoever is convinced and believes that what they are taught and told by us is the truth, and professes to be able to live accordingly, is instructed to pray and to beseech God in fasting for the remission of their former sins, while we pray and fast with them. Then they are led by us to a place where there is water; and there they are reborn in the same kind of rebirth in which we ourselves were reborn. (*First Apology* 61)

268

The testimony of Hippolytus concerning baptismal practices in the early third century are significant for at least two reasons: First, he lived in Rome, the cosmopolitan center of the empire, where he would have become aware of church practices throughout the empire. Second, his book *Apostolic Tradition* is a remarkable manual of church practices generally in his day. The actual ritual of baptizing is described with some detail. It was to take place using whatever amount of water was at hand, and while the preference was for immersion, pouring was also sanctioned; the baptized was to be naked in the water; ceremonial oil was to be used; and the person was to be baptized three times (a custom followed in the Orthodox churches today). Prior to baptism, the recipient was asked to make a confession of faith in each person of the divine Trinity (21). Faith in Christ and commitment to Christ preceded the sacrament. Hippolytus makes it clear that the practice in the churches he knew took a "disciple," or a catechumen, through a rigorous educational process of several years before he or she could enter the church (13).

The earliest reference to infant baptism is found in Irenaeus's *Against Heresies* (2.22.4).[5] Tertullian, a contemporary of Irenaeus' in North Africa, was aware of the practice of baptizing "little children" and opposed it (*On Baptism* 18), as Hippolytus appears to have done also. Origen was the first to argue for the validity of infant baptism by claiming that it was an apostolic custom. He wrote, "The church received from the Apostles the tradition of giving Baptism even to infants. . . . [They] knew that there is in everyone the innate stains of sin, which must be washed away through water" (*Commentaries on Romans* 5.9).

The Eucharist. The apologists viewed the Eucharist as a celebration of thanksgiving and a real presence of Christ in the bread and wine, as had the earliest Fathers. Justin Martyr spoke of it in these graphic terms: "So likewise have we been taught that the food which is blessed by the prayer of His word, and from which our blood and flesh by transmutation are nourished, is the flesh and blood of that Jesus who was made flesh" (*First Apology* 66). Origen of Alexandria explained the Eucharist as having a symbolic significance as well as a realistic effect through the Word of God. "It is not the material of the bread but the word which is said over it which is of advantage to the one who eats it. . . . Everyone who eats of this Bread shall live forever" (*Commentaries on Matthew* 11.4). For Origen, the efficacy of the sacrament was not in the outward elements but in the truth they symbolized, which is God's Word. It is the Word that nourishes the believer, strengthening his or her faith. Irenaeus suggested that the observance of the Eucharist—the celebration of the gospel in symbol—effects a cleansing of sin in believers (*Against Heresies* 4.18.4). While Irenaeus refers to the Eucharist as an offering to God, it was an uplifting of thanksgiving. "Now we make offering to Him, not as though He stood in need of it, but rendering thanks for His gift, and sanctifying what he has created" (4.18.6).

THE THEOLOGIANS
AND THE DOCTRINE OF THE CHURCH (300–600)

*A*s we arrive at the theologians, those great thinkers of late Christian antiquity, we begin seeing some serious new development in the doctrine of the church. Here we see the foundations laid for the medieval church that would dominate Europe for centuries.

The Theologians and the Nature of the Church

*I*n the struggle between Augustine (354–430) and the Donatists, the nature of the church was poignantly defined. The Donatists—a fourth-century North African holiness movement—suggested that the toleration of unworthy members was proof that a church was not catholic. Further, they argued that the benefits of the work done by an unworthy bishop were ineffectual. In contrast to the Donatist pleas that the mark of the true church was holiness, Augustine argued that it was membership in the historic church. Neither the unholiness of a member nor the unholiness of a bishop obstructed the one, single Catholic Church from its function of dispensing grace.

Like Cyprian (who struggled against a similar movement in his day, the Novatians), Augustine maintained that the one, true church was alone the Catholic Church. The authority and apostolicity of the church was established through apostolic succession, an uninterrupted lineage from Peter through all the churches. "What the universal

270

Church holds, not as instituted by councils but as something always held, is most correctly believed to have been handed down by apostolic authority" (*Baptism* 4.24). Thus, the church is identified by the truth it professes and dispenses, as well as an unbroken lineage of bishops from the apostles who perpetuated that truth within the church. Other characteristics of the church are unity and love. Outside of the one Catholic Church, the body of Christ, there is no truth, no gospel, no salvation. Though Augustine appears to have differed with Cyprian in that he did not stress the divine right of the bishop's office, he clearly connected a Christian's faith to the authority of the church. He went so far as to argue that it was sufficient to believe in the gospel simply because the Catholic Church proclaimed it to be true. In his polemic against Manichaeanism, a Gnostic religion he had once embraced, Augustine answered the question of the authority of faith this way: "Should you meet with a person not yet believing the gospel, how would you reply to him were he to say, I do not believe? For my part, I should not believe the gospel except as moved by the authority of the Catholic Church" (*Epistle* 5).

Augustine is a fair lens by which to view the state of the church in his day. Indeed, his insights continue to shape the church even today. As the expression of truth has been fashioned by polemical considerations through the centuries, it was no less for the greatest of all early church leaders. The true church is the one, single, holy Catholic Church rooted in the apostles (priority, though not superiority, given to Peter and Rome) and identified by an unbroken lineage of successors. In this church is salvation. In it alone the sacred gospel has been preserved.

The issue of the relationship of the principal churches in the empire (Alexandria, Antioch, Rome, and later Constantinople) was a continual point of wrangling among the bishops. The issue was not so much one of political and administrative authority as a pecking order of highest honors. While the place of honor was granted to Rome because of the primacy of Peter, the tendency of the Roman bishops was to guard that honor and press for more than mere prominence from the other churches. In the first ecumenical gathering of the church at Nicaea in 325, the sixth canon deposited the administration of the churches under the three regional bishops in Antioch, Alexandria, and Rome. These three bishops were viewed as belonging to a confederation of equals in their administrative functions, with the bishops throughout each region operating in a community of equals. By the time of the Council of Constantinople in 381, a priority of honor was assigned to Rome; Antioch and Alexandria were placed after Constantinople. "The Bishop of Constantinople shall have the primacy of honor after the Bishop of Rome, because it is the New Rome" (Canon 3). In affirming that the Council of Constantinople was ecumenical, since it was made up of Eastern bishops, the Council of Chalcedon (451) in its twenty-eighth canon clarified the third canon of Constantinople by interpreting it to mean that the two were equal in honor. The church at Rome accepted the decrees of Chalcedon but rejected the clarification. The issue of the primacy of honor continued to be a point of contention between the two churches. For example, Bishop Leo I (who is known for his defense of Rome against the ravages of Attila the Hun as well as his Christological insights) pressed for a recognition of the primacy of his church, being conscious of inherited Petrine rights as the head of the church. Leo was the first of the Roman bishops whose sermons have been preserved in large number. In one he wrote:

> The dispensation of Truth . . . abides, and the blessed Peter persevering in the strength of the Rock, which he has received, has not abandoned the helm of the Church, which he undertook. For he was ordained before the rest in such a way that from his being called the Rock, from his being pronounced the Foundation, from his being constituted the Doorkeeper of the kingdom of heaven. . . . And so if anything is won from the mercy of God by our daily supplications, it is of his work and merits whose power lives and whose authority prevails in his see. (*Sermons* 3.3)

The Theologians and the Sacraments of the Church

These early church leaders appear to have viewed the sacraments as having two parts: an outward appearance, which functioned as a material symbol, and an internal significance. The efficacy of the symbol depended upon a heartfelt attachment to the thing it symbolized. The grace conveyed through the outer form was not automatic; it was faith in the meaning expressed through the form that brought the promise of the forgiveness of sin. Augustine, for example, noted:

> God is present in his own Gospel words, without which words the Baptism of Christ is unable to be consecrated; and He Himself sanctifies His Sacrament, so that the sacrament may be availing unto salvation for the man who receives it, either before He is baptized, or while he is being baptized, or afterwards, whenever he turns in truth to God, which Sacrament, if he does not turn to God, will be availing to his destruction. Is there anyone who does not know that it is not the Baptism of Christ if the Gospel words, to which the sign consists, should be lacking there? (*Baptism* 6.25.47)

Baptism. The sacrament of baptism was viewed as the rite of admission into the church; it had the power to effect forgiveness, the water being a symbol of the cleansing that Christ effects. St. Ambrose (c.339–397) described baptism this way: "The Lord was baptized, not to be cleansed Himself but to cleanse the waters, so that those waters, cleansed by the flesh of Christ which knew no sin, might have the power of Baptism. Whoever comes, therefore, to the washing of Christ lays aside his sins" (*Commentary on Luke* 83). It was abundantly plain to him, as well as the church in general, that "no one ascends into the kingdom of heaven except through the sacrament of Baptism" (*Abraham* 2.11.79). The mixing of the water as a symbol with faith in Christ effects the removal of the guilt of Adam's sin, leaving only a tendency in human nature to succumb to the remnants of sin's once-universal grip. "If there is any grace in the water, it is not from the nature of water but from the presence of the Holy Spirit" (*The Holy Spirit* 1.6.77).

The same line of thinking is evident in Cyril of Jerusalem (c.315–387). Clinging to Jesus' phrase to Nicodemus, "of water and the

Spirit" (John 3:5), he argued that baptism, if it is to be effectual, is really two simultaneous baptisms: a washing with water and a renewing of the Holy Spirit (to use the phrase in Titus 3:5). Again, the symbol and the thing symbolized are united. He bluntly stated, "If any man does not receive Baptism, he does not have salvation" (*Catechetical Lectures* 3.10).

The practice of extending baptism to all was a permanent practice of the church by this time. Apart from faith, since babies could not receive instruction or express faith, baptism functioned to cleanse the guilt of Adam's inheritance, leaving only the residual effects of sin's presence for removal. Gregory of Nazianzus (329/30–389/90) stated:

> "Well enough," some will say, "for those who ask for Baptism; but what do you have to say about those who are still children, and are unaware neither of loss nor of grace? Shall we baptize them too?" Certainly, if there is any pressing danger. Better that they be sanctified unaware, than they depart unsealed and uninitiated. (*Oration on the Holy Lights* 40.28)

Statements such as this one appear to obliterate the unity of symbol and the thing symbolized in faith. Augustine championed these sentiments in his doctrine of inherited guilt from the charge that it implied that all infants are lost, thus impugning the compassionate mercies of God. He wrote of infants, "They are also freed from the serpent's venomous bite" (*Forgiveness . . . and the Baptism of Infants* 2.27.43).

The Eucharist. The theologians in the church viewed the Eucharist as had their predecessors. First, they saw the Lord's Supper with a strong degree of realism, though with a spiritualizing tendency. The elements really and truly were the body and blood of Christ, yet not in such a way as to be identical with the historical body of the Savior. Christ's literal body had ascended into heaven, to be brought from heaven only in His return in the last great judgment. Second, for the theologians, the sacrament conveyed the grace of life to the baptized. A person received the benefit of the sacrament when it was mixed with faith.

The realism with which the church interpreted the elements in the Eucharist, as well as its sanctifying benefit, was captured by Cyril of Jerusalem.

> Wherefore let us partake as of the Body and Blood of Christ; for in the figure of Bread is given thee His Body, and in the figure of Wine His Blood; that thou by partaking of the Body and Blood of Christ, mayest be made of the same body and the same blood with Him. For thus we come to bear Christ in us . . . we become partakers of the divine nature. (*Catechetical Lectures* 23.3)

Gregory of Nyssa (c.330–c.395) spoke of the benefits of the Eucharist, in terms characteristic of the Eastern churches, as effecting our assimilation into Christ or our deification ("becoming partakers of the divine nature"). He spoke of a spiritual eating of Christ through partaking of the elements.

> He disseminates Himself in every believer through that flesh, whose substance comes from bread and wine, blending Himself with the bodies of believers, to secure that, by this union with the immortal, man, may be a sharer in corruption. He gives these gifts by virtue of the benediction through which He trans-elements the natural. (*The Great Catechism* 37)

Augustine's interpretation of the Eucharist appears not to have embraced the realism of other writers. For him, the outward symbols of bread and wine possessed a spiritual meaning. The Holy Spirit revealed through faith the deeper meaning of the elements and effected spiritual renewal and edification. The Lord's Table was a nonmeritorious, spiritually real experience of receiving the gift of life. "Jesus answered and said to them, 'This is the work of God, that

275

ye believe on Him whom He has sent.' This is for them to eat the meat, not that which perisheth, but that which endureth unto eternal life. To what purpose dost thou make ready teeth and stomach? Believe, and thou hast eaten already" (*Commentary on John* 25.12).

THE MEDIEVAL CHURCH AND THE DOCTRINE OF THE CHURCH (600–1500)

Never before or since has the Christian church held such power as it did in Europe during the medieval years. Much of this had to do with the doctrine of the church itself. The medieval church wielded massive power because, according to its own statements, it controlled the means of grace.

We'll look at the medieval period in two separate eras. In the early medieval period the church established itself as the major power in Europe, reshaping its own structure in the process. In the late medieval period church leaders struggled to define the role of the papacy and the relationship of the church to the state. Throughout both periods the theology of the sacraments was advanced.

THE EARLY MEDIEVAL CHURCH AND THE DOCTRINE OF THE CHURCH (600–1000)

The last vestiges of the once-dominant Roman Empire vanished in 476 when the last Roman emperor was deposed and a Gothic king took his place. The resultant political chaos had a profound impact on the church. The church at Rome, perhaps prepared by Leo I's remarkable confrontation with Attila the Hun, not only remained intact through the period but emerged in the early medieval period to play an enlarged religious and political role. At this important juncture, Gregory I (c.540–604; pope 590–604) had an enduring influence on the church. One has summarized his role in the church this way: "It was Gregory who led antiquity into the middle ages, and he laid the foundations of the medieval papacy that governed the Western world after the calamitous wars and invasions that completed the fall of the western empire in the sixth century."[6]

276

The Early Medieval Church
and the Structure of the Church

In his understanding of the nature of the church, Gregory I embraced the tradition that emerged from the time of Cyprian and was expressed most cogently by Augustine. Though composed of wheat and tares, the saved and lost, the church was viewed as the kingdom of God on the earth; the church is one, holy, and universal. In this institution alone is salvation, for it alone dispenses the grace of God through the ministry of the Word and the sacraments. The unique contribution of Gregory was that he greatly expanded the ecclesiastical power and prestige of Rome. For example, he assumed the functions of civil government at a time of a political power vacuum; increased the revenues of the church and administered them equitably; drew the churches in the West more closely to Rome; initiated successful missionary expeditions, such as sending Augustine (not Augustine of Hippo) to England; and upheld the claims of his church against Constantinople. In regard to the prestige of the Roman church, Gregory claimed that it was supreme over all the churches, believing that the decrees of the ecumenical councils had no force without the authority and consent of his Apostolic See. He was the first to style himself as the pope, the supreme leader over the one, holy, and universal church ("the servant of the servants of God"). Gregory wrote John of Constantinople, objecting to his claim of being the universal bishop. In Gregory's judgment, that office belonged exclusively to the bishop of Rome. "Certainly Peter, the first of the apostles, himself a member of the holy and universal Church, Paul, Andrew, John—what were they but heads of particular communities? . . . Was it not the case, as your Fraternity knows that the prelates of the Apostolic See, which by the providence of God I serve, had the honour offered them of being called universal?" (*Epistle* 18). In Gregory the transition from a plurality of leadership in each church to a singularity of rule by a bishop to a single leader over all the churches was complete, though this was never acceptable to the churches in the East.

In the political realm, Gregory believed that the church did not have sufficient strength, so that it must seek the aid of the unchristianized state, calling it "that rhinoceros." One of the major themes in the medieval period is that of defining the relationship of the church

277

to the state and vice versa. The church needed the state to protect it from its many military adversaries, yet it feared the state's intrusive powers. During the reign of Pépin the Short in the eighth century, the Carolingian dynasty (a powerful kingdom that dominated Europe for two centuries) preserved the papacy from the menacing Lombard tribe. Pépin was crowned by popes for his efforts, and he gave extensive lands in central Italy to the papacy, the Donation of Pépin. Perhaps, the high-water mark of state-church relations was the crowning of Charlemagne, the greatest of the Carolingian kings, by Pope Leo III on Christmas Day in the year 800 in St. Peter's, placing Charlemagne in the great succession of the Roman emperors from the first century.

It was also through Gregory that ritual became more dominant in the church with the introduction of Gregorian chants and other forms. He also stressed miracles and angelic agents, both fallen and unfallen, that stretched the limits of reason and evidence. Justo Gonzalez capsulized Gregory's influence this way: "Gregory is an indication of the manner in which, in the midst of a period of political and intellectual decline. Augustine's theology was accommodated to popular faith in two main ways: by mitigating the most extreme aspects of the doctrines of grace and predestination, and by making room for superstitious beliefs and practices."[7]

The Early Medieval Church
and the Sacraments of the Church

The emphasis on ritual by Gregory is evident in his understanding of the Eucharist. The early church viewed the Lord's Table with a profound realism as a memorializing of the sacrifice of Christ. In Gregory this realism was extended into an actual recrucifixion of Christ, the Mass, for the living and those in purgatory. According to Gregory, in the ritual of the priest at the altar Christ truly materialized in the elements. In the elevation of the host, Christ was again sacrificed and sins were remitted.

> He is for us again immolated in this mystery of sacred oblation. For His body is eaten there, His flesh is distributed among the people unto salvation, His blood is poured out. . . . Let us take

thought, therefore, of what this sacrifice means for us, which is in constant representation of the suffering of the Only-begotten Son, for the sake of our forgiveness. (*Dialogues* 4.60)

The manner of the presence of Christ was not resolved with Gregory's materialistic view on the matter; indeed, church leaders held varying views until the Fourth Lateran Council in 1215 mandated a corporealist view. The issue boiled to the point of open controversy during the height of the Carolingian Empire of the ninth century. Charles the Bald had proposed two questions: Is Christ physically present in the Eucharist and, if physically present, is it the same flesh as of His birth? The monk and scholar Paschasius Radbertus (c.790–c.860) argued that Christ was truly present—a presence granted literally to the eyes of the particularly faithful at times (otherwise, it was seen only through the eyes of faith)—and that His presence entailed an actual repetition of His sacrifice. All could not agree with Radbertus's judgment, particularly those in the spiritualist tradition of Augustine, such as Ratramnus (9th c.). He argued that Christ was truly in the elements, but the manner of His presence was spiritual. The body that was present in the Eucharist was Christ's resurrected body, not that born of Mary. Further, Christ's death was not physically reenacted, because of the spiritual nature of His presence.

The controversy erupted again in the eleventh century between Berengar of Tours (c.1010–1088) and Lanfranc (c.1010–1089), the archbishop of Canterbury. The immediate cause for the discussion was the writings of Ratramnus on the Eucharist. Berengar defended them, taking the view that the presence of Christ in the Eucharist is His postresurrection body, a spiritual presence. Thus, the Lord's Table was a memorial of Christ's once-for-all death. However, it was more than a bare memorial of a historic event, because it was a spiritually edifying sacrament. Lanfranc, however, argued that Christ is present in the Eucharist in the flesh of His birth by a miracle of transformation; the bread and wine are symbols of the bread and wine that were there before Christ's true presence replaced them. Berengar seems to have confessed the error of his views, church leaders at that time threatening him with death, only to revert to his former teaching when the

279

danger subsided. The importance of this discussion is that it lead to a formal resolution on the meaning of Christ's presence in the Eucharist in the thirteenth century. The Fourth Lateran Council in 1215 argued that Christ's incarnate flesh was transubstantiated in the Eucharist. "Jesus Christ . . . whose body and blood are truly contained in the sacrament of the altar under the figures of bread and wine, the bread having been transubstantiated into His body and the wine into His blood by divine power."[8]

In the early medieval period the doctrine of purgatory (an interim state after death wherein the last remnants of sin are purged through suffering prior to entrance into heaven) emerged into widespread acceptance. Gregory I appears to have read Augustine widely but at times twisted Augustine's insights in the process of popularizing them. However, Gregory faithfully mirrored Augustine when he wrote, "Everyone is presented in judgment just as he is when he departs this life. But, nevertheless, it must be believed that there is, for the sake of certain lesser faults, a purgatorial fire before the judgment" (*Dialogues* 4.40). Augustine based his belief in "a certain purgational fire" (*Handbook of Faith, Hope, and Love* 18.69) on 2 Maccabees 12:38-45, a passage he understood to be canonical, as well as on "the authority of the universal church" (*The Care That Should Be Taken of the Dead* 1.3). In this transitory state the departed, though yet to be purified, are benefited through the prayers of the living. "By the prayers of the Holy Church, and by the salvific sacrifice, and by the alms which are given for the spirits, there is no doubt that the dead are aided, that the Lord might deal more mercifully with them than their sins would deserve" (*Sermons* 172.2). Influenced deeply by Augustine's orthodoxy, Gregory gave the doctrine of an interim purgational state its most dogmatic expression, largely based upon a series of visions and appeals to the miraculous.[9]

THE LATE MEDIEVAL CHURCH
AND THE DOCTRINE OF THE CHURCH (1000–1500)

The medieval period is often looked upon as a time of unchanging social conditions. But in fact, much was happening in Europe during those centuries, and the church was changing too. The late medieval church was not the same as the early medieval church. In regard to the authority of the church, two issues appear to have been central concerns in the late medieval period: first, the relationship of the church to the state; and second, the authority of the popes in the church. As for the sacraments, it was in the late medieval period that their number and function were solidified in the later sanctioned teachings of Roman Catholic theology.

The Late Medieval Church
and the Authority of the Church

As noted earlier, the church at Rome survived the turbulent collapse of the Roman Empire and the intrusion of pagan tribes. It was at this time that Gregory I assumed not only religious prerogatives but political ones as well. With the emergence of the Franks and the establishment of another political entity in the Merovingian dynasty (418–714), which was succeeded by the expansive Carolingian kingdom (714–843), the relationship of the state to the church was frequently acted out. Popes often crowned kings, indicating that the church was superior to the state, though kings aided the popes by granting them lands. The chaotic demise of the Carolingian Empire, a state that geographically had embraced most of modern Europe, plunged the West into what was truly a Dark Age. Out of this difficult period, where strong political alliances did not exist, the modern nation-states of France and Germany emerged, along with a revived and strident papacy. The secular and religious powers, however, were on a collision course as the state assumed powers accorded to the church. The summit of the controversy was reached when Gregory VII, a reforming pope, clashed with the king of Germany, Henry IV, in what has been called the Investiture Struggle. In the quest to lift the church from a nadir of influence, Gregory VII (d. c.1085; pope 1073–1085) asserted the supremacy of the church over kings and princes. Among his claims was the insistence that princes were subject to popes before kings, that popes ought to be allowed to depose monarchs, and that Christ's vicar had the authority to absolve vassals from their political allegiances. The Investiture Struggle concerned the practice in the early Middle Ages of an emperor or prince crowning abbots or bishops-elect with the emblems of spiritual authority.

281

Gregory VII attacked this custom, asserting the superiority of the church over the state in ecclesiastical confirmations. Under the threat of a church-sanctioned rebellion by his princes as well as excommunication from the church, Henry begged for forgiveness at Canossa in 1076. At that moment Gregory's claim to the church's superiority over the state was confirmed. Though the issue was far from being resolved, an agreement was struck in the Concordat at Worms (1122). Emperors would forfeit the right to appoint bishops, creating the distinctively Western notion of the separation of church and state. The church, however, sought to dominate the state, not merely to regain religious privileges, as the pontificates of Innocent III (1160/1–1216; pope 1198–1216) and Boniface VIII (c.1234–1303; pope 1294–1303) evidence. Innocent exercised unparalleled power over nations, claiming to be "a God of Pharaoh, set between God and man, lower than God but higher than man." Boniface issued *Unam Sanctum* (1302), arguing that the church possessed the sword of the state, since "the temporal sword is in the power of Peter." Steven Ozment has made the acute observation that "many of the papacy's problems in the late Middle Ages stemmed directly from the pope's continuing conception of himself as more politically powerful than he could be in the new world of ascendant secular nation-states."[10]

A second claim by the papacy of earthly preeminence concerned the authority of church councils. From the time of the papacy of Gelasius I (d. 496), Roman bishops claimed priority over earthly monarchs. Basing their view upon Matthew 16:19, they asserted the same over the church universal. Against this medieval papal claim, John of Paris (c.1255–1306) and Marsilius of Padua (c.1275–1342) argued that popes should be subject to the people of God as kings should be to the citizenry. For much of the thirteenth and fourteenth centuries, the issue of the authority of the popes was argued in the Conciliar Movement, an attempt to reverse the embarrassment to the church's prestige and decline of power in the context of simultaneously reigning popes wherein each claimed to be the sole Vicar of Christ. Some within the church called for a subordination of the councils to the pope, a circumstance evident in the Fourth Lateran Council (1215). Others wanted a mutual sharing of power. Still others sought to subject the papacy to a general council of the church that represented the

282

faithful. The Conciliar Movement gradually lost momentum in the fourteenth century. Pius II (1405–1464; pope 1458–1464) delivered the deathblow in 1460 when he issued a bull condemning any appeals beyond the pope to councils. While the popes had difficulty applying the prerogatives of Peter and Matthew 16 to rulers, they managed to have their way in the late medieval church. Such was one of the causes of the Reformation in the sixteenth century.

The Late Medieval Church and the Sacraments of the Church

The evolution of the number of sacraments from two to seven in the church is difficult to trace. Some, such as Bernard of Clairvaux (1090–1153), taught that there were ten or eleven of them. In retrospect, it was the influential scholar Peter Lombard (c.1100–1160), in *The Four Sentences,* who limited the number to the seven. The dominance of his work in the curriculum of the universities (as well as the works of Thomas Aquinas, who followed Lombard at this point) made the teaching of the seven sacraments standard in the period. The Council of Florence (1438–1445) was the first gathering of the church to mandate it. "There are seven sacraments of the New Law, viz. baptism, confirmation, the eucharist, penance, extreme unction, orders, and marriage."

The meaning and role of the sacraments in the late medieval church are more important than the number for an understanding of subsequent ecclesiastical events. Medieval Christians viewed themselves as on an earthly salvation pilgrimage. They were as unworthy of salvation as uncertain of its obtainment. Salvation was understood to come to fallen creatures by an infusion of God's grace through the church and its sacraments and to be realized through priestly pronouncement. Teachers in the church generally agreed that sacraments had an objective function; that is, it was through them that God's grace was conveyed to the Christian, causing an increase of grace and charity that had the potential of such degrees of personal purification that it was possible to go to heaven—the state of a final justification. However, the teachers were not agreed on whether the grace necessary for salvation was of one's own nature and efforts or whether it was from God. Lombard, for example, argued in *The Four Sentences* that the increase of grace came only from the Holy Spirit and was not the result of human striving, at least in its formative, though expansive, stages. Thomas Aquinas (c.1225–1274) opposed this teaching by arguing that saving grace emerged from a divine and personal mutual endeavor; otherwise, it could not be said to be voluntary. John Duns Scotus (c.1265–1308) put the cause of infused grace in the will of God rather than in a gracious cooperation. Others, such as William of Ockham (c.1285–1347), Robert Holcot (d. 1349), and Gabriel Biel (c.1420–1495), taught that grace was an appropriate reward of human effort. Said Holcot, "According to God's established law the pilgrim who does what he can to dispose himself to grace always receives grace."[11]

Whether grace was brought to the Christian by the Holy Spirit, through a cooperation with God, or as a reward for self-effort, the scholars of the church agreed that the means of the grace were the sacraments. The sacrament of baptism was believed to wash away the effects of original sin, remove any actual sins, and weaken the hold of any subsequent allurements to sins. Other sacraments, such as the Eucharist, confirmation, and orders, granted an increase of grace. Penance and extreme unction replaced degrees of grace lost by sinning. Ozment summarized the viewpoint of the medieval saint like this: "In theological doctrine the medieval Christian was always sinning, always beginning anew, always returning to the sacraments for short-lived strength and assurance."[12]

The first general council of the church to specify the number, meaning, and role of the sacraments was the Council of Florence (1438–1445). Three sacraments indelibly imprint the soul and are not repeatable: baptism, confirmation, and orders. Two deal with the maintenance of the church: through orders the church is to be governed; through marriage it increases numerically. The formula produced by the council set forth the meaning and function of the others.

Our sacraments, however, not only contain grace, but also confer it on those who receive them worthily. . . . Through baptism we are spiritually reborn; through confirmation we grow in grace and are strengthened in faith. Having been regenerated and strengthened, we are sustained by the divine

284

food of the eucharist. But if we become sick in soul through sin, we are healed spiritually as well as physically, in proportion as it benefits the soul, through extreme unction.[13]

THE EARLY MODERN CHURCHES AND THE DOCTRINE OF THE CHURCH (1500–1750)

From a religious viewpoint, the most stunning event in the sixteenth century was the schism of the Western Catholic Church and the emergence of both Roman Catholicism and the Protestant churches. Each claimed to be the heir of the fifteen previous centuries, though each selectively appealed to the past to justify their claims. In the spheres of the structure of the church and the role and meaning of the sacraments, the two parties held widely different perspectives.

THE ROMAN CATHOLIC CHURCH AND THE DOCTRINE OF THE CHURCH

In some respects, the early modern period was not a period of great change for the Roman Catholic Church. But during this period, the Roman Catholic Church cemented its own traditional view on its structure and sacraments.

The Roman Catholic Church and the Structure of the Church

The Roman Catholic Church embraced the governmental framework of the medieval church, a rule through bishops. The episcopal structure—a hierarchical rule—was presided over by a pope, a man recognized as the successor of St. Peter and the Vicar of Christ on earth, though the prerogative of infallibility was centuries from recognition. The *Tridentine Profession of Faith* (1564), a doctrinal summary derived from the *Canons and Dogmatic Decrees of the Council of Trent*, calls the faithful to confess: "I acknowledge the holy Catholic Apostolic Roman Church for the mother and mistress of all churches; and I promise and swear true obedience to the Bishop of

285

Rome, successor to St. Peter, Prince of the Apostles, and Vicar of Jesus Christ" (X).

The Roman Catholic Church and the Sacraments of the Church

The grand defining moment of the Roman Catholic Church as it evolved in conflict with a myriad of social, religious, and political forces in the late fifteenth and early sixteenth centuries was the Council of Trent (1545–1563). There the issues of controversy with Protestants were carefully delineated and mandated. The greater part of the council's findings concern the role and meaning of the sacraments since the larger issue of concern was the manner in which righteousness and life is brought to pilgrim sinners. In numerous ways Trent reflects the earlier Council of Florence. The number of sacraments was fixed at seven ("Decrees on the Sacraments," "On Sacraments in General" 1); three of them (baptism, confirmation, and orders) imprint a spiritual character on the soul and are nonrepeatable (11). Further, sacraments convey and confer grace objectively; that is, the sacraments do not witness to grace already received but rather are the means of receiving grace. Trent makes this quite emphatic in the condemnatory decrees. "If any one saith, that these sacraments were instituted for the sake of nourishing faith alone, let him be anathema" (5). "If anyone saith, the sacraments of the New Law do not contain the grace which they signify; or that they do not confer that grace . . . as though they were merely outward signs of grace or justice received through faith . . . let him be anathema" (6).

Having established that the sacraments are means of justifying grace, Trent elaborated on the meaning and function of each sacrament. For example, baptism is the instrumental cause of justification. It inaugurates the gradual attainment of greater degrees of righteousness, which include sanctification and renewal ("Decrees on Justification" 7), while the meritorious cause is Christ. Concerning the Eucharist, Trent defined the presence of Christ as an actual, miraculous, corporeal presence; the common elements are transubstantiated (changed in substance) into the body and blood of Christ ("Decree concerning the Most Holy Sacrament of the Eucharist" 4). The fruit of the Eucharistic observance is that of gaining forgiveness for postbaptismal sins. "This sacrifice is truly propitiatory. . . . For the

286

Lord, appeased by the oblation thereof, and granting the grace and gift of penitence, forgives even heinous crimes and sins" ("Doctrine of the Sacrifice of the Mass" 2). The faithful are called upon to confess, "I profess, likewise, that in the mass there is offered to God a true, proper, and propitiatory sacrifice for the living and the dead; and that in the most holy sacrament of the eucharist there is truly, really, and substantially, the body and blood, together with the soul and divinity of our Lord Jesus Christ" ("Tridentine Profession of Faith" 6).

The sacrament of penance functions like baptism to forgive sins, but in an entirely different circumstance and manner. Baptism is a laver of washing and an entrance into life; penance is a renewing and restoration from a lapse into sin after having received life. Baptism is once for all time; penance is repeatable. "This sacrament of penance is, for those who have fallen after baptism, necessary unto salvation; as baptism itself is for those who have not as yet been regenerated" ("On the Most Holy Sacraments of Penance and Extreme Unction" 2).

The sacrament of extreme unction is administered to those in the state of bodily weakness. It signifies the giving of the grace of the Spirit, "whose anointing cleanses away sins, if there be any to be expiated . . . and strengthens the soul of the sick person" ("On the Sacrament of Extreme Unction" 2). Unlike penance, it is not dependent on contrition, confession, or works of satisfaction; it is a granting of grace in weakness.

The Protestant Churches and the Doctrine of the Church

While the Protestant Reformers were unified in their perception that the late medieval church was in need of reform (in this they had some commonality with their Roman Catholic counterparts) and agreed essentially on grace and forgiveness, their deepest internal conflicts were over the structure of the church and the meaning of the sacraments. Thus, in discussing the history of the Protestant movement, scholars speak of various traditions, primarily the Lutheran, Calvinist, Anglican, and Anabaptist traditions.

The Lutheran Churches and the Doctrine of the Church

*M*artin Luther (1483–1546), as the fountainhead of the Reformation, had a greater influence on Protestants' conceptions of what the church should be than did perhaps any other individual. Though some Protestant bodies would go further than Luther in redefining the church, the churches that bear his name stuck fairly close to his teachings on the matter.

Lutheranism, the church, and society. Luther conceived of the church as one, apostolic, and invisible, though the visible manifestation of the church was composed of believers and unbelievers. "The church be properly the congregation of saints and true believers, yet see that in this life many hypocrites and evil persons are mingled with it" (*Augsburg Confession* 8). The church is where you find two identifying characteristics: It is where there is accurate doctrinal preaching and where the sacraments are correctly taught and administered. The churches in Germany were essentially congregational in polity on the local level, with an equality of all ministers; there was no episcopal hierarchy. However, a hierarchy of sorts did prevail as Luther substituted a lay-civil magistrate for a clerical one. Ecclesiastical power rested in the hands of civil magistrates who appointed ministers and superintendents for the churches. In the matter of the relationship of the church to the state, Luther argued that the two were distinct and separate spheres. The state was godless and ruthless, capable of great evil but entrusted by God to alone bear the sword and maintain the civil peace; it was the realm answerable to reason. The church, however, was the community of faith and godliness; there the authority of Scripture prevailed over reason. Rebellion against the state for even the most just cause was treason, anarchy, and godlessness. Rightly would rebels be subjected by the state to the most forceful recrimination. In Luther's judgment, it was never right to rise up against the state in the name of Christianity, though he did not take the abuses of the state with silence. He strongly urged the state to address its oppressive measures; however, arguments and righteous living, not swords, were the weapons of the church in a wicked world. Quite clearly, Luther's view has been adjusted in subsequent centuries as the Lutheran community has found its place in different social and political settings.

288

Lutheranism and the sacraments. The Protestant churches reduced the number of sacraments from seven (the Roman Catholic position) to two. More importantly, they renounced the idea that the function of the sacraments was to convey to the saint increases of justifying grace. According to the *Augsburg Confession,* the sacraments are "signs and testimonies of the will of God to us, set forth to stir up and confirm faith" (13). They function subjectively, calling the saint to faith in the thing signified in the sacrament; they do not objectively deliver grace.[14] Luther spoke of baptism in this fashion: "It worketh forgiveness, delivers from death and the devil, and gives everlasting life to all who believe" (*Small Catechism* IV.2). But then he posed the question "How can water do such great things?" His answer was that "it is not water, indeed, that does it, but the Word of God which is with and in the water, and faith, which trusts in the Word of God in the water. For without the Word of God it is nothing but water, and no baptism" (IV.3). According to Luther, the sinful nature inherited from Adam is not purged away in baptism, leaving only residual remnants that require purgation before salvation is realized. Baptism breaks the universal hold of Adam's inheritance in us; salvation is immediately granted by divine reckoning for Christ's sake; and the saint is to labor to reduce the remnants of Adam's nature as long as life lasts. When life ends, the saint is immediately glorified and the sin nature is finally and completely removed in the resurrection body. Though Luther advocated the baptism of those incapable of faith in the Word, he recognized that it was only the faith of those who brought the child.

> Such faith cannot save the child but through its intercession and help the child may receive his own faith from God; and this faith will save him. Children are not baptized because of the faith of sponsors or of the church; rather the faith of sponsors and of the church gains their own faith for them and it is this faith that they are baptized and believe for themselves. (*Works* 17.82–83)

289

The baptism of infants places them in the church; it is an "ecclesiastical salvation" whereby they are placed in a community of faith so that they can be instructed to embrace and confirm the thing signified at their baptism, when they were incapable of faith in the Word of God.

Luther argued, in the tradition of Irenaeus, for a realistic, corporeal, nontransubstantial, nonmeritorious view of the Eucharist. It is a sacrifice of praise and a means of Christian grace because Christ is truly and really present in it (consubstantially). The effect of this sacrament, like baptism, is that it strengthens faith. The Word and symbol are needed because in this life we are constantly attacked and endangered. Faith in the thing symbolized by the sacrament, which is verbally expressed in the Word, brings to the saint the assurance of God's good pleasure and mercy. Luther asks the question "How can bodily eating and drinking do such great things?" His reply is consistent with his view of the subjective means of the efficacy of baptism. "Eating and drinking, indeed, do not do them, but the words which stand here: 'Given and shed for you, for the remission of sins.' Which words, besides the bodily eating and drinking, are the main point in the sacrament; and he who believes these words has that which they declare, namely, forgiveness of sins" (*Small Catechism* V).[15]

The Calvinist Churches and the Doctrine of the Church

The second great stream of the Magisterial Reformation (along with Lutheranism) is Calvinism. Though heavily influenced by Martin Luther, John Calvin (1509–1564) modified Luther's thought with several original ideas. The Reformed, or Calvinistic, churches took these ideas and ran with them.

Calvinism, the church, and society. According to Calvin, there is but one universal, Catholic Church. This church is both visible and invisible; the invisible church is comprised of all the saints of God, the elect, of all ages. The visible church is a professing community composed of both "wheat and tares" ("We are not bidden to distinguish between reprobate and elect—that is for God alone, not for us, to do" [*Institutes of the Christian Religion* VI.1.3]). This church began in the promises God made to Abraham and was formed in the Egyptian exodus when God redeemed a people from the land of bondage through the sprinkling of blood. In the giving of the law at Sinai, God instructed the professing community on how to walk before Him, pointing them to Christ, the true Passover, who would seal a new covenant with God's new people, the "New Israel," since at that time He would extend His covenantal blessings beyond Israel to all nations.

Like Luther, Calvin envisioned two distinguishing marks of the true church. The church is to be found where the Word of God is proclaimed and the sacraments are observed according to the biblical pattern. "Wherever we see the Word of God purely preached and heard, and the sacraments administered according to Christ's institution, there, it is not to be doubted, a church of God exists" (*Institutes of the Christian Religion* IV.1.9). Calvin explained the governance of the church using the Ephesians 4:11 passage. He believed that apostles, prophets, and evangelists were offices given in the early Christian era and, while they may arise periodically as need may require, pastors and teachers are the ordinary, permanent offices in the churches since that time. These pastors and teachers form the presbytery of leaders, each having separate duties in each local church. Pastors are appointed by the approval of the people under the direction of the presbytery of other recognized ministers in the church. Calvin, at least in incipient form, recognized a rule by leaders over the church by the vote of the people; it was a modest presbyterial form of government. The pastors of the churches in Geneva did meet periodically, and this may be thought of as a presbytery. There were also to be deacons, whose service was to care for the poor (*Institutes of the Christian Religion* IV.1.4–9). The purpose of the church is to renew the earth from the devastating effects consequent to Adam's first sin.

Calvin viewed the state more positively than Luther, though he did view it as having a sphere of authority separate from that of the church. The state had religious obligations "to cherish and protect the outward worship of God, to defend sound doctrine," as well as to maintain civil order and employ the sword (*Institutes of the Christian Religion* IV.20.2). While lower magistrates might legitimately overthrow a bad government, it was never the right or duty of a citizen or collection of private persons to resist or overthrow a government. In this, Calvin agreed with Luther and Zwingli (1484–1531), though Thomas Münzer (c.1468 or 1489/90–1525) and John Knox (c.1513–1572) dissented. Knox, the fiery Scot, believed it was sin for citizens not to rebel against a political tyrant—a view adopted by Scots Presbyterians.

Calvinism and the sacraments. Calvin viewed the sacraments as related to the Word of God, being marks of the church, each setting forth Christ and in Him the treasures of heavenly grace. Sacraments related to the Word in their function as outward signs, which confirmed the Word. He defined them by saying, "It is an outward sign by which the Lord seals on our conscience the promises of his good will toward us in order to sustain the weakness of our faith. . . . One may call it a testimony of divine grace to us, confirmed by an outward sign, with mutual attestation of our piety toward him" (*Institutes of the Christian Religion* IV.14.1). Baptism is defined as a "sign of initiation by which we are received into the society of the church, in order that, ingrafted in Christ, we may be reckoned among God's children" (IV.15.1). The purposes of baptism are three: to attest to forgiveness, to teach us death to sin, and to assure us that we are partakers of God's blessings. Like Luther, Calvin understood that the efficacy of the sign or sacrament was dependent upon a hearty faith in the thing it signified, that is, the Word of God. It is the Word in the sign that defines the sacrament. In answer to the question of why the apostle Paul referred to baptism as a washing of rebirth in Titus 3:5, the *Heidelberg Catechism* notes, "By the divine pledge and sign he wishes to assure us that we are just as truly washed from our sins spiritually as our bodies are washed with water" (Q. 73). Calvin defended the baptism of infants, believing that children of the godly are born members of the church by virtue of the hereditary nature of the Abrahamic covenant, circumcision having been replaced in the New Covenant with baptism as a sign. At times, he seems to suggest that infants are regenerated, though they are so without faith ("God declares that he adopts our babies as his own before they are born" [*Institutes of the Christian Religion* IV.15.20]) and speaks of baptism as regenerative (IV.17.1). At other times he views infant baptism as a sign of faith to come at a future time ("Infants are baptized into a future repentance and faith, and even though these have not yet been formed in them, the seed of both lies within them by the secret working of the Spirit" [IV.16.19]).

Calvin defined the Eucharist as "a spiritual banquet, wherein Christ attests himself to be the life-giving bread" (*Institutes of the Christian*

Religion IV.17.1). Rejecting the materialist interpretation of Luther and the memorialism of Zwingli, Calvin viewed the Lord's Table with a mystical realism. In meditation on the deeper significance of the outward forms in the Eucharist, the believer is lifted spiritually heavenward, where he or she enjoys spiritual union with the resurrected Christ (IV.17.31). As to how this "spiritual feeding" takes place, Calvin wrote: "If anyone should ask me how this takes place, I shall not be ashamed to confess that it is a secret too lofty for either my mind to comprehend or my words to declare. And to speak more plainly, I rather experience than understand it" (IV.17.32).

While Calvin, Luther, and Zwingli maintained views concerning the Eucharist in a strident, nonconcessionary fashion, such was not the case of the later Reformers. Calvin and Theodore Beza (1519–1605) reached a rapprochement with Heinrich Bullinger (1504–1575), Zwingli's successor, allowing the German Swiss and French Swiss reformations to unite. Beza reached agreement with Luther's successor, Philipp Melanchthon (1497–1560), and others, such as Thomas Cranmer (1489–1556) of England, on the Eucharist as well.

The Anabaptist Churches and the Doctrine of the Church

In discussions of the Protestant Reformation, it has been generally helpful to see two broad types of reform. First, the Magisterial Reformation of Luther, Calvin, and Zwingli, which envisioned mutual cooperation between church and state in perpetuating reform. Second, the Radical Reformation, or those groups that rejected the role of the state in religious change, advocating the idea of the separation of church and state. Scholars in the study of the Radical Reformation have recognized three subgroups: Rationalists or Antitrinitarians, Spiritualists, and Anabaptists. Though this latter group is actually a spectrum of groups with differing beliefs at certain points, for the sake of tracing the origin of the Baptist tradition the focus must be on one particular Anabaptist group, the Swiss Brethren, followers of the Swiss reformer Ulrich Zwingli. The Swiss Brethren, or Anabaptists, appear to have been the root source in Europe of the later English and American Baptists, at least as far as doctrinal distinctives are concerned.

293

Anabaptism, the church, and society. In contrast to the major Reformers, the earliest Anabaptists took a negative, separatist view of the role of the church in the state. Their view of the church would directly impact their understanding of the sacrament of baptism. The state was viewed as the domain of the devil, and unbelievers should not be forced into any religious affirmation by either the state or the church; the church is a voluntary society where coercion is restricted. Some, though not all, in the Anabaptist tradition forbade participation in government entirely.

For the Anabaptists, then, the church was a called-out assembly of people who gather to worship God, attend the sacraments, submit to pastors, and do good in the world. Each church was independent, with a staunch aversion to any outside control, whether it be from the state or an ecclesiastical court.

Anabaptism and the sacraments. Ulrich Zwingli nurtured a group of reform-minded men and attempted, with their assistance, to introduce Protestant principles in Zürich. However, after Reformation was secured in principle in 1523, the outworking of it in the life of the church revealed that Zwingli and Conrad Grebel (c.1498–1526), the leader of the Swiss Brethren, had significant differences. Zwingli's belief in the necessity of state support for reform made him leery and cautious of quick changes. This and the Anabaptist vision that a church should be a voluntary community caused him to distance himself from his own followers. Among the many issues that eventually separated Reformer from Reformer, the central one was the matter of baptism. At issue were the nature of the church and role of the state. Anabaptists insisted that a sign should follow the thing it figures, not anticipate it. People are born into the world lost and need to be regenerated. One does not enter the church as a citizen as one enters the state. In the latter one is naturally born into it; in the former one is spiritually reborn into it. The state is not the church; the church is not the state. The earliest Anabaptist confession, The *Schleitheim Confession* of 1527, states: "Baptism shall be given to all those who have learned repentance and amendment of life, and to all those who walk in the resurrection of Jesus Christ, and wish to be buried with him in death. . . . This excludes all infant baptism, the highest and chief abomination of the pope." While the mode of baptism was not

294

an issue to the earliest Anabaptists, immersion became the common practice among some Dutch Anabaptists, who influenced the emergence of English Baptists (*The London Confession of 1689*, "On Baptism" 4).

On the issue of the Lord's Table, the Anabaptist tradition followed closely the teachings of Ulrich Zwingli. In contrast to Luther, Zwingli rejected the notion that physical things can contain or dispense spiritual realities, the physical and spiritual being separate entities. The elements of bread and wine were only bread and wine; the resurrected Christ was not present. Therefore, Zwingli conceived in the Eucharist a physical reminder of Christ's sacrifice, though it was still more than a bare memorial to him. In the *Sixty-Seven Articles* of 1523, Zwingli argued "that Christ, having sacrificed Himself once, is to eternity a certain and valid sacrifice for the sins of all the faithful, where from it follows that the mass is not a sacrifice, but is a remembrance of the sacrifice and assurance of the salvation which Christ has given us" (18). *The Schleitheim Confession* states: "In the breaking of bread we are of one mind and are agreed [as follows]: All those who wish to break one bread in remembrance of the broken body of Christ, and who wish to drink of one drink as a remembrance of the shed blood of Christ, shall be united beforehand by baptism in one body of Christ."

The Anglican Churches and the Doctrine of the Church

Forming later than other major streams of the Reformation, Anglicanism shows signs of having done some picking and choosing among the existing options. But these options were welded together into a structure that has endured.

Anglicanism, the church, and society. The Anglican community finds its roots in the Magisterial Reformation. That is, its view of the relationship of church and state is generally reflective of the continental Calvinist tradition. In ecclesiastical structure, the church is episcopal or hierarchical. The head of the Church of England is the reigning monarch, with the leadership of the church under the direction of two archbishops, those of York and Canterbury, with the latter being the oldest church in the land. The flow of authority proceeds from the archbishops to bishops, who preside over various dioceses, to rectors or priests, and finally to the laity. The marks of the church are the same as those expressed by Luther and Calvin; true congregations are those where the Word of God is faithfully preached and the two sacraments are observed (*Thirty-Nine Articles* 19).

Anglicanism and the sacraments. The sacraments are defined in a manner reflective of the Calvinist tradition. "Sacraments ordained of Christ be not only badges or tokens of Christian men's profession, but rather they be certain sure witnesses, and effectual signs of grace, and God's good will to us" (*Thirty-Nine Articles* 25). Baptism is defined as a "sign of profession," and a "sign of Regeneration or New-Birth." Those who receive it "rightly are grafted into the Church; the promises of the forgiveness of sin, and of our adoption to be the sons of God by the Holy Spirit are visibly signed and sealed" (27). Consistent with the outlook of the Magisterial Reformation, baptism is extended to infants. The sacrament of the Eucharist, "the sacrament of Redemption," is defined as a "heavenly and spiritual" eating in faith (28), seemingly reflective of the agreements forged among the later Reformers.

THE LATE MODERN CHURCHES AND THE DOCTRINE OF THE CHURCH (1750–PRESENT)

The issues that have preoccupied the church in recent centuries have largely concerned the possibility and nature of Christianity in an Enlightenment and post-Enlightenment world. Some in the church have been consumed with refashioning the old faith in light of the advances in the sciences and philosophy in order to preserve it. For others in the church, the task has been to demonstrate the viability of the old faith. Hence, the scholars and writers of recent centuries have been concerned with polemics and apologetics.

The doctrine of the church and the sacraments has not been the subject of detailed new studies. New discoveries and options in ecclesiology have not been the focus of heated discussions, though new emphases have arisen now and again. While advances in our knowledge of the nature of language and hermeneutics have resulted in significant discussions, the major ecclesiastical traditions have remained within the structures developed in the sixteenth century and before.

THE PROTESTANT TRADITIONS AND THE DOCTRINE OF THE CHURCH

In an era when the liberal and conservative wings of Protestantism were growing more and more unlike each other, in regard to the doctrine of the church they were not in as much disagreement. Some new ideas about the church were, however, advanced in both wings.

The Liberal Protestant Tradition and the Doctrine of the Church

*F*riedrich Schleiermacher (1768–1834), generally recognized as the "father of religious liberalism," is an illustration of this point. While the structure of his theology is reflective of a subjective impulse in defining the essence of religion, his doctrine of the church was largely quite traditional (though, as we have seen, his understanding of the Trinity and Christology were quite nontraditional, even heterodox). He defined the church as a religious, self-conscious, dependent community or fellowship of believers. Membership in that community is based upon the psychological perception of dependence on Christ through faith in Jesus as Redeemer. Said Schleiermacher, "The Christian Church takes shape through the coming together of regenerate individuals to form a system of mutual interaction and co-operation."[16]

For Schleiermacher, the distinguishing features of the church, as Luther and Calvin suggested, are two: the ministry of the Word of God and the observance of the sacraments in the gathering of the faithful to worship.[17] Schleiermacher understood that baptism confers membership in the Christian church and salvation through divine grace in regeneration to each individual. Like Luther, he was careful to distinguish an external washing, which cannot produce any spiritual effects, and an internal washing by the Word through faith. "Baptism . . . is ineffectual only when it is imparted prematurely, before the work of preaching is complete and has awakened faith. It is different with the

297

assertation that faith springs from baptism as a fruit. This is obviously in contradiction to the whole practice of the apostles and the whole experience of the church."[18] He believed that the practice of baptizing infants was not an apostolic custom but quickly became assimilated into the church. Infant baptism was a symbolic, dedicatory action and was only complete when a profession of faith followed after instruction.

Schleiermacher recognized the sacrament of the Lord's Table to be the highest act and the climax of worship in the church. Its function was to strengthen believers in the Christian faith. Schleiermacher was willing to reject what he felt were two interpretative extremes: the Roman Catholic corporeal view (because it attached magical effects to physical properties) and the Anabaptist view (which interpreted the Eucharist as a bare sign or memorial). He was willing to advocate any theories between the two as long as a spiritual, participationalist meaning was attached to the elements. The fruit of participating in the Supper is that it confirms union with Christ and the community of Christians one with another.

The Plymouth Brethren Tradition and the Doctrine of the Church

The distinctive feature in Brethren ecclesiology is the heightened role of laity in the ordering of the church, accompanied by a rejection of a professional clergy. The roots of this 1820s movement are this found in the Church of England and the experience of John Nelson Darby, among others. Darby (1800–1882), an Anglican priest-missionary to Roman Catholics in Wicklow County, south of Dublin in Ireland, felt the repressive measures of state influence on the Church of England, which greatly curtailed his activities of evangelism. From that disappointment, he came to see the negative potential of state-controlled religions firsthand and quickly found others who felt the same way. Groups of like-minded people began to meet both in Dublin and Plymouth, England. These groups were characterized by the rejection of an ordained and trained clergy as well as simplicity of meetings to "break bread" and hear teaching from the Bible. When meeting houses emerged from living-room studies, they were denominated as chapels, not churches. No one was referred to by the title of pastor. "Brother" and "sister" were the accepted terms of recognition, and elders directed the chapels. Though the Brethren distinguished themselves by devotion to the Scriptures and a primitive simplicity of worship style, the distinctive features of the movement stand in marked antithesis to the experience of state-church religion at its worst. Darby particularly embraced the belief that all denominations were corrupt and antichrist organizations, and he exhorted believers to leave them. He was amazed that, while many embraced one or another of his personal views, many in America did not embrace his negative views of the established churches. The Brethren, however, did attempt to grant the laity a greater role in the life of the church. Having provided a corrective to professionally led, laity-marginalized churches, they have made and continue to make a major contribution to the life of all the churches.

The Roman Catholic Tradition and the Doctrine of the Church

One is hard pressed to find a truly radical departure in any area of the Roman Catholic Church's doctrine of its own nature in recent centuries. Mostly what has taken place is some development and some hardening of previous positions.

The Roman Catholic Tradition and Ecclesiastical Authority

One recent change within the Roman Catholic community has been the recognition of papal infallibility. That is, while the church has recognized since Trent that the Vicar of Christ is the teacher of orthodoxy in the church, he was not accorded the status that, in his official capacity as teacher (being the true successor of Peter), he functioned errorlessly. In historic context it would seem that the impetus to grant the popes this additional prestige was the same reason why the church produced the famous Syllabus of Errors (1864) and called Vatican I (1869): to address the threats to the church in the nineteenth century from without and within, and to provide another bulwark against unwanted teachings and influences upon the church. The official statement of infallibility issued by Vatican I is as follows:

The Roman Pontiff, when he speaks *ex cathedra,* that is, when in discharge of the office of pastor and doctor of all Christians, by virtue of his supreme Apostolic authority, he defines a doctrine regarding faith or morals to be held by the universal church . . . is possessed of that divine infallibility with which the divine redeemer willed that his church should be endowed for defining doctrine regarding faith and morals. (*Dogmatic Decrees,* "First Dogmatic Constitution" 4)

The *Catechism of the Catholic Church* (1994) does not discuss the insights of Vatican I directly as it relates to papal infallibility. However, it does state, "The task of interpreting the Word of God [that is, sacred Tradition and sacred Scripture] authentically has been entrusted solely to the Magisterium of the Church, that is, to the Pope and to the bishops in communion with him" (100).

The Roman Catholic Tradition and the Sacraments

The somewhat recent *Catechism of the Catholic Church* (1994) can serve as a lens for determining trends within the Roman community. The sacraments are defined in number and function as they were by the definitive Council of Trent in the sixteenth century. "The sacraments confer the grace that they signify. They are efficacious because in them Christ is at work" (1127). Grace is conferred in the manner described at the councils of Florence and Trent, *ex opere operato,* that is, by the fact of the act being performed (1128). The sacrament of baptism "erases original sin and turns a man toward God" (405), incorporating the recipient into the body of Christ (1267). Specifically, by baptism all sins, original and personal, are forgiven (1263); sins committed through weakness after baptism are forgiven through penance and extreme unction, a sacrament also referred to as the "Anointing of the Sick" (1459, 1520). According to the church, those who are ignorant of the gospel, but who are sincere in seeking truth and doing God's will as best they can, are eligible for salvation

(1260). The sacrament of the Eucharist strengthens the spiritual life, forgives sin for the living and the dead (1371), and increases baptismal grace (1392). The manner of Christ's presence is a miraculous corporeal presence, "a sacrifice because it represents (makes present) the sacrifice of the cross" (1366).

THE ORTHODOX TRADITION AND THE CHURCH

The Orthodox Church, commonly referred to as the Eastern Orthodox Church in the West, is actually composed of fourteen or so autonomous and self-governing churches. Within the Orthodox community four churches rank first in honor (Constantinople, Alexandria, Antioch, and Jerusalem), with the patriarch of Constantinople alone receiving the title of "Ecumenical," or universal, though he does not function in the same sort of authoritative role as the pope in Rome. The patriarch does not have the authority to impose his views on any of the churches (his authority is akin to that of the archbishop of Canterbury within the Anglican community). The unity in the Orthodox churches is a shared commonality of faith and the sacraments.

The Orthodox churches generally recognize seven sacraments, although it was not until the seventeenth century that that number was fixed. Further, the church does not restrict the channels of grace to these alone, because special events, such as the celebration at Epiphany, and other times of blessings are recognized as sacramentals. Through baptism all sins are forgiven, both original and actual; Christ is "put on" and the recipient becomes a member of the body of Christ. Trifold immersion is mandated lest the sacrament have no significance, and a small necklace with a cross is to be worn for the rest of life as a symbol of Christian identity. According to the *Confession of Dositheus* (1672), "those that are not regenerated, since they have not received the remission of hereditary sin, are, of necessity, subject to eternal punishment, and consequently cannot without Baptism be saved, so that infants ought, of necessity, to be baptized" (16). Unlike the Roman community, the Orthodox churches celebrate the sacrament of confirmation immediately after baptism; it marks the reception of the Holy Spirit.

For the Orthodox, the presence of Christ in the Eucharist is defined, as in the Roman Church, as a real corporeal presence, though the manner of Christ's presence is not delineated. It is explained as both a true sacrifice and yet not as one, because Christ was sacrificed once forever. An Orthodox child receives communion from infancy. Once a child understands right from wrong, the sacrament of repentance is urged, since through it postbaptismal sins are forgiven.

The other sacraments in the church are holy orders, marriage, and the anointing of the sick. The latter is given both to those sick of body and those sick of soul, not merely when physical life is threatened. It works forgiveness of sin and, sometimes, relief from sickness.

8

The End Times: Fulfillment of Our Blessed Hope

A teenage girl is struck by a drunk driver and left a "vegetable." The drunk driver escapes punishment through a legal technicality.

During an outbreak of tribal warfare in Africa, the Christians in one village run to their church building for safety. Some of the women are raped; all the believers are beaten to death with rifle butts.

A Texas church group is coming back from a ski trip in Colorado when a tire blows and the bus careens five hundred feet down the mountainside. Thirty-four of thirty-six die.

What can make right such terrible losses and such injustices? Can there be any hope left when all hope seems to be gone?

Called in the Scriptures "the blessed hope and the appearing of the glory of our great God and Savior, Christ Jesus" (Titus 2:13), the coming of the Redeemer to triumph over all His enemies is something Christians have universally longed for. While they have reckoned the insight of Jesus that "in the world you have tribulation" (John 16:33) to be a true description of things, Christians have found solace and confidence that the purposes of the ages will climax in Christ's return for His people. The world will not end in some tragic event like a madman unleashing nuclear destruction; rather, it will be consummated in the coming of Christ to judge this world and to gather His people out of it to enjoy His presence and reflect His glory forever. That is, there is a grand purpose in history; it will end not in a chaotic, random manner but instead with design and purpose, even glory. Jonathan Edwards, the American Puritan pastor-writer, struggled to explain to

303

his parishioners the ordering of all history by a divine directive and purpose in his great work *A History of Redemption* (1739). In it he argued that the purpose of time is a divine one: God is preparing a people for Himself, whom His Son came to purchase. These purchased people will be gathered to Him finally and completely when Christ comes again at the end of time.

For Christians, human history is the stage of a divine drama. It is the unfolding of a story that has left even the angels spellbound. It is this providential understanding of purpose behind the events of history that has sustained the people of God in their deepest sorrows and tempered their earthly joys. In reading the history of the church in this regard, at least three things are impressive. First, Christians have grasped from the earliest times the concept of the "blessed hope." Jesus spoke of it frequently; the writers of the Scriptures explained it; and the church has grasped it throughout the centuries. Second,

The Development of Millennialism

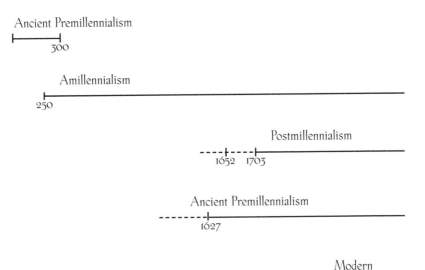

304

though the church embraced the notion of the Second Coming, often misapplying the teaching, there has not been agreement throughout the centuries concerning the chronology of events that precede it. Third, no doctrine has been so influenced by sociological context than the interpretation of the Second Coming. It appears that the experiences of God's people—times of suffering or times of prosperity—have provided a lens through which they have read the Bible.

The task before us is to trace out the major interpretations of the chronology of the end times, called the "blessed hope."

THE ANCIENT CHURCH AND THE END TIMES
(100–600)

It's an interesting but not an easy task to piece together a picture of what early Christians thought about the end times. Unfortunately, our sources for their thought in this area are relatively limited. Furthermore, this is another area where the early Christians evidently only gradually began to feel a need to develop an extensive theology. Nevertheless, most of the elements of later eschatologies can be found in this early period.

THE CHURCH FATHERS AND THE END TIMES (100–150)

The earliest Fathers in the church—those writings in the late first century and early second centuries that are not accorded the status of Scripture in either the Roman Catholic or Protestant traditions—did not attempt a synthesis of doctrine in any area. While it would be erroneous to suggest that they were ignorant of the great themes of Christian truth, it is valid to say that the tendency to systematize teachings did not preoccupy them. The evidence suggests that they viewed the coming of Christ as a vibrant hope embracing such ideas as the consummation of the ages, the resurrection of the dead, and the blessing of believers with everlasting life in Christ. J. N. D. Kelley described the understanding of the early church in this fashion:

305

Four chief moments dominate the eschatological expectation of early Christian theology—the return of Christ, known as the Parousia, the resurrection, the judgment, and the catastrophic ending of the present world-order. In the primitive period they were held together in a naive, unreflective fashion, with little or no attempt to work out their implications or solve the problems they raise.[1]

In discussing future events, the Fathers embraced a premillennial understanding; that is, the earliest writers after the apostles understood that Christ would return to earth and physically reign before the Final Judgment. They all anticipated a future bodily resurrection of believers. For example, Ignatius (c.35–c.107), after speaking of the bodily resurrection of Christ by the Father, stated, "[The Lord] in like fashion will so raise us also who believe on Him—His Father, I say, will raise us also—in Christ Jesus, apart from whom we have no true life" (*To the Trallians* 9). Interestingly, the writers of this period speak of the resurrection of believers without discussing the resurrection of the wicked dead; their focus was clearly upon the hope of believers (*1 Clement* 11:1; 12:7; 26:1; 27:1; 28:1; 51:1; 57:2; 58:1). In the resurrection to heavenly blessing, the heretic has no part (Ignatius, *To the Smyrneans* 7; *To the Ephesians* 11; *To the Romans* 4; *To the Trallians* 9). There is no consistent pattern of when these writers/writings viewed the time of the resurrection. Clement (d. 101?) placed it at the second advent of Christ (*1 Clement* 24); Barnabas placed it before the kingdom (*Epistle* 5); and the writer of the *Didache* put it after the Tribulation but before the Second Advent (16).

The second advent of Christ is a predominating theme in the Fathers; it is an imminent hope, a visible appearing of Christ in the Last Day. The Fathers associated the coming of Christ with the establishment of an earthly kingdom, though they were not in agreement on the details and did not suggest that it was to be one thousand years in duration. The purpose of the kingdom also varied among them. *Second Clement* saw it as a time of rest for believers (6) and worldwide rule by Christ (17); Barnabas spoke of it as a time of holiness in which

Christians live and rule the earth (6); the *Didache* portrayed it as a time prepared for the church (9); and Ignatius saw it as the future residence for believers (*To the Ephesians* 16; *To the Magnesians* 5). The time of the judgment of the wicked is seen to be at the Second Advent (*2 Clement* 16,17; *Barnabas* 15).

THE APOLOGISTS AND THE END TIMES (150–300)

Church leaders in this era manifested two tendencies in interpreting futuristic themes. Some, such as Justin Martyr and Tertullian, viewed prophetic passages with a literalistic sense, seeing a coming kingdom on the earth and a triumphant King. Others, such as Origen and Dionysius of Alexandria, spiritualized the same passages, arguing for a reign of Christ through the church in the redeemed. Scholars have suggested that the cause for such a shift in the church's interpretive outlook may have been the emergence of Platonism, the tendency to deemphasize the physical aspects of life for an inner spiritual reality. Also, the observation has been made that in times of persecution, as was the case in the early centuries, the church has looked for a dramatic deliverance from heaven, while in times of peace and triumph, such as that after the third century, the perspective changed to His victory over the church as individuals. In either case, the church continued to warmly embrace the hope of Christ's Second Coming. Finally, premillennialism may have suffered a loss of respectability in the Catholic Church when radical, reform-minded groups, such as the Montanists, adopted it. When the church condemned Montanism for its alleged excesses, it sought to distance itself from any affinity with its teachings so as to safeguard the purity of doctrine.

The Apologists' Nonspiritualizing Tradition and the End Times

Justin Martyr (c.100–c.165) is generally regarded as the most important second-century apologist. Understanding his insights is crucial to understanding the early church's view of future things because he wrote extensively on the subject, particularly for apologetical purposes. Justin connected three events: the second coming of Christ, the resurrection of the living and the dead, and the inauguration of a kingdom on the earth for one thousand years. His view of prophetic events has been described as ancient premillennialism. With a sense of immediacy, he awaited the literal coming of Christ to the earth to bless and to judge.

> The prophets have proclaimed two advents of His: the one already past . . . but the second when, according to prophecy, He shall come from heaven with glory, accompanied by His angelic host, when also He shall raise the bodies of all men who have lived, and shall clothe those of the worthy with immortality and send those of the wicked . . . into everlasting fire with the wicked devils. (*First Apology* 52)

Following these events, Christ would establish Himself in Jerusalem and reign as King for one thousand years. These insights he gained from the Revelation.

> We have perceived, moreover, that the expression, "The day of the Lord is as a thousand years," is connected with this subject. And further, there is a certain man, whose name was John, one of the apostles of Christ, who prophesied, by a revelation that was made to him, that those who believed in our Christ would dwell a thousand years in Jerusalem; and that thereafter the general, and in short, the eternal resurrection and judgment of all men would likewise take place. (*Dialogue to Trypho* 81)

The earliest Fathers in the church did not identify the Old Testament people of God with the New Testament church. For example, Barnabas made a clear distinction between Israel and the church (5). Clement of Rome did make a reference to Israel (*Letter to the Corinthians* 29), but he avoided making the assertion of an Israel-church identity. Further, in a lengthy discussion of the church in *The Shepherd*, Hermas is silent concerning an Israel identity ("Similitudes"

308

8–9). It is Justin, seeking to convert a Jewish man, Trypho, who made the Israel-church identity for the first time. Peter Richardson has made the point clearly. "The word 'Israel' is applied to the Christian Church for the first time by Justin Martyr c. A.D. 160."[2] "Nowhere from the close of the New Testament canon to Justin is the Church explicitly said to be Israel."[3] The identity of the church as the "true Israel" may have been occasioned by at least two factors. First, until the destruction of Israel following the Bar Kochba rebellion of 132–134, Christians avoided identity with Israel either because they were persecuted by the Jews or because they were treated with hostility by outsiders for being a Jewish sect. It would have been a common reaction by early Christians to avoid all identification with the cause of their affliction. Second, Martyr's intent in writing the *Dialogue* was to win a Jewish man to Christ. He seems to have employed a method of apologetics reminiscent of his apologetic to pagan philosophers. If there is any truth in such philosophers, it was because they derived it from Moses (a true philosopher is one who follows Moses, who followed Christ). So a true Jew, a true son of Israel, is a follower of the Christ and His people, who are now the true Israel of God. As the people of Israel were the "shadowy" people of God, Christians are the highest fulfillment of God's promises. In a direct sense, the church is Israel.

The same ancient premillennialist understanding of history is found in Irenaeus (c.130–c.200) and Tertullian (c.160–c.225). Such a view of future events appears to have been widely held in the churches at this time. Irenaeus, who claims to have derived his view of these things from Papias's writings (thus demonstrating continuity of perspective with the early first century), divided history into seven epics or thousand-year increments, with the last being an era of peace, the era of Sabbath-rest. Hence, he thought that he was living in the sixth period, which would end with the intense, destructive activity of Satan in the person of the Antichrist. After citing 2 Thessalonians 2:3 ("unless the apostasy comes first, and the man of lawlessness is revealed"), he stated, "For he [the Antichrist], being endued with all the power of the devil, shall come" (*Against Heresies* 5.25.1). After a time of Satanic deception, which concludes the sixth era, Christ will return, the resurrection of the righteous will take place, and the Millennium will begin. He described it as follows:

309

> These are [the calling of people to a banquet] in the times of
> the kingdom, that is, upon the seventh day, which has been
> sanctified, in which God rested from all the works which He
> had created, which is the true sabbath of the righteous, which
> they shall not be engaged in any earthly occupation; but shall
> have a table at hand prepared for them by God, supplying
> them with all sorts of dishes. (*Against Heresies* 5.33.2)

After the Millennium, the earth will be destroyed in judgment, the
final resurrection will occur, and the eternal state will begin with a
new heaven and a new earth.

Tertullian of North Africa did not differ from the eschatological
opinions of either Justin or Irenaeus, holding to a sevenfold millennial
theory of time. The seventh period will commence with the resurrection or transformation of the righteous into a subcelestial kingdom at
Christ's coming. He noted:

> We confess that a kingdom has been promised to us on earth,
> but before heaven and in another state of existence. It will be
> after the resurrection for a thousand years in the divinely
> built city of Jerusalem, let down from heaven. . . . After its
> thousand years are over, during which period the resurrection
> of the saints will be completed, who will rise earlier or later
> according to their merits, there will be the destruction of the
> world and the conflagration at the judgment. (*Against Marcion*
> 3.24.3)

The Apologists' Spiritualizing Tradition and the End Times

The debate about the interpretation of texts relative to eschatology is
not so much about a literal versus a nonliteral approach as it is about

the meaning of a literal interpretation. The question is, what clues within or without a given text entitle a particular way of interpreting it? A "spiritualizing" view of the meaning of the text may be the correct and "literal" way to view it. These are not easy matters to decide; it accounts for the oft-heated manner of the discussion of these matters. Further, one's viewpoint or approach to the meaning of a particular group of texts is often subject to sociological factors. However, both approaches attempt to treat the Bible with integrity and defend its teachings. This was certainly the case in the spiritualizing tradition of the "blessed hope." What is certain is the steadfast anticipation of the "blessed hope," though the interpretation of details about it are widely contrastive.

It was that outstanding student of the Scriptures Origen (c.185–c.254) who appears to have been the first in the church to spiritualize the "future kingdom," as a "literal earthly reign" of Christ. Given his Platonic perspective of viewing material things as a shadow of a greater nonphysical significance, as well as his willingness to interpret difficult sayings nonliterally to defend the trustworthiness of the Bible, he heaped scorn on the concept of a millennial rest. What makes him somewhat distinct is that he came to a nonliteral meaning of future events in turbulent times. He spoke of those who believed in a future millennium as "certain persons . . . refusing the labor of thinking, and adopting a superficial view of the letter of the law, and yielding rather in some measure to the indulgence of their own desires and lust . . . [who] are of the opinion that the fulfillment of the promises of the future are to be looked for in bodily pleasure" (*The Fundamental Doctrines* 2.11.2). He often chided church leaders for interpreting the Scriptures in strict accord with Jewish literalism. For example, he stated that whereas in reading the Scriptures in a Judaistic fashion one can obtain an "elementary knowledge," a higher sense may be obtained by interpreting the text "spiritually." The "kingdom of heaven" is to be interpreted as a maturity of faith and life by believers now; the "kingdom" is not a geographic concept so much as it is a spiritualized realm in the hearts of God's people (*Commentary on Matthew* 10.14). So, for Origen, the kingdom is not a future rule of Christ over the earth; it is the reign of God in the saint presently ("The kingdom of God is in your midst" Luke 17:21). His future anticipation is that of the coming of Christ at the end of the ages in judgment on the wicked and blessing for the righteous followed by the eternal state where saints, fully transformed in body and soul, enjoy proper benefits befitting their spiritual natures.

By the end of the third century, chiliasm, a belief in a physical reign of Christ over the earth, had fallen into disfavor, and in the next century it was nearly nonexistent. Because the view had found extensive support in the book of the Revelation, some writers, such as Dionysius of Alexandria (d. c.264), a pupil of Origen and later bishop in the city, denied that John the apostle had written it. "I conjecture, both from the general tenor of both [the gospel and his general epistles], and the form and complexion of the composition, and the execution of the whole book, that it is not from him" (quoted in Eusebius, *Ecclesiastical History* 7.25). To sustain that a book was not apostolic, directly or through apostolic sanction, was tantamount to proving that it was not trustworthy.

THE THEOLOGIANS AND THE END TIMES (300–600)

*A*s usual, in this area of doctrine the theologians were less polemical and more systematic than the apologists. And as usual, Augustine stands out as one who developed a body of teachings that would have powerful influence for centuries to come. Nevertheless, we can detect among the theologians the same nonspiritualizing/spiritualizing split that we saw among the apologists.

The Theologians' Nonspiritualizing Tradition and the End Times

*P*erhaps the clearest example of the continuance of a more literal interpretation of future biblical events (though, admittedly, ancient premillennialism quickly passed away in this era) is in the writings of Lactantius (c.250–c.325), a teacher of rhetoric. While many stopped looking for a divine Deliverer when they had an earthly defender in the person of Emperor Constantine, this teacher of one of Constantine's sons embraced fading themes. That is, he looked forward to the coming of the Savior to rule on the earth in righteousness for a thousand years before the end of time. "The Son of the Most High and Mighty God will come. . . . He will remain among men for a thousand years" (*Divine Institutes* 7.24.1,3).

312

> When, however, the thousand years are over, the world will be renewed by God, and the heavens will be folded together, and earth will be changed. . . . At that same time there will be that second [the first coming prior to the Millennium] and public resurrection of all, in which the unrighteous will be raised up for everlasting tortures." (7.26.5,6)

Like his predecessors in this tradition of interpretation, he believed that the world was six thousand years old and that he was in the sixth millennium. The climax of this era, which he felt would end within two hundred years (about 500) would be a time of increased satanic activity, divine judgment on the nations (pagans), and the passing of all Christians into a world of peace at the coming of Christ.

The Theologians' Spiritualizing Tradition and the End Times

The growing disdain for a literal Millennium was expressed by Eusebius (c.260–c.340), the "father of church history." This bishop of Caesarea heaped scorn on Papias, the early church leader, calling him a "man of very little intelligence," likely because Papias embraced a view that Eusebius found objectionable.[4]

Augustine (354–430) was the first church leader to attempt a comprehensive history of the world from a Christian perspective. What he created was a theory of divine workings in the affairs of life that went well beyond questions about the fall of the Roman Empire and the rise and fall of nations. He argued that two contemporaneous yet incompatible societies exist, one controlled by Satan and the other controlled by God, the community of self-love and the community of the love of God. "What we see, then, is that two societies have issued from two kinds of love. Worldly society has flowered from selfish love which dared to despise even God, whereas the communion of saints is rooted in a love of God that is ready to trample on self" (*The City of God* 14.28). Augustine used this theory to refute the charge that Rome fell due to a neglect of the gods; he pointed out that empires come and go as God wills. Having been preserved to accomplish its earthly mission (for example, peace for

313

the extension of the gospel), Rome collapsed on its own accord because God withdrew His preventive mercies from it.

In eschatological matters Augustine had a grasp of ancient premillennialism but was overwhelmed in disgust for the materialist nature of an earthly rest of indulgence. He noted:

> I myself at one time accepted such an opinion. But when these interpreters say that the rising saints are to spend their time in limitless gormandizing with such heaps of food and drink as not only goes beyond all sense of decent restraint but go utterly beyond belief, then such an interpretation becomes wholly unacceptable save to the carnal-minded. (*The City of God* 20.7)

In its place he argued persuasively for a spiritualizing of the prophetic passages, advocating amillennialism. Augustine maintained two resurrections—one the rebirth of individual Christians into the invisible kingdom of divine love, another at the end of time consisting of both the redeemed and lost raised unto their respective judgments.

> To conclude, then, just as there are two births, of which I spoke earlier—one in time by faith and baptism, the other in the last judgment by the incorruptibility and immortality of the flesh—so there are two resurrections, the first of which is temporal and spiritual and allows no second death, while the other is not spiritual but corporeal and is to be at the end of time. This resurrection, though the last judgment, will send some into the second death, others into that life which knows no death. (20.6)

The "kingdom" is also spiritualized to mean the existence of the church in the world. "During the 'thousand years' when the Devil is bound, the saints also reign for a 'thousand' and doubtless the two periods are identical and mean the span between Christ's first and second coming" (20.9). At the end of the "Millennium," or this present age, Satan will be loosed, having been bound by God at the beginning of the church, to wreak havoc before he is consigned in the Final Judgment forever. Thus, to Augustine, there is not a gradual improvement of world conditions before the final coming on judgment of Christ. Nor is there a gradual degeneration. The two kingdoms coexist with things overall becoming neither better nor worse until the end when Satan is loosed for a short period.

THE MEDIEVAL CHURCH AND THE END TIMES (600–1500)

The era between Augustine and the Renaissance was a time of the unparalleled triumph of the church in the West. Christianity was the unchallenged, supreme religion of Europe, defining social and cultural values from kings to the lowest serf. Augustine's understanding of the church, and his spiritualization of the Millennium as the reign of Christ in the saints, predominated.

Though hardly of significant interest during this period, there were sporadic discussions here and there of a literal, future Millennium. In the tenth century, for example, there was interest in the thousand-year reign of Christ; however, it was perceived as a past event. Given the fact that churchmen generally believed that world history could be divided into six periods of one thousand years each from Adam to the end of time, the last millennium being the final Sabbath-rest, an air of expectancy was aroused in anticipation of the end of the sixth era and Christ's return. Further, marginalized sects periodically advocated one form or another of millennialistic and apocalyptic teaching, but such teachings attracted the religious fringe and brought the condemnation of the church.

Apocalyptic speculation can be seen in the panorama of history as explained by Joachim of Fiore (c.1135–1202). This Cistercian spent much of his time in the study of the Bible, particularly Revelation. He suggested that the persons of the Trinity could also be viewed as periods of human existence, the eras of the Father and the Son being a

315

span of forty-two generations, or 1,260 years. The era of the Father began with Adam and ended with Christ; the era of Christ would end in 1260 and then the final period of uncertain length would commence, the Age of the Holy Spirit. The period would be characterized by unprecedented spiritual vitality; at its termination, the end of time would come.

With this said, the succinct way to look at the medieval period has been summarized by Henry Sheldon. "In general, the medieval mind seems to have imitated Augustine in looking to the past, rather than to the future, for the beginning of the millennial reign."[5]

THE EARLY MODERN CHURCHES AND THE END TIMES (1500–1750)

The interpretation of the events that characterize the end of time was not an issue that divided Europe in the late medieval period; it was not a contributing cause of the schism in the Catholic Church. As indicated earlier, the points of conflict concerned the criteria of religious authority, the accomplishments of Christ's redemptive sacrifice, the degree of human sinfulness and inability, and the means of the acquisition of God's grace. Generally, partisans on both sides of the schism embraced the outline of history, past and future, delineated by Augustine in *The City of God*. However, it is enlightening to discuss the Reformers' understanding of their time and future events, as well as the emergence of new perspectives in the era of the Reformation.

THE EARLY REFORMERS AND AUGUSTINIAN ESCHATOLOGY

Luther and Calvin remained more firmly in the tradition of eschatology set out by Augustine than would later Reformers. Yet each had certain emphases unique to him.

The Lutheran Churches and the End Times

In looking to the future, Luther did so from his understanding of the present. First, as to the future, Luther envisioned a time of great tribulation that would immediately be followed by the return of Christ. He believed that he was someplace in the midst of the first of these two events, and he hoped for the second. Second, it is only fair to argue that he did not develop a synthesis of his views on these matters; his focus was on human inability and justification through faith alone. In these matters Luther was content to continue in the themes advocated by Augustine, the spiritualization of the Millennium, an end-time upheaval of the church by the Antichrist, and the imminent return of Christ to judge the living and the dead. Third, he interpreted Scripture, even the visionary books such as Daniel and Revelation, with an immediatist or presentist perspective for its apologetical and polemical value.

In terms of an overall understanding of history, Luther followed the consensus of the church leaders before him in dividing it into six 1,000-year periods concluding with a "Sabbath," or the eternal rest. Luther wrote:

> I divide the [history of the world] into six ages: the age of Adam, of Noah, of Abraham, of David, of Christ, and of the Pope. Each of the first five has attained about a thousand years together with its prosperity. The Pope began about five thousand years after the creation of the world, this is, when Hildebrand [Pope Gregory VII] openly ridiculed the marriage of priests in the time of Henry VI. . . . But the Pope won't complete his thousand years. (*Works* 54.407)

Thus, Luther found himself poised on the edge of eternity with such biblical books as Daniel, 2 Thessalonians, and Revelation holding the clues to his day and the future. In Daniel, for example, he interpreted the "little horn" as either the papacy or the onrushing Islamic Ottoman Turks, depending on the immediate threatening circumstance, and the "willful king" of Daniel 11:36 as the papacy. Clearly these eschatological insights provided comfort and hope to the Reformer. The images of judgment in Revelation portrayed the persecution of the church in the Age of the Pope that would shortly end in the coming of Christ. The two beasts of Revelation 13 were political

"Rome" and the papacy, which are judged in chapters 15–19. After all this, Christ would return in the Final Judgment as time expires and eternity commences, the human drama being concluded.

The Augsburg Confession (1530), an explanation of Lutheran faith presented to the emperor, Charles V, expressed the Augustinian view of the future, a nonmillennial interpretation, warning of the errors of millennialism.

> Also they teach that, in the consummation of the world [at the last day], Christ will appear to judge, and shall raise up all the dead, and shall give unto the godly and elect eternal life and everlasting joys; but ungodly men and the devils shall be condemned unto endless torments. . . . They condemn others also, who now scatter Jewish opinions, that, before the resurrection of the dead, the godly shall occupy the kingdom of the world. (Article XVII)

The Calvinist Churches and the End Times

While Calvinists are not unified in understanding future events, the position of Augustine and Calvin predominates. That is, Calvinists have generally perceived the coming of Christ in judgment at the end of the age as the hope of the church and the transition into the eternal state.

For Calvin, the "blessed hope" was the glorious appearing of Christ in the final day to redeem His children. This hope was a sustaining, uplifting promise from God that should be the meditation of all believers, giving strength in trials and growth in grace. Calvin pressed the importance of this by alerting his readers that this event is called in Scripture "our redemption." At Christ's coming, all who have lived on the earth will be separated into two groups, the redeemed and the reprobate. "This fact remains firm: one will be a resurrection to judgment, the other to life (John 5:29), and that Christ will come to 'separate the kids from the goats' (Matthew 25:32)."[6] The lost are cast to a Christless, tormented eternity apart from the mercies of God; the

318

redeemed enter into the indescribable joys and delights of heaven. The practical hope for Christians in Christ's return is captured by the *Heidelberg Catechism* (1563) in answer to the question "What comfort does the return of Christ 'to judge the living and the dead' give you? (Q. 15)."

> That in all affliction and persecution I may await with head held high the very judge from heaven who has already submitted himself to the judgment of God for me and has removed all the curse from me; that he will cast all his enemies and mine into everlasting condemnation, but he shall take me, together with all his elect, to himself into heavenly joy and glory.

The Belgic Confession of Faith (1561) has a rather full and detailed chronology of last events (Article XXXVII): the coming of Christ and the destruction of the earth, the resurrection of all the deceased as well as the translation of the living, the judgment of each, and the just assignment of destinies (some being cast out of His presence, others entering into it). Unlike the ancient premillennarian understanding of events, Christ is not viewed as first coming to reign on the earth, followed by a final judgment.

THE LATER REFORMERS AND MILLENNIALISM

The history of belief in a literal reign of Christ on the earth, a millennium, prior to the Final Judgment has been succinctly described this way: "Though Millennialism has never been formally rejected by the larger Christian bodies, they have treated the subject with the greatest reserve."[7] The hostility expressed by Augustine reemerges in Luther, Calvin, and Zwingli. Unfortunately for conservative advocates of a literal reign of righteousness on earth, such teaching has often been accompanied by political, even moral, extremism. This has allowed many to quickly dismiss it. In the early church the view was obscured by the embrace of it by both the heretical Gnostic sects and the radically separatist Montanists. A tendency to radicalism, antiestablishmentarianism, and hatred by its unsympathetic opponents caused it to be the teaching of the marginalized through the Reformation. The lens through which Luther viewed millennialist claims was the teachings of Thomas Münzer, whose charismatic preaching and truth claims led to the Peasants' Revolt and his beheading in 1525. Further, the tragic episode in 1534 at Münster, a city in Holland, where a group of radicals with millennialistic hopes exhibited wild behavior, turned most people away from any thought of a literal millennial reign of Christ. Sadly, much distortion prevailed by both critic and proponent. Calvin, a severe opponent, like Augustine before him, must have encountered only the most radical expressions of this view.

> [After the apostle Paul] there followed the chiliasts, who limited the reign of Christ to a thousand years. Now their fiction is too childish to need or to be worth a refutation. And the Apocalypse, from which they undoubtedly drew a pretext for their error, does not support them. . . . All Scripture proclaims that there will be no end to the blessedness of the elect or the punishment of the wicked. (Matthew 25:41,46)[8]

The Reformation in the sixteenth century was occasioned, at least in part, by a renewal of interest in biblical studies. This intense study of the Scriptures in the seventeenth century brought about a revival of interest in gaining perspective on the times as well as the future. In essence, the hegemony of the Augustinian understanding of history, an amillennial view, was broken. While the events of a Final Judgment at the coming of Christ and the destruction of the present earth remained firm, events leading to them were cast in a slightly different light. For some, a greater optimism about the possibility of gospel progress was the cause; for others, the root appears to have been a discouragement about the same possibility. In either case, the prevailing notion that times remain the same, neither declining nor improving overall, was reinterpreted. The willingness to open the question of the experience of the church in the world as it related to gospel progress appears to have been rooted in at least three factors. First, the emergence of the study of biblical Hebrew in Protestant universities after 1549 caused a proliferation of language tools as well as a rethinking of such things as how promises of future glory given to the ancient people of God might relate to the church. Second, the triumph of the Reformation, particularly in England, created a groundswell of optimism that the Antichrist had been conquered and that the church was on the verge of an unprecedented era of success. Reading the Scriptures through this lens had the net effect of bringing into question the things-are-about-the-same understanding of Augustine (this is a bit unfair because amillennialists do see a progressive unfolding of the kingdom of God in time, yet not to the extent of postmillennialists). The experience of difficult times for the church, such as the tragedy in Germany during the Thirty Years War, had the effect of producing the opposite understanding of the church's "progress." Third, the appearance of the work of Thomas Brightman (1562–1607), an English Calvinist, broke the spell of the Origen-Augustine understanding of history, though his particular views bordered on the fantastic. Regardless of the validity of Brightman's view, some Protestant clerics departed from Augustine.

The Rise of the Postmillennial Interpretation of History

Thomas Brightman, the English Presbyterian, assembled in his commentary of Revelation, *A Revelation of Revelation,* the seeds of the postmillennial view. Though he rejected a visible return of Christ at the inauguration of a literal kingdom on earth, he argued for a Christianizing of the earth through a progressive triumph of the church before the return of Christ in the Last Day. Brightman did not see the Millennium as the entire church age but postulated two millennia in the period before Christ returns. Interpreting most of Revelation as a time line of the initial millennium, he thought that he was in the era of the judgments of chapters 16–18, the destruction of Roman Catholicism and the Islamic faith. Revelation 20 described for him the second millennium, one near beginning in God's judgment, characterized by the recalling of the Jews, the revitalization of Jerusalem, and the proliferation of the gospel throughout the world. Whereas Augustine placed the Tribulation just prior to the return of Christ, Brightman placed it at the end of the first millennium. Christ will return in judgment after the second millennium.

Brightman's influence became readily apparent as his ideas were taken up by his contemporaries and modified in one way or another. His view impacted the thought of Henry Finch, who wrote *The Calling of the Jews* (1621), as well as John Cotton and Jonathan Edwards. The most important formulator of the postmillennial view was John Owen (1616–1683), a Puritan Congregationalist or Independent who was deeply influential during the time of Oliver Cromwell. Basking in the glow of Protestant triumphalism in England, he spoke of a reign of Christ through the church before His coming. He described the Millennium as a time of many conversions from all over the world, purity of worship and sacrament observance, and the victory of Christ over His enemies. Being the chief architect of the Savoy Declaration of Faith (1658), an English Congregationalist confession, Owen's view of the future progress of the church before Christ's coming is evident.

> As the Lord is in care and love towards his Church . . . we expect that in the latter days, Antichrist being destroyed, the Jews called, and the adversaries of the kingdom of his dear Son broken, the churches of Christ being enlarged and edified through a free and plentiful communication of light and grace, shall enjoy in this world a more quiet, peaceful, and glorious condition than they have enjoyed. (Article XXVI.5)

A major influence in the propagation of postmillennialism was Daniel Whitby (1638–1726). While Whitby was not the originator of the views expressed in his *Paraphrase and Commentary on the New Testament* (1703), his advocacy of Unitarianism has been cited to disavow the legitimacy of his views. This is quite unfortunate because postmillennialism has had many fine, orthodox defenders, and it does not find its roots in a heterodox movement. Whitby echoed

322

Brightman (the borders of eschatological views not being as rigid as they became in later years) in that he expected the defeat of the Antichrist and the binding of Satan before the "Millennium," an unprecedented time of gospel prosperity, followed by the return of Christ. A lengthy subtitle of his work explained his view: "A Treatise of the True Millennium: showing that it is not a reign of persons raised from the dead, but of the church flourishing gloriously for a thousand years after the conversion of the Jews, and the flowing-in of all nations to them thus converted to the Christian Faith."[9] Thus, the "fall" or binding of the Antichrist does not characterize this age as advocated by Augustine, nor does it come at the end of the age as in premillennialist thinking, but it occurs before a period of prosperity for the church and before His coming in judgment. After the "literal" reign of the saints in peace, Christ will return in judgment at the end of the age.

The Renewal of the Ancient Premillennialist Interpretation of History

In the 1620s not a few English Puritans were moving both by the logic of their biblical exegesis and the signs of the times in the direction of interpreting the "thousand years" of Revelation 20 literally. However, they hesitated to take the final step, to advocate the doctrine of a future reign of Christ on earth, because of the onus placed upon the teaching by Augustine, Luther, and Calvin. The way was made easier when a prominent German Calvinist, Johann Heinrich Alsted (1588–1638), adopted chiliasm. Alsted's teachings—unlike later adaptations of premillennialism, but more aligned with the earliest form of it—argued that the Bible presented a single program for the one people of God, a people restricted to Abraham's descendants through faith in God's promises in the Old Testament, though expanded in the New Testament to embrace both Jews and Gentiles in a single, extended family. He divided the New Testament era into four segments, the third of these segments stretching from John the Baptist to Christ's return in judgment. This lengthy period was subdivided into four parts also. The third of these periods followed the judgment of God on the papacy and the renewal of the church in the Reformation, a period ending sometime in the late seventeenth century. This would be followed by a thousand-year reign of Christ, a period characterized by the reigning of resurrected saints, the end of persecutions, the growth of the church, and an upsurge of spiritual vitality. Then, after a final time of misery for the church in a final satanic rebellion by Gog and Magog, Christ will come to judge His enemies and lift the church to its final victory in the eternal state.

It is interesting to note that one's view of circumstances, the perception of fears and threats, influences one's perspectives on the Scriptures. This seems most clearly evident when it comes to the need for hope. Alsted turned from the amillennial view of end-times events, a theory that suggests times exist in a generally steady state until the Final Judgment, because of the tragedies and devastations connected with the Thirty Years War that ravished Germany. He identified the horrors of the war with judgmental descriptions in various prophetic passages, particularly Revelation, concluding that destruction would be followed by peace (Revelation 20), a final evil rebellion at its end, and the return of Christ in judgment at the end of the age. These insights, sustained from his understanding of the Bible, gave him comfort in the midst of uncertainty, even hope, as fear was circumscribed by the knowledge of its ultimate termination.

England's counterpart of Alsted was Joseph Mede (1586–1638). This Puritan and biblical scholar at Cambridge University, Christ Church College, was the first in England to advocate a return to the premillennial view of end-time events. The immediate circumstance for his advocacy of premillennialism appears to have been the oppression of the Puritan movement within the Church of England. Clergy who refused to wear certain clothing, light candles, or read from the *Book of Common Prayer* were oppressed by the state. Though the Reformation in England toppled the papal "antichrist" and Protestant doctrine flourished, some Puritans found it difficult to embrace a triumphalist theory of the prosperity of the church when they were being called into court, the king was less than congenial to their views, and the archbishop despised Calvinism. Accordingly, Mede set forth his views in *The Key of the Revelation* (1627) and *The Apostacy of the Latter Times* (1641). He saw his day as one of persecution that would be followed by a literal reign of Christ on the earth for one thousand years. Mede's influence was enormous; some claim him as the "father of premillennialism." Among those who found his insights particularly

324

insightful were John Milton, Isaac Newton, Thomas Goodwin, and William Twisse, the leader of the Westminster Assembly of Divines.

The Early American Puritans and Premillennialism

The hostility of king and archbishop, in the early 1600s, to the reforming attempts of the Puritans led to the Puritans' flight to Holland and to British North America, specifically New England. A sense that England and Europe would not be the place of Christ's reign over the churches filled the Puritans with disappointment but also infused them with hope that the New World would be the scene of the inauguration of Christ's reign. Like so many before them, the Puritans represented a blend of eschatological insights that makes them difficult to categorize strictly; the various views often overlapped among them. Further, such a difference of views was not a ground of division among Christians as it would become later. With this stated, the earliest Puritans to venture to Cambridge and Boston in New England brought with them broad premillennial views.

Illustrative of this understanding of history was the Mather family. Spanning three generations of prominent Bostonian clerics, Richard (1596–1669), Increase (1639–1723), and Cotton (1663–1728) embraced historicist or ancient premillennialism. The record suggests that the Mathers were not alone in following the insights of Mede in the study of prophetic materials in the Bible. That approach was widely embraced by the early American Puritans, granting them a lens for interpreting their disappointments with the English church, justifying the exodus from their homeland, and inspiring them with hope in their new struggles.

The Early American Puritans and Postmillennialism

Puritan eschatology was by no means uniform in the exodus to British America, as has been demonstrated among their counterparts who remained in the homeland. The optimistic understanding of history held by John Owen had its heirs as well. The prince of them was John Cotton (1585–1652). Prophecy was an interest to most Puritans, and the book of Revelation was the testing ground. In 1642 Cotton published *The Churches Resurrected, or the Opening of the Fifth and Sixth Verses of the 20th of the Revelation.* Through it, he not only described future events but also organized the events of the past into a cogent argument for hope in a howling wilderness.

Cotton situated the experiences of himself and his Puritan stalwarts into the events of his day with amazing clarity. The church that had suffered persecution for 1,260 years (the period of state religion) had been ended as of 1630 with Christ establishing His reign through the wilderness churches in and about Boston! The resurrection of saints was interpreted in a nonliteral, spiritual sense to mean a quickening and revitalizing of the church, inaugurating a period of prosperity and success. Christ began His reign in the 1630s, not immediately in His kingly rulership, but mediately through the church. This would be fully accomplished, Cotton taught, in New England through the regulations of church censures and the threat of punishment by the state.

THE LATE MODERN CHURCHES AND THE END TIMES (1750–PRESENT)

Christians of the late modern period, at least in the Protestant traditions, have not been entirely satisfied with the eschatological formulations bequeathed them by earlier Christians. Late modern Protestants have tinkered in many ways with theology of the end times. Theologians within Roman Catholicism and the Orthodox churches, on the other hand, have tended to hold on to past beliefs to a much greater degree.

THE PROTESTANT TRADITIONS AND THE END TIMES

The conservative-liberal split within Protestantism during the late modern period has made for radically different theologies in many areas, including eschatology. Liberal Protestants have had a hard time accepting a literal return of Jesus Christ to the earth, and so their "blessed hope" is something much different from what it was for earlier Christians. Meanwhile, even conservative Protestants have made some developments of their own, more so in postmillennialism and premillennialism than in amillennialism.

326

The Liberal Protestant Tradition and the End Times

The fountainhead of the Protestant liberal tradition, a school of Christian interpretation that sought to make the faith more plausible to an increasingly skeptical Western world, was Friedrich Schleiermacher (1768–1834). Influencing subsequent centuries of scholarly religious endeavor, he substituted "feeling" for historical objectivity and established the witness of the Holy Spirit through the Scriptures as the basis of the faith. Schleiermacher argued that there are two ways of viewing this present age: an introductory period of preparation and development or a period of trial leading to spiritual life or death in judgment in a physical resurrection; he preferred the former. After a belief in a future Millennium was purged from the early church, he affirmed, Christianity embraced the idea of the return of Christ at the end of the age, though unfortunately in a literalistic way. He confidently assured his readers that such a doctrine should not be taken literally, implying a reward unto eternal life for the faithful and of judgment for the wicked. Instead, the "return" of Christ will be in a sudden moment when wavering and development will be consummated by a leap to perfection and of cosmic fellowship with God, the achievement of a divine consciousness exemplified in Christ. He denied the idea of a future judgment or the eternal damnation of the wicked ("Through the power of the redemption there will one day be a universal restoration of all souls" [10]). Life gradually reaches higher levels of divine oneness until the oneness dissolves into the One. Schleiermacher was a universalist, the "return" of Christ was a non-literal divine absorption, and " hell" was merely the immaturity of religious existence in the present life.

Within the liberal tradition in Europe and America, the idea of an apocalyptic intervention of God into human history to bring it to a culmination was gradually set aside for a concept of the gradual improvement of humankind in the social context. The concept of the "kingdom of God" ceased to be a branch of theology and, like theology itself, became a subdivision of ethics. Redemption talk became a moral discourse. For Albrecht Ritschl (1822–1889), the kingdom of God was actually moral values, those exemplified in Jesus, toward which society is inexorably progressing. Ritschl and the coterie of scholars who followed his insights argued that Christianity, as it had

327

evolved, had become a distortion of the simple moral teachings of Jesus. The focus of Christianity, he suggested, should be upon the practical side of things, the theological side being obscure and uncertain. The kingdom, then, is not an order that will be brought about by a divine intervention; it is the moral rule of God in all of present life. The passion for the ethical was the focus of Jesus' calling and is the essence of the faith; it is the kingdom of God. Sadly, according to Ritschl, the disciples distorted Jesus' teachings and established the church. In essence, the liberal movement discounted the eschatological aspects of the kingdom and substituted human actions inspired by love as the "blessed hope."

Within the liberal tradition, a serious critique was mounted against the nonapocalyptic interpretation of the kingdom, principally by Johannes Weiss (1863–1914) and Albert Schweitzer (1875–1965). These scholars understood the kingdom of God in Jesus' preaching as completely eschatological, having no present dimension. Weiss reacted against the Ritschlian assertion that the kingdom was a moral ideal or rule; he believed that Jesus preached the intervention of God into human history. By so doing, he also questioned the movement's portrait of Jesus as a mere human educator. Schweitzer concluded from his study that Jesus' life and ministry were determined by an eschatological passion, an imminent apocalyptic end to the world, though He was mistaken in His belief.

Whereas the Ritschlian school collapsed the kingdom into a noneschatological, present reign of moral idealism without the intervention of God into human affairs in any apocalyptic way, and whereas others found the essence of Jesus' preaching to be exclusively otherworldly, C. H. Dodd (1884–1973), an English New Testament scholar, argued that the kingdom of God is best viewed as having several aspects, principally a "now" and a "not yet." He felt that the term "kingdom" should be defined as both a reign and a realm. Christ inaugurated His reign in His first coming in that His influence broke into human history and is spreading today. However, the kingdom is still to come upon the earth as a geographic realm through an abrupt, divine intervention. Dodd's insights, which have had a significant impact in conservative circles, have been defined as "realized eschatology."

The American liberal movement at the end of the nineteenth century and prior to World War I followed the European Ritschlian school. The kingdom of God was stripped of any futurist and interventionist importance, being moralized into a present and increasing reign of the idealistic spirit of Jesus within societal conventions. Shailer Mathews, perhaps the most influential scholar in the liberal tradition in the 1920s, argued that Jesus proclaimed "a very real kingdom," a new social order of human relationships. Said Mathews, "Heaven is the absolute, ideal social order. And it is for the coming of the ideal that we portray when we say 'Thy kingdom come'."[11] The kingdom, then, is an ethical ideal, not an eschatological intrusion, that was expected to gradually appear as humankind progressed in the spirit of Christ. It is valid to say that the liberal movement substituted the fruit of Christianity (its ethical ideals) for the essence of Christianity (the historical gospel concerning the person and accomplishments of Christ) and in the process of forfeiting the latter also lost the former. Such is the state of much of Christendom today; the essence of Christianity has become little more than the natural person's sense of moral rectitude.

The concept of a temporal, moral rule as the essence of Christ's kingdom was most cogently expressed in the social gospel movement, a movement within the liberal movement that reached its maturity between 1900 and 1918 in the writings of Walter Rauschenbusch (1861–1918). The magnum opus of the movement was his *A Theology of the Social Gospel* (1918). The work was not novel in its interpretation of the kingdom, but its linkage to the progressive movement made it a powerful force. Rauschenbusch was correct that the starting point for understanding the future should be the teachings of Jesus, though he felt that there were few reliable sources, even in the Gospel narratives as we now have them, to form a judgment.[12] He felt that Jesus would have rejected all ideas of an apocalyptic kingdom and taught that the kingdom would come gradually through people committed to His moral ideals. He even argued that the early Christians rightly embraced the ideal of a millennium, though they defined it wrongly by filling it with apocalyptic nuances and materialistic tendencies. Instead, the kingdom should be interpreted in a nonliteral way as representing moral rightness in society. On realizing this interpretation of the kingdom/Millennium, Rauschenbusch stated, "This process will have to utilize all constructive and educational forces in humanity. . . . The coming of the kingdom of God will be the regeneration of the super-personal life of the race, and will work out a social expression of what was contained in the personality of Christ."[13]

Factors evident at the turn of the century spelled the death of this phase of the liberal movement; the unprecedented atrocities related to the World War demanded a revising of the optimistic, progressive features of it. Such circumstances opened the possibility that humanity, despite the rhetoric of improvement, possessed a sinister dimension. In all this, the kingdom seemed an impossible dream of morally blinded and disconnected idealists. Thus, there occurred the rise of neo-liberalism within the liberal tradition that dominated the scene from 1930 to 1960.

Other than Karl Barth, who unfortunately trivialized and downplayed the discussion of the kingdom of God, the most influential theologian in the twentieth century was Rudolf Bultmann (1884–1976), a New Testament scholar at Marburg University. Bultmann argued that the New Testament is unreliable, being made impure by mythological elements. The most impressive case in point, according to Bultmann, was the myth of a divine intervention into human history in judgment. Thus, these "untruthful" additions to the Bible must be interpreted existentially to have any meaning. Jesus' supposed apocalyptic teachings have meaning only as they can be appropriated personally and immediately. The Final Judgment, for example, is not about a future event; it is a symbol of the need to regard ourselves from a proper perspective now. Biblical symbols, events, and metaphors are only the occasion of a self-exploration. In his famous Gifford Lectures in 1955 he stated, "The menacing in history lies always in the present, and when the present is conceived as the eschatological present by Christian faith the meaning of history is realized. . . . Do not look into your own universal history, you must look into your own personal history. Always in your present lies the meaning in history."[14]

The eschatological element reemerged in the liberal tradition in the 1960s through the work of Jürgen Moltmann (b. 1926), who attempted to make hope the central factor in Christian life and thought. For Moltmann, "hope" is not so much an eschatological event (a view he

330

finds particularly barren) as one that inspires a present consciousness that eternal reality is temporally present. It is, in his view, not an event so much as it is "a medium of thinking."[15] The hope that is at the very core of Christianity is not so much about heavenly bliss but about the possibility of harmony on earth. Ultimately, Moltmann's hope is a hope that this world can become a better place. "Peace with God means conflict with the world, for the goad of the promised future stabs inexorably into the flesh of every unfulfilled present."[16]

The Conservative Protestant Tradition and the End Times

While many conservative Protestants have held on to amillennialism, others have developed preexisting eschatologies, postmillennialism and premillennialism.

Amillennialism. The Augustinian interpretation of history has continued from the time of Origen and others to be widely embraced within Christendom. It remains the majority view embraced in the Roman Catholic and Orthodox communities as well as the confessional Protestant churches.

Postmillennialism. As a theological interpretation of history, postmillennialism emerged among English Puritans in the seventeenth century when Protestantism showed promise of religious triumph in the nation. Though the differences among the various millennial positions tended to blur at points (unlike today, when the positions often define themselves by their discontinuities with the other views), an end-time triumphalism (a view slightly more optimistic and graphic than amillennial triumphalism) was embraced by some Puritans and was brought with them into the British colonial experiment in North America, most clearly by John Cotton in New England. The popularity of the view, which seemed so in tune with the fortunes and unbridled optimism of the new nation in the nineteenth century, emerged through the popular advocacy of one of the most important defenders of conservative Christianity, Jonathan Edwards (1703–1758).

The famous Northampton pastor embraced postmillennialism as the hope for the renewal of the churches in the context of what he viewed as particularly dark days. In the revivals of his day he envisioned the harbinger of a glorious advance of the kingdom of God before the coming of Christ. Edwards searched the newspapers for

events described in the Scriptures, signs of the defeat of God's enemies, which he felt would precede a time of spiritual renewal. Writing
in the 1740s, he felt that the evidence was such that he was living in
the time of the sixth vial, the last of the three series of judgments, of
Revelation, the final one before the advent of Christ. This particular
judgment would flow from the 1746 defeat of France and Spain by
England ruining papal revenues. This happened, according to
Edwards, about 220 years after the outpouring of the fifth vial of judgment on the Roman Catholic Church, the Antichrist, in the
Reformation, causing Edwards to speculate that the seventh vial, the
coming of Christ, was less than two hundred years away.[17] Under the
shadow of the sixth vial and anticipating a prerequisite mighty work
of the Holy Spirit to bring about the coming of Christ, expressed in
the success of the gospel through the church, Edwards viewed the
Great Awakening of the 1740s with great anticipation. This time of the
advancement of the church and the reign of Christ would last until
Christ returns in judgment and time is no more. The reign through
Christ in the churches for a "thousand years" was interpreted to be "a
very long time." Said Edwards, "When once this day of the church's
advancement and peace is begun, it shall never end, till the world
ends; or at least, that there shall be no more a return of her troubles
and adversity for any considerable continuance; that then 'the days of
her mourning shall be ended'."[18] He waxed eloquent before his congregation in 1739, describing the features of the reign of Christ that
was soon to break forth.

> Great knowledge shall prevail everywhere. It may be hoped
> that then many of the Negroes and the Indians will be divines,
> and that excellent books will be published in Africa, in
> Ethiopia, in Turkey—and not only very learned men, but oth-
> ers that are ordinary men, shall then be very knowing in reli-
> gion, Is. 32:3-4.[19]

This era of churchly prosperity will end in a final great apostasy and
the coming of Christ in the clouds, bringing gladness to His saints and

the Final Judgment. This final time of spiritual darkness would not be long, he assured his parishioners, because the real darkness was that day in which they were living. "God won't suffer it to continue long because this is not the proper day of the church's trouble; that was ended at the fall of Antichrist. . . . And therefore a time as this won't continue long."[20] Then would end the stirring apocalyptic times he saw beginning to unfold in his day. Heaven, the place of divine love, would become the abode of the saints forever.

Postmillennial eschatology, through the influence of Edwards' enormous hegemony in nineteenth-century conservative Christianity, won numerous advocates across denominational frontiers. Within Congregationalism there was Joseph Bellamy, Samuel Hopkins, and Nathaniel Taylor; among the Baptists was Augustus H. Strong; and within Presbyterianism, Charles Hodge. Both Strong and Hodge wrote eminently successful systematic theologies that remained centerpieces of their respective denominations. The influence of Hodge (1797–1878) has been succinctly captured in the sentence, "If less an original thinker than a systematizer and defender of traditional Calvinism, Hodge has a real claim to be considered one of the great-est of American theologians, and he had a great influence and follow-ing."[21] Hodge rejected the notion of an immediate reign of Christ in an earthly kingdom as a "relic of Judaism, and out of keeping with the spirituality of the gospel." Instead, he believed that following the suc-cess of the gospel in the mediate reign of Christ through the church, as witnessed in the proclamation of the gospel worldwide, the redraft-ing of the Jews into the blessings "of their own live-tree and knowl-edge our Lord to be their God and Savior," and the defeat of anti-Christian powers, Christ will come in judgment upon all humankind, the redeemed to inherit a spiritual kingdom.[22]

Postmillennialism seems to have fallen out of favor at the end of the nineteenth century, largely due to the embrace of a progressive, temporal millennialism by the growing liberal movement in American Christianity. Since the 1970s, it has had a strident, though modest, renewal of interest. This has been particularly so in the Christian reconstruction movement, which has infused the political Religious Right with much of its optimism in its social and political activism.

THE END TIMES: FULFILLMENT OF OUR BLESSED HOPE

Premillennialism. Premillennialism reemerged in the Reformation era, having once been widely held by church leaders. In the eighteenth and nineteenth centuries, it experienced significant development, which continues to be felt.

Interest in a nonprogressive, generally pessimistic interpretation of history gained momentum at the time of the disheartening French Revolution. Many came to see in the events of the 1790s a key to understanding the future in a new way as well as maintaining hope in precarious times. Interest in understanding future events was spurred by the emerging English and Irish Bible and prophetic conferences, such as the Albany (1826–30) and Powerscourt (1830–1833) meetings, which gradually became immensely popular and transdenominational in nature. The Albany conferences produced a statement of belief that said Christ would descend from heaven to inaugurate a kingdom on the earth, followed by the Final Judgment. The 1,260 days of Daniel 7 and Revelation 13 were interpreted literally as the time between the reign of Emperor Justinian to the French Revolution. The vials of Revelation 16 were being poured out and the coming of Christ to reign for one thousand years on the earth was imminent.

The Powerscourt conferences of the 1830s continued the prophetic emphasis but additionally witnessed, largely through the influential John Nelson Darby (1800–1882), a growing Brethren dominance. Darby, a disillusioned former Anglican missionary to Roman Catholics in Ireland, moved away from ancient premillennialism to futurist premillennialism. He divided the Bible into eight periods from Noah to the end of the Millennium, characterized by divine regulations and promises, failure, and judgment. The period of most of the Old Testament, the period of the Law, was composed of promises and threats that God made to His ancient people, Israel. The failure of Israel culminated in the rejection of the Messiah, which brought about the postponement of His promises of a literal reign of righteousness on the earth for His ancient people. Though God would return to His ancient people to fulfill His promises, the church, the new people, are beneficiaries of His promises of blessing until the church is gathered to heaven in a Rapture.[23] Following this event, the world and its inhab-

itants will suffer a terrible tribulation for seven years. At its end Christ will return to reign on earth, fulfilling His promises to Israel in a thousand-year kingdom. These turbulent events will conclude with one final rebellion, Satan and his minions will be crushed, then Christ will come in judgment and time will be no more.

Premillennialism began to show evidence of some impact within American Christianity in the 1840s but received negative press through the apocalyptic fervor created by the disappointing Adventist movement, which set a specific date for the Lord's return. After the Civil War, a type of premillennialism emerged that eschewed date setting but insisted on the imminent return of Christ. Revelation was interpreted as largely futuristic, so the problem of date setting was avoided. The teaching of the any-moment return of Christ in a secret Rapture accomplished the same purpose in that it created expectancy. This form of premillennialism became increasingly popular through the Bible conference movement, particularly through the Believer's Meetings for Bible Study (later called the Niagara Bible Conferences), and the American Bible and Prophetic movement. A schism occurred among the Niagara Bible Conference leadership in the 1890s that eventually brought about its discontinuance. It was a rift of opinion over the timing of Christ's premillennial return; would it be before or after the Tribulation? Was there a "secret Rapture"?

Differences have emerged among modern premillennialists, particularly in the latter decades of the twentieth century. The work of George Ladd of Fuller Theological Seminary caused a stir among modern premillennialists in the 1950s. He searched for a way to biblically amalgamate the futurist millennial tradition with a presentist interpretation of aspects of it. He found C. H. Dodd's writings insightful and brought up the issue of a now-and-not-yet aspect of the kingdom. Ladd came to believe that the kingdom of God has a present fulfillment in the church and a future consummation in the coming of Christ. Ladd, as well as Robert Gundry, adopted a posttribulational view of the church, a denial of a Rapture prior to the Tribulation.

Dispensationalism, an inseparable twin of modern premillennialism, has experienced changes also. Some have observed that there are three discernible emphases in the development of this particular way of viewing the unity of the Scriptures: classical dispensationalism, such as presented by the *Scofield Reference Bible* and the theology of

Lewis Sperry Chafer, the founder of Dallas Theological Seminary; revised dispensationalism, such as reflected in the *New Scofield Reference Bible* (1967) and the works of Charles Ryrie, John F. Walvoord, and Dwight Pentecost; and progressive dispensationalism.[24] Revisionist dispensationalists sought to answer certain criticisms leveled by covenantalists, such as the charge that their systems advocated two ways of salvation (law keeping in the Old Testament and grace in the New Testament), rejected the notion of two New Covenants, and argued that Matthew's gospel was for the church. Progressives maintain the seminal distinctive of the two peoples of God but have ameliorated the sharpness of the separation by suggesting that Christ is now on the throne of David and the promises made to Israel are now being fulfilled in the church, though the fullest manifestation of them awaits the millennial kingdom.

The Roman Catholic Tradition and the End Times

The most recent catechism of the Roman Catholic community in 1994 suggests the church has continued to officially embrace an amillennial interpretation of history. The newest catechism is clear in its teachings that the church officially opposes any concept of the triumph of Christ in the present age. "The antichrist's deception already begins to take shape in the world every time the claim is made to realize within history that messianic hope which can only be realized beyond history through the eschatological judgment."[25] The kingdom of Christ, in its fullest manifestation, awaits an age to come.

In a significantly qualified sense, the "kingdom of Christ" is present in a mystery form as the church struggles against the evil of pseudomessianisms in the present age. The reign of Christ, therefore, is the hope for the church; it is an imminent event that will take place when the Jews will be returned to a place of blessing, the Gentiles having been brought into the church of God, at Christ's literal return to earth in judgment upon His enemies. "The kingdom will be fulfilled, then, not by a historic triumph of the Church through progressive ascendancy, but only by God's victory over the final unleashing of evil, which will cause his Bride to come down from heaven."[26] At that time,

Christ will judge the living and the resurrected dead, assigning their just destinies, and consummate the kingdom, the reign of God, without hindrances forever.

THE ORTHODOX TRADITION AND THE END TIMES

The Orthodox churches follow the lead of the Eastern Fathers, who envisioned a now-and-not-yet kingdom. That is, present aspects of Christ's reign, such as His dominion over nature and the church, do not exclude a future triumph in glory. Orthodox creeds align with the amillennial eschatology argued in Augustine's *City of God.* While the first coming of Christ was in humility, the second coming of Christ will be one of judgment. It is an imminent hope because foreboding signs offer comfort that it is not a distant one. In answer to the question "Are there not, however, revealed to us some signs of the nearer approach of Christ's coming?" the *Longer Catechism of the Eastern Church* states: "In the Word of God certain signs are revealed, as the decrease of faith and love among men, the abounding of iniquity and calamities, the preaching of the Gospel to all nations, and the coming of Antichrist" (Q. 234). The Orthodox tradition sees a return of Christ at the end of the age to destroy His enemies, casting them into a literal hell,[27] and bringing all His children into a kingdom without end in a new heaven and earth.[28] This Second Coming is the "blessed hope."

337

9

Conclusion: What's Most Important

In chapters two through eight we have taken a detailed, historical look at seven great themes of systematic theology. In an age when it seems people are ready to forget the past, want easy answers to complex problems, and are loath to put in the hard effort that mental understanding requires, this careful, historical study of Christian thought is just what is needed. Yet in all the mass of detail, amid descriptions of the mutating and contradictory doctrines, one could easily lose track of what really matters. So I want to help you refocus on what's most important.

THE PLACE OF THEOLOGY IN THE POSTMODERN WORLD

I endeavored to write this book because we are living in a world that is without direction or moral compass. As I stated in chapter 1, Christians are in a world that has repudiated many of the assumptions of modernity: the importance of the rational, the propriety of the orderly, and the possibility of objective truth. Ours is a culture where personality has more street value than character, psychological wholeness than spiritual authenticity. We find ourselves in a world where pleasures are embraced without moral norms and social responsibility.

Christian truth is attacked not so much for its particular assertions, but for its fundamental claim that there is such a thing as binding, objective truth. The quest for truth has been replaced with an emphasis on pleasure and entertainment. We live in a world of the therapeutic and the psychological, an endless quest for self-fulfillment and entitlement. Sin has become little more than the infringement of personal rights and privileges; there is little thought of defining it by the standard of the holiness of God. With so much interest in the management of life, what is the benefit of a volume on such a seemingly esoteric topic as timeless, transcendent, historic truth?

This question is complicated by the fact that modern Evangelicalism is in a state of crisis. The very community that historically has been deeply interested in transcendent, timeless truth seems more focused on the merely private, personal, and temporal than ever before. If I could be so blunt, the church has lost its soul, at least some think so. The Evangelical Church, I believe, is on the brink of becoming another of the many social, do-good agencies whose mission-purpose is to help people to more fully enjoy this life, but neglect the implications of eternity.

As our culture has shown a marked inclination to secularism, the church seems to have followed suit. One of our recent Christian social critics has summarized the problem quite succinctly: "The stream of historic orthodoxy that once watered the evangelical soul is now dammed by a worldliness that many fail to recognize as worldliness because of the cultural innocence with which it presents itself."[1]

Another has described the current situation in the church as an "ecclesiastical swamp." In accepting the vogue of postmodernity, Thomas Oden suggests that segments of the contemporary church have fallen victim to "an intellectual immune deficiency syndrome." This malaise is characterized by a decline of Christian content in teaching and preaching with an accompanying increased interest in self-help directions that merely promise a better management of everyday crises.[2]

There is also an appalling ignorance in the church of its rich Christian heritage. Mark Noll speaks of "the scandal of the evangelical mind," the denigration of the intellectual content of the faith accompanied by the elevation of the subjective and personal.[3] George Barna complains that the average Christian is uninterested in life-changing religious convictions, having little more than the most superficial awareness of sin, grace, and redemption.[4]

This moral and intellectual crisis comes to the Evangelical Church when Christianity is without a serious opponent; there are no potent rivals in our culture making claims to having objective, final truth. Such truth claims have been abandoned in the postmodern experience. David Wells has found a general parallel to the situation in the churches today in the era prior to the Reformation in the sixteenth century.

First, the two churches, he suggests, are similar in that they each manifest a lack of confidence in the Word of God. In the fourteenth and fifteenth centuries the denigration of the Scriptures was manifested in the church's reversion to papal pronouncements, today to business know-how and psychological counseling. Second, both churches reflect a flawed understanding of the seriousness of sin. One of our philosophers, having reflected on the decline of the discussion of sin within his own religious heritage, simply has stated: "The new language of Zion fudges: 'Let us confess our problem with human relational adjustment dynamics, and especially our feebleness in networking' . . . . 'Peanut Butter Binge' and 'Chocolate Decadence' are sinful; lying is not. The measure of sin is caloric."[5] Third, in both instances the church, having lost its grasp on sin, has minimized the glory and efficacy of the death of Christ.[6]

These very circumstances (the moralizing of virtue and the trivializing of sin, the psychologizing of the Scriptures to make it user friendly and inoffensive, and the marginalizing of the centrality of the cross of Christ) are the reasons for this book. This is a call for the church (its pastors, teachers, and laity) to reverse the trends that pose a threat to the historic gospel of Christ and speak so lightly of the work of the Savior. It is time for us to listen to the Scriptures for our message, not the beckoning cry of a pleasure-inebriated culture. The need of the hour is not for revival; it is for something even more fundamental. It is time for a reformation in the church. Revival has to do with the extension of the gospel; the greatest need in the contemporary church is to rediscover the gospel, its glory and its power. It is time to return to the fundamentals of the faith and be refreshed in its truths, to gain anew a love and respect for the Holy Scriptures. Revival without Reformation is religious enthusiasm at best; revival out of reformation is the only hope of the church.

341

THE CENTRALITY OF THE GOSPEL
IN CHRISTIAN PROCLAMATION

Doctrines are not all created equal: some are more important than others. Consequently, the Christian theologian finds it useful to talk of gradations of convictions. Think of three concentric circles.

First, in the center ring, there are the essential beliefs of Christianity. These are the core doctrines of Christianity—those beliefs without which there can be no Christianity; those beliefs so central that one should have a willingness to die for them. Among these, in my view, are the existence of God, the deity of Christ, the atoning sacrifice of Christ, and salvation by grace without any human merit.

Second, moving outward by ring one, there are beliefs that are reckoned to be important but about which there is legitimate debate among Christians. Examples of these convictions might be particular views of baptism or the Eucharist, church polity, or the chronology of last things. While Christians may hold such convictions with a significant degree of fervency, they are nonetheless subject to a variance of opinion and are not issues that should divide the fellowship of the saints in the broadest sense. Nor should such doctrines hold center stage in our discussions of the Bible. The central things, the topics that should be our most frequent, fervent topics are those in the center circle.

Third, in the outermost of the concentric circles, there are distinctly personal beliefs. They are neither core doctrines of Christianity nor those embraced in a creedal statement by any particular Christian group. They are simply private, personal views that arise from the study of the Bible and the experience of life. Traditionally these have been defined as *adiaphora*, "things in difference." They might have to do with certain moral issues that are neither prohibited nor propounded by the Scriptures.

While it is useful to think of concentric circles of beliefs, these three categories are often blended in practice. Sometimes, for example, mere personal beliefs are treated as core truths. My plea is that these distinctions be recognized and that our Christian pastors, teachers, missionaries, and laity make sure that the central truths be foremost in our proclamation of Christianity.

The most important person in all of history is Jesus Christ; he must always be the passionate message of the church. Without Christ, there can be no gospel that is really good news. While there are teachings that are important, greatly adding to the maturity of the church, Christ is the keystone of all.

We know this is so because Christ is the very center of Scripture. The Old Testament is the book of shadows; it describes darkly what the New Testament elucidates with clarity and profundity. If the centuries before the coming of Christ can be described as anticipatory of Him, the centuries after the death, resurrection, and ascension of Christ can be described as an era of reflection and anticipation. In our private and collective worship as Christians we rehearse the events of His first coming and anticipate His coming again to fulfill the promise of rest for His people.

Christ, then, is the center of the Bible. The cross of Christ is the great moment of redemptive history. Along with all the teachings of Christ that fill out its deepest meaning, the Cross should always be the essential proclamation of the Christian community.

THE CENTRALITY OF CHRISTIAN ORTHODOXY IN THE CHURCH

The Church of Jesus Christ is at risk when the ancillary becomes a preoccupation, when the core doctrines of the faith are superseded by others (even if they are solid and wonderful teachings). I see at least two negative consequences in this.

First, when nonessential teachings are taught over and over again to the virtual exclusion of the essential doctrines, an impression is conveyed that these nonessential teachings are the very heart of the faith. But to be biblical means, at least in part, that one not only derives the content of one's teaching from the Bible but that one maintains the priorities of the Bible in teaching from it. The pages of history are replete with examples of people who have majored on the minors. Such a tendency distorts the gospel of Jesus Christ when the particular insights of a teacher or a group—teaching not shared by the entire Christian community—are substituted for the time-honored, central teachings of the church. Let us become "catholic" in our profession of Christianity, standing together on the historic Christian doctrines. Let us major on the major doctrines in our proclamation of Christ and not be drawn away by the attractions of novelty and complexity.

Second, there is also a danger in majoring on minors for those who preach and proclaim them. Novelty will always get a crowd and build a following, but it does not last beyond the gifted and winsome teacher or teachers who proclaim it. There is a rather wonderful dynamic in all this. Christ has so ordered things, it appears, that the enduring truths of Scripture last from generation to generation, but novelty is short-lived. Those who teach other than the core truths of the gospel as gospel truth can be compared to a person who walks along a beach in the soft, moist sand when the tide is out. This person leaves footprints in the sand, but the tide eventually comes and washes them away. In the past centuries of the church, many have taught novel insights, but most of it has passed with the tide of time. In refusing to major on the great and timeless truths of the gospel, they have poorly managed their precious time, have distorted the gospel, and have confused the Lord's people.

The history of Christian thought suggests that there is a timeless core of Christian truth. It has survived the battering of those unsympathetic with it and the minimalization of it by its advocates. Because Christ and His gospel have come to us from heaven, they will survive the ravages of friend and foe.

Help us, O Lord, not to be ashamed of the simplicity and wonder of the gospel of Jesus Christ. Enable us to preach nothing other than Christ and Him crucified, calling men and women, boys and girls, to this One who has loved us and loosed us from our sins by His precious blood. Amen!

—John D. Hannah

344

Notes

PREFACE

1. David F. Wells, *No Place for Truth: Or, Whatever Happened to Evangelical Theology?* (Grand Rapids, Mich.: Eerdmans, 1993), p. 300.
2. Thomas C. Oden, "On Whoring after the Spirit of the Age," in *No God but God: Breaking with the Idols of Our Age,* eds. Os Guinness and John Seel (Chicago: Moody Press, 1992), p. 196.

CHAPTER ONE: INTRODUCTION

1. David F. Wells, *No Place for Truth: Or, Whatever Happened to Evangelical Theology?* (Grand Rapids, Mich.: Eerdmans, 1993), p. 11.
2. Mark A. Noll, *The Scandal of the Evangelical Mind* (Grand Rapids, Mich.: Eerdmans, 1994), pp. 35–36.
3. George Barna, *The Barna Report* (Ventura, Calif.: Regal, 1994), pp. 44, 58.
4. Cornelius Plantinga, "Natural Born Sinners: Why We Flee from Guilt and the Notion of Sin," *Christianity Today* 38 (November 14, 1995): 26.
5. David F. Wells, *Losing Our Virtue* (Grand Rapids, Mich.: Eerdmans, 1998), pp. 28–29.
6. The substance of this section has been derived from Peter Toon, *The Development of Doctrine in the Church* (Grand Rapids, Mich.: Eerdmans, 1979). I am deeply indebted to him for his careful research and illuminating discussion.
7. Scottish Common Sense moral philosophy was dominant in America in the nineteenth century. Rooted in Baconianism, or the inductive

method of knowledge acquisition, Common Sense philosophy argued that self-consciousness or intuition was a reliable instrument of observation. Thus, knowledge is seen as prior to and independent of experience. See *Encyclopedia of Philosophy*, s.v. "Common Sense," and Irving H. Bartlett, *The American Mind in the Mid-Nineteenth Century* (New York: Crowell, 1967), pp. 18–20.

8. The date of the separation of the ancient period from the medieval period is admittedly arbitrary. Some scholars have seen the period as ending with the death of Augustine, "the last of the church fathers"; others have seen it as ending with the demise of the last Roman emperor, Augustus Romulus, in 476, and the emergence of the Frankish Empire. I have chosen as a date the emergence of Gregory the Great, the bishop of Rome, who pressed Petrine prerogatives to a previously unknown level. His claim, it seems, marks the beginning of an era.

9. It is customary to view the Reformation era, the early modern period, as ending with the Peace of Westphalia in 1648, followed by the rise of the Enlightenment. While the Enlightenment is more akin to the late modern period than the previous one, I have chosen to use the arbitrary date of 1750 as the dividing point between them because that appears to be more accurate in dating the change of eras in North America.

10. The beginning of the postmodern era is the subject of considerable discussion. While 1900 is, perhaps, accurate for the European context, 1960 is more accurate in North America. American disillusionment with the assumptions of the Enlightenment appears to have been a postwar phenomena. Because this book has been written for a North American audience, I define the postmodern era as beginning about 1960. I have determined, further, to blend the treatment of the most recent doctrinal developments within the discussion of the modern era for at least two reasons: first, because of the interconnectedness of the two eras; and second, because of the nature of the impact of postmodernity on theology. The influence has not been so much on how theology is expressed as on its relevancy in the personal lives of professing Christians.

CHAPTER TWO: AUTHORITY

1. The term *church father* admits to various referents. It can mean those earliest writers in the church through Augustine and Chrysostom in

the fifth century. I am using the term to refer to those writers (or writings) that immediately followed, and perhaps overlapped with, the apostles. The corpus of their literature is unique in its nonstrident, moral, and nonpolemical tone. J. B. Lightfoot, the English scholar of the previous century, edited the several small works of this corpus, designating them as the writings of the church fathers. They are enormously important to us in that they provide our first glimpse into the church after the death of the apostles.

2. The apologists were second- and third-century writers whose strident, defensive literary tone in part defines the corpus of their writings. By the second century, the church was recognized as a threat both to the state and to the false cults that flourished within it. These writers argued that the Christian faith was a true friend of the state, and they attacked the credibility of the false religions, principally Gnosticism, that were making inroads into the churches, disturbing the faith of some, perverting that of others. In the process of defending the church from adversaries from without and within, they commenced the task of systematic theology, the explanation and reasoned defense of our right to believe the gospel. These pastor-philosopher-writers became our first theologians.

3. The idea of the continuation of the "sign gifts" or "miraculous gifts" (for example, prophecy and tongues) after the apostolic era, along with canonical cessation, are issues that continue to divide the church. The Fathers indicate that the spiritual gifts continued after the first century, though they were progressively less evident in the church. Origen indicates that the gifts were less numerous in his time, the third century. Augustine and Chrysostom said that they were rare, if not extinct, in their time, the fifth century. The reason for the decline is uncertain. Some feel that the New Testament predicted their extinction with the end of the apostolic era; others feel that the troubles in the church, coupled with the rise of a power-oriented leadership, drove the gifts from the laity. For whatever reason, the gifts were not tied to an evidence of spiritual progress or a second, postconversion baptism of the Spirit. The issue of the cessation of revelation is difficult in part because the term *revelation* is not carefully nuanced. To the question "Is God today giving divine disclosures that are equal in authority to those of the apostles?" most would

347

answer with a resounding no! The Bible is the revelation of God, final and complete. However, to the question "Does God direct His people from sources other than the Bible?" the answer would be yes, though there are vast differences of opinion on the issue. God's providences in daily life, both negative and positive, are promised "revelations" of God to His children. The same can be argued for prayer, the counsel of a trustworthy friend, or the preaching of a dutiful pastor. As revelation is spoken of as both special (the Bible) and general (the order and regularity of the universe), the one perfect and the other impartial and incomplete, so "revelation" is complete and perfect, yet God reveals Himself and His ways through perfect and imperfect means. The validity of the latter, the imperfect, is derived from its compatibility and conformity with the former, the perfect.

4. Justo L. Gonzalez (*A History of Christian Thought* [Nashville: Abingdon, 1970], 1:151) summarizes the point in this way: "What we have just summarized is that which may be found in early antiheretical writers such as Irenaeus and Tertullian. But one must point out that at this time the understanding of apostolic succession was still not such that succession is required to confer validity to the episcopal office. On the contrary, some bishops had that succession and others did not have it; but all their churches were apostolic because their faith agreed with the faith of the apostles as it had been preserved in churches whose bishops were in their succession."

5. Bruce Vawter, *Biblical Inspiration* (Philadelphia: Westminster, 1972), pp. 26–27. See also R. P. C. Hanson, *Allegory and Event: A Study of the Sources and Interpretation of Origen's Interpretation of Scripture* (Richmond, Va.: John Knox, 1959), p. 187.

6. The *New Catholic Encyclopedia* (I:390) confirms this point. "St. Jerome distinguished between canonical books and ecclesiastical books. The latter he judges were circulated by the Church as good spiritual reading but were not recognized as authoritative Scripture."

7. A. D. R. Polman, *The Word of God According to St. Augustine* (Grand Rapids, Mich.: Eerdmans, 1969), pp. 53–54.

8. These dates are arbitrary, though generally a millennium of years marks out the period. It was a prosperous era in the history of the church, a period of triumph as the Mediterranean world and Europe were Christianized. However, the unity of the Catholic Church was

rent in the eleventh century, and the church was increasingly beset by an aggressive Islamic religion in Africa and the Near East.

9. The rise of the Renaissance in the late medieval period gave birth to the modern era (1500–1900). Scholars have generally divided the period into two eras: the early modern period (1500–1750) and the modern period (1750–1900). These dates are approximations of the periods. Both eras evidence an immeasurable debt to the Renaissance with its numerous intellectual forces that inspired advances in the sciences and arts. The early modern period, as expressed in the Protestant movements, took an increasingly disparaging view of medieval tradition as authority; the Roman Catholic Church followed the path of a historically inaccurate embrace of it. The late modern period rejected the role of both tradition and Scripture for the insights and promises of enlightened reasonability, an inward authority.

10. William Ames, *The Marrow of Theology,* trans. and ed. John D. Eusden (1629; reprint, Boston: Pilgrim, 1968), p. 186.

11. Cited in the *New International Dictionary of the Christian Church,* s.v. "Enlightenment."

12. Clyde L. Manschreck, *The Church from the Reformation to the Present,* vol. 2 of *A History of Christianity* (Grand Rapids, Mich.: Baker, 1981), p. 219.

13. Karl Barth, *Protestant Thought: From Rousseau to Ritschl,* trans. Brian Cozens (New York: Simon & Schuster, 1969), p. 306.

CHAPTER THREE: THE TRINITY

1. J. L. Neve, *A History of Christian Thought* (Philadelphia: United Lutheran Publishing House, 1943), I:6.

2. J. N. D. Kelley, *Early Christian Doctrines* (New York: Harper & Row, 1978), p. 95.

3. William Cunningham, *Historical Theology* (1862; reprint, London: Banner of Truth Trust, 1969), 1:305.

4. Adolf von Harnack, *History of Dogma,* trans. Neil Buchanan (1900; reprint, New York: Dover, 1961), 4:112.

5. Tony Lane, "A 12th-Century Man for All Seasons: The Life and Thought of Bernard of Clairvaux," *Church History Magazine* 8 (1990): 23.

6. Reinhold Seeberg, *Text-Book of the History of Doctrine,* trans. Charles E. Hay (Grand Rapids, Mich.: Baker, 1977), 2:54.

7. Colin Brown, *Christianity and Western Thought* (Downers Grove, Ill.: InterVarsity Press, 1990), p. 123.

8. H. John McLachlan, *Socinianism in Seventeenth-Century England* (London: Oxford University Press, 1951), p. 337.

9. James Orr, *English Deism: Its Roots and Its Fruits* (Grand Rapids, Mich.: Eerdmans, 1934), p. 34. Unitarians generally differed from the Deists over the relationship of the deity to the creation and the creature. Deists envisioned God as the great watchmaker who created the world as a fine-running mechanism that operates by natural forces that do not require His intervention. Hence, God was neither personal nor a worker of miracles; He was lost to His creation by an overemphasis on transcendence. Unitarians embraced the idea that God could and did intervene in the world He had made; they attempted to maintain transcendence and immanence. Thomas Jefferson, the third president of the United States, was a Unitarian by his own profession. Benjamin Franklin was a Deist.

10. Conrad Wright, *The Beginnings of Unitarianism in America* (Boston: Starr King, 1955), p. 10.

11. See chapter 2 for a discussion of the Enlightenment and its impact.

12. Albrecht Ritschl, *The Christian Doctrine of Justification and Reconciliation* (Edinburgh: Clark, 1902), p. 13.

13. Stanley Grenz and Roger Olsen have assessed Barth's contribution at this point by stating, "One of Barth's greatest contributions to twentieth-century theology is his recovery of the doctrine of the Trinity from obscurity" (*20th Century Theology* [Downers Grove, Ill.: InterVarsity Press, 1992], p. 77).

14. William Newton Clarke, *An Outline of Christian Theology* (New York: Scribner's, 1899), p. 154.

15. William Newton Clarke, *The Christian Doctrine of God* (Edinburgh: Clark, 1909), p. 229.

16. Harry Emerson Fosdick, *The Idea of God: Its Development within the Old and New Testaments* (New York: Harper & Brothers, 1938), p. 53.

17. Paul Tillich, *Systematic Theology* (Chicago: University of Chicago Press, 1951–1957), I:245.

18. R. Allan Killen, *The Ontological Theology of Paul Tillich* (Kampen: Kok, 1956), p. 132.

19. Ewert H. Cousins, "Process Models in Culture, Philosophy, and

Theology" in *Process Theology*, ed. Ewert H. Cousins (New York: Newman, 1971), p. 15.

20. For this neo-classicist interpretation of the doctrine of God, see Clark Pinnock et al., *The Openness of God* (Downers Grove, Ill.: InterVarsity Press, 1994).

21. Demetrios J. Constantelos, *The Greek Orthodox Church: Faith, History, and Practice* (New York: Seabury, 1967), p. 65. I have found three other volumes to be of significant help in understanding the Orthodox churches: Timothy Ware, *The Orthodox Church* (New York: Viking Penguin, 1984); Daniel B. Clendenin, *Eastern Orthodox Christianity: A Western Perspective* (Grand Rapids, Mich.: Baker, 1994); and Daniel B. Clendenin, *Eastern Orthodoxy: A Contemporary Reader* (Grand Rapids, Mich.: Baker, 1995).

22. Clendenin, *Eastern Orthodox Christianity*, p. 53.

CHAPTER FOUR: THE PERSON OF CHRIST

1. Jonathan Edwards, *A History of the Work of Redemption* (1782; reprint, New Haven: Yale University Press, 1989), 9:116.

2. Edwards, *History of the Work of Redemption*, 9:513.

3. Alois Grillmeier, *Christ in Christian Tradition* (Atlanta: John Knox, 1975), I:105.

4. Grillmeier, *Christ in Christian Tradition*, I:149.

5. The issue of whether the virgin Mary bore only a human or the God-man has had some important ramifications, at least for some. When the Roman Catholic Church accorded increasing importance to Mary, it did so on the basis that she is the "mother of God," that she bore deity in her womb. The declaration of this ecumenical council that she bore God was a pivotal interpretative point in the much later movement in the church to increase Mary's redemptive role by asserting her immaculate conception, beatific assumption, and comediation. These doctrines, however, emerged definitively only in the nineteenth and twentieth centuries.

6. This was not the first instance of the destruction of the external unity of the catholic or universal church. The second century witnessed the disruptive Marcionite movement and the pneumatic Montanists; in the third and fourth centuries the schismatic Novatians and Donatists emerged. In each of these cases, the dissenting purists were relatively

351

small in number and short-lived. Eventually, they either ceased to exist as a discernible entity or were reassimilated into the Catholic Church.

7. The condemnation of the bishop of Rome for advocating the Monothelite error has interesting implications relative to papal infallibility, a doctrine that emerged in the nineteenth century.

8. Paul Althaus, *The Theology of Martin Luther* (Philadelphia: Fortress, 1966), p. 197. Dennis Duling has written, "Luther attempted to be orthodox, but he did not present Jesus Christ in the orthodox manner, that is, with a systematic and well formulated doctrinal position" (*Jesus Christ through History* [New York: Harcourt Brace Jovanovich, 1979], p. 109).

9. *The Racovian Catechism,* trans. Thomas Rees (1562; reprint, London: Longman, Hurst, Rees, Orme, and Brown, 1818), pp. 55–56.

10. William Ellery Channing, *The Complete Works of William Ellery Channing* (Boston: American Unitarian Association, 1879), p. 373.

11. Friedrich Schleiermacher, *The Christian Faith* (1830; reprint, New York: Harper & Row, 1963), II:389.

12. Schleiermacher, *Christian Faith,* II:424.

13. Albrecht Ritschl, *The Christian Doctrine of Justification and Reconciliation* (Edinburgh: Clark, 1900), p. 470.

14. Karl Barth, *Church Dogmatics,* eds. G. W. Bromiley and Thomas F. Torrance (Edinburgh: Clark, 1956), I.2.132.

15. Barth, *Church Dogmatics,* I.2.160–161.

16. Lyman Abbott, *The Theology of an Evolutionist* (New York: Outlook, 1925), p. 173.

17. Lyman Abbott, *Reminiscences* (New York: Houghton Mifflin, 1915), p. 170.

18. Arthur Cushman McGiffert, *The God of the Early Christians* (New York: Scribner's, 1924), p. 22.

19. McGiffert, *God of the Early Christians,* p. 28.

20. Harry Emerson Fosdick, *The Modern Use of the Bible* (New York: Macmillan, 1924), p. 245.

21. Fosdick, *Modern Use,* p. 257.

22. Fosdick, *Modern Use,* p. 272.

23. Walter Rauschenbusch, *Christianity and the Social Crisis* (New York: Macmillan, 1907), pp. 44–71.

24. Alexander J. McKelway, *The Systematic Theology of Paul Tillich* (Richmond, Va.: John Knox, 1964), p. 168.

25. J. Gresham Machen, *What Is Faith?* (New York: Macmillan, 1935), p. 88.

26. J. Gresham Machen, *Christianity and Liberalism* (1923; reprint, Grand Rapids, Mich.: Eerdmans, 1981), p. 2.

27. Machen, *Christianity and Liberalism,* pp. 7–8.

28. Machen, *Christianity and Liberalism,* p. 6.

29. Machen, *Christianity and Liberalism,* p. 96.

30. Machen, *What Is Faith?* p. 116.

31. Timothy Ware, *The Orthodox Church* (New York: Viking Penguin, 1984), p. 218.

CHAPTER FIVE: THE WORK OF CHRIST

1. James Orr, *The Progress of Dogma* (London: Hodder and Stoughton, 1901), p. 210.

2. For a very readable explanation of the atonement as a ransom, see Alister E. McGrath, *Christian Theology: An Introduction* (Cambridge, Mass.: Blackwell, 1994), p. 345. I am dependent on his discussion for my information at this point.

3. John K. Mozley, *The Doctrine of the Atonement* (London: Duckworth, 1915), p. 110.

4. Adolf von Harnack, *History of Dogma,* trans. Neil Buchanan (1900; reprint, New York: Dover, 1961), 2:367.

5. Justo Gonzalez, *History of Christian Thought* (Nashville: Abingdon, 1971), I:166.

6. Paul Althaus, *A Theology of Martin Luther,* trans. Robert C. Shultz (Philadelphia: Fortress, 1966), p. 203.

7. Gonzalez, *History of Christian Thought,* III:261–262.

8. Friedrich Schleiermacher, *The Christian Faith* (1830; reprint, New York: Harper & Row, 1963), II:456–460.

9. Schleiermacher, *Christian Faith,* II:456.

10. Otto Pfleiderer, *The Development of Theology in Germany since Kant,* trans. J. Frederick Smith (London: Allen & Unwin, 1893), p. 117.

11. Albrecht Ritschl, *The Christian Doctrine of Justification and Reconciliation* (Edinburgh: Clark, 1900), pp. 473–474.

12. Karl Barth, *Church Dogmatics,* eds. G. W. Bromiley and T. F. Torrance, trans. G. W. Bromiley (Edinburgh: Clark, 1956), 4.1,222.

13. Barth, *Church Dogmatics,* 4.1.253.

14. Donald Bloesch, *Jesus Is Victor!* (Nashville: Abingdon, 1976), p. 52.

15. Barth's interpretation of the atonement cannot be understood without grasping his view of history and election. Concerning the former, Barth separates event from meaning; that is, there is an inner, sacred notion of history and an outer, nonobjective history. What the eye can observe is merely the outer shell of an interior and profound significance. The outer may contain error, but it somehow errorlessly conveys truth. An event and the words describing it are separated from its meaning. The redemptive event was really a declarative event speaking of a salvation similarly announced at the Incarnation; it was finished before He came. This directly relates to Barth's view of election, which he treats with primacy. Obsessed with the transcendent, sovereign actions of God, and failing to see salvation as being a process entailing past, present, and future aspects, he argued strongly that election saves, not that it procures objects of salvation. Since we are saved before the Incarnation by God's decree, says Barth, the death of Christ can only be the proclamation or announcement of it.

16. Conrad Wright, *The Beginnings of Unitarianism in America* (Boston: Starr King, 1955), p. 10.

17. Richard D. Mosier, *The American Temper: Patterns of Our Intellectual Heritage* (Berkeley: University of California Press, 1952), pp. 69–70.

18. Jonathan Edwards Jr., *Works,* ed. Tryon Edwards (1842; reprint, New York: Garland, 1987), 2:24–27.

19. Robert L. Ferm, *Jonathan Edwards the Younger* (Grand Rapids, Mich.: Eerdmans, 1976), p. 119.

20. Charles G. Finney, *Systematic Theology,* ed. James H. Fairchild (1846; reprint, Minneapolis: Bethany, 1976), p. 271.

21. Finney, *Systematic Theology,* p. 271.

22. Lyman Abbott, *Reminiscences* (New York: Houghton Mifflin, 1915), p. viii.

23. Lyman Abbott, *The Theology of an Evolutionist* (New York: Outlook, 1925), p. 108.

24. William Newton Clarke, *An Outline of Christian Theology* (New York: Scribner's, 1899), p. 352.

25. Clarke, *Outline of Christian Theology,* pp. 352–353.

26. Harry Emerson Fosdick, *The Modern Use of the Bible* (New York: Macmillan, 1924), pp. 230–231.

27. Shailer Mathews, *The Faith of Modernism* (1924; reprint, New York: AMS, 1969), p. 160.

28. Shailer Mathews, *The Atonement and the Social Process* (New York: Macmillan, 1930), p. 208.

29. George F. Thomas, "Central Christian Affirmations" in H. P. Van Dusen, ed., *The Christian Answer* (London: Nisbet, 1946), pp. 160–161.

30. Paul Tillich, *Systematic Theology* (Chicago: University of Chicago Press, 1951, 1957), 1:282, 2:172.

31. Tillich, *Systematic Theology*, 2:176.

32. Norman Pittenger, *Freed to Love: A Process Interpretation of Redemption* (Wilton, Conn.: Morehouse-Barlow, 1987), p. 63.

33. J. Greshem Machen, *What Is Faith?* (Macmillan, 1935), pp. 144–146.

34. J. Greshem Machen, *Christianity and Liberalism* (1923; reprint, Grand Rapids, Mich.: Eerdmans, 1981), p. 121. See also *What Is Faith?* pp. 148–151. The arguments subsequently referred to by Machen are to be found in *Christianity and Liberalism* (pp. 125–136).

35. Daniel B. Clendenin, *Eastern Orthodox Christianity: A Western Perspective* (Grand Rapids, Mich.: Baker, 1994), p. 122.

36. Clendenin, *Eastern Orthodox Christianity,* pp. 120–125, and Timothy Ware, *The Orthodox Church* (New York: Viking Penguin, 1984), p. 234.

CHAPTER SIX: SALVATION

1. George P. Fisher, "The Augustinian and the Federal Theories of Original Sin Compared," *New Englander* 27 (July 1868): 468.

2. J. N. D. Kelley, *Early Christian Doctrines* (New York: Harper & Row, 1978), p. 163.

3. William G. T. Shedd, *A History of Christian Doctrine* (1889; reprint, Minneapolis: Klock & Klock, 1978), 2:29. Typically, the apologists define the foreknowledge of God as foresight and make the determinations of God dependent upon a knowledge of what humanity would do if provided the opportunity to do it. This, it would seem, was the result of the blinders placed on them by their opponents, the Gnostics, who accused Christians of fatalism. Thinking that a denial of fatalism was tantamount to the assertion of orthodoxy, they defended an understanding of free will that included the power to determine choices, not merely to choose an available one. Said Martyr: "So, if we declare that future events have been predicted, by

355

that we do not claim that they take place by the necessity of fate. But, since God has foreknowledge of what all men will do, and has ordained that each man will be rewarded in accordance with the merit of his actions, foretells through the prophetic Spirit that He Himself will reward them in accordance with the merit of their deeds, ever urging him to reflection and remembrance, proving that He both cares and provides for them" (*Apology* I.84).

4. John Calvin, *The Institutes of the Christian Religion in the Library of Christian Classics,* ed. John T. Neill, trans. Ford Lewis Battles (Philadelphia: Westminster, 1960), II.2.4.

5. Justo L. Gonzalez (*A History of Christian Thought* [Nashville: Abingdon, 1971], 2:44) summarized this point. "In summary, natural man is free only inasmuch as he is free to sin. 'Thus we always enjoy a free will; but this will is not always good.' This does not mean that freedom has lost its meaning in fallen man, who is only able to choose a particular sinful alternative. On the contrary, natural man has true freedom to choose between alternatives, although, given his condition as a sinner subject to concupiscence, as a member of this 'mass of damnation,' all the alternatives that are really open to him are sin. The option not to sin does not exist. This is what is meant by the saying that he has freedom to sin but does not have freedom not to sin." Justo Gonzalez sees in the semi-Augustinianism of the synod an ill-boding future for the church. The synod connected God's grace to baptism in canon 8 in a way that is novel. Grace gradually would be perceived as a process that begins with baptism, rather than a once-for-all act of God. Of this gradual shift, he wrote, "The overwhelming and dynamic experience set forth in the confession is being transformed into an entire system of grace—a process that was perhaps inevitable, but nonetheless unfortunate" (2:61).

6. Jasper Hopkins, *A Companion to the Study of St. Anselm* (Minneapolis: University of Minnesota, 1972), p. 158.

7. Marianne Sawicki, *The Gospel in History* (New York: Paulist, 1988), pp. 184–185.

8. Robert Holcot, "Lectures on the Wisdom of Solomon" in *Forerunners of the Reformation,* ed. Heiko Oberman (New York: Holt, Rinehart and Winston, 1966), p. 149.

9. Michael Horton, "The Crisis of Evangelical Christianity," *Modern Reformation* (January–February 1994): 17.

10. Alister McGrath, "The State of the Church before the Reformation," *Modern Reformation* (January–February 1994): 10.

11. Martin Luther, *The Bondage of the Will*, trans. J. I. Packer and O. R. Johnston (Grand Rapids, Mich.: Revell, 1958), p. 310.

12. Luther, *Bondage of the Will*, pp. 295–296.

13. In reading Lutheran literature on the meaning of baptism, there appears to be confusion. This relates to the necessity of faith in the thing symbolized by the sacrament when it comes to that category of children who, due to their infantile state, come to the water incapable of either receiving instruction or believing. While Luther's answer will be noted later, Lutheranism seems to suggest that infants in this state receive regeneration apart from faith, or at least through the faith of others. It is difficult to see how the sacrament does not have an objective function, though confessedly the Lutheran tradition differs greatly from their Roman Catholic opponents in defining the doctrines of sin and grace. For example, while not referring to infants, the *Saxon Visitation Articles* (1592) stated that through baptism "God saves us, and works in us . . . justice and purgation from our sins" (III.2). How can one "in it [baptism] be born again" (III.4) if one comes having already received the reality as evidenced by faith which is strengthened by the symbol? How does this relate to declarative righteousness through faith?

14. J. I. Packer and O. R. Johnston, introduction to *The Bondage of the Will*, p. xxxx.

15. Calvin, *Institutes of the Christian Religion*, III.11.3.

16. Calvin, *Institutes of the Christian Religion*, III.17.2.

17. Jacob Arminius, *The Works of Jacob Arminius*, trans. James Nichols and William Nichols (1825–1875; reprint, Grand Rapids, Mich.: Baker, 1986), I:374.

18. The Arminian tradition faithfully teaches that salvation is through the grace of God alone. It is the explanation of it, as a miraculous cooperative moment in regeneration, that has caused considerable discussion. A corollary to the Arminian view of human ability and cooperative grace is their understanding of foreknowledge, a prior covenantal love, to be foreseen human faith. Seeking to preserve the

freedom of humanity and the justice of God, Arminians consistently make the creature the determinative agent to the degree that God can effect His will, since He is not willing for any to perish. A second corollary is that continuance in grace is dependent upon willingness to persevere; this semi-bilateral contractualism for salvation can be forfeited through negligence. A third corollary is the Arminian understanding of the atonement described in the previous chapter. Christ died for the concept of sin, not for the sins of selected sinners.

19. *New International Dictionary of the Christian Church,* s.v. "Enlightenment."

20. Friedrich Schleiermacher, *The Christian Faith* (1830; reprint, New York: Harper & Row, 1963), II:494.

21. Albrecht Ritschl, *The Christian Doctrine of Justification and Reconciliation* (Edinburgh: Clark, 1900), p. 592.

22. Karl Barth, *Church Dogmatics,* eds. G. W. Bromiley and T. F. Torrance, trans. G. W. Bromiley (Edinburgh: Clark, 1956), IV.1.479.

23. Barth, *Church Dogmatics,* IV.1.596.

24. Perhaps catapulted by the excessive immanentism of the nineteenth century, Barth stressed the transcendence of God to such a degree that historic events lost their normal significance. Such events as Christ's death were only witnesses to eternal decisions by the Trinity. History became a stage to dramatize events that had already transpired. History, like the Bible, is a witness to something greater.

25. Lyman Abbott, *The Theology of an Evolutionist* (New York: Outlook, 1925), p. 85.

26. Abbott, *Theology of an Evolutionist,* p. 48.

27. Shailer Mathews, *The Faith of Modernism* (1924; reprint, New York: AMS, 1969), pp. 95, 97.

28. Mathews, *Faith of a Modernist,* p. 108.

29. Mathews, *Faith of a Modernist,* p. 124.

30. Paul Tillich, *Systematic Theology* (Chicago: University of Chicago, 1951, 1957), II:29.

31. Tillich, *Systematic Theology,* II:177.

32. J. Greshem Machen, *Christianity and Liberalism* (1923; reprint, Grand Rapids, Mich.: Eerdmans, 1981), p. 64.

33. Machen, *Christianity and Liberalism,* p. 117.

34. Machen, *Christianity and Liberalism,* p. 134.

NOTES

35. Samuel Hopkins, *The Works of Samuel Hopkins* (1852–1854; reprint, New York: Garland, 1987), I:218.

36. Nathaniel Emmons, *The Works Nathaniel Emmons* (1860–1863; reprint, New York: Garland, 1987), III:123.

37. Charles Grandison Finney, *Systematic Theology* (1846; reprint, Minneapolis: Bethany, 1976), p. 231.

38. Finney, *Systematic Theology,* p. 285.

39. Walter M. Abbott, gen. ed., *The Documents of Vatican II* (New York: Herder, 1966), p. 90.

40. Daniel B. Clendenin, *Eastern Orthodox Christianity: A Western Perspective* (Grand Rapids, Mich.: Baker, 1994), p. 123.

41. Timothy Ware, *The Orthodox Church* (New York: Viking Penguin, 1984), p. 226.

42. Ware, *Orthodox Church,* p. 229.

43. The parallels between the Roman Catholic Church and the Orthodox churches in these matters are remarkable. They possess similar views on the nature of the human condition and the workings of God, the cleansing sacramental effectiveness of baptism and penance, and the certainty of heaven in death after the residual effects of sin are removed (though the Roman Church argues for a purgatory and the Eastern churches do not). Further, both insist on the perpetual virginity of Mary.

    Differences are also discernible. For example, each church confesses the importance of sacraments and defines their functions similarly; however, the Roman Catholic Church limits them to seven while the Orthodox do not.

CHAPTER SEVEN: THE CHURCH

1. J. N. D. Kelley, *Early Christian Doctrines* (New York: Harper & Row, 1978), p. 194.

2. For a discussion of the issue of infant baptism in the early church, the research of David F. Wright seems to be both extensive and unmarred by prior ecclesiastical commitments. See particularly his "One Baptism or Two? Reflections on the History of Christian Baptism" *Vox Evangelica* 18 (1988): 7–23.

3. Justo L. Gonzalez makes a rather remarkable qualifying statement about the nature of apostolic succession at this time. "One must point out that at this time the understanding of apostolic succession was

359

still not such that succession is required to confer validity to the episcopal office. On the contrary, some bishops had that succession and others did not have it; but all their churches were apostolic because their faith agreed with the faith of the apostles whose bishops were in their succession. Later, and through much development that would take centuries, this doctrine of apostolic succession would be developed to a point that would never be recognized by those who first advocated it" (*A History of Christian Thought* [Nashville: Abingdon, 1971], I:151).

4. The term *pope* was used in the church at this time for its bishops and was not restricted to one of the bishops in particular. In a letter from the clergy of Rome, for example, Cyprian is referred to as Pope Cyprian and "most blessed and glorious Pope" (*Epistle* 30). William A. Jurgens, a Roman Catholic scholar, commented on the usage of this term as well as Cyprian's understanding of the independent authority of each bishop as expressed in a council he convened in Carthage in 256. "It was not at this time a special title assigned to the Bishop of Rome; and the attitude expressed in regard to the jurisdictional autonomy of individual bishop is Cyprian's constant attitude" (*The Faith of the Early Fathers* [Collegeville, Minn.: Liturgical, 1970], I:241). He states that the term *episcopus episcoporum* (supreme bishop) was used as a grand title to designate various persons of authority in the early fourth century.

5. See note 2. David Wright is impressed that the first attestation of "infant baptism" concerns those who can receive instruction and confess faith (Hippolytus, *Apostolic Traditions*). He suggests that a distinction should be made between infant baptism and baby baptism. The original language did not differentiate between a small child capable of receiving instruction and intellectually responding and one who could not. He suggests that this led to the error that babies were baptized in the earliest decades of the church. He believes that babies were baptized only after a century or so, when the stigma of Jewish identity had ceased to be a problem in the church. It was only then that the identities between the sign of the Old Covenant (circumcision) and the sign of the New Covenant (baptism) were equated. When the Jewish threat diminished, a cogent biblical argument could then be made for baby baptism.

6. William A. Jurgens, *The Faith of the Early Fathers* (Collegeville, Minn.: Liturgical, 1970), III:308.

7. Justo L. Gonzalez, *A History of Christian Thought* (Nashville: Abingdon, 1971), II:72.

8. Quoted in John H. Leith, ed., *Creeds of the Churches: A Reader in Christian Doctrine from the Bible to the Present* (Garden City, N.Y.: Anchor/Doubleday, 1963), 58.

9. There are references to prayers for the dead in writers before Augustine. Tertullian, for example, stated, "We offer sacrifices for the dead on their birthday anniversaries" (*The Crown* 3.2). However, it seems that the prayers are for the refreshment of souls disengaged momentarily from their bodies, not for souls to be spared of suffering for any unforgiven sins. In another place he wrote of the duties of a wife to her deceased husband: "Indeed, she prays for his soul and asks that he may, while waiting, find rest; and that he may share in the first resurrection. And each year, on the anniversary of his death, she offers the sacrifice" (*Monogamy* 10.1).

10. Steven Ozment, *The Age of Reform, 1250–1550* (New Haven: Yale University Press, 1980), p. 144.

11. Quoted in Heiko Oberman, *Forerunners of the Reformation,* trans. Paul L. Nyhus (New York: Holt, Rinehart and Winston, 1966), p. 149.

12. Ozment, *Age of Reform,* p. 30.

13. Leith, *Creeds of the Churches,* p. 60.

14. This is a point of contention within modern Lutheran circles. Some Lutheran communities, such as the Wisconsin Lutheran Synod, teach that baptism objectively conveys salvation grace apart from faith for every child who is brought to it.

15. *The Augsburg Confession* (1530) was a statement of Lutheran Protestantism created to explain the viability of the "new" faith to the emperor, Charles V. It was framed in such a way as to distance Lutheranism from the Anabaptists, who had troubled the empire by misapplying Luther's teachings. Accordingly, the statements on baptism and the Eucharist have a decidedly anti-Anabaptist ring to them. *The Formula of Concord* (1576), the second profound statement of Lutheran orthodoxy, has a decidedly anti-Zwinglian flavor relative to the Eucharist. Could it be that Lutheranism was slanted by apologetical and political concerns in defining the sacraments?

16. Friedrich Schleiermacher, *The Christian Faith* (Edinburgh: Clark, 1928), p. 532.

17. Schleiermacher, *Christian Faith*, p. 586.

18. Schleiermacher, *Christian Faith*, pp. 630–631.

CHAPTER EIGHT: THE END TIMES

1. J. N. D. Kelley, *Early Christian Doctrines* (New York: Harper & Row, 1978), p. 462.

2. Peter Richardson, *Israel in the Apostolic Church* (London: Cambridge University Press, 1969), p. 1.

3. Richardson, *Israel in the Apostolic Church*, p. 16.

4. William A. Jurgens, *The Faith of the Early Fathers* (Collegeville, Minn.: Liturgical, 1970), 1:38.

5. Henry C. Sheldon, *History of Christian Doctrines* (New York: Eaton & Mains, 1906), 1:405.

6. John Calvin, *Institutes of the Christian Religion* (Philadelphia: Westminster, 1960), 3.25.9.

7. *The Oxford Dictionary of the Christian Church,* s.v. "Millenarianism."

8. Calvin, *Institutes of the Christian Religion,* 3.25.5.

9. Daniel Whitby, *Paraphrase and Commentary on the New Testament* (London: Clarke, 1760), p. 687.

10. Friedrich Schleiermacher, *The Christian Faith* (Edinburgh: Clark, 1928), p. 722.

11. Shailer Mathews, *The Social Gospel* (Philadelphia: Griffith & Rowland, 1910), p. 20.

12. Walter Rauschenbusch, *A Theology of the Social Gospel* (New York: Macmillan, 1918), pp. 218–219.

13. Rauschenbusch, *Theology of the Social Gospel*, p. 226.

14. Rudolf Bultmann, *History and Eschatology* (Edinburgh: Edinburgh University Press, 1957), p. 155.

15. Jürgen Moltmann, *Theology of Hope* (New York: Harper & Row, 1967), p. 41.

16. Moltmann, *Theology of Hope*, p. 21.

17. Jonathan Edwards, *The Complete Works of Jonathan Edwards, Apocalyptic Writings: An Humble Attempt* (1747; reprint, New Haven: Yale University Press, 1977), 5:421.

18. Edwards, *Apocalyptic Writings,* 5:335.

19. Jonathan Edwards, *A History of the Work of Redemption* (1782; reprint, New Haven: Yale University Press, 1989), 9:480.

20. Edwards, *History of the Work of Redemption,* 9:489.

21. *Oxford Dictionary of the Christian Church,* s.v. "Charles Hodge."

22. Charles Hodge, *Systematic Theology* (New York: Scribners, 1872), 3:866.

23. One of the most controversial aspects of modern or futurist premillennialism has been the doctrine of the Rapture, a teaching that split the Brethren movement in 1845 when B. W. Newton opposed Darby's view. Even those who are most adamant in defending the view find little support for it in the early church. One has confessed that "it is hard to find clear pretribulationalism spelled out in the fathers. . . . " Instead, the weight of argument seems to rest on the idea that the church expected the any-moment return of Christ though crucial accompanying teachings, such as the two people's doctrine appears unknown." Advocates cite the work of Ephraem the Syrian, a fourth-century writer, and the American Baptist Benjamin Morgan of the eighteenth century. When imminency faded as a doctrine in the church, proponents suggest that a secret Rapture was suppressed. For a discussion of this important point, see *The Dictionary of Premillennialism,* s.v. "Rapture, History of the."

24. *The Dictionary of Premillennial Theology,* s.v. "Dispensationalism."

25. *Catechism of the Catholic Church* (Morristown, N.J.: Silver Burdett Gin, 1994), p. 177. This statement is followed by a sentence that indicates that the intent of it is to prohibit the propagation of politico-religious theories of liberationism through secular messianisms, issues of concern to the conservative Catholic hierarchy.

26. *Catechism of the Catholic Church,* p. 177.

27. Timothy Ware (*The Orthodox Church* [New York: Viking Penguin, 1984], pp. 265–267) is rather strident in the defense of this teaching in the church. It appears to have been motivated by the fear that some in the church are rejecting the truth.

28. There has been some discussion in the Orthodox community concerning what the Roman Catholic Church calls purgatory, the abode of unpurified deceased believers effecting purgation before entrance into heaven. *The Acts and Decrees of the Synod of Jerusalem* (1672), directed by Dositheus, implies an interim state for the unpurified,

though the term "purgatory" was not used. "Of these and such like souls depart into Hades, and there endure the punishment due to the sins they have committed. But they are aware of their future release from hence" (XVIII). Timothy Ware has argued that Dositheus for some time embraced such a doctrine as well as prayer for the dead, but most in the Orthodox community reject the view. He says that most in the church teach that the dead depart to blessedness immediately; some teach that there is suffering after death but that it is not redeeming; and others prefer to leave the question unresolved (*Orthodox Church,* p. 259).

CHAPTER 9: CONCLUSION

1. David F. Wells, *No Place for Truth: Or, Whatever Happened to Evangelical Theology?* (Grand Rapids, Mich.: Eerdmans, 1993), p. 300.
2. Thomas C. Oden, "On Whoring after the Spirit of the Age," in *No God but God: Breaking with the Idols of Our Age,* eds. Os Guinness and John Seel (Chicago: Moody Press, 1992), p. 196.
3. Mark A. Noll, *The Scandal of the Evangelical Mind* (Grand Rapids, Mich.: Eerdmans, 1994), pp. 35–36.
4. George Barna, *The Barna Report* (Ventura, Calif.: Regal, 1994), pp. 44, 58.
5. Cornelius Plantinga, "Natural Born Sinners: Why We Flee from Guilt and the Notion of Sin," *Christianity Today* 38 (November 14, 1995): 26.
6. David F. Wells, *Losing Our Virtue* (Grand Rapids, Mich.: Eerdmans, 1998), pp. 28–29.

Glossary

Adoptionism: A heretical teaching that denies Christ's absolute deity, affirming that He was a human being merely endowed with unusual powers from God.

Amillennialism: A teaching that the glorious reign of Christ is synonymous with the eternal state, that the promises of God to His people are not fulfilled in the eternal state.

Anabaptism: A movement of broad constituency that emerged in the sixteenth century and shared with Lutheranism and Calvinism a rejection of Roman Catholic distinctives while differing from them by insisting that baptism should not be extended to infants and that the roles of the church and state should remain separated.

Ancient Premillennialism: A teaching concerning future events in history, the triumph of God, and the final coming of Christ at the end of time. While agreeing with modern premillennialism that there will be a physical reign of Christ on the earth for one thousand years, advocates of ancient premillennialism identified Israel and the church as the one people of God.

Anglicanism: A term referring to the Church of England that was defined during the reign of Elizabeth I, a compromise of sorts to minimize the strident religious conflicts in England between Protestants and Catholics.

Anselmic Theory: The teaching that the meaning of Christ's death on the cross was a divine transaction in which Christ placated the wrath of God for sin by becoming the sinner's penalty-bearing substitute.

Because of this substitution, God could truly remain just in forgiving sinners and clothing them with the righteousness of God. Anselm was an eleventh-century theologian living in England.

Apocalyptic: A type of literature, largely metaphorical and symbolic, dealing with the ultimate destruction of evil, the triumph of God in the world, and the events that characterize the judgments of God and the end of the world.

Apollinarianism: A heretical teaching that denigrated the humanity of Christ, making Him less than fully human while affirming His absolute deity. Apollinarius was a fourth-century bishop from Asia Minor.

Apologists: The writers of the second and third centuries of the church who sought to defend the Christian faith against false accusations from opponents outside the church as well as heretical teaching propagated within the community.

Apostolic Succession: An early defense of the Christian faith, before the collection of the new canonical writings, by an appeal to the passing of the gospel from Christ to the apostles and then to their disciples. Later, the term came to mean the succession of men in an office.

Arianism: A heretical teaching that endeavored to explain the preincarnate relationship of the Father to the Son by viewing the Son as less than God. Arius was an Alexandrian presbyter who died in the fourth century.

Arminianism: A teaching that emerged in Holland and was concerned that the prevailing Calvinist interpretation of the Christian faith did not do justice to the biblical stress on the freedom of individuals to choose the gospel. It redefined such doctrines as human depravity, election, and the atonement. Jacob Arminius lived from 1560 to 1609.

Baptists: A tradition within the Protestant Reformation with European antecedents and English origins from the seventeenth century. Special teachings of Baptists include a stress on regenerate church membership, believer's baptism, a memorialist understanding of the Eucharist, and the separation of church and state.

Blessed Hope: The assurance that Christ will return again to gather His own to Himself and judge unbelievers before the Great White Throne.

Calvinism: A system of Protestant teaching that has its fountainhead in Calvin's *Institutes of the Christian Religion* and interprets the Bible

GLOSSARY

through the grid of the omnipotence of God in all of life. John Calvin was a French theologian who led the Protestant Reformation in Geneva, Switzerland, in the sixteenth century.

Canon: The term generally means a standard by which a thing is judged. Eventually the term came to signify the list of books that were to be recognized as authoritative in the church.

Cassianism: A teaching that sought to explain the relationship between the work of God in salvation and the activity of the sinner. This view argues that God's action may at times follow the sinner's repentance and at other times may precede it. Though condemned in the sixth century, Cassianism was widespread in the centuries before the Reformation. It is also called semi-Pelagianism. John Cassian was a monk who lived in the fourth and fifth centuries.

Catechism: A doctrinal confession set in the form of questions and answers that is used to educate people in the beliefs of the Christian faith and the distinctive teachings of the group that formulated it.

Church Fathers: A term that can mean any church scholar or writer through the centuries. More precisely, the term indicates those scholars and writers who lived in the initial centuries of the church, especially those who came immediately after the apostles.

Conciliar Movement: An organized attempt in the fourteenth century to resolve the question of who had supreme authority in the church—the Roman pontiff or the church councils?

Congregationalism: A form of church government that puts decision making in the hands of members of the local assembly.

Conservative Movement: A term expressing an attempt to maintain the status quo. It generally indicates the organized endeavor to foster traditional and orthodox theology, as opposed to revisionist interpretations of Scripture and doctrine.

Covenant Theology: An attempt to organize the data of the Bible by emphasizing the unity of the Scriptures, seeing the Old Testament people and the New Testament saints as being one.

Creed: A concise summary of doctrine produced by a church council. It is what a religious body confesses to be true. The earliest creeds functioned as baptismal formulas.

Deism: A form of rationalistic religious faith that viewed God as the Creator of the universe who directs the world through established laws

367

rather than providential control. It viewed Christ as the best human example of virtue and morality.

Dispensationalism: An attempt to find continuity in the seeming discontinuities of the Bible by arguing for a distinction between the ancient people of God (Israel) and the new people (the church). The essence of it is that there are two distinct peoples of God with two separate purposes and two unique destinies.

Doctrine: A term referring to the teaching of the church or to what has been set forth by the church as its understanding of the Bible.

Dogma: A religious teaching established from the Scriptures and stated in a formal fashion by an ecclesiastical body.

Donatism: A movement largely within the North African churches, from the fourth to eighth centuries, concerned with the spiritual and moral vitality of the church. According to Donatism, the spiritual benefit of church offices and sacraments was determined by the purity of the officeholder. Donatus was a North African bishop.

Ecumenical Councils: While the term may indicate any large ecclesiastical decision-making body, it more specifically refers to the gatherings of the bishops of the church, after the fourth century through the sixth, that dealt with questions concerning the Trinity and the person of Christ and issued creeds describing their binding decisions.

Empiricism: A method of searching for knowledge through experiment and experience. The potential difficulty with this approach to knowledge is the assumption that all that is knowable may be obtained by this method. In Pascal's famous line, "the heart has ways of knowing the mind knows not of."

Enlightenment: An intellectual movement that emerged in the seventeenth century and sought to base knowledge on an empiricist foundation rather than on an external authority, such as revelation or church dogma.

Episcopalianism: Though often a synonym for the Church of England or the Anglican community worldwide, the term may refer to the hierarchical form of government, a rule through bishops.

Eschatology: Teaching concerning future events in the church and the world, especially regarding ultimate judgment and triumph.

Evangelicalism: As used of a branch of Christendom, the term refers to the embracing of conservative perspectives on such doctrines as the Trinity, the deity of Christ, the inability of humankind to merit salvation, substitutionary atonement, and salvation by grace alone. At the core of the movement are a set of religious values that center on the necessity of personal conversion and the spreading of the gospel.

Filioque Controversy: A controversy in the medieval church concerning the relationship of Christ to the sending of the Holy Spirit into the world. Did both the Father and the Son send the Spirit, or did the Father alone send the Spirit? (*Filioque* is Latin for "and from the Son.") The discussion encompassed the issues of the authority of Roman bishops in Eastern church affairs and the role of church councils.

Fundamentalism: The term historically is a synonym for evangelicalism or conservatism relative to the embrace of orthodox doctrine. In twentieth-century American religious life, it came to mean a party within the evangelical movement that was separatistic and morally restrictive.

Gnosticism: A religious movement in the early church that embraced some of the features of Christianity but rejected its essential teachings. *Gnosis* is Greek for "knowledge." Gnostics denied God as the Creator of the universe, the incarnation of Christ, and the salvation of the body.

Governmental Theory: An understanding of the atonement of Christ that viewed the death of Christ as a demonstration of God's rightness in judging violations of His law. Christ's death is a lesson on the seriousness of obedience. Advocates of this theory, such as Charles Finney, deny that Christ's death was the literal payment for the penalty of sin in the sinner's place.

Hegelianism: A teaching that history is subject to evolutionary laws of progress, that society is pressing toward a utopia by natural forces. When Hegelianism is applied to religion, the foundation of Christianity is undercut, since it is rooted in a nonprogressive understanding of history. Georg Wilhelm Friedrich Hegel was a German philosopher who lived from 1770 to 1831.

Higher Criticism: A term referring to questions about the authorship and date of the books of the Bible. "Lower Criticism" refers to restoration of the text itself.

History-of-Religions School: An approach to religious truth that developed in Germany in the late nineteenth century. It sought to establish the essence of religion in the discovery of the common ingredients of all religions, thus denying the finality of Christianity and reducing religion to morality.

Imputation: The term means "to reckon." There are three such divine declarations in the Bible: the imputation of Adam's sin to the entire race, the imputation of humankind's sin to Christ on the cross, and the imputation of Christ's righteousness to the believing sinner.

Justification: A theological term with strong legal connotations, it means "to declare righteous" and is the pronouncement of God based on the satisfaction of His divine wrath through the atonement of Christ in the place of the sinner.

Liberal Movement: An attempt by church leaders from the nineteenth century and afterward to adjust Christianity in light of the findings of science. Scholars of this tradition sought to preserve the faith by reducing the essence of Christianity to its moral teachings while rejecting the complete truthfulness and sufficiency of the Bible, the absolute deity of Christ, the necessity of blood atonement, and salvation by divine declaration through grace alone based on the work of Christ.

Liberation Theology: A kind of theology, begun in the twentieth century, in which humanity's problems are seen in terms of social injustice and oppressive authority structures, whether they be political, racial, or gender-based in nature. Salvation is seen in changing social attitudes through political legislation, suggesting that sin is largely relational in nature and that redemption is equivalent to moral harmony and social equality.

Lutheranism: A major branch of Protestantism that emerged in the reformation of the late medieval church in the sixteenth century. While Lutherans embrace the concept of salvation apart from human cooperation and merit, they are distinct from other Protestants in their views on the sacraments, the role of the state, the function of the law in Christian experience, and the centrality of justification. Martin Luther, the father of the Protestant Reformation, lived from 1483 to 1546.

Magisterium: A term that refers to the teaching ministry of the church. Within Roman Catholicism, it denotes the church's authority to correctly teach the Bible.

Manichaeanism: An influential religious movement founded by Mani in the early centuries of the church and manifesting Gnostic emphases, such as the teaching that matter is evil and salvation is through deliverance from physical appetites.

Modalism: A heretical teaching that the Son is a manifestation of the one God but not a distinct person. In Modalism, God is one in person and

370

three in separate appearances.

Modernism: A term—synonymous with religious liberalism—that indicates the attempt by church leaders, beginning in the nineteenth century, to redefine Christianity in light of certain advances in the sciences, philosophy, and a new understanding of history.

Monarchianism: A term that identified a movement in the early centuries of the church to safeguard the oneness and unity of the Godhead. It became heretical in that it either denied the equality of Father and Son (Adoptionism) or the separateness of the Father and Son (Modalism).

Monophysitism: A teaching, originating in the early church, that Christ possessed one nature, a mixture of the divine and the human. This is in contradiction to the Chalcedon creed, which asserted that Christ possessed two distinct natures in one person.

Monothelitism: A controversy in the medieval church over Christology. Particularly, it concerned the issue of whether the incarnate Christ possessed two wills or a single will.

Montanism: A second- and third-century restorationist movement within the church. Montanists believed that the church was becoming morally lax and needed to return to the primitive ideals and practices, including an emphasis on healing, continual revelation, and (perhaps) tongues. Montanus, who gave his name to the movement, lived in the second century in Phrygia.

Neo-Orthodoxy: A movement of many varieties that emerged in the twentieth century and viewed liberalism as having gone too far in adjusting its teachings but agreed with liberalism that evangelicalism had not gone far enough. A common thread in the movement is a denial of the intregity and sufficiency of the Bible.

Nestorianism: A Christological heresy of the fourth century that denied the unity of the two natures of Christ in one person, the divine and the human joined in a moral union but not an organic one. Nestorius, patriarch of Constantinople, lived in the fourth and fifth centuries.

New England Theology: A theological tradition that emerged in the late eighteenth century as an answer to the encroachment of Enlightenment Rationalism upon New England Congregationalism. While the movement initially showed promise of responding to Unitarian and Deist critics, it paved the way for liberalism by gradually denying imputed sin, substitutionary atonement, and the deity of Christ.

New Theology: The original term designating American liberalism and later modernism.

Patripassianism: A synonym for Modalism, a second-century heresy. Since the terms "Father," "Son," and "Spirit" are names for the one God in His various roles, Modalists believed the Father (*pater* in Latin) suffered upon the cross (the Passion).

Pelagianism: A heretical teaching, strenuously opposed by Augustine in the fifth century, asserting that people can earn salvation based on natural ability and that divine intervention is unnecessary. Today's version of this view is expressed by the proverb "God helps those who help themselves" and is common among secular humanists and postmodernists. The monk Pelagius was a teacher in Rome in the early fifth century.

Postmillennialism: A teaching concerning future events in history, the triumph of God, and the final coming of Christ at the end of time. Advocates of postmillennialism believe that the reign of Christ over His kingdom is ever increasing and will reach its greatest extent before Christ comes in judgment. They neither confine the Millennium to a thousand years, as do premillennialists, nor assign it to the eternal state, as do amillennialists.

Postmodernism: An emerging worldview whose advocates reject the progressive idealism, trust in education, and adulation of science and technology that characterized the modern era. In postmodernism the hope for a corporate ethic has lost out in favor of individualism, privatism, and toleration.

Predestination: A doctrine concerning the activity of God in determining the destiny of those whom He gathers out of humankind as recipients of His grace, bringing them to eternal salvation through divine adoption as the children of God through Christ.

Premillennialism: A teaching concerning future events in history, the triumph of God, and the final coming of Christ at the end of time. Advocates of premillennialism believe that Christ will return twice, first to establish a literal thousand-year reign on the earth, fulfilling God's promises to Israel, and a second time in the final judgment.

Presbyterianism: Though the term often refers to various churches, it may denote either the form of government in the churches (a rule by presbytery and session rather than by membership or bishop) or the form of doctrine embraced in the churches (Calvinism).

Process Theology: A contemporary theological movement of transdenominational character that gathers insights from the assumptions of evolution. Specifically, process theism teaches that God does not know the future and is not all-knowing or all-powerful but rather is a being who is defining Himself through time. In this way, supporters believe, God can be shown to be more aware of the human dilemma and more compassionate.

Ransom Theory: A teaching in the early church concerning the death of Christ. Its advocates taught that Christ died on the cross to offer a payment of Himself to the devil, who had captured humankind.

Recapitulation Theory: The teaching that Christ, as the perfect second Adam, on the cross made up for the error of Adam's disobedience. Adam broke the Law; Christ fulfilled it. Adam caused the loss of righteousness through disobedience; Christ gained for us righteousness through obedience. This understanding of the atonement has also been called reinstitutionalism.

Reformation: An intellectual and religious movement in the sixteenth century that was a corrective to late-medieval corruptions in the church. Concern for reformation led to two mutually hostile movements—the Roman Catholic Church and the Protestant churches—as well as a host of other religious movements.

Reformed: A term that is generally synonymous with the teachings of Calvin as expressed in his *Institutes of the Christian Religion* and adopted to various settings as Calvinism spread across Europe and into America.

Remonstrants: A politico-religious party in Holland that petitioned for a redefining of national Calvinism in the seventeenth century. Remonstrants believed that Calvinism had overstated the depravity of humanity, denying the freedom of the will and making humans too passive in salvation.

Renaissance: An intellectual movement of the fourteenth and fifteenth centuries that spread through the universities, creating an interest in learning, and spawned the reformation of the late medieval church.

Revelation: A term that literally means "disclosure," or a revealing of what had previously been unknown. In the theological realm it refers to the disclosure of the mind of God, which led to the inspiring of men to write the Bible. The Bible is the Word of God, His thoughts recorded for all people.

Roman Catholic Church: A reform movement in the late medieval period that agreed with the emerging Protestants on the issue of the corruption of church life and practices but disagreed on such cardinal teachings as justification, the role of the sacraments, and papal authority.

Sabellianism: A synonym for Modalism and Patripassianism, a second- and third-century heresy that denied the distinction of persons in the Godhead in order to preserve monotheism. Sabellius was a teacher in Rome in the early third century.

Sacrament: A term that literally means "mystery," a divine secret subsequently revealed. In Protestant circles the sacraments are two: baptism and the Eucharist. The Roman Catholic Church teaches that there are seven sacraments: baptism, confirmation, the Eucharist, holy orders, marriage, penance, and extreme unction. The Protestants view the sacraments as supplying *sanctifying* grace, whereas Roman Catholics see them as imparting degrees of *justifying* grace.

Sanctification: The term literally means "to separate" and has the idea of increasing obedience to God in morals and lifestyle. Protestants understand sanctification to be the fruit of salvation; Roman Catholics think that sanctification is the cause of the grace of final justification. For the former, practical holiness is the expression of gratitude for a completed redemption; for the latter, it is the cause of salvation.

Saumurianism: A theological movement within seventeenth-century French Calvinism and identified with an academy in the city of Saumur. Its teachings reflect a revision of traditional Calvinism by emphasizing justification over predestination and advocating a hypothetical or unlimited view of the atonement, the idea that Christ died in the same sense for all persons and not merely for the elect.

Scholasticism: An intellectual movement identified with the rise of the universities of Europe in the twelfth and thirteenth centuries. Scholastics were teachers—loyal churchmen such as Anselm and Aquinas—who attempted to expand the role of rational argument and reason in the explanation and defense of the Christian faith.

Semi-Pelagianism: See Cassianism.

Septuagint: A Greek translation of the Old Testament writings and apocryphal works done in the third century B.C. in Alexandria, Egypt, by seventy scholars of the Jewish Diaspora.

Social Gospel: A branch of the liberal movement in American theology in the late nineteenth and early twentieth centuries that emphasized the societal nature of evil and sought to remedy the dark side of industrialism through political endeavor. It shared the goals and assumptions of the American progressive movement in the same era.

Socinianism: A sixteenth-century revival of the Arian heresy of the fourth century. Advocated by Laelius and Faustus Socinus, it rejected the orthodox doctrine of the triunity of God, denied the deity of Christ, and defined His uniqueness according to His adoption by God.

Subordinationism: A heresy in the early church, and in the religious liberal movements since the Enlightenment, that denies the absolute equality of the Son and the Father. All Subordinationists are Adoptionists; Christ is "God" because He was uniquely pious and otherworldly—a human ideal.

Theologians: A term used in a specific sense to refer to the writers, mostly bishops, in the church of the fourth and fifth centuries, the era after the persecutions and during the great ecumenical councils.

Theology: In the early church the term referred narrowly to the discussion of the Trinity, though it later came to mean the study of our knowledge of God in general. Specialization of the study of the knowledge of God has led to segmentation: systematic theology, dogmatic theology, historical theology, and practical theology.

Tradition: A term that in the early centuries meant the revelation of God delivered in oral form by apostles and prophets. This included what we later called the Bible but was expanded to include the writings of church leaders and the findings of the early councils as well as various customs. After the third century, the term was narrowed to mean the written teachings of the apostles, particularly the gospel. Today, the Orthodox churches define authority in the former, broader sense, while the Western churches define it in the latter, narrower sense.

Traducianism: The teaching that the human soul is generated in a child by the parents just as is the body. In this way original sin is passed down from Adam and Eve to every person, as the soul is generated in a spiritually blighted condition. This position stands in contrast to creationism, which suggests that God supernaturally creates the soul at conception for each child.

Trinity: The teaching of the church, as expressed in the Nicene Creed, that God is a triunity—one in the possession of the same characteristics or attributes, three in persons, and equal in every respect in the community of characteristics.

Tritheism: The belief in three Gods. This view is attributed to teachers in the church who did not seem to grasp that God, while three in persons, is one in essence. Often the quest to defend the unity of God led to a denigration of the triplicity of God's persons.

Unitarianism: A belief that God is one in nature as well as person. Its advocates deny the deity of Christ, viewing Him as a superb model of humanity but nothing more.

Universalism: A movement that shares the same view of Christ and God as the Unitarians. Universalists believe that all humankind will be saved, since God is love and grace. The ground of unlimited salvation is slightly different between Unitarians and Universalists: Unitarians believe that God is too good to condemn people, while Universalists believe that people are too good to be condemned by God.

Vulgate: A Latin translation of the Scriptures by St. Jerome in the fifth century. This was "the Bible" throughout the medieval period.

Wesleyanism: A term that often refers to John Wesley's understanding of the relationship of the divine and human elements in salvation. He taught two works of grace to save a sinner: prevenient grace and saving grace. Prevenient grace supplies the sinner with the ability to turn from sin so that God can redeem him or her. In this way Wesley felt that he had resolved the complexities of divine grace and free will.

Bibliography

CHRISTIAN DOCUMENTS

This portion of the bibliography contains complete information for those
works cited parenthetically in *Our Legacy: A History of Christian
Doctrine.*

Anselm. *Anselm of Canterbury.* 4 vols. Edited and translated by Jasper
Hopkins and Herbert Richardson. Toronto and New York: Mellen, 1975.

Aquinas, Thomas. *Summa Theologica.* 5 vols. Translated by Fathers of the
English Dominican Province. Allen, Texas: Christian Classics, 1981.

Arminius, James. *The Works of Arminius.* 3 vols. Translated by James
Nichols and William Nichols. Grand Rapids, Mich.: Baker, 1986.

Barth, Karl. *Church Dogmatics.* 5 vols. Translated by G. W. Bromiley. Edited
by G. W. Bromiley and T. F. Torrance. Edinburgh: Clark, 1975.

Calvin, Jean. *Institutes of the Christian Religion.* 2 vols. Translated by Ford
Lewis Battles. Edited by John T. McNeill. Philadelphia: Westminster,
1960.

Catechism of the Catholic Church. Morristown, N.J.: Silver Burdett Gin, 1994.

Lightfoot, J. B., and J. R. Harmer, eds. and trans. *The Apostolic Fathers:
Greek Texts and English Translations of Their Writings.* Revised by
Michael W. Holmes. Grand Rapids, Mich.: Baker, 1992. This collection
includes the following works: *2 Clement; Didache; Epistle of Barnabas.*

Pelagius. *Pelagius's Commentary on St. Paul's Epistle to the Romans.*
Translated by Theodore de Bruyn. New York: Oxford University Press,
1993.

Roberts, Alexander, and James Donaldson, eds. 10 vols. *The Ante-Nicene Fathers: Translations of the Writings of the Fathers Down to* A.D. *325.* Grand Rapids, Mich.: Eerdmans, 1973. This collection includes the following works: *Epistle to Diognetus;* Athenagoras, *Apology;* Clement of Alexandria, *Exhortation to the Heathen, The Instructor, Who Is the Rich Man That Shall Be Saved?* Clement of Rome, *First Epistle to the Corinthians;* Cyprian of Carthage, *Epistle, Unity of the Church;* Hermas, *The Shepherd;* Hippolytus, *Apostolic Tradition, A Refutation of All Heresies;* Ignatius, *To the Ephesians, To the Magnesians, To the Philadelphians, To the Smyrneans, To the Trallians;* Irenaeus, *Against Heresies;* Justin Martyr, *Address to the Greeks, Apology, Dialogue to Trypho;* Lactantius, *Divine Institutes;* Origen, *Commentaries on John, Commentaries on Matthew, Commentaries on Romans, The Fundamental Doctrines;* Tertullian, *Against Celsus, Against Praxeas, Against Marcion, The Crown, Monogamy, On Baptism, Prescription against Heretics, The Soul;* Theophilus of Antioch, *To Autolycus.*

Schaff, Philip, ed. 14 vols. *A Select Library of the Nicene and Post-Nicene Fathers of the Christian Church.* First Series. Grand Rapids, Mich.: Eerdmans, 1979. This collection includes the following works by Augustine: *Baptism, The Care That Should Be Taken of the Dead, The City of God, Commentary on John, Enchiridion, Epistles, Forgiveness . . . and the Baptism of Infants, Handbook of Faith, Hope, and Love, On Nature and Free Will, Sermons, The Trinity.*

Schaff, Philip, and Henry Wace, eds. *A Select Library of Nicene and Post-Nicene Fathers of the Christian Church.* Second Series. 14 vols. Grand Rapids, Mich.: Eerdmans,1952. This collection includes the following works: Ambrose of Milan, *Abraham, Commentary on Luke, The Holy Spirit;* Athanasius, *1 Serapion, Orations against Arius, On the Incarnation;* Basil of Caesarea, *On the Holy Spirit;* Cyril of Jerusalem, *Catechetical Lectures;* Eusebius, *Ecclesiastical History;* Gregory of Nazianzus, *Letter to Nectarius, Oration on the Holy Lights, Theological Orations;* Gregory of Nyssa, *The Great Catechism;* Gregory the Great, *Dialogues, Epistles, Moralia;* Hilary of Poitiers, *Commentaries on the Psalms;* John of Damascus, *The Orthodox Faith;* Leo I, *Sermons.*

Schaff, Philip. *The Creeds of Christendom with a History of Critical Notes.* 3 vols. Grand Rapids, Mich.: Baker, 1977.

Schleiermacher, Friedrich. *The Christian Faith*. Edited by H. R. Mackintosh and J. S. Stewart. Edinburgh: Clark, 1928.

Shedd, William G. T. *A History of Christian Doctrine*. 2 vols. New York: Scribner's, 1902. These volumes contain quotes from the following works: Cassian, *Spiritual Discourse;* Curcellaeus, *Opera Theologica;* Epiphanes, *Heresies;* Faustus of Riez, *On Grace and Free Will;* Limborch, *Theologia Christiana;* Melito of Sardis, *The Guide;* Faustus Socinus, *Works;* Vincent of Lérins, *Commonitorium.*

Wesley, John. *The Bicentennial Edition of the Works of John Wesley*. 23 vols. Edited by Frank Baker. Nashville: Abingdon, 1984.

CREEDS AND SOURCEBOOKS

Cross, F. L., and E. A. Livingstone, eds. *The Oxford Dictionary of the Christian Church*. 3d ed. Oxford: Oxford University Press, 1997. One of the standard dictionaries of the history of the church. It is a must for the serious student.

Jurgens, William A. *The Faith of the Early Fathers*. 3 vols. Collegeville, Minn.: Liturgical, 1970, 1979. A very usable guide to the writers and writings of the early church. The work introduces each father of the church with a synopsis of his works followed by quotations from each of them. The footnotes provide further insight into the works themselves.

Leith, John, ed. *Creeds of the Churches*. Garden City, N.Y.: Doubleday, 1963. A single volume of the creeds of the church. While not as complete as Schaff's, it makes the major creeds available at less cost.

Schaff, Philip. *The Creeds of Christendom with a History of Critical Notes*. 3 vols. Grand Rapids, Mich.: Baker, 1977. The most complete edition of creeds available today for the student of church history.

SURVEYS OF THE HISTORY OF DOCTRINE

Berkhof, Louis. *The History of Christian Doctrines*. 1937. Reprint. Grand Rapids, Mich.: Baker, 1975. A general survey of the history of doctrine. Originally, it was a part of Berkhof's systematic theology volume.

Bromiley, Geoffrey W. *Historical Theology: An Introduction*. Grand Rapids, Mich.: Eerdmans, 1978. A history of doctrine that traces the development century by century rather than by individual doctrines, as in the case of Berkhof.

Cuncliffe-Jones, Hubert, with Benjamin Drewery, eds. *A History of Christian Doctrine.* Edinburgh: Clark, 1978. A detailed and scholarly delineation of the history of doctrine.

Cunningham, William. *Historical Theology.* 2 vols. 1862. Reprint. London: Banner of Truth Trust, 1969. An older history of doctrine by a Scottish divine of the previous century. It is a classic defense of orthodoxy from a Reformed perspective.

Gonzalez, Justo L. *A History of Christian Thought.* 3 vols. Nashville: Abingdon, 1970, 1971, 1975. In my judgment, this is the best of the major histories currently in print. It is a highly readable work and was written by a scholar who is well acquainted with the sources.

Harnack, Adolf. *History of Dogma.* 7 vols. 1900. Reprint. New York: Dover, 1961. This work is an older, classic history reflective of the liberal biases that informed scholarship in the nineteenth century. It is still a must for the serious student.

Heick, Otto W. *A History of Christian Thought.* Philadelphia: Fortress, 1965. This is a rather well-written history, with materials unavailable in other volumes, though it is somewhat dated.

Klotsche, E. H. *The History of Christian Doctrine.* 1945. Reprint. Rev. ed. Grand Rapids, Mich.: Baker, 1979. A general, brief survey of history much like Berkhof's volume.

McGrath, Alister E. *Christian Theology: An Introduction.* Oxford and Cambridge, Mass.: Blackwell, 1994. A recent history written by an English scholar. It reflects the scholarly abilities of its author and has the advantage of dealing with contemporary issues in a readable style.

Olson, Roger E. *The Story of Christian Theology: Twenty Centuries of Tradition & Reform.* Downers Grove, Ill.: InterVarsity Press, 1999. A fine new history written from an Arminian perspective.

Pelican, Jaroslav. *The Christian Tradition: A History of the Development of Doctrine.* 5 vols. Chicago: University of Chicago Press, 1989. This is the standard currently in the field of historical theology. The author is a scholar without peer in his field. The work is a research tool for students.

Seeburg, Reinhold. *The History of Christian Doctrines.* 2 vols. 1895, 1898. Reprint. Grand Rapids, Mich.: Baker, 1977. Though an older history of Christian thought, it is a classic.

Shedd, William G. T. *A History of Christian Doctrine.* 2 vols. 1889. Reprint. Minneapolis, Minn.: Klock & Klock, 1978. This is an older history written by an American scholar. Shedd wrote in a very clear style.

WORKS ON SPECIFIC TOPICS

Catechism of the Catholic Church. Morristown, N.J.: Silver Burdett Gin, 1994. The most recent catechism of the Roman Catholic Church. It is a must for the student who would seek to understand the official position of the church on most matters.

Clendenin, Daniel B. *Eastern Orthodox Christianity: A Western Perspective.* Grand Rapids, Mich.: Baker, 1994. This is an introduction to the Orthodox churches. It contains a useful description of the history and theology of this particular branch of Christianity.

Gonzalez, Justo L. *The Story of Christianity.* 2 vols. San Francisco: Harper & Row, 1984. In my judgment, this is the best available history of the Christian church. It is a wonderful companion to the author's history of Christian doctrine.

Kelley, J. N. D. *Early Christian Doctrines.* 1960. Reprint. San Francisco: Harper & Row, 1978. This is a classic volume on the history of doctrine in the early church. It is an important volume to anyone interested in this particular period.

Ware, Timothy. *The Orthodox Church.* 1963. Reprint. New York: Penguin, 1985. Like Clendenin's volume, this work is a very fine introduction to the Orthodox churches.

Index

385

INDEX

387

INDEX

Author

Dr. John D. Hannah is the department chairman and distinguished professor of historical theology at Dallas Theological Seminary in Dallas, Texas. He holds a BS from Philadelphia College of the Bible, an MA from Southern Methodist University, a ThM and ThD from Dallas Theological Seminary, and a PhD from the University of Texas at Dallas. Further, he was granted a post-doctoral fellowship at Yale University. Dr. Hannah has written extensively for journals including *Bibliotheca Sacra, Front Lines, Fundamentalist Journal, Discipleship Journal, Modern Reformation,* and *Trinity Journal*. His books include *The Glory of God Alone* (Crossway) and *The Kregel Pictorial Guide to Church History* (Kregel). Dr. Hannah is a frequent conference and church speaker both in the United States and abroad.

The joy and freedom of faith.

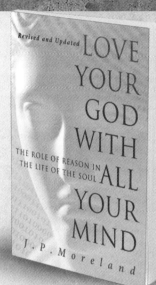